P9-DVD-090

My
iPhone®

NINTH EDITION

Brad Miser

800 East 96th Street,
Indianapolis, Indiana 46240 USA

My iPhone®, Ninth Edition

Copyright © 2016 by Pearson Education, Inc.

ISBN-13: 978-0-7897-5539-1
ISBN-10: 0-7897-5539-4

Costco Edition ISBN 13: 978-0-7897-5822-4
Costco Edition ISBN 10: 0-7897-5822-9

Library of Congress Control Number: 2015954100

Printed in the United States of America

First Printing: November 2015

Trademarks

All terms mentioned in this book that are known to be trademarks or service marks have been appropriately capitalized. Que Publishing cannot attest to the accuracy of this information. Use of a term in this book should not be regarded as affecting the validity of any trademark or service mark.

Warning and Disclaimer

Every effort has been made to make this book as complete and as accurate as possible, but no warranty or fitness is implied. The information provided is on an "as is" basis. The author and the publisher shall have neither liability nor responsibility to any person or entity with respect to any loss or damages arising from the information contained in this book.

Special Sales

For information about buying this title in bulk quantities, or for special sales opportunities (which may include electronic versions; custom cover designs; and content particular to your business, training goals, marketing focus, or branding interests), please contact our corporate sales department at corpsales@pearsoned.com or (800) 382-3419.

For government sales inquiries, please contact governmentsales@pearsoned.com.

For questions about sales outside the U.S., please contact international@pearsoned.com.

Editor-in-Chief
Greg Wiegand

Senior Acquisitions Editor and Senior Development Editor
Laura Norman

Managing Editor
Sandra Schroeder

Project Editor
Mandie Frank

Senior Indexer
Cheryl Lenser

Proofreader
Debbie Williams

Technical Editor
Greg Kettell

Editorial Assistant
Cindy Teeters

Designer
Mark Shirar

Compositor
Tricia Bronkella

Contents at a Glance

Table of Contents

7 Managing Contacts   **211**

8 Communicating with the Phone and FaceTime Apps   **233**

About the Author

Brad Miser has written extensively about technology, with his favorite topics being the amazing "i" devices, especially the iPhone, that make it possible to take our lives with us while we are on the move. In addition to *My iPhone*, Ninth Edition, Brad has written many other books, including *My iPhone for Seniors*, Second Edition; and *My Pages, Keynote, and Numbers*. He has also been an author, development editor, or technical editor for more than 50 other titles.

Brad is or has been a sales support specialist, the director of product and customer services, and the manager of education and support services for several software development companies. Previously, he was the lead proposal specialist for an aircraft engine manufacturer, a development editor for a computer book publisher, and a civilian aviation test officer/engineer for the U.S. Army. Brad holds a bachelor of science degree in mechanical engineering from California Polytechnic State University at San Luis Obispo and has received advanced education in maintainability engineering, business, and other topics.

Brad would love to hear about your experiences with this book (the good, the bad, and the ugly). You can write to him at bradmiser@icloud.com.

Dedication

To those who have given the last full measure of devotion so that the rest of us can be free.

Acknowledgments

To the following people on the *My iPhone* project team, my sincere appreciation for your hard work on this book:

Laura Norman, my acquisitions and development editor, who envisioned the original concept for *My iPhone* and works very difficult and long hours to ensure the success of each edition. Laura and I have worked on many books together, and I appreciate her professional and effective approach to these projects. Thanks for putting up with me yet one more time! Frankly, I have no idea how she does all the things she does and manages to be so great to work with given the incredible work and pressure books like this one involve!

Mandie Frank, my project editor, who skillfully managed the hundreds of files and production process that it took to make this book. Imagine keeping dozens of plates spinning on top of poles and you get a glimpse into Mandie's daily life! (And no plates have been broken in the production of this book!)

Mark Shirar, for the interior design and cover of the book.

Que's production and sales team for printing the book and getting it into your hands.

We Want to Hear from You!

As the reader of this book, *you* are our most important critic and commentator. We value your opinion and want to know what we're doing right, what we could do better, what areas you'd like to see us publish in, and any other words of wisdom you're willing to pass our way.

We welcome your comments. You can email or write to let us know what you did or didn't like about this book—as well as what we can do to make our books better.

Please note that we cannot help you with technical problems related to the topic of this book.

When you write, please be sure to include this book's title and author as well as your name and email address. We will carefully review your comments and share them with the author and editors who worked on the book.

Email: feedback@quepublishing.com

Mail: Que Publishing
         ATTN: Reader Feedback
         800 East 96th Street
         Indianapolis, IN 46240 USA

Reader Services

Visit our website and register this book at quepublishing.com/register for convenient access to any updates, downloads, or errata that might be available for this book.

Using This Book

This book has been designed to help you transform an iPhone into *your* iPhone by helping you learn to use it easily and quickly. As you can tell, the book relies heavily on pictures to show you how an iPhone works. It is also task-focused so that you can quickly learn the specific steps to follow to do lots of cool things with your iPhone.

Using an iPhone involves lots of touching its screen with your fingers. When you need to tap part of the screen, such as a button or keyboard, you see a callout with the step number pointing to where you need to tap. When you need to swipe your finger along the screen, such as to browse lists, you see the following icons:

The directions in which you should slide your finger on the screen are indicated with arrows. When the arrow points both ways, you can move your finger in either direction. When the arrows point in all four directions, you can move your finger in any direction on the screen.

To zoom in or zoom out on screens, you unpinch or pinch, respectively, your fingers on the screen. These motions are indicated by the following icons:

When you need to tap once or twice, such as to zoom out or in, you see the following icons matching the number of times you need to tap:

If you use an iPhone 6s or iPhone 6s Plus, you can use pressure on the screen to activate certain functions. The following icons indicate when you should apply some pressure (called a peek) or slightly more pressure (called a pop):

When you can rotate your iPhone, you see this icon:

Occasionally, you shake the iPhone to activate a control. When you do, you see this icon:

As you can see on its cover, this book provides information about a number of iPhone models, which are the iPhone 4s, iPhone 5, iPhone 5s, iPhone 5c, iPhone 6, iPhone 6 Plus, iPhone 6s, and iPhone 6s Plus. Each of these models has specific features and capabilities that vary slightly from the others. Additionally, they have different screen sizes with the 4s being the smallest and the iPhone 6 Plus and iPhone 6s Plus being the largest.

Because of the variations between the models, the figures you see in this book may be slightly different than the screens you see on your iPhone. For example, the iPhone 6 has settings that aren't on the iPhone 5s, while the 5s and later models support Touch ID (fingerprint recognition), although the 4s and 5 don't. In most cases, you can follow the steps as they are written with any of these models even if there are minor differences between the figures and your screens.

When the model you are using doesn't support a feature being described, such as the Display Zoom that is on the iPhone 6 and later but not on earlier models, you can skip that information or read it to help you decide if you want to upgrade to a newer model.

Although there are many changes in iOS 9 that you will notice, some are significant and still others are entirely new. In the case of those features that have changed significantly, or are completely new, we have added indicator to the text and table of contents to help you easily locate them. When you see **New!** be sure to check out those tasks to quickly get up to speed on what's new in iOS 9.

You'll soon wonder
how you ever got along
without one!

In this chapter, you get introduced to the amazing iPhone! Topics include the following:

→ Getting to know your iPhone's external features
→ Getting to know your iPhone's software

Getting Started with Your iPhone

Your iPhone is one of the most amazing handheld devices ever because of how well it is designed. It has only a few external features you need to understand. For most of the things you do, you just use your fingers on your iPhone's screen (which just seems natural), and the iPhone's consistent interface enables you to accomplish most tasks with similar steps.

Getting to Know Your iPhone's External Features

Take a quick look at the iPhone's physical attributes. It doesn't have many physical buttons or controls because you mostly use software to control it.

Note: on the 5s and earlier models, the Wake/Sleep button is here

Camera

Mute switch

Volume buttons

Wake/Sleep button (iPhone 6/6s and 6/6s Plus)

Touch ID/Home button

Headphone jack   Docking port

- **Cameras**—One of the iPhone's camera lenses is located on its backside near the top-left corner; the other is on the front at the top at the center of the phone. When you take photos or video, you can choose either camera to use. All iPhone models have a flash located near the camera on the backside. The iPhone 6s and 6s Plus also have a flash on the front that comes from the screen; for all other models, there is no flash when you use the camera on the front.

- **Wake/Sleep button**—Press this to lock the iPhone's screen and put it to sleep. Press it again to wake the iPhone from Sleep mode. You also use this button to shut down the iPhone and to power it up.

- **Mute switch**—This switch determines whether the iPhone makes sounds, such as ringing when a call comes in or making the alert noise for notifications, such as an event on a calendar. Slide it toward the front of the iPhone to hear sounds. Slide it toward the back of the iPhone to mute all sound. When muted, you see orange in the switch.

- **Headphone jack**—Plug the iPhone's EarPods or self-powered, external speakers into this jack.

- **Volume**—Press the upper button to increase volume; press the lower button to decrease volume. This is contextual; for example, when you are listening to music, it controls the music's volume, but when you aren't, it controls the ringer volume. When you are using the Camera app, pressing either button takes a photo.

- **Docking port**—Use this port, located on the bottom side of the iPhone, to connect it to a computer or power adapter using the included USB cable. There are also accessories that connect to this port. The iPhone 5s, 5c, 6/6s, and 6/6s Plus have the Lightning port, which uses a flat, thin plug. It doesn't matter which side is up when you plug something into this port. The iPhone 4s uses the 30-pin port, which is much larger and has to be inserted "top side up."

- **Touch ID/Home button (iPhone 5s, 6/6s, and 6/6s Plus)**—This serves two functions. The Touch ID sensor recognizes your fingerprint, so you can simply touch it to unlock your iPhone, sign into the iTunes Store, and use Apple Pay to confirm your information to complete a transaction. It also functions just like the Home button described in the following bullet.

- **Home button (iPhone 5c, 5, and 4s)**—When the iPhone is asleep, press it to wake up the iPhone. When the iPhone is awake and unlocked, press this button to move to the all-important Home screens; press it twice quickly to open the App Switcher. Press and hold the Home button to activate Siri to speak to your iPhone.

So Many iPhones, So Few Pages

The iPhone is now in its ninth generation of software that runs on multiple generations of hardware. Each successive generation has added features and capabilities to the previous version. All iPhone hardware runs the iOS operating system. However, this book is based on the current version of this operating system, iOS 9. Only the iPhone 4s and newer can run this version of the software. If you have an older version of the iPhone, this book helps you see why it is time to upgrade, but most of the information contained herein won't apply to your iPhone until you do.

There are also differences even among the models of iPhones that can run iOS 9. For example, the iPhone 5s, 6, 6 Plus, 6s, and 6s Plus models have Touch ID that uses your fingerprint to unlock your iPhone, to sign into your Apple ID, and for other purposes (such as Apple Pay). The iPhone 4s, 5, and 5c do not have this capability.

This book is primarily based on the latest generation of iPhones, the iPhone 6s and 6s Plus. If you use one of the other models that can run iOS 9, there might be some differences between the details you read in this book and your phone. Those differences aren't significant and shouldn't stop you from accomplishing the tasks as described in this book.

Getting to Know Your iPhone's Software

You might not suspect it based on the iPhone's simple and elegant exterior, but this powerhouse runs very sophisticated software that enables you to do all sorts of great things. The beauty of the iPhone's software is that it is both very powerful and also easy to use—once you get used to its User Interface (UI for the more technical among you). The iPhone's UI is so well designed that after a few minutes, you may wish everything worked so well and was so easy to use.

Using Your Fingers to Control Your iPhone

Apple designed the iPhone to be touched. Most of the time, you control your iPhone by using your fingers on its screen to tap buttons, select items, swipe on the screen, zoom, type text, and so on. If you want to get technical, this method of interacting with software is called the multi-touch interface.

Going Home

Almost all iPhone activities start at the Home screen, or Home screens, to be more accurate, because the Home screen consists of multiple pages. You get to the Home screen by pressing the Touch ID/Home button once. Along the bottom of the Home screen (or along the side on an iPhone 6 Plus/6s Plus held horizontally) is the Dock, which is always visible on the Home screen. This gives you easy access to the icons it contains (more on the Home screens shortly); up to four icons can be placed on this Dock. Above the Dock are apps that do all sorts of cool things. As you install apps, the number of icons increases. You can also create bookmarks for websites and store them on the Home screens. You can organize the pages of the Home screens in any way you like, and you can place icons into folders to keep your Home screens tidy. At the top of the screen are status icons that provide you with important information, such as whether you are connected to a Wi-Fi network and the current charge of your iPhone's battery.

Touching the iPhone's Screen

The following figures highlight the major ways you control an iPhone:

- **Tap:** briefly touch a finger to the iPhone's screen and then lift your finger again. For example, to open an app, you tap its icon.

Tap an app's icon to launch it

- **Double-tap:** tap twice.

- **Swipe:** touch the screen at any location and slide your finger in one direction.

- **Drag:** tap and hold an object and move your finger across the screen without lifting it up; the faster you move your finger, the faster the resulting action happens. (You don't need to apply pressure, just make contact.)

- **Pinch or unpinch:** place two fingers on the screen and drag them together or move them apart; the faster and more you pinch or unpinch, the "more" the action happens (such as a zoom in).

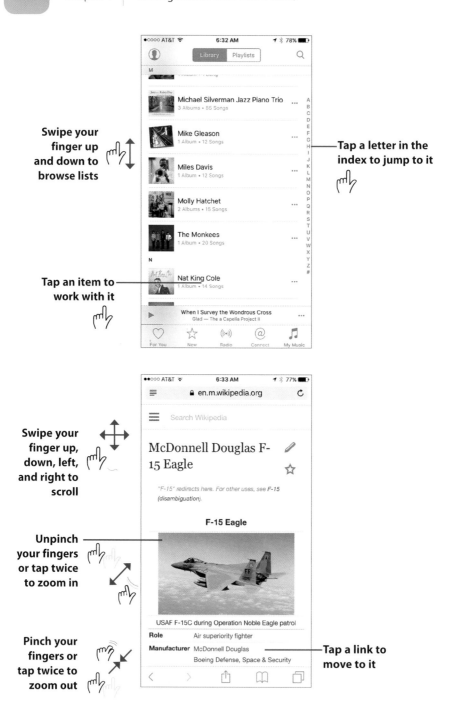

Swipe your finger up and down to browse lists

Tap a letter in the index to jump to it

Tap an item to work with it

Swipe your finger up, down, left, and right to scroll

Unpinch your fingers or tap twice to zoom in

Tap a link to move to it

Pinch your fingers or tap twice to zoom out

Swipe your finger to the right to move to the previous screen

Swipe your finger to the left to move to the next screen

Tap the screen to show/hide toolbars

Tap controls to activate them

- **Rotate:** rotate the iPhone to change the screen's orientation.

Rotate the iPhone to change the screen's orientation

New! On an iPhone 6s or iPhone 6s Plus, you can take advantage of 3D Touch that enables you to perform tasks by applying pressure on the screen in addition to just touching it.

When you are looking at a preview of something, such as an email, tap and put a small amount of pressure on the screen to perform a Peek. A Peek causes a window to open that shows a preview of the object. You can preview the object in the Peek window; if you swipe up on a Peek, you get a menu of commands related to the object. For example, when you perform a Peek on an email and then swipe up on the Peek, you can tap Reply to reply to the email.

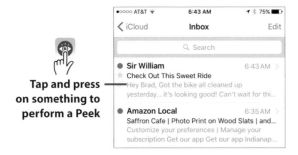

Tap and press on something to perform a Peek

When you swipe up on a Peek, you get a menu; tap an action to perform it

A Peek is a quick way to look at something without actually opening it

Swipe up on a Peek to reveal menus with actions you can select to perform them

When you are looking at a Peek, apply slightly more pressure on the screen to perform a Pop, which opens the object in its app. For example, you can perform a Peek on a photo's thumbnail to preview it. Apply a bit more pressure (a Pop) on the preview to "pop" it open in the Photos app (for example, to crop your finger out of the photo).

Tap and press on something to perform a Peek

Press slightly harder on a Peek to perform a Pop

When you perform a Pop, the object opens in the associated app

Peeks and Pops can take a little bit of experimentation to get the amount of pressure you need just right, but after a few tries, you'll find these to be handy techniques to access content.

Working with iPhone Apps

When you tap an app's icon, it opens and fills the iPhone's screen

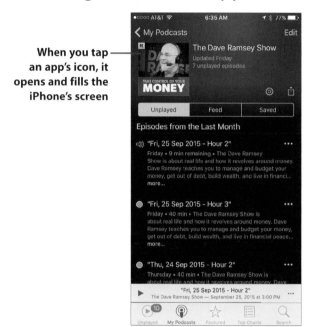

One of the best things about an iPhone is that it can run all sorts of applications, or in iPhone lingo, *apps*. It includes a number of preinstalled apps, such as Mail, Safari, and so on, but you can download and use thousands of other apps through the App Store. You learn about many of the iPhone's preinstalled apps as you read through this book. And as you learned earlier, to launch an app, you simply tap its icon. The app launches and fills the iPhone's screen.

Tap a Quick Action to perform it

Pressing on an app's icon pops open the Quick Actions menu

New! On an iPhone 6s or iPhone 6s Plus, 3D Touch enables you to perform tasks by applying pressure on the screen in addition to just touching it. When you press on an app's icon, the Quick Actions menu appears; tap an action to take it. For example, when you open the Quick Actions menu for the Phone app, you can place calls to people you have recently communicated with or create a new contact.

Tap a folder to access its icons

Folder name

Open folder

Tap an icon to open it

Icons within the folder

Swipe to the right or left to move between a folder's pages

Tap outside a folder or press the Home/Touch ID button to close it

In Chapter 5, "Customizing How Your iPhone Looks and Sounds," you learn how you can organize icons in folders to keep your Home screens tidy and make getting to icons faster and easier. To access an icon that is in a folder, tap the folder. It opens and takes over the screen. Under its name is a box showing the apps or website bookmarks it contains. Like the Home screens, folders can have multiple pages. To move between a folder's pages, swipe to the left to move to the next screen or to the right to move to the previous one. Each time you "flip" a page, you see another set of icons. You can close a folder without opening an app by tapping outside its borders or by pressing the Home/Touch ID button.

To launch an app or open a website bookmark within a folder, tap its icon.

When you are done using an app, press the Home button. You return to the Home screen you were most recently using.

When you move out of an app by pressing the Home button, the app moves into the background but doesn't stop running (you can control whether or not apps are allowed to work in the background, as you learn in a later section). So, if the app has a task to complete, such as uploading photos or playing audio, it continues to work behind-the-scenes. In some cases, most notably games, the app becomes suspended at the point you move it into the background by switching to a different app or moving to a Home screen. In addition to the benefit of completing tasks when you move into another app, the iPhone's capability to multitask means that you can run multiple apps at the same time. For example, you can run an Internet radio app to listen to music while you switch over to the Mail app to work on your email.

The App Switcher enables you to quickly move among open apps

Swipe to the left or right to move among the running apps

The current screen in the app

Tap an app's screen to move into it

Running apps

You can control apps by using the App Switcher. To see this, quickly press the Touch ID/Home button twice. The App Switcher appears.

At the top of the App Switcher, you see icons for apps you have used recently. Under each app's icon, you see a thumbnail of that app's screen. You can swipe to the left or right to move among the apps you see. You can tap an app's screen to move into it. That app takes over the screen, and you can work with it, picking up right where you left off the last time you used it.

When you open the App Switcher, the app you were using most recently comes to the center to make it easy to return to. This enables you to toggle between two apps easily. For example, suppose you need to enter a confirmation number from one app into another app. Open the app into which you want to enter the number. Then open the app containing the number you need to enter. Open the App Switcher and tap the pervious app to return to it quickly so that you can enter the number.

To close the App Switcher without moving into a different app, press the Home button once. You move back into the app or Home screen you were most recently using.

Swipe up on an app's screen to force it to close

In some cases (such as when it's using up your battery too quickly or it has stopped responding to you), you might want to force an app to quit. To do this, open the App Switcher by quickly pressing the Touch ID/Home button twice. Swipe up on the app you want to stop. The app is forced to quit, its icon and screen disappear, and you remain in the App Switcher. You should be careful about this, though, because if the app has unsaved data, that data is lost when you force the app to quit. The app is not deleted from the iPhone—it is just shut down until you open it again (which you can do by returning to the Home screen and tapping the app's icon).

Tap to return to the app you were previously using

New! Sometimes, a link in one app takes you into a different app. When this happens, you see the Back to *App*, where *App* button is the name of the app in which you tapped the link, in the upper-left corner of the screen. You can tap this button to return to the app you came from. For example, you can tap a link in a Mail email message to open the associated web page in Safari. To return to the email you were reading in the Mail app, tap the Back to Mail button in the upper-left corner of the screen.

Using the Home Screens

Previously in this chapter, you read that the Home screen is the jumping-off point for many of the things you do with your iPhone because that is where you access the icons you tap to launch things such as apps or website bookmarks you've saved there.

Swipe to the left or right to move between pages of your Home screen

The white dot indicates the page you are currently viewing

Tap to the left or right of the current page (white dot) to move to the previous or the next page

The Dock is visible on every page

When you move to a different page, you see a different set of icons and folders

The Home screen has multiple pages. To change the page you are viewing, swipe to the left to move to later pages or to the right to move to earlier pages. The dots above the toolbar represent the pages of the Home screen. The white dot represents the page being displayed. You can also change the page by tapping to the left of the white dot to move to the previous page or to the right of it to move to the next page.

Using the iPhone 6 Plus/6s Plus' Split-Screen

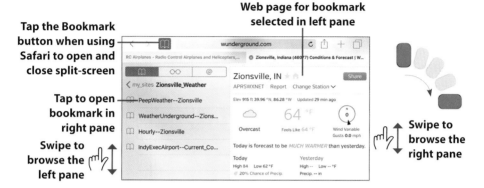

Web page for bookmark selected in left pane

Tap the Bookmark button when using Safari to open and close split-screen

Tap to open bookmark in right pane

Swipe to browse the left pane

Swipe to browse the right pane

When you hold an iPhone 6 Plus/6s Plus in the horizontal orientation, you can take advantage of the iPhone 6 Plus/6s Plus' Split-screen feature in many apps (not all apps support this). In Split-screen mode, the screen has two panes. The left pane is for navigation, while the right pane shows the content selected in the left pane. The two panes are independent, so you can swipe up and down on one side without affecting the other. In most apps that support this functionality, there is a button you can use to open or close the split screen. This button changes depending on the app you are using. For example, when you are using Safari to browse the Web, tap the Bookmark button to open the left pane and tap it again to close the left pane (while the left pane is open, you can select bookmarks in and see the associated web pages in the right pane). As another example, in the Mail app, you tap the Full Screen button (two arrows pointing diagonally away from each other) to open or close the left pane.

Apps that support this functionality include Settings, Mail, Safari, and Messages; you see examples showing how Split-screen works in those apps later in this book. You should hold the iPhone 6 Plus/6s Plus horizontally when using your favorite apps to see if they support this feature.

Dock

Home screen pages

When you hold the iPhone 6 Plus/6s Plus horizontally and move to the Home screen, the Dock moves to the right side of the screen and you see the Home screen's pages in the left part of the window. Though this looks a bit different, it works the same as when you hold an iPhone vertically.

Searching on Your iPhone

Swipe down from the center part of the screen to open the Spotlight search tool

You can use the Spotlight Search tool to search your iPhone. To open this tool, move to a Home screen and swipe down from the center part of the screen. (Be careful not to swipe down from the very top of the screen because that opens the Notification Center instead.) The Search bar appears at the top of the screen and the keyboard opens.

Type what you want to search for

Current results

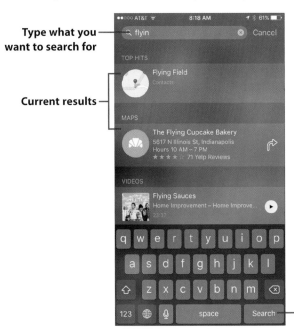

When you're done entering your search term, tap Search

To perform a search, tap in the Search bar and type the search term using the onscreen keyboard. As you type, items that meet your search are shown on the list below the Search bar. When you finish typing the search term, tap Search.

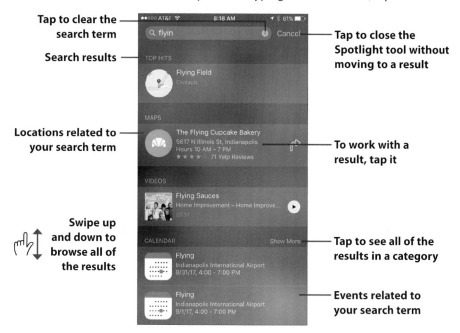

Tap to clear the search term

Search results

Locations related to your search term

Swipe up and down to browse all of the results

Tap to close the Spotlight tool without moving to a result

To work with a result, tap it

Tap to see all of the results in a category

Events related to your search term

The results are organized into sections, such as TOP HITS, CONTACTS, MAIL, MUSIC, and so on. Swipe up and down the screen to browse all of the results. To work with an item you find, such as to view an event you found, tap it; you move into the associated app and see the search result that you tapped. The results remain in the Spotlight Search tool. Move back to the Home screen and open the Spotlight tool again. The results of the most recent search are still listed. To clear the search term, tap the Clear button (x). To close the Spotlight tool without going to one of the results, tap Cancel.

Working with Siri Suggestions

New! When you move to a Home page and swipe all the way to the right, you see the SIRI SUGGESTIONS page. This page shows you people you communicate with, apps you use, items that might of interest that are near you, and news you might be interested in. You can also search from this screen just like from other Home screens.

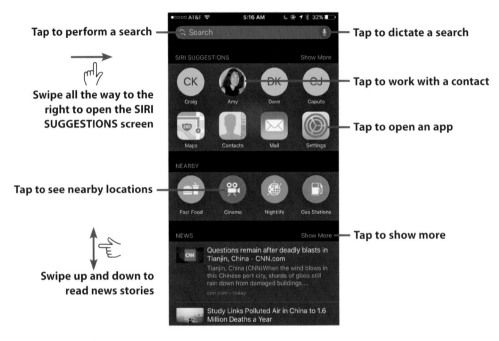

Tap to perform a search

Swipe all the way to the right to open the SIRI SUGGESTIONS screen

Tap to see nearby locations

Swipe up and down to read news stories

Tap to dictate a search

Tap to work with a contact

Tap to open an app

Tap to show more

On the SIRI SUGGESTIONS screen, you can do the following tasks:

- Tap in the Search bar to type a search or tap the Microphone to dictate a search. This works just like the searching you learned about in the previous section.

- Tap a contact to reveal options you can use to communicate with her.

- Tap an app you've used recently to return to it.

- Tap a category of location shown in the NEARBY section to move to the Maps app and see a list of places of that type.

- Swipe up and down in the NEWS section to browse news stories. Tap a story to read its detail in the News app.

Working with the Control Center

On the Home screen or when you are using apps, swipe up from the bottom of the screen to open the Control Center

On the Lock screen, the place you swipe up on to open the Control Center is marked with a line

On some app screens, where you swipe up to open the Control Center is indicated by an upward-facing arrow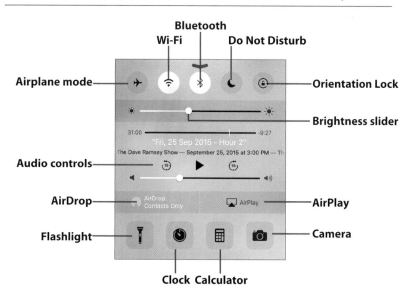

The Control Center provides quick access to a number of very useful controls. To access it, swipe up from the bottom of the screen. If your iPhone is asleep/ locked, press the Sleep/Wake or Touch ID/Home button to wake up the phone and then swipe up from the bottom of the screen from the area of the horizontal line. Sometimes when you are using an app, the place you swipe up on is marked with an upward-facing arrow. Regardless of the screen you are on, when you swipe up, the Control Center opens and gives you quick access to a number of controls.

Control Center Tip

Some apps have a Dock at the bottom of the screen. When you are using such an app, make sure you don't touch a button on the Dock when you are trying to open the Control Center because you'll do whatever the button is for instead. Just swipe up on an empty area of the Dock and the Control Center opens.

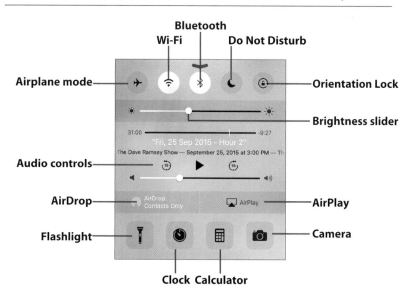

At the top of the Control Center are buttons you can use to turn on or turn off important functions. To activate a function, tap the button, which becomes white to show the function is active. To disable a function, tap the button so that it becomes dark to show you it is inactive. For example, to lock the orientation of the iPhone's screen in its current position, tap the Orientation Lock button so it becomes white. Your iPhone screen's orientation no longer changes when you rotate the phone. To make the orientation change when you rotate the phone again, turn off the Orientation Lock button. You learn about Airplane mode and Do Not Disturb later in this chapter. Wi-Fi and Bluetooth are explained in Chapter 2, "Connecting Your iPhone to the Internet, Bluetooth Devices, and iPhones/iPods/iPads."

Below the top function buttons is the Brightness slider. Drag the slider to the right to make the screen brighter or to the left to make it dimmer.

In the center of the Control Center are the audio controls you can use with whatever audio is playing, such as music from the Music app, podcasts from the Podcasts app, and so on. Music and podcasts are covered in Chapter 14, "Finding and Listening to Music," and Chapter 16, "Using Other Cool iPhone Apps and Features," respectively.

The AirDrop button enables you to share content with other iOS device and Mac users in the same vicinity; this is covered in Chapter 2. The AirPlay button enables you to stream your iPhone's music, podcasts, photos, and video onto other devices, such as a TV to which an Apple TV is connected; using AirPlay is covered in Chapters 14 and 15, "Working with Photos and Video You Take with Your iPhone."

At the bottom of the Control Center are four app icons; tap an icon to open the app, just as you do on the Home screens. The Flashlight app uses your iPhone's flash as a flashlight. The Clock app provides you with a number of time-related functions, which are world clocks, alarms, timer, and stopwatch; when you open this app from the Control Center, it opens in the timer, but you can use its other functions by tapping the function you want to use. The Calculator does just what it sounds like it does; when you hold the iPhone vertically, you see a simple calculator, while if you rotate the iPhone to horizontal, the calculator becomes more powerful. The Camera app enables you to capture photos and video (this is covered in Chapter 15).

Working with Notifications and the Notification Center

Your iPhone has a lot of activity going on, from new emails to reminders to calendar events. The iOS notification system keeps you informed of these happenings through a number of means. Visual notifications include alerts, banners, and badges. Alert sounds can also let you know something has happened, and vibrations make you feel the new activity. There are a variety of notification options for each app. You learn how to customize the notifications your iPhone uses in Chapter 5.

Working with visual notifications is pretty straightforward.

Banner notification — Sir William ★ now / Flying Today? / If so, what time are you heading out? Best, Will — **Tap to move into the app**

Swipe down to respond (some apps, such as Messages) — **Swipe up to close the banner**

Sir William now / Are you flying today? If so, what time?

Type your reply — Yes, about 2. | Send — **Send your reply**

When a banner appears, you can do one of several things. You can view and then ignore it (it rotates off the screen after displaying for a few seconds). You can tap it to move into the app to take some action, such as to read an email. You can swipe up from the bottom of the banner to close it. For some apps, such as Messages, you can swipe down on the banner to respond directly in the notification.

Reminder
Finish Ch 5
— **Alert notification**

Mark as Completed

Later

When an alert appears, you must either take action, such as marking a reminder as completed or listening to a voice message, tap the Options button to take one of a number of actions, or tap the Later, Dismiss, Close, or Ignore button (the button you see depends on the app the alert comes from) to close the alert and keep doing what you were doing.

— **Badge**

Mail

Badges appear on an app's or a folder's icon to let you know something has changed, such as when you have received new email.

Badges are purely informational as are sounds and vibrations; you can't take any action on these directly. They inform you about an event so that you can take action, such as to download and install an update to your iPhone's iOS software.

Notifications on the Lock Screen

Notifications can appear on the Lock screen. This is useful because you can see them when your iPhone is locked. If your phone is asleep, the notifications appear briefly on the screen and then it goes dark again; you can press the Wake/Sleep button or the Touch/ID Home button to see your notifications without unlocking the iPhone. You can swipe up or down the screen to browse the notifications on the Lock screen or swipe to the right on them to move to the related app, too (you need to enter your passcode or touch the Touch ID button to move into the associated app).

The Notification Center organizes and displays a variety of information for you. To open the Notification Center, swipe down from the top of the iPhone's screen; if your iPhone is currently asleep/locked, press the Home/Touch ID or Sleep/Wake button and then swipe down from the top of the screen to open the Notification Center.

Today's information

Tap to move into the related app

Swipe down from the top of the screen to open the Notification Center

Swipe up or down to browse all of today's information

Tap the Today tab to see the day and date along with weather information. Under that, you see any information that impacts your day; this information is organized in sections based on its type, such as Reminders, Calendar events, and so on. If you swipe up far enough, you see the Tomorrow section that presents information about tomorrow's activities, too.

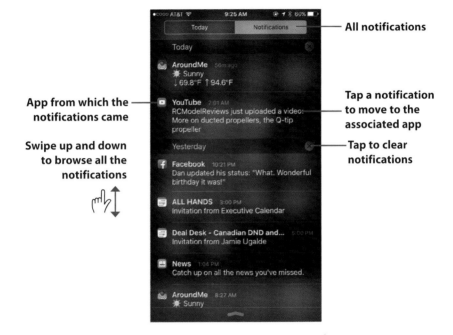

All notifications

App from which the notifications came

Tap a notification to move to the associated app

Swipe up and down to browse all the notifications

Tap to clear notifications

Tap the Notifications tab to see all your current notifications, such as for new email or text messages. These are organized by the app from which they come. Like the Today tab, you can swipe up and down to browse all the notifications, tap a notification to move to the related app, and so on. To remove all the notifications for an app, tap its Clear button (x) and then tap Clear.

Active Notifications

Some of the notifications can show more information than can fit on the screen (examples include the Weather and Stocks apps). Swipe to the left or right on these notifications to see more information. Some notifications have links that take you to the Web to get more detailed information.

Using the Do Not Disturb Mode

All the notifications you read about in the previous section are useful, but at times, they can be annoying or distracting. When you put your iPhone in Do Not Disturb mode, its visual, audible, and vibration notifications are disabled so that they won't bother you. It won't ring if someone calls you, unless you specify certain contacts to override the Do Not Disturb.

Tap to keep your iPhone from bothering you

Do Not Disturb is on

To put your iPhone in Do Not Disturb mode, open the Control Center and tap the Do Not Disturb button. It becomes white and the Do Not Disturb: On status appears at the top of the Control Center. Your iPhone stops its notifications and does not ring if someone calls. To make your notifications active again, tap the Do Not Disturb button so it is black; your iPhone resumes trying to get your attention when it is needed.

In Chapter 4, "Configuring an iPhone to Suit Your Preferences," you learn how to set a schedule for Do Not Disturb so that your iPhone goes into this mode automatically at certain times, such as from 10 p.m. to 6 a.m. You can also configure certain exceptions, including whose calls come in even when your iPhone is in Do Not Disturb mode.

Working with Text

You can do lots of things with an iPhone that require you to provide text input. There are a couple of ways you can do this, the most obvious of which is by typing. The iPhone's keyboard is quite amazing. Whenever you need it, whether it's for emailing, entering a website URL, performing a search, or any other typing function, it pops up automatically.

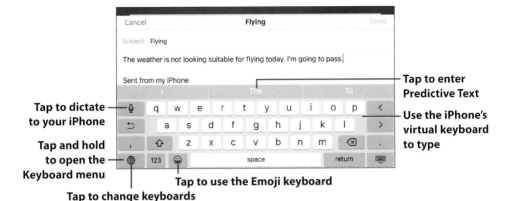

Tap to dictate to your iPhone

Tap and hold to open the Keyboard menu

Tap to change keyboards

Tap to enter Predictive Text

Use the iPhone's virtual keyboard to type

Tap to use the Emoji keyboard

To type, just tap the keys. As you tap each key, you hear audio feedback (you can disable this sound if you want to) and the key you tapped pops up in a magnified view on the screen. The keyboard includes all the standard keys, plus a few for special uses. To change from letters to numbers and special characters, just tap the 123 key. Tap the #+= key to see more special characters. Tap the 123 key to move back to the numbers and special characters or the ABC key to return to letters. The keyboard also has contextual keys that appear when you need them. For example, when you enter a website address, the .com key appears so you can enter these four characters with a single tap.

You can also use Predictive Text, which is the feature that tries to predict text you want to enter based on the context of what you are currently typing and what you have typed before. Predictive Text appears in the bar between the text and the keyboard and presents you with three options. If one of those is what you want to enter, tap it and it is added to the text at the current location of the cursor. If you don't see an option you want to enter, keep typing and the options change as the text changes. You can tap an option at any time to enter it. The nice thing about Predictive Text is that it gets better at predicting your text needs over time. In other words, the more you use it, the better it gets at predicting what you want to type. You can also enable or disable Predictive Text, as you see shortly.

Predictive Text Need Not Apply

When you are entering text where Predictive Text doesn't apply, such as when you are typing email addresses, the Predictive Text bar is hidden and can't be enabled. This makes sense because there's no way text in things such as email addresses can be predicted. When you move back into an area where it does apply, Predictive Text becomes active again.

The great thing about a virtual keyboard like the iPhone has is that it can change to reflect the language or symbols you want to type. As you learn in Chapter 4, you can install multiple keyboards, such as one for your primary language and more for your secondary languages. You can also install third-party keyboards to take advantage of their features (this is also covered in Chapter 4).

By default, two keyboards are available for you to use. One is for the primary language configured for your iPhone (for example, mine is U.S. English). The other is the Emoji keyboard (more on this shortly). How you change the keyboard you are using depends on if you have installed additional keyboards and the orientation of the iPhone.

If you haven't installed additional keyboards, you can change keyboards by tapping the Emoji key, which has a smiley face on it.

If you have installed other keyboards, you change keyboards by tapping the Globe key.

Each time you tap this key (Globe if available, Emoji if there isn't a Globe), the keyboard changes to be the next keyboard installed; along with the available keys changing, you briefly see the name of the current keyboard in the Space bar. When you have cycled through all the keyboards, you return to the one where you started.

The Keys, They Are A-Changin'

The keys on the keyboard can change depending on the orientation of the iPhone. For example, when you have more than one keyboard installed and hold the iPhone vertically, the Emoji key disappears and you see only the Globe key. Not to worry though, you can still get to the Emoji keyboard by tapping the Globe key until the Emoji keyboard appears, or by opening the Keyboard menu and tapping Emoji. When you have installed additional keyboards and hold the iPhone horizontally, you see both the Globe and Emoji keys. Tap the Emoji key to switch to that keyboard or the Globe key to cycle through all the keyboards.

Tap to enable/disable Predictive Text

Tap to use a keyboard

You can also select the specific keyboard you want to use and enable/disable Predictive Text by tapping and holding on the Globe key (or the Emoji key, if you don't see the Globe key). The Keyboard menu appears. Tap a keyboard to switch to it. Tap the Predictive Text switch to enable or disable it; when the switch is green Predictive Text is enabled, when the switch is white, it is disabled.

Swipe to browse icons

Everyone loves the Emoji keyboard!

Tap to change keyboards

Tap to see groups of icons

Tap to see icons you've used before

Tap to return to the previous keyboard

The Emoji keyboard allows you to insert a variety of icons into your text to liven things up, communicate your feelings, or just to have some fun (if you don't have this keyboard installed, see Chapter 4). You can open this keyboard by tapping its key (the smiley face) or by tapping it on the Keyboard menu. You see a palette containing many icons, organized into groups. You can change the groups of icons you are browsing by tapping the buttons at the bottom of the screen. Swipe to the left or right on the icons to browse the icons in the current group. Tap an icon to enter it at the cursor's location in your message, email, or other type of document. To use an icon you've used before, tap the Clock button; you'll probably find that you use this recent set of icons regularly so this can save a lot of time. To return to the mundane world of letters and symbols, tap the Emoji or Globe key again.

Another Reason It's Called a Plus

When you rotate an iPhone 6Plus/6s Plus to the horizontal position, the keyboard gains some extra keys. These include Cut (scissors), Copy (two squares), Paste (paper and clipboard), Format (**B**/U), and Undo (curved arrow).

What's Your Typing Orientation?

Like many other tasks, you can rotate the iPhone to change the screen's orientation while you type. When the iPhone is in the horizontal orientation, the keyboard is wider, making it easier to tap individual keys. When the iPhone is in vertical orientation, the keyboard is narrower, but you can see more of the typing area. So, try both to see which mode is most effective for you.

If you type a word that the iPhone doesn't recognize, that word is flagged as a possible mistake and suggestions are made to help you correct it. How this happens depends on whether or not Predictive Text is enabled.

Tap to change the suspicious word to be the suggested word

Suspicious word

If Predictive Text is enabled, potential replacements for suspicious words appear in the Predictive Text bar. Tap a word to replace what you've typed with the suggested word.

Suspicious word

Tap X to reject the suggestion

If Predictive Text isn't enabled, a suspicious word is highlighted and a suggestion about what it thinks is the correct word appears in a pop-up box. To accept the suggestion, tap the Space key. To reject the suggestion, tap the pop-up box to close it and keep what you typed. You can also use this feature for shorthand typing. For example, to type "I've" you can simply type "Ive" and iPhone suggests "I've," which you can accept by tapping the Space key.

Typing Tricks

Many keys, especially symbols and punctuation, have additional characters. To see a character's options, tap it and hold down. If it has options, a menu pops up after a second or so. To enter one of the optional characters, drag over the menu until the one you want to enter is highlighted, and then lift your finger off the screen. The optional character you selected is entered. For example, if you tap and hold on the period, you can select .com, .edu, and so on, which is very helpful when you are typing a website or email addresses.

By default, the iPhone attempts to correct the capitalization of what you type. It also automatically selects the Shift key when you start a new sentence, start a new paragraph, or in other places where its best guess is that you need a capital letter. If you don't want to enter a capital character, simply tap the Shift key before you type. You can enable the Caps Lock key by tapping the Shift key twice. When the key is highlighted, everything you type is in uppercase letters.

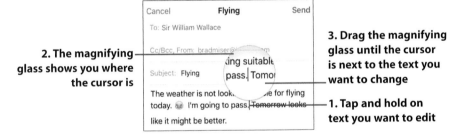

2. The magnifying glass shows you where the cursor is

3. Drag the magnifying glass until the cursor is next to the text you want to change

1. Tap and hold on text you want to edit

To edit text you've typed, tap and hold on the text you want to edit. A magnifying glass icon appears on the screen, and within it you see a magnified view of the location of the cursor. Drag the magnifying glass to where you want to make changes (to position the cursor where you want to start making changes), and then lift your finger from the screen. The cursor remains in that location, and you can use the keyboard to make changes to the text or to add text at that location.

Using 3D Touch with Text

When you are using an iPhone 6s or 6s Plus, you can apply slight pressure when you touch the screen to have the closest word selected automatically; it is highlighted in blue to show you that it is selected. To place the cursor without selecting words that are near your finger, just touch the screen without applying any pressure.

Your Own Text Replacements

You can create your own text shortcuts so you can type something like "eadd" and it is automatically replaced with your email address. See Chapter 4 for the details.

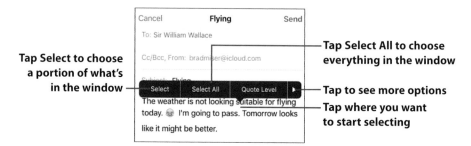

Tap Select to choose a portion of what's in the window

Tap Select All to choose everything in the window

Tap to see more options

Tap where you want to start selecting

You can also select text or images to copy and paste the selected content into a new location or to replace that content. Tap and hold down briefly where you want to start the selection until the magnifying glass icon appears; then lift your finger off the screen. The Select menu appears. Tap Select to select part of the content on the screen, or tap Select All to select everything in the current window.

More Commands

Some menus that appear when you are making selections and performing actions have a right-facing arrow at the right end. Tap this to see a new menu that contains additional commands. These commands are contextual, meaning that you see different commands depending on what you are doing at that specific time. You can tap the left-facing arrow to move back to a previous menu.

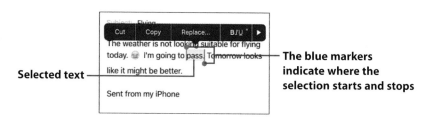

Selected text

The blue markers indicate where the selection starts and stops

You see markers indicating where the selection starts and stops. (The iPhone attempts to select something logical, such as the word or sentence.) New commands appear on the menu; these provide actions for the text currently selected.

Magnified view of what you are selecting

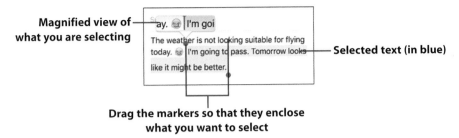

Selected text (in blue)

Drag the markers so that they enclose what you want to select

Drag the two markers so that the content you want to select is between them; the selected portion is highlighted in blue. As you drag, you see a magnified view of where the selection marker is, which helps you place it more accurately. When the selection markers are located correctly, lift your finger from the screen. (If you tapped the Select All command, you don't need to do this because the content you want is already selected.)

Have I Got a Suggestion for You!

Tap the Suggestion option to see items that might be useful to you. These are also contextual. For example, when you have a word selected, one of the suggestions might be Define, which looks up the selected word in the Dictionary (tap Done to return to where you came from). As you use your iPhone, check out the Suggestions because you'll find some very useful options tucked away there.

Tap Cut or Copy

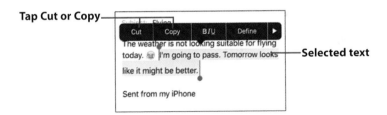

Selected text

Tap Cut to remove the content from the current window, or tap Copy to just copy it.

Format It!

If you tap the **B**/U button, you can tap Bold, Italics, or Underline to apply those formatting options to the selected text. You also can tap multiple format options to apply them at the same time. You might need to tap the right-facing arrow at the end of the menu to see this command, depending on how many commands are on the menu.

Tap where you want to paste

Tap Paste

Move to where you want to paste the content you selected; for example, use the App Switcher to change to a different app. Tap where you want the content to be pasted. For a more precise location, tap and hold and then use the magnifying glass icon to move to a specific location. Lift your finger off the screen and the menu appears. Then tap Paste.

Pasted content

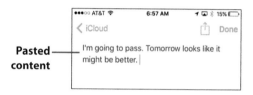

The content you copied or cut appears where you placed the cursor.

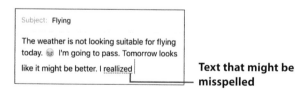

Text that might be misspelled

The iPhone also has a spell-checking feature that comes into play after you have entered text (as opposed to the Predictive Text and autocorrect/suggests feature that change text as you type it). When you've entered text the iPhone doesn't recognize, it is underlined in red.

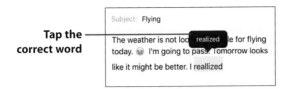

Tap the correct word

Tap the underlined word. It is shaded in red to show you what is being checked, and a menu appears with one or more replacements that might be the correct spelling. If one of the options is the one you want, tap it. The incorrect word is replaced with the one you tapped.

Contextual Menus and You

In some apps, tapping a word causes a menu with other kinds of actions to appear; you can tap an action to make it happen. For example, in the iBooks app, when you tap a word, the resulting menu enables you to look up the word in a dictionary. Other apps support different kinds of actions, so it's a good idea to try tapping words in apps that involve text to see which commands are available.

Dictating Text

You can also enter text by dictating it. This is a fast and easy way to type and you'll be amazed at how accurate the iPhone is at translating your speech into typed words. Dictation is available almost anywhere you need to enter text. (Exceptions are passcodes and passwords, such as for your Apple ID.)

Tap to put the cursor where you want dictated text to start

Tap the Microphone key to start dictation

To start dictating, tap the Microphone key. The iPhone goes into Dictation mode. A gray bar appears at the bottom of the window. As the iPhone "hears" you, the line oscillates.

The iPhone is taking dictation ⎯⎯

I'm heading out to Muncie to fly in a little while.

Sent from my iPhone

Tap Done when you're done speaking ⎯⎯⎯⎯⎯⎯⎯⎯ Done

Start speaking the text you want the iPhone to type. As you speak, the text is entered starting from the location of the cursor.

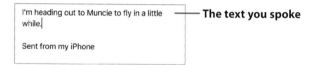

I'm heading out to Muncie to fly in a little while. ⎯⎯ **The text you spoke**

Sent from my iPhone

When you've finished dictating, tap Done. The keyboard reappears and you see the text you spoke. This feature is amazingly accurate and can be a much faster and more convenient way to enter text than typing it.

You can edit the text you dictated just like text you entered using the keyboard.

Meeting Siri

Siri is the iPhone's voice-recognition and control software. This feature enables you to accomplish many tasks by speaking. For example, you can create and send text messages, reply to emails, make phone calls, and much more. (Using Siri is explained in detail in Chapter 12, "Working with Siri.")

When you perform actions, Siri uses the related apps to accomplish what you've asked it to do. For example, when you create a meeting, Siri uses the Calendar app.

Siri is a great way to control your iPhone, especially when you are working in handsfree mode.

Your iPhone has to be connected to the Internet for Siri (and dictation for that matter) to work. That's because the words you speak are sent over the Internet, transcribed into text, and then sent back to your iPhone. If your iPhone isn't connected to the Internet, this can't happen and Siri reports that it can't connect to the network or simply that it can't do what you ask right now.

Using Siri is pretty simple because it follows a consistent pattern and prompts you for input and direction.

Siri is ready to do your bidding

This line shows what Siri is hearing

Activate Siri by pressing and holding down the Touch ID/Home button or pressing and holding down the center part of the buttons on the right EarPod wire until you hear the Siri chime. If so configured (see Chapter 12), you can say "Hey Siri" to activate it, too. This puts Siri in "listening" mode and the "What can I help you with?" text appears on the screen. This indicates Siri is ready for your command.

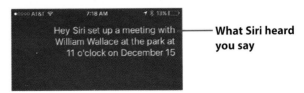

What Siri heard you say

Speak your command or ask a question. When you stop speaking, Siri goes into processing mode. After Siri interprets what you've said, it provides two kinds of feedback to confirm what it heard: it displays what it heard on the screen and provides audible feedback to you. Siri then tries to do what it thinks you've asked and shows you what it is doing. If it needs more input from you, you're prompted to provide it and Siri moves into "listening" mode automatically.

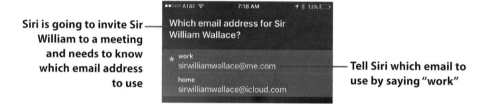

Siri is going to invite Sir William to a meeting and needs to know which email address to use

Tell Siri which email to use by saying "work"

If Siri requests that you confirm what it is doing or to make a selection, do so. Siri completes the action and displays what it has done; it also audibly confirms the result.

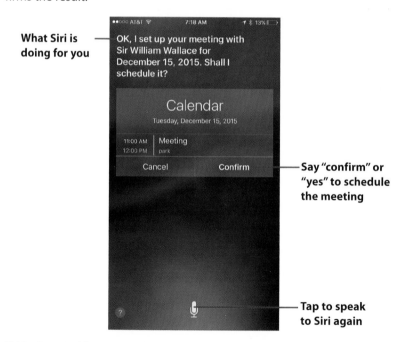

What Siri is doing for you

Say "confirm" or "yes" to schedule the meeting

Tap to speak to Siri again

Siri isn't quite like using the computer on the Starship Enterprise on *Star Trek*, but it's pretty darn close. Mostly, you can just speak to Siri as you would talk to someone else, and it is able to do what you want or asks you the information it needs to do what you want.

Understanding iPhone Status Icons

At the top of the screen is the Status bar with various icons that provide you with information, such as whether you are connected to a Wi-Fi or cellular data network, the time, sync in process, whether the iPhone's orientation is locked, the state of the iPhone's battery, and so on. Keep an eye on this area as you use your iPhone. The following table provides a guide to the most common of these icons.

iPhone Status Icons

Icon	Description	Where to Learn More
●●○○○	Signal Strength—Indicates how strong the cellular signal is.	Chapter 2
AT&T	Provider name—The provider of the current cellular network.	Chapter 2
LTE	Cellular data network—Indicates which cellular network your iPhone is using to connect to the Internet.	Chapter 2
📶	Wi-Fi—Indicates your phone is connected to a Wi-Fi network.	Chapter 2
Wi-Fi 📶	Wi-Fi calling—Indicates your phone can make voice calls over a Wi-Fi network.	Chapter 2
🌙	Do Not Disturb—Your iPhone's notifications and ringer are silenced.	Chapters 1, 4
✳	Bluetooth—Indicates if Bluetooth is turned on or off and if your phone is connected to a device.	Chapter 2
15%	Battery percentage—Percentage of charge remaining in the battery.	Chapter 17
🔋	Battery status—Relative level of charge of the battery.	Chapter 17
🔋	Low Battery status—The battery has less than 20% power remaining.	Chapter 17
🔋	Low Power mode—The iPhone is operating in Low Power mode.	Chapter 17
🔒	Orientation Lock—Your iPhone's screen won't change when you rotate your iPhone.	Chapter 1
⚡	Charging—The battery in the iPhone is being charged.	Chapter 17
➤	Location Services—An app is using the Location Services feature to track your iPhone's location.	Chapter 4
✈	Airplane mode—The transmit and receive functions are disabled.	Chapter 1

Turning Your iPhone On or Off

Swipe to the right to turn your iPhone off

If you want to turn off your iPhone, press and hold the Wake/Sleep button until the slider appears at the top of the screen. Swipe the slider to the right to shut down the iPhone. The iPhone shuts down.

To restart your iPhone, press and hold the Wake/Sleep button until the Apple logo appears on the screen, and then let go of the button.

After it starts up, and you have a passcode, you see the Lock screen. Swipe to the right and enter your passcode to start using your phone. (Even if you have Touch ID enabled to unlock your phone, you must enter your passcode the first time you unlock it after a restart.)

If you don't have a passcode configured, you move directly to the Home screen when the phone starts and it's ready for you to use. Keep in mind, if you do not have a passcode configured, your phone is vulnerable to anyone who gets a hold of it.

Sleeping/Locking and Waking/Unlocking Your iPhone

When an iPhone is asleep/locked, you need to wake it up and then unlock it to use it. How you do this depends on the type of iPhone you have.

If you have an iPhone 5s or later, and have configured it to recognize your fingerprint to unlock it, press the Touch ID/Home button once, and then touch the Touch ID button with your finger. When your fingerprint is recognized, your iPhone unlocks and you can start using it.

Be Recognized

To use the Touch ID, you need to train your iPhone to recognize the fingerprints you want to use. You were prompted to configure one fingerprint when you started your iPhone for the first time. You can change or add fingerprints for Touch ID at any time; see Chapter 4 for the details of configuring Touch ID.

Swipe to the right to unlock your iPhone

If you have an iPhone 5c or older, or you don't have any Touch ID configured to unlock your phone, you first press the Wake/Sleep button or the Home button. The iPhone wakes up, the Lock screen appears, and at the bottom of the screen, the Unlock slider appears. Swipe on the slider to the right to unlock the iPhone so you can work with it.

Enter your passcode to start using your iPhone

If you require a passcode to unlock your iPhone—which you should for security—type your passcode at the prompt.

When you unlock the phone, or swipe to open it if no passcode is configured, you move to the last screen you were using before it was locked.

The Time Is Always Handy

If you use your iPhone as a watch the way I do, just press the Wake/Sleep button. The current time and date appear; if you don't unlock it, the iPhone goes back to sleep after a few seconds.

In most cases, you should just put the iPhone to sleep when you aren't using it instead of shutting it off. It doesn't use much power when it sleeps, and it wakes up immediately when you want to start using it again. Also, when you put your iPhone to sleep, it can't be used until it is unlocked. If you set it to require a passcode to unlock, this also protects your information. (You seldom need to turn off an iPhone.) Even when the iPhone is asleep, you can receive notifications, such as when you receive emails or text messages. (See Chapter 4 to configure which notifications you see on the Lock screen.)

To put your iPhone to sleep and lock it, press the Wake/Sleep button.

Signing Into Your Apple ID

As you learn throughout this book, an Apple ID is useful in many situations, such as to access iCloud services; purchase music, movies, and other content from the iTunes Store; download apps from the App Store; and so on. If you have an iPhone 5s or later, you can quickly sign into your Apple ID by using the iPhone's Touch ID/Home button. (As referenced in the prior note, you need to configure your iPhone to recognize your fingerprint to use Touch ID; see Chapter 4 for details.)

Touch the Touch ID button to sign in **You need to sign into your Apple ID to complete an action**

When you need to sign into your Apple ID, you see a prompt. Simply touch your finger to the Touch ID/Home button. When your fingerprint is recognized, you sign into your Apple ID and can complete whatever you were doing, such as downloading music from the iTunes Store.

You need to sign into your Apple ID to complete an action **Enter your Apple ID password and tap OK**

If you have an older model or you don't have the settings configured to enable you to use Touch ID with your Apple ID, you need to provide your Apple ID password to sign in by typing it and tapping OK. Whatever action you were performing is completed.

Setting the Volume

Setting the ringer volume

To change the iPhone's volume, press the up or down Volume button on the side of the iPhone. When you change the volume, your change affects the current activity. For example, if you are on a phone call, the call volume changes or if you are listening to music, the music's volume changes. If you aren't on a screen that shows the Volume slider, an icon pops up to show you the relative volume you are setting and the type, such as setting the ringer's volume. When the volume is right, release the Volume button.

Drag to the left or right to change the volume level

When you are using an audio app, such as the Music app, you can also drag the volume slider in that app or on the Control Center to increase or decrease the volume.

When you use the iPhone's EarPods, you can change the volume by pressing the upper part of the switch on the right EarPod's wire to increase volume or the lower part to decrease it.

Using Airplane Mode

Although there's a debate about whether devices such as iPhones pose any real danger to the operation of aircraft, there's no reason to run any risk by using your iPhone while you are on an airplane. (Besides, not following crew instructions on airplanes can lead you to less-than-desirable interactions with the flight crew.) When you place your iPhone in Airplane mode, its transmitting and receiving functions are disabled, so it poses no threat to the operation of the aircraft. While it is in Airplane mode, you can't use the phone, the Web, Siri, or any other functions that require communication between your iPhone and other devices or networks.

Tap to put your iPhone in Airplane mode

To put your iPhone in Airplane mode, swipe up from the bottom of the screen to open the Control Center and tap the Airplane mode button. All connections to the Internet and the cell network stop, and your iPhone goes into quiet mode in which it doesn't broadcast or receive any signals. The Airplane mode button becomes white and you see the Airplane mode icon at the top of the screen.

In Airplane mode, you can use your iPhone for all your apps that don't require an Internet connection, such as iBooks, Music, Videos, Photos, and so on.

To turn off Airplane mode, open the Control Center and tap the Airplane mode button; it becomes black again and the Airplane mode icon disappears. The iPhone resumes transmitting and receiving signals, and all the functions that require a connection start working again.

Wi-Fi in Airplane Mode

Many airplanes support Wi-Fi on board. To access a Wi-Fi network without violating the requirement not to use a cell network, put the iPhone in Airplane mode, which turns off Wi-Fi. On the Control Center, tap the Wi-Fi button to turn Wi-Fi back on. Wi-Fi starts up and you can select the network you want to join (see Chapter 2). You can use this configuration at other times, too, such as when you want to access the Internet but don't want to be bothered with phone calls. When your iPhone is in Airplane mode and Wi-Fi is on, all your calls (including Wi-Fi calls) go straight to voicemail but you can use your Internet-related apps. (I would never do this, you understand.)

Using the Settings App

Tap to open the Settings app

Swipe up or down to browse all the settings options

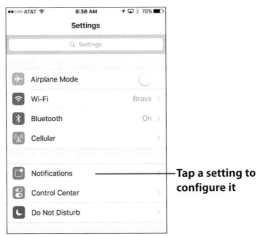

Tap a setting to configure it

The Settings app is where you do almost all of your iPhone's configuration, and you use it frequently throughout this book. To use the Settings app, tap Settings on the Home screen. The app opens. Swipe up and down the screen to browse the various settings tools. Tap an item to configure its settings. For example, to configure your notifications, tap Notifications. (You use the Settings app in a number of chapters in this book, especially in Chapter 4.)

Printing from Your iPhone

You can also print from your iPhone to AirPrint-compatible printers.

Share button

Swipe to see the Print button if it isn't visible

Tap to print

First, set up and configure your AirPrint printer (see the instructions that came with the printer you use).

It Depends

When you tap the Share button, you might see a menu containing commands instead of the grid of icons shown in the figure. The way it appears is dependent upon the app you are using. Either way, tap Print to move to the Printer Options screen.

When you are in the app from which you want to print, tap the Share button. Tap Print on the resulting menu. You might need to swipe to the right to expose the Print command. (If you don't see the Share button or the Print command, the app you are using doesn't support printing.) The Share button looks a bit different in some apps, but it works similarly.

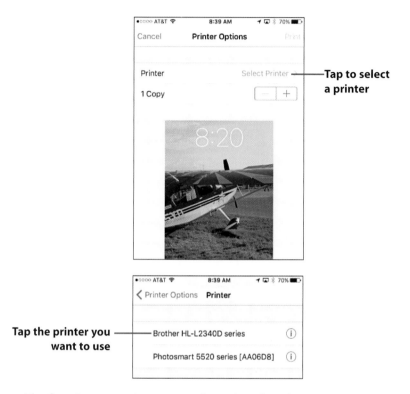

Tap to select
a printer

Tap the printer you
want to use

The first time you print, you need to select the printer you want to use. On the Printer Options screen, tap Select Printer. Then tap the printer you want to use. You move back to the Printer Options screen and see the printer you selected.

Don't Have an AirPrint Printer?

If you don't have an AirPrint printer, do a web search for a tool called "AirPrint for Windows" if you have a Windows PC or "handyPrint for Mac" if you have a Mac. Download and install the software on a computer that is capable of sharing its printers. Configure your computer to share the printer you want to use with your iPhone. Then launch the software on your computer and start it. The printers you configure in the AirPrint software are available for printing from your iPhone.

Tap to print

Current printer

Current number of copies

Tap to set the number of copies

Preview of what you are printing

Tap the – or + to set the number of copies; the current number of copies is shown to the left of the buttons. Tap Print to print the document.

The next time you print, if you want to use the same printer, you can skip the printer selection process because the iPhone remembers the last printer you used. To change the printer, tap Printer and tap the printer you want to use.

Connect to the
Internet via Wi-Fi or
a cellular network

Use AirDrop to
share content
with other iOS
devices

Tap here to join
Wi-Fi networks
to connect to
the Internet
and configure
Bluetooth to
connect to
other devices

Take
advantage of
an Internet
connection in
many different
apps

In this chapter, you explore how to connect your iPhone to the Internet; Bluetooth devices; and other iPhones, iPod touches, and iPads. Topics include the following:

→ Using Wi-Fi networks to connect to the Internet
→ Using cellular data networks to connect to the Internet
→ Using Bluetooth to connect to other devices
→ Connecting your iPhone to other iPhones, iPod touches, or iPads
→ Using AirDrop to share content with Macs, other iPhones, iPod Touches, or iPads

Connecting Your iPhone to the Internet, Bluetooth Devices, and iPhones/iPods/iPads

Your iPhone has many functions that rely on an Internet connection. Fortunately, you can connect your iPhone to the Internet by connecting it to a Wi-Fi network that provides Internet access. You can also connect to the Internet through a cellular data network operated by your cell phone provider.

Using Bluetooth, you can wirelessly connect your iPhone to other devices, including keyboards, headsets, headphones, and so on.

There are a number of ways to connect your iPhone to other iPhones, iPod touches, iPads, and Macintosh computers. This is useful to use collaborative apps, play games, and share information. For example, using AirDrop, you can quickly and easily share photos and other content with other people using iOS devices and Macintosh computers.

Using Wi-Fi Networks to Connect to the Internet

Almost all Wi-Fi networks broadcast their information so that you can easily see them with your iPhone; these are called *open networks* because anyone who is in range can attempt to join one since they appear on Wi-Fi devices automatically. The Wi-Fi networks you can access in public places (such as airports and hotels) are all open, and you can see them on your iPhone. Likewise, any Wi-Fi networks in your home or office are very likely to be open as well. Connecting to an open network typically requires selecting the network you want to join, based on its name, and then entering its password (if required).

By default, when you access one of your iPhone's Internet functions, such as Safari, your iPhone automatically searches for Wi-Fi networks to join if you aren't already connected to one. A box appears showing all the networks available. You can select and join one of these networks. You learn how to do this in the following steps.

Connecting to Open Wi-Fi Networks

To connect to a Wi-Fi network, perform the following steps:

1. On the Home screen, tap Settings. Next to Wi-Fi, you see the status of your Wi-Fi connection. It is Off if Wi-Fi is turned off, Not Connected if Wi-Fi is turned on and your phone isn't currently connected to Wi-Fi, or the name of the Wi-Fi network to which your iPhone is connected.

2. Tap Wi-Fi.

Current Wi-Fi status

3. If Wi-Fi isn't enabled already, slide the Wi-Fi switch to on (green) to allow your iPhone to start searching for available networks. When Wi-Fi is turned on, a list of available networks is displayed in the CHOOSE A NETWORK section (it can take a moment or two for your iPhone to list all the networks in the area). Along with each network's name, icons indicating whether it requires a password (the padlock icon) to join and the current signal strength (the radio signal icon) are displayed.

4. Tap the network you want to join. If a network requires a password, you must know what that password is to be able to join it. Another consideration should be signal strength; the more waves in the network's signal strength icon, the stronger the connection will be.

5. At the prompt, enter the password for the network. If you aren't prompted for a password, you selected a network that doesn't require one and can skip to step 7. You're likely to find networks that don't require a password in public places (hotels, airports, and so on); see the next section for information on using these types of networks.

6. Tap Join. If you provided the correct password, your iPhone connects to the network and gets the information it needs to connect to the Internet. If not, you're prompted to enter the password again. After you successfully connect to the network, you return to the Wi-Fi screen.

Wi-Fi network provided by an iPad

Network name

Requires a password

Signal strength

Info button

Does not require a password

Typing Passwords

As you type a password, each character is hidden by dots in the Password field except for the last character you entered, which is displayed on the screen for a few moments. This is helpful because you see each character as you type it, so you always see the most recent character you entered, which can prevent you from getting all the way to the end of a long password only to discover you've made a mistake along the way and have to start all over again.

7. Review the network information. The network to which you are connected appears just below the Wi-Fi switch and is marked with a check mark. You also see the signal strength for that network. (This indication is typically more accurate than the one you see before you are connected.) Assuming the Wi-Fi network is providing Internet access, you're able to use apps that require the Internet to work.

The network your iPhone is using

Changing Networks

You can use these same steps to change the Wi-Fi network you are using at any time. For example, if you have to pay to use one network while a different one is free, simply choose the free network in step 4.

8. Try to move to a web page, such as www.weather.com, to test your Wi-Fi connection. (See Chapter 13, "Surfing the Web," for details on using the web browser.) If the web page opens, you are ready to use the Internet on your phone. If you are taken to a login web page for a Wi-Fi provider rather than the page you were trying to access, see the next task. If you see a message saying the Internet is not available, there is a problem with the network you joined. Go back to step 4 to select a different network.

Be Known

After your iPhone connects to a Wi-Fi network successfully, it becomes a known network. This means that your iPhone remembers its information so you don't have to enter it again. Your iPhone automatically connects to known networks when it needs to access the Internet. So unless you tell your iPhone to forget a network (explained later in this chapter), you need to log in to it only the first time you connect to it.

>>>Go Further

PERSONAL HOTSPOTS

In the PERSONAL HOTSPOTS section, you might see networks being provided by individual devices such as iPhones and iPads. These devices can share their cellular Internet connection (how to do this is covered in a later Go Further sidebar) with other devices. The icons for these networks are a bit different; along with the name of the network, you see its type of connection (such as LTE), the charge state of the device providing the network, and two connected loops that indicate the network is from a hotspot. You can select and use these networks just like the other types of networks being described in this chapter. Select the hotspot you want to use, and enter the correct password to join it. After you've joined a hotspot's network, you can access the Internet. The speed of your access is determined mostly by the speed of the device's cellular data connection.

Connecting to Public Wi-Fi Networks

Many Wi-Fi networks in public places, such as hotels or airports, require that you pay a fee or provide other information to access the Internet through that network; even if access is free, you usually have to accept the terms and conditions for the network to be able to use it.

When you connect to one of these public networks, you're prompted to provide whatever information is required. This can involve different details for different networks, but the general steps are the same. You're prompted to provide whatever information required. Then, follow the instructions that appear.

Following are the general steps to connect to many types of public Wi-Fi networks:

1. Use the steps in the previous task to move to and tap the public network you want to join. The iPhone connects to the network, and you see the Log In screen for that network.

2. If prompted to do so, provide the information required to join the network, such as a name and room number. If a fee is required, you'll have to provide payment information. In almost all cases, you at least have to indicate that you accept the terms and conditions for using the network, which you typically do by checking a check box.

3. Tap the button to join the network. This button can have different labels depending on the type of access, such as Authenticate, Done, Free Access, Login, and so on.

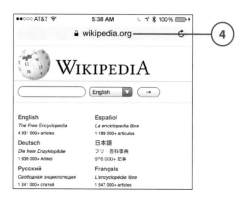

4. Try to move to a web page, such as www.wikipedia.org, to test your Wi-Fi connection. (See Chapter 13 for details.) If the web page opens, you are ready to use the Internet on your phone. If you are taken to a login web page for the Wi-Fi network's provider, you need to provide the required information to be able to use the Internet.

No Prompt?

Not all public networks prompt you to log in as these steps explain. Sometimes, you use the network's website to log in instead. After you join the network (step 1), your iPhone is connected to the network without any prompts. When you try to move to a web page as explained in step 4, you're prompted to log in to or create an account with the network's provider on the web page that appears.

A Closed Network

Some Wi-Fi networks are closed, which means they don't broadcast their names. This means that you don't see closed networks listed in the CHOOSE A NETWORK on the Wi-Fi screen. To be able to access a closed network, you need to know its name, its password, and the type of security it uses. With this information in hand, tap Other in the CHOOSE A NETWORK section. Then type the network's name. Tap Security, choose the appropriate type, and tap Back. Enter the required password and tap Join.

Disabling Automatic Prompting

When your iPhone can't find a known network—meaning one that you've used before—it presents a prompt showing you the currently available networks. You can use this prompt to select and join one of these networks. This can be useful because you don't have to use the Settings app to find a network to which you are going to connect; instead, you can just tap a network at the prompt to join it.

However, this automatic prompting for networks can be as annoying as it is helpful. It is helpful in that your iPhone prompts you when it comes into range of a network it doesn't know, which can make it easier to know when a network is available to you. It can be annoying when you are moving around a lot because what you are doing can be constantly interrupted by the prompt, even if you don't want to connect to one of the available networks. For example, when you walk through an airport, the prompt can appear multiple times as you move between networks.

To disable automatic network prompting, perform the following steps:

1. Open the Settings app and move to the Wi-Fi screen.

2. Set the Ask to Join Networks switch to off (white). To connect to unknown networks, you need to use the Settings app as described in the previous tasks because your iPhone no longer automatically prompts you to join unknown networks. (Remember that it will still join known networks, meaning those you have used before, automatically.)

Forgetting Wi-Fi Networks

As you learned earlier, your iPhone remembers networks you have joined and connects to them automatically as needed; these are known networks. Although this is mostly a good thing, there are times when you no longer want to use a particular network any more. For example, when in an airport, you might decide to connect to a network for which you have to pay for Internet access. Each time you move through that airport, your iPhone connects to that network again automatically, which might not be what you want it to do.

To have your iPhone forget a network so it doesn't automatically connect to it in the future, do the following:

1. Tap Wi-Fi in the Settings app to view the Wi-Fi screen.

2. Tap the Info button for the network that you want your iPhone to forget. (You can forget a network only if you are currently connected to it.)

3. Tap Forget this Network.

4. Tap Forget in the resulting prompt. Your iPhone stops using and forgets the network.

5. Tap Wi-Fi. You return to the Wi-Fi screen. If another known network is available, your iPhone connects to it automatically. If a network you've forgotten is still in range of your iPhone, it continues to appear in the CHOOSE A NETWORK section, but your iPhone no longer automatically connects to it. You can rejoin the forgotten network at any time, just as you did the first time you connected to it.

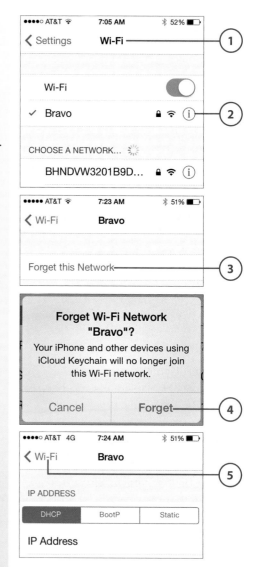

Cell Phone Provider Wi-Fi Networks

Many cell phone providers also provide other services, particularly public Wi-Fi networks. In some cases, you can access that provider's Internet service through a Wi-Fi network that it provides; often, you can do this at no additional charge. So, you can take advantage of the speed a Wi-Fi connection provides without paying more for it. You start connecting to these networks just like any other by selecting them on the available network list. What happens next depends on the specific network. In some cases, you need to enter your mobile phone number and then respond to a text message to that phone number. Check your provider's website to find out whether it offers this service and where you can access it.

Using Cellular Data Networks to Connect to the Internet

The provider for your iPhone also provides a cellular data connection your iPhone uses to connect to the Internet automatically when a Wi-Fi connection isn't available. (Your iPhone tries to connect to an available Wi-Fi network before connecting to a cellular data connection, because Wi-Fi is typically less expensive and faster to use.) These networks cover large geographic areas and the connection to them is automatic; your iPhone chooses and connects to the best cellular network currently available. Access to these networks is part of your monthly account fee; you choose from among various amounts of data per month at different monthly charges.

Most providers have multiple cellular data networks, such as a low-speed network that is available widely and one or more higher-speed networks that have a more limited coverage area. Your iPhone chooses the best connection available automatically. (If a low-speed network is all that is currently available, you might find its performance unusable for web browsing or other data-intensive tasks; in which case, you should try to connect to a Wi-Fi network.)

The cellular data networks you can use are determined based on your provider, your data plan, the model of iPhone you are using, and your location within your provider's networks or the roaming networks available, when you are outside of your provider's coverage area. The iPhone automatically uses the fastest connection available to it at any given time (assuming you haven't disabled that option, as explained later).

In the United States, the major iPhone providers are AT&T, Verizon, T-Mobile, and Sprint. There are also other smaller providers, such as Virgin Mobile. All these companies offer high-speed Long Term Evolution (LTE) cellular networks (these are also referred to as *true 4G networks*) along with the slower 4G and 3G networks. In other locations, the names and speeds of the networks available might be different.

As noted earlier, the speed of the cellular data network you can access depends on the model of iPhone you are using. The iPhone 5, 5c, 5s, 6/6s, and 6/6s Plus can use the fastest possible connection. The iPhone 4s can connect to the next fastest networks.

The following information is focused on LTE networks because I happen to live in the United States, use an iPhone 6s and 6 Plus, and use AT&T and Sprint as my cell phone providers. If you use another provider or a different iPhone model, you are able to access your provider's networks similarly, though your details might be different. For example, the icon on the Home screen reflects the name of your provider's network, which might or might not be LTE.

This iPhone is connected to a high-speed LTE cellular network

LTE high-speed wireless networks provide very fast Internet access from many locations. (Note: LTE networks might not be available everywhere, but you can usually access them near densely populated areas.) To connect to the LTE network, you don't need to do anything. If you aren't connected to a Wi-Fi network, you haven't turned off LTE, and your iPhone isn't in Airplane mode, the iPhone automatically connects to the LTE network if it is available in your current location. When you are connected to the LTE network, you see the LTE indicator at the top of the iPhone's screen. If you can't access the LTE network, such as when you aren't in range of it, the iPhone automatically connects to the next fastest network available, such as 4G. If that isn't available, it connects to the next fastest and so on until it finds a network to which it can connect if at least one network is available. If it can't connect to any network, you see No Service instead of a network's name; this indicates that you currently can't connect to any network, and so you aren't able to access the Internet.

One thing you do need to keep in mind when using a cellular network is that your account might include a limited amount of data per month. When your data use exceeds this limit, you might be charged overage fees, which can be very expensive. Most providers send you warning texts or emails as your data use approaches your plan's limit, at which point you need to be careful about what you do while using the cellular data network to avoid an overage fee. Some tasks, such as watching YouTube videos or downloading large movie files, can chew up a lot of data and should be saved for when you are on a Wi-Fi network to avoid running out of data. Others, such as using email, typically don't use very much.

An App for That

Various apps are available in the App Store that you can install on your iPhone that monitor how much data you are using. These apps are a good way to know where your data use is relative to your plan's monthly allowance so that you can avoid an overage situation. To get information on finding, downloading, and installing apps, see Chapter 6, "Downloading Apps, Music, Movies, TV Shows, and More onto Your iPhone." (To find an app for this purpose, search for "data monitoring app.")

When you move outside of your primary network's geographic coverage area, you are in roaming territory, which means a different provider might provide cellular phone or data access, or both. The iPhone automatically selects a roaming provider, if there is only one available, or allows you to choose one, if there is more than one available.

When you are outside of your primary provider's coverage area, roaming charges can be associated with calls or data use. These charges are often very expensive. The roaming charges associated with phone calls are easier to manage, because it's more obvious when you make or receive a phone call in a roaming area. However, data roaming charges are much more insidious, especially if Push functionality (where emails are pushed to iPhone from the server automatically) is active. And when you use some applications, such as Maps to navigate, you don't really know how much data is involved. Because data roaming charges are harder to notice, the iPhone is configured by default to prevent data roaming. When data roaming is disabled, the iPhone is unable to access the Internet when you are outside of your cellular network, unless you connect to a Wi-Fi network. (You can still use the cellular roaming network for telephone calls.)

You can configure some aspects of how your cellular network is used, as this task demonstrates. You can also allow individual apps to use, or prevent them from using, your cellular data network. This is important when your data plan has a monthly limit.

In most cases, the first time you launch an app, you're prompted to allow or prevent it from using cellular data. At any time, you can use the Cellular Data options in the Settings app to enable or disable an app's access to your cellular data network.

To configure how your iPhone uses its cellular network for data, perform the following steps:

1. Open the Settings app.

2. Tap Cellular.

3. To disable all cellular data connections, set the Cellular Data switch to off (white) and skip the rest of these steps. The iPhone is no longer able to connect to any cellular data networks. To use the Internet when the Cellular Data switch is off, you have to connect to a Wi-Fi network that provides Internet access.

Monitoring Data Use

In the CELLULAR DATA USAGE section toward the bottom of the Cellular screen, you see how much data you've used for the current period and how much you've used while roaming. This can help you see where your use is compared to your monthly plan allowance, so you know whether you are getting close to exceeding that allowance (thus incurring overage charges). This isn't proactive at all, as you have to remember to go and check the information. If you are concerned about data use, you're better off getting an app with more active monitoring.

4. To disable the high-speed network, set the Enable *high-speed network*, where *high-speed* network is the network name (such as LTE) switch to off (white). The iPhone is no longer able to use the higher-speed network, but can access other, slower cellular data networks.

Higher-speed Networks Use More Power

Using a higher-speed network, such as an LTE network, also uses somewhat more battery power than using a slower network. If getting the absolute maximum time on a charge is important, you might want to disable the high-speed network.

5. To configure roaming, tap Roaming.

6. To prevent voice calls when you are roaming, set the Voice Roaming switch to off (white). When you are outside of your provider's network, you won't be able to make or receive voice calls. If you want to tightly control roaming charges, leave this switch off except for periods of time during which you want to make or receive calls. When you disable Voice Roaming, Data Roaming is disabled automatically so you can skip to step 9.

7. If you want to allow data roaming, slide the Data Roaming switch to the on (green) position. When you move outside your primary network, data comes to iPhone via an available roaming cellular data network. You should disable it again by sliding the Data Roaming switch to off (white) as soon as you're done with a specific task to limit roaming charges.

8. Use the other options you see to complete the Roaming configuration. For example, if your phone uses a CDMA (Code division multiple access) network, you can disable International CDMA to try to improve your phone's performance.

9. Tap Cellular.

Provider Differences

The configuration of roaming depends on the provider your iPhone is connected to. Steps 4 through 9 show the details for Sprint in the United States. Other providers have different options. For example, when you use AT&T in the United States, you can enable LTE for voice or data, and you can turn Data Roaming off or on. You don't have a separate control for Voice Roaming. Regardless of the specific options you see on your phone, the basic purpose is the same, which is to configure how your iPhone uses its high-speed network and to enable and disable roaming. You can configure cellular data use by apps for all providers as shown, starting with step 10.

10.   Swipe up the screen until you see the
USE CELLULAR DATA FOR: section.
This section enables you to allow or
prevent individual apps from accessing a cellular data network. To limit the
amount of data you use, it's a good
idea to review this list and allow only
those apps that you rely on to use the
cellular data network. (Of course, if you
are fortunate enough to have an unlimited data plan, you can leave all the
apps enabled.)

**Amount of data
the app has used
since last reset**

Monitoring an App's Data Use

Just under each app's name, you see how
much data the app has used since the counter was reset. This number can help you determine how much data a particular app uses.
For example, if an app's use is shown in Mega
Bytes (MB), it's used a lot more data than an
app whose use is shown in Kilo Bytes (KB).

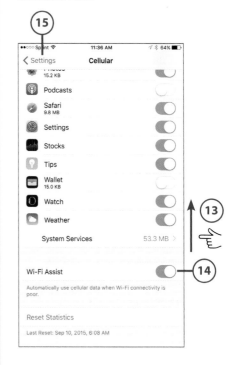

11.   Set an app's switch to on (green) if you
want it to be able to use a cellular data
network.

12.   Set an app's switch to off (white) if you
want it to be able to access the Internet only when you are connected to a
Wi-Fi network.

13.   Swipe up until you reach the bottom
of the screen.

14.   Set the Wi-Fi Assist switch to on (green)
if you want your iPhone to automatically switch to its cellular connection
when the Wi-Fi connection is weak.

15.   Tap Settings when you're done configuring your cellular network use.

Erase the Past

You can reset all of the statistics on the Cellular screen by swiping up until you reach the bottom
of the screen and tapping Reset Statistics. Tap Reset Statistics again.

PERSONAL HOTSPOT

The iPhone can be a personal hotspot, which is when it provides an Internet connection to computers or other devices. This is useful when you are in a location where you can't connect a computer or other device to a Wi-Fi or cellular network with Internet access (or don't want to spend the money to do so) but can access the Internet with the iPhone's cellular data connection.

There are a lot of caveats to this service, including whether your provider offers it, additional costs, and so on. Check with your provider to see if the personal hotspot feature is supported and if there are additional fees to use it. If it is provided and the fees are acceptable, this is a good way to provide Internet access to other devices when a Wi-Fi or cellular connection either isn't available or is too expensive.

First, add the personal hotspot service to your cellular account. Second, move to the Cellular screen in the Settings app, and then tap Set Up Personal Hotspot (if you don't see this option, your provider doesn't offer personal hotspot service). Follow the onscreen prompts to complete the configuration of the personal hotspot; the details depend on the specific provider you are using. After your iPhone is configured as a hotspot, it can share its Internet connection with other devices.Your iPhone's network appears in the PERSONAL HOTSPOTS section on the Wi-Fi screen.

Using Bluetooth to Connect to Other Devices

The iPhone includes built-in Bluetooth support so you can use this wireless technology to connect to other Bluetooth-capable devices. The most likely devices to connect to iPhone in this way are Bluetooth headphones, speakers, headsets, or car audio/entertainment/information systems, but you can also use Bluetooth to connect to other kinds of devices, most notably keyboards, headphones, computers, iPod touches, iPads, and other iPhones.

To connect Bluetooth devices together, you *pair* them. In Bluetooth, pairing enables two Bluetooth devices to communicate with each other. The one constant requirement is that the devices can communicate with each other via Bluetooth. For devices to find and identify each other so they can communicate, one or both must be *discoverable*, which means they broadcast a Bluetooth signal other devices can detect and connect to.

There is also a "sometimes" requirement, which is a pairing code, passkey, or PIN. All those terms refer to the same thing, which is a series of numbers, letters, or both, entered on one or both devices being paired. Sometimes you enter this code on both devices, whereas for other devices you enter the first device's code on the second device. Some devices don't require a pairing code at all.

When you have to pair devices, you're prompted to do so, and you have to complete the actions required by the prompts to communicate via Bluetooth. This might be just tapping Connect, or you might have to enter a passcode on one or both devices.

Connecting to Bluetooth Devices

This task demonstrates pairing an iPhone with a Bluetooth keyboard; you can pair it with other devices similarly.

1. Move to the Settings screen. The current status of Bluetooth on your iPhone is shown.

2. Tap Bluetooth.

3. If Bluetooth isn't on (green), tap the Bluetooth switch to turn it on. If it isn't running already, Bluetooth starts up. The iPhone immediately begins searching for Bluetooth devices. You also see the status Now Discoverable, which means other Bluetooth devices can discover the iPhone. In the OTHER DEVICES section, you see the devices that are discoverable to your iPhone but that are not paired with it.

4. If the device you want to use isn't shown in the OTHER DEVICES section, put it into Discoverable mode. (Not shown; see the instructions provided with the device.) When it is discoverable, it appears in the OTHER DEVICES section.

5. Tap the device to which you want to connect. If a passkey is required, you see a prompt to enter it on the device with which you are pairing.

Bluetooth is on

Device that isn't paired with the iPhone

6. If it is required, input the pairing code, passkey, or PIN on the device, such as typing the passkey on a keyboard if you are pairing your iPhone with a Bluetooth keyboard.

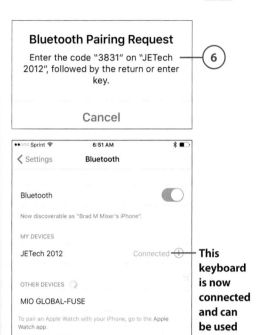

Bluetooth Pairing Request

Enter the code "3831" on "JETech 2012", followed by the return or enter key. ——6

Cancel

7. If required, tap Connect (not shown in the figures)—some devices connect as soon as you enter the passkey and you won't need to do this. If a passkey isn't required, such as with a Bluetooth speaker, you tap Connect instead. You see the device to which the iPhone is connected in the MY DEVICES section of the Bluetooth screen, and its status is Connected, indicating that your iPhone can communicate with and use the device.

••○○○ Sprint 🗢   6:51 AM   ✶ ■▷

< Settings   **Bluetooth**

Bluetooth   ⬤

Now discoverable as "Brad M Miser's iPhone".

MY DEVICES

JETech 2012   Connected ⓘ —— **This keyboard is now connected and can be used**

OTHER DEVICES ⁙

MIO GLOBAL-FUSE

To pair an Apple Watch with your iPhone, go to the Apple Watch app.

>>>Go Further
MANAGING BLUETOOTH

Following are a few pointers for using Bluetooth with other devices:

- Like other connections you make, the iPhone remembers Bluetooth devices to which you've connected before and reconnects to them automatically, which is convenient—most of the time anyway. If you don't want your iPhone to keep connecting to a device, move to the Bluetooth screen and tap the device's Info (i) button. Tap the Forget this Device button and then tap Forget Device. The pairing is removed. Of course, you can always pair the devices again at any time. If you just want to stop using the device, but keep the pairing in place, you can tap Disconnect instead.

- If a device is already paired but has the Not Connected status, you need to connect it to use it. Move to the Bluetooth screen and tap the device to connect it to your iPhone. Once its status becomes Connected, your iPhone can communicate with the device again.

- You can use multiple Bluetooth devices with your iPhone at the same time. For example, you might want to be connected to a Bluetooth speaker and a keyboard at the same time.

Connecting Your iPhone to Other iPhones, iPod Touches, or iPads

The iPhone (and other devices that run the iOS software, including iPod touches and iPads) supports peer-to-peer connectivity, which is the technical way of saying that these devices can communicate with one another directly via a Wi-Fi network or Bluetooth. This capability is used in a number of apps, especially multiplayer gaming, for information sharing, and for other collaborative purposes.

If the app you want to use communicates over a Wi-Fi network, such as a network you use to access the Internet, all the devices with which you want to communicate must be on that same network. If the application uses Bluetooth, you must enable Bluetooth on each device and pair them (as described in the previous task) so they can communicate with one another.

The specific steps you use to connect to other iOS devices using a collaborative app depend on the specific app you are using. The general steps are typically as follows:

1. Ensure the devices can communicate with each other. If the app uses Wi-Fi, each device must be on the same Wi-Fi network. If the app uses Bluetooth, the devices must be paired.

2. Each person opens the app on his device.

3. Use the app's controls to select the devices with which you'll be collaborating. Usually, this involves a confirmation process in which one person selects another person's device and that person confirms that the connection should be allowed.

4. Use the app's features to collaborate. For example, if the app is a game, each person can interact with the group members. Or, you can directly collaborate on a document with all parties providing input into the document.

---

iPhone and Apple Watch

The Apple Watch is designed to be a perfect partner device for your iPhone and can work with it in many ways. For detailed information about the Apple Watch, see the book *My Apple Watch*.

Using AirDrop to Share Content with Other iPhones, iPod Touches, iPads, or a Mac

You can use the iOS AirDrop feature to share content directly with people using a Mac running OS X Yosemite or later, or using a device running iOS 7 or later. For example, if you capture a great photo on your iPhone, you can use AirDrop to instantly share that photo with iOS device and Mac users near you.

AirDrop can use Wi-Fi or Bluetooth to share, but the nice thing about AirDrop is that it manages the details for you. You simply open the Share menu—which is available in most apps—tap AirDrop, and tap the people with whom you want to share.

When you activate AirDrop, you can select Everyone, which means you will see anyone who has a Mac running OS X Yosemite or later, or an iOS device running version iOS 7 or newer and is on the same Wi-Fi network with you (or has a paired Bluetooth device); those people can see you, too. Or, you can select Contacts Only, which means only people who are in your Contacts app are able to use AirDrop to communicate with you. In most cases, you should choose the Contacts Only option so you have more control over who uses AirDrop with you.

When enabled, you can use AirDrop by opening the Action menu while using an app. Then, tap the people with whom you want to share content.

Is AirDrop Safe?
Anything you share with AirDrop is encrypted, so the chances of someone else being able to intercept and use what you share are quite low. Likewise, you don't have to worry about someone using AirDrop to access your information or to add information to your device without your permission. However, like any networking technology, there's always some chance—quite small in this case—that someone will figure out how to use this technology for nefarious purposes. The best thing you can do is to be wary of any requests you receive to share information and ensure they are from people you know and trust before you accept them.

Enabling AirDrop

To use AirDrop, you must enable it on your iPhone.

1. Swipe up from the bottom of the screen to open the Control Center.

2. If AirDrop is not active—indicated by the text "AirDrop" being in black—tap AirDrop. If it is active, the "AirDrop" text is in white and you see its status (Everyone or Contacts Only); if it is already active, skip the next two steps.

Current AirDrop status (disabled)

3. Tap Contacts Only to allow only people in your Contacts app to communicate with you via AirDrop, or tap Everyone to allow anyone using a device running iOS 7 or later or a Mac running OS X Yosemite or later in your area to do so.

4. Swipe down from the top of the Control Center to close it. You're ready to use AirDrop to share.

Share and Share Alike?

You should disable AirDrop when you aren't using it, especially if you use the Everyone option. By disabling it, you avoid having people in your area be able to try to communicate with you without you wanting them to do so. Generally, you should enable AirDrop only when you are actively using it and disable it when you aren't. To disable AirDrop, open the Control Center, tap AirDrop, and then tap Off.

People in your Contacts app can use AirDrop to communicate with you

Using AirDrop to Share Your Content

To use AirDrop to share your content, do the following:

1. Open the content you want to share. This example shows sharing a photo using the Photos app. The steps to share content from any other app are quite similar.

2. Tap the Share button.

3. Tap AirDrop or just wait a couple of seconds. The AirDrop button is replaced with icons for each person in your area who has AirDrop enabled that you have permission to access (such as being in her Contacts app if she is using the Contacts Only option).

4. Swipe to the left or right to browse all the people with whom you can share.

5. Tap the people with whom you want to share the content. A sharing request is sent to those people's devices. Under their icons, the Waiting status is displayed. When a recipient accepts your content, the status changes to Sent. If a recipient rejects your content, the status changes to Declined.

Photo selected to share

6. If the app supports it, browse and select more content to share.

7. Tap the people with whom you want to share the content.

8. When you're done sharing, tap Done.

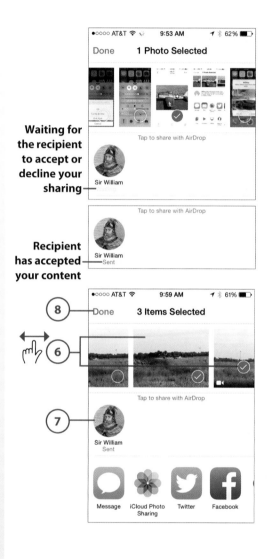

Waiting for the recipient to accept or decline your sharing

Recipient has accepted your content

Using AirDrop to Work with Content Shared with You

When someone wants to share content with you, you receive an AirDrop sharing request; if you have previously accepted content from that person, you might not receive a request, because it is accepted by default. Respond to sharing requests by doing the following:

1. Make sure you know the person attempting to share with you.

2. Make sure the content being shared with you is something you want. In this case, a photo is being shared.

3. To accept the content on your iPhone, tap Accept. To reject it, tap Decline.

4. If you accepted the content and the app enables you to review it in detail or edit it before saving it on your iPhone, swipe up and down the screen to see the detail of what you are accepting, or use the app's controls to edit it. For example, you can review the details of contact information being shared, you can edit photos shared with you, and so on.

5. Use the app's controls to work with the shared content. For example, the Photos app provides tools to edit and share photos that are shared with you. In some cases, such as saving a contact shared with you, you need to tap Save to save the content on your iPhone or Cancel to not save it. (Other apps provide different controls depending on the type of content and the app it opens in.)

Use iCloud and other accounts to store the data your apps use on the cloud

Go here to configure and manage iCloud and your other online accounts

Store files on the cloud

In this chapter, you learn how to connect your iPhone to various types of accounts, such as iCloud, Exchange, and Google, so that apps on your iPhone can access their data stored on the Internet cloud. The topics include the following:

→ Configuring and using iCloud

→ Setting up other types of online accounts on your iPhone

→ Configuring other types of online accounts

→ Setting how and when your accounts are updated

Setting Up and Using iCloud and Other Online Accounts

No iPhone is an island. Connecting your iPhone to the Internet enables you to share and sync a wide variety of content using popular online accounts such as iCloud, Exchange, and Google. Using iCloud, you can put your email, contacts, calendars, photos, and more on the Internet so that multiple devices—most importantly your iPhone—can connect to and use that information. There are lots of other accounts you might also want to use, such as Exchange and Google for email, calendars, and contacts as well as Twitter and Facebook for accessing social networks.

You need to configure these accounts on your iPhone to be able to use them; in this chapter, you'll see sections for several different accounts you might want to use. Of course, you only need to refer to the sections related to the accounts you actually use. You should also understand how you can determine how and when your information is updated along with tasks you might find valuable as you manage the various accounts on your iPhone.

Configuring and Using iCloud

iCloud is a service provided by Apple that provides you with your own storage space on the Internet. You can store content from your computer or devices in your storage space on the cloud, and because it is on the Internet, all your devices are able to access that information at the same time. This means you can easily share your information on your iPhone, a computer, an iPad, and so on, so that the same information and content is available to you no matter which device you are using at any one time.

Although your iPhone can work with many types of online/Internet accounts, iCloud is integrated into the iPhone like no other type of account (not surprising because the iPhone and iCloud are both Apple technology). An iCloud account is really useful in a number of ways. For example, iCloud can be used for the following:

- **Family Sharing**—With Family Sharing, you can designate up to six people with whom you want to automatically share your iTunes and apps down-loads, calendars, reminders, and more.

- **Files**—iCloud Drive enables you to store your documents and other files on the cloud so that you can seamlessly work with them using different devices.

- **Photos**—You can store your photos in iCloud to back them up and to make them easy to share.

- **Email**—An iCloud account includes an @icloud.com email address. You can configure any device to use your iCloud email account, including an iPhone, an iPad, an iPod, and a computer.

- **Contacts**—You can store your contact information in iCloud.

- **Calendars**—Putting your calendars in iCloud makes it much easier to manage your time.

- **Reminders**—Through iCloud, you can be reminded of things you need to do or anything else you want to make sure you don't forget.

- **Safari**—iCloud can store your bookmarks, letting you easily access the same websites from all your devices. And you can easily access websites currently open on other devices, such as a Mac, on your iPhone.

- **Notes**—With the Notes app, you can create text notes, draw sketches, and capture photos for many purposes; iCloud enables you to use these notes on any iCloud-enabled device.

- **News**—iCloud can store information from the News app online, making reading news on multiple devices easier.

- **Wallet**—The Wallet app stores coupons, tickets, boarding passes, and other documents so you can access them quickly and easily. With iCloud, you can ensure that these documents are available on any iCloud-enabled device.

- **Backup**—You can back up your iPhone to the cloud so that you can recover your data and your phone's configuration should something ever happen to it.

- **Keychain**—The Keychain securely stores sensitive data, such as passwords, so that you can easily use that data without having to remember it.

- **Find My iPhone**—This service enables you to locate and secure your iPhone and other devices.

You'll learn about iCloud's many useful features throughout this book (such as using iCloud with your photos, which is covered in Chapter 15, "Working with Photos and Video You Take with Your iPhone"). The tasks in this chapter show you how to set up and configure the iCloud features you want to use.

Obtaining an iCloud Account

Of course, to use iCloud on your iPhone, you need to have an iCloud account. The good news is that you probably already have one. The other good news is that even if you don't, obtaining one is simple and free.

If you have any of the following accounts, you already have an iCloud account and are ready to start using iCloud and can skip ahead to the next section:

- **iTunes Store**—If you've ever shopped at the iTunes Store, you created an account with an Apple ID and password. You can use that Apple ID and password to access iCloud.

- **Apple Online Store**—As with the iTunes Store, if you made purchases from Apple's online store, you created an account with an Apple ID and password that also enables you to use iCloud.

- **Find My iPhone**—If you obtained a free Find My iPhone account, you can log in to iCloud using that Apple ID.

During the initial iPhone startup process, you were prompted to sign into or create an iCloud account. If you created one at that time, you are also good to go and can move to the next task.

If you don't have an iCloud account, you can use your iPhone to create one by performing the following steps:

1. On the Home screen, tap Settings.

2. Swipe up the screen and tap iCloud.

3. Tap Create a new Apple ID.

4. Provide the information required on the following screens; tap Next to move to the next screen after you've entered the required information. You start by entering your birthday.

During the process, you'll be prompted to use an existing email address or to create a free iCloud email account. You can choose either option. The email address you use becomes your Apple ID that you use to sign into iCloud. If you create a new email account, you can use that account from any email app on any device, just like other email accounts you have.

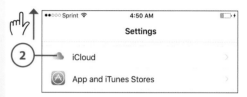

You'll also create a password, set up security questions, enter a rescue email address (optional), choose email updates you want to receive, and agree to license terms. When your account has been created, you're prompted to enter your password.

After you successfully create your password, you are logged into your iCloud account and might be prompted to merge information already stored on your iPhone, such as Safari bookmarks, onto iCloud. Tap Merge to move your existing data to the cloud or Don't Merge to keep it out of the cloud.

When you've worked through merging your information, you see that iCloud will track the location of your iPhone through the Find My iPhone feature.

5. Tap OK. You are ready to complete the configuration of your iCloud account, which is covered in the next section.

Multiple iCloud Accounts

You can have more than one iCloud account. However, you can have only one iCloud account active on your iPhone at a time.

> ### Find My iPhone Enabled
>
> This allows you to locate, lock, or erase your iPhone. Your Apple ID and password will be required to reactivate your iPhone.
>
> OK ——⑤

Signing Into Your iCloud Account

To be able to use an iCloud account on your iPhone, you need to first sign into your account and then enable the services you want to use and disable those that you don't want to use. After iCloud is set up on your iPhone, you rarely need to change your account settings. If you restore your iPhone at some point, you might need to revisit these steps to ensure iCloud remains set up as you want it.

To get started, sign into your iCloud account—if you created your iCloud account on your iPhone, you don't need to perform these steps because you signed in when you created the account; in that case, skip to the next task.

1. On the Home screen, tap Settings.

2. Swipe up the screen and tap iCloud.

3. Enter your Apple ID. If you see account information instead of the Apple ID field, an iCloud account is already signed into on the iPhone. If it is your account, skip to the next task. If it isn't your account, swipe up the screen and tap Sign Out; tap Delete to delete various data from your iPhone at the prompts and continue with these steps.

4. Enter your Apple ID password.

5. Tap Sign In. You are logged in to your iCloud account.

6. If prompted to do so, tap Merge to merge existing data, such as Safari bookmarks, already stored on the iPhone onto the cloud.

7. At the prompt, tap OK indicating that you realize Find My iPhone is enabled. You're ready to configure the rest of iCloud's services.

Enabling iCloud to Store Your Information on the Cloud

One of the best things about iCloud is that it stores email, contacts, calendars, reminders, bookmarks, notes, photos, and other data on the cloud so that all your iCloud-enabled devices can access the same information. You can choose the types of data stored on the cloud by performing the following steps:

1. Move to the iCloud screen by tapping Settings, iCloud. Just below the Storage information are the iCloud data options. Some of these have a right-facing arrow that you tap to configure options, while others have a two-position switch. When a switch is green, it means that switch is turned on and the related data is stored to your iCloud account and kept in sync with the information on the iPhone.

Account currently signed in (tap to make changes)

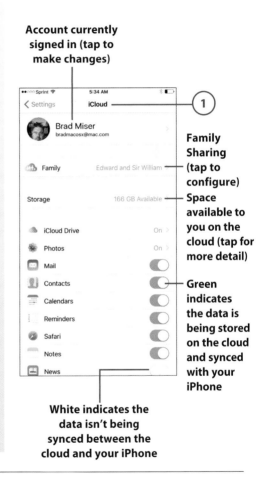

Family Sharing (tap to configure)

Space available to you on the cloud (tap for more detail)

Green indicates the data is being stored on the cloud and synced with your iPhone

White indicates the data isn't being synced between the cloud and your iPhone

Share and Share Alike

Family Sharing enables you to share iTunes and App Store downloads, reminders, photos, and other information with a group of people. Configuring Family Sharing is explained in "Using Family Share to Share your iTunes Store Content" in Chapter 6, "Downloading Apps, Music, Movies, TV Shows, and More onto Your iPhone."

2. If you don't want a specific type of data to be stored on the cloud and synced to your iPhone, tap its switch to turn that data off (the switch becomes white instead of green). The types of data that have switches are: Mail, Contacts, Calendars, Reminders, Safari, Notes, News, and Wallet.

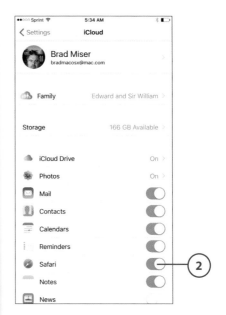

When you turn a switch off because you don't want that information stored on the cloud any more, you might be prompted to keep the associated information on your iPhone or delete it.

If you choose Keep on My iPhone, the information remains on your iPhone but is no longer con-nected to the cloud; this means any changes you make exist only on the iPhone. If you choose Delete from My iPhone, the information is erased from your iPhone. Whether you choose to keep or delete the information, any information of that type that was previously stored on the cloud remains available there; the delete action only impacts the information stored on the iPhone.

After you've configured each data switch on the iCloud screen, you're ready to configure the rest of the data options, which are explained in the following tasks.

Configuring iCloud Drive

iCloud drive, which is enabled by default, stores files (such as Keynote presentations) on the cloud so that you can work with those documents on any device. For example, you can create a Keynote presentation on a Mac and then access it on your iPhone to present it. To configure your iCloud drive, perform the following steps:

1. On the iCloud screen in the Settings app, tap iCloud Drive.

2. To enable your documents to be stored in iCloud, set the iCloud Drive switch to on (green).

3. To show the iCloud Drive icon on the Home screens, set the Show on Home Screen switch to on (green). Using this icon, you can open and view files in folders just like on a computer. If you prefer not to display the icon, your apps can still use the iCloud Drive, you just can't get to the files stored there without using an app.

4. Set the switch to off (white) for any apps currently saving data to your iCloud Drive that you don't want to use your iCloud Drive; set the switch to on (green) for those apps that you do want to use the iCloud Drive to store data.

5. To prevent file data from being copied to and from the cloud while your iPhone is using a cellular data network, set the Use Cellular Data switch to off (white). In this case, when your iPhone connects to a Wi-Fi network, your documents are synced with the cloud.

6. Tap iCloud.

Look Me Up

Some iCloud-aware apps can look you up via your email address/Apple ID to determine your first and last name. Apps that allow this are shown in the Look Me Up By Email section. For example, if someone knows your email/Apple ID, they can look for it in apps that support this feature; when your email/Apple ID is found, the person sees your first and last name.

Configuring iCloud to Store Photos

Storing your photos on the cloud provides many benefits, not the least of which is that the photos you take with your iPhone are automatically saved on the cloud so that you can access them from computers and other iOS devices (such as iPads) and your photos remain available even if something happens to your iPhone, such as you lose it. Using iCloud also makes it easy for you to share your photos with others. To configure your photos to be stored in iCloud, do the following:

1. On the iCloud screen, tap Photos.

2. To store your entire photo library on the cloud, set the iCloud Photo Library switch to on (green). This stores all of your photos and video in iCloud, which both protects them by backing them up and makes them accessible on other iOS devices (iPads, iPod touches, and iPhones) and via the Web.

Photos Revealed

Using the iCloud-enabled photo features is explained in detail in Chapter 15.

---

3. If you enable the iCloud Photo Library feature, tap Optimize iPhone Storage to keep lower resolution versions of photos and videos on your iPhone (this means the file sizes are smaller so that you can store more of them on your phone) or Download and Keep Originals if you want to keep the full-resolution photos on your iPhone. In most cases, you should choose the Optimize option so that you don't use as much of your iPhone's storage space for photos.

4. Ensure the Upload to My Photo Stream switch is on (green) (if you aren't using the iCloud Photo Library, this switch is called My Photo Stream); if you disabled this, skip to step 6. Any photos you take with the iPhone's camera are copied onto iCloud, and from there they are copied to your other devices on which the Photo Stream is enabled. Note that Photo Stream only affects photos that you take with the iPhone from the time you enable it, while the iCloud Photo Library feature uploads all of your photos, those you took in the past and will take in the future.

5. If you want all of your burst photos (see Chapter 15) to be uploaded to iCloud, set the Upload Burst Photos switch to on (green). In most cases, you should leave this off (white) because you typically don't want to keep all the photos in a burst. When you review and select photos to keep, the ones you keep are uploaded through Photo Stream.

6. To be able to share your photos and to share other people's photos, set the iCloud Photo Sharing switch to on (green).

7. Tap iCloud.

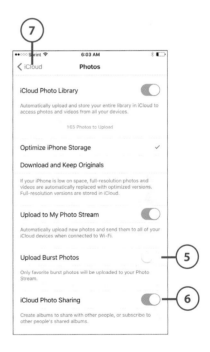

Configuring Your iCloud Backup

Like other digital devices, it is important to back up your iPhone's data so that you can recover should something bad happen to your iPhone. You can back up your iPhone's data and settings to iCloud, which is really useful because that means you can recover the backed-up data using a different device, such as a replacement iPhone. Configure your iCloud backup with the following steps:

1. On the iCloud screen, tap Backup.

2. Set the iCloud Backup switch to on (green). Your iPhone's data and settings are backed up to the cloud automatically.

3. Tap iCloud.

Back Me Up on This

You can manually back up your iPhone's data and settings at any time by tapping Back Up Now on the Backup screen. This can be useful to ensure recent data or settings changes are captured in your backup. For example, if you know you are going to be without a Wi-Fi connection to the Internet for a while, back up your phone to ensure that your current data is saved in the backup.

Configuring Your iCloud Keychain

A keychain can be used to store usernames, passwords, and credit cards so you can access this information without retyping it every time you need it. Enabling keychain syncing through iCloud makes this information available on multiple devices. For example, if you've configured a credit card on your keychain on a Mac, that credit card is available though the keychain being synced via iCloud. Follow these steps to enable keychain syncing through iCloud:

1. On the iCloud screen, tap Keychain.

2. Enter your Apple ID password and tap OK. Next, you need to approve with your security code or via another device that uses your keychain.

3. Set the iCloud Keychain switch to on (green). You need to verify you want the keychain to be enabled on the device. You can do this by entering your security code or approving on another device that has access to your keychain. When you enable the keychain, approval requests are sent to the other devices that have access to your keychain. You can enter your Apple ID password at the prompt on those devices to approve the keychain on your iPhone or continue with these steps to use your security code to do so.

4. Tap Approve with Security Code.

Assumptions

These steps assume you have a keychain already configured for iCloud syncing on another device, such as a Mac or iPad, and that you know your security code. If not, your steps may be slightly different than those shown here. For example, you create a security code if this is the first time you set up keychain syncing.

5. Enter your security code. You're prompted to enter a verification code, which is texted to your phone.

6. Enter the verification code you receive via text. Your keychain syncing starts and your keychain information is stored on the cloud and synced onto your iPhone.

Advanced Keychain Syncing

When keychain syncing has been enabled, Advanced appears on the Keychain screen. Tap this to access additional Keychain commands. Use the Approve with Security Code switch to determine if your code can be used to set up keychain syncing on other devices. Tap Change Security Code to change your security code. Use the controls in the VERIFICATION NUMBER section to see or change the phone number to which the verification code is texted.

It's Not All Good

If you store a lot of sensitive information in your keychain on a Mac, such as usernames and passwords to websites, credit cards, and such, be careful about enabling keychain syncing. When you enable that, all this data becomes available on your iPhone and can be used by anyone who can use your phone. Assuming you have a passcode to the phone, you are protected from someone using your phone without you knowing it, but if you let someone use your phone, they can also use your sensitive information. You may choose to leave keychain syncing off and just keep a minimum amount of sensitive information on your phone.

>>>Go Further

CONFIGURING FIND MY iPHONE

Find My iPhone enables you to locate and secure your iPhone if you lose it. This feature is enabled by default when you sign into your iCloud account. You should usually leave it enabled so that you have a better chance of locating your iPhone should you lose it or to be able to delete its data should you decide you won't be getting it back. There are a couple of configuration tasks you can do for Find My iPhone:

- To disable Find My iPhone, open Settings and tap the iCloud option, and then tap Find My iPhone. Set the Find My iPhone switch to off (white) and enter your Apple ID password at the prompt. You can longer access your iPhone via the Find My iPhone feature.

- To send the last known location of the iPhone to Apple when power is critically low, open the Find My iPhone screen and set the Send Last Location switch to on (green). When your iPhone is nearly out of power, its location is sent to Apple. You can contact Apple to try to locate your iPhone should it run out of power while it isn't in your possession.

Performing Advanced Configuration of Your iCloud Account

Most of the time, you can use your iCloud account just fine if you only configure it as described in the previous tasks. However, there are a number of other configuration options that you might want to use at some point. Tap the Settings app on your Home screen, and then tap iCloud. Each setting is explained in the following table.

Advanced iCloud Settings

iCloud Settings Area	Location	Setting	Description
Your iCloud account (tap your account shown at the top of the iCloud screen)	Apple ID	Edit	Enables you to change the image or name associated with your account.
Your iCloud account	Apple ID	Contact Information	Enables you to view and change your contact information, including the email and physical addresses associated with your account.

iCloud Settings Area	Location	Setting	Description
Your iCloud account	Apple ID	Password & Security	Enables you to change your password and other security related information.
Your iCloud account	Apple ID	Devices	Enables you to see all the devices that are currently using your iCloud account. You can locate the devices using Find My iPhone, see their details, or remove them from the account.
Your iCloud account	Apple ID	Payment	Displays and enables you to change the payment information associated with your Apple ID.
ADVANCED	Mail	ICLOUD ACCOUNT INFORMATION	Enables you to change the name associated with your email and to choose the default email address should you have more than one.
ADVANCED	Mail	ALLOW SENDING FROM	Enables you to allow or prevent email from being sent from the email addresses associated with your account.
ADVANCED	Mail	OUTGOING MAIL SERVER	Enables you to see and configure information about the Simple Mail Transfer Protocol (SMTP) server your account uses to send email.
ADVANCED	Mail	Advanced	Enables you to configure where email in various stages is stored. For example, you can choose to store draft email on your iPhone or in a mailbox on the cloud (which is useful because you can then work on that email from multiple devices). You can also configure where discarded (deleted) messages are stored and how long they are kept there.
ADVANCED	Share My Location	N/A	Use the upper part of the Share My Location screen to determine if your location is shared and which device is used to indicate your location.
ADVANCED	Share My Location	FAMILY	Enables you to determine if people in your Family Sharing group can access your location.

>>>Go Further

EMAIL ALIASES

One of the great features of iCloud is using email aliases. You can create alias addresses for specific purposes, such as avoiding spam or just to use an email address you prefer. Email sent to one of your aliases comes into your normal inbox. When you send email from an alias, it appears to be from the alias address, even though any aliases are still related to the same email account. You can create email aliases for your iCloud account using your iCloud website, available at www.icloud.com. Log into your iCloud account, and then open the Mail app. Open the Mail Preferences dialog by clicking the gear icon, and then choosing Preferences. Then, click the Accounts tab. Here you can create and manage up to three aliases.

Setting Up Other Types of Online Accounts on Your iPhone

Many types of online accounts provide different services, including email, calendars, contacts, social networking, and so on. To use these accounts, you need to configure them on your iPhone. The process you use for most types of accounts is similar to the steps you used to set up your iCloud account. In this section, you'll learn how to configure Exchange, Google, and Facebook accounts.

Configuring an Exchange Account

Microsoft Exchange is the most widely used system for corporate email. Your iPhone is compatible with Exchange, which is good news indeed. (You can even configure multiple Exchange accounts on your iPhone if you can't get by with just one.) You can sync Exchange email, contact, calendar, reminder, and notes information on your iPhone; this works similarly to synchronizing with your iPhone using an iCloud account.

Before you can use Exchange on your iPhone, the Exchange server for your account must be configured to support iOS devices. Almost all are these days. You need to contact the IT organization providing the Exchange account to get the information you need to be able to configure it on your iPhone if you don't know it. You need to have your email address, username, password, server address, and domain. With this information in hand, you can use the following steps to configure the Exchange account:

1. On the Home screen, tap Settings.

2. Tap Mail, Contacts, Calendars.

3. Tap Add Account.

4. Tap Exchange.

5. Enter your email address.

6. Enter your password.

7. Change the description of the account if you want to use something more specific than Exchange.

8. Tap Next. The information you've entered is verified. If it can't be, you might see a dialog box saying so and you'll need to add more information to complete the account configuration; continue to step 9. If the information is verified, your account is configured and you see the sync screen with switches for the types of data you can sync; skip to step 14.

9. Tap Continue.

10. Enter the server address.

11. Enter the domain for the account.

12. If your username and password weren't carried forward from the previous screen, enter them.

13. Tap Next.

14. Slide the switch to off (white) for any of the information you don't want to be moved onto the iPhone. (If a switch is green, that type of information will be synced on your iPhone.)

15. Tap Save. The account configuration is saved, and you move back to the Mail, Contacts, Calendars screen where your Exchange account is displayed. Under the account description is the information that is synced with the account, such as Mail, Contacts, Calendars.

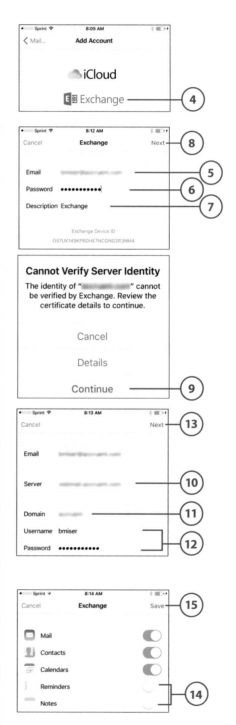

16. Tap the Exchange account you configured.

17. Tap Mail Days to Sync.

18. Tap the time period over which you want emails to be synced; for example, tap 2 Weeks to have email sent to you within the past two weeks synced onto your iPhone.

19. Tap Exchange. Your Exchange account information is available in the apps being synced on your iPhone.

Not Working?

If you see an error message after step 13, go back and make sure you've entered the information correctly. If you have entered the information exactly as it was provided to you, you'll need to contact the IT department that supports the Exchange system you use to get help setting up the account on your iPhone.

Annoying Warnings

Sometimes, you might need to change your account's password if it gets reset (most organizations require that Exchange passwords be reset after a certain amount of time, such as 90 days). Because your iPhone won't be able to connect your account with the current password, you see messages telling you the iPhone can't access your account. These can be quite annoying as you have to keep clearing them and they keep reappearing immediately. They might even get your Exchange account locked if the iPhone tries and fails to connect a certain number of times. If this happens, you can disable the account by turning off all the data options so your phone won't try to connect to the account. After you get a new password, update it on the account screen and then turn on the data options again. Or, use the technique my great acquisitions editor employs; when she encounters a password issue, she puts the iPhone in Airplane mode so it won't present annoying warnings until she updates the password.

>>>Go Further

MORE ON EXCHANGE CONFIGURATION

There are several other things you may need to do to keep your Exchange account working as you want it to:

- To make changes to the account configuration, including changing your password, move to the Exchange account's Settings screen and tap the account shown at the top of the screen. Change any of the information you see, such as the password, to update it, and then tap Done. You aren't likely to need to change any of the other settings on this screen; however, if the administrator of the Exchange account instructs you to make changes to its configurations, you would enter them on this screen.

- At the bottom of the Account Settings screen for the Exchange account, you see the Advanced Settings option. This enables you to determine if you use the Secure Sockets Layer (SSL) setting. SSL is a means of encrypting data; most organizations use it, so this should be on (green). You can also choose where discarded messages are stored.

- You can have a reply automatically sent in response to email you receive. To configure an automatic reply, move to the Exchange account's Settings screen. Tap Automatic Reply at the bottom of the screen. Set the Automatic Reply switch to on (green) and type the text to be sent in the automatic reply. Swipe down the screen and tap End Date at the top of the screen. Use the resulting date and time wheels to set when you want the automatic reply to stop being sent. Tap Save. From the current time until the one you set as the End Date, the automatic reply is sent to any email that is received by your Exchange account. You can stop the reply at any time by moving to the Automatic Reply screen and setting the Automatic Reply switch to off (white). You can also edit the text in the automatic reply on this screen.

Configuring a Google Account

A Google account provides email, contacts, calendar, and note syncing that is similar to iCloud and Exchange. To set up a Google account on your iPhone, do the following:

1. On the Home screen, tap Settings.

2. Tap Mail, Contacts, Calendars.

3. Tap Add Account.

4. Tap Google.

5. Enter your Google email address.

6. Enter your Google account password.

7. Tap Sign In.

8. Tap Allow to allow Google to use your information or Deny to prevent it.

9. Enable the features of the account you want to access on the iPhone, which are Mail, Contacts, Calendars, and Notes.

10. Tap Save. The account is saved, and the data you enabled becomes available on your iPhone.

Advanced Google

Similar to iCloud and Exchange, a Google account has some settings you aren't likely to use, but it's good to know how to get to them in case you do. To access these settings, move to the Mail, Contacts, Calendars screen and tap your Google account. On the Gmail account's screen, you can change the types of data you are syncing by setting the switches to on or off. Tap Account, and then tap Advanced to see additional settings. Working with these is similar to iCloud and Exchange. For example, you can determine where draft email messages are stored, such as on the Gmail server or on your iPhone.

Configuring Other Types of Online Accounts

You can access many types of online accounts on your iPhone. These include accounts that are "built in," which include iCloud, Exchange, Google, Yahoo!, AOL, and Outlook.com. Setting up a Yahoo!, AOL, or Outlook.com account is similar to iCloud, Exchange, and Google. Just select the account type you want to use and provide the information for which you are prompted.

There are lots of other accounts you might want to use. An email account included with an Internet access account, such as one from a cable Internet provider, is one example. Support for these accounts isn't built in to the iOS; however, you can usually set up such accounts on your iPhone fairly easily.

When you obtain an account, such as email accounts that are part of your Internet service, you should receive all the information you need to configure those accounts on your iPhone. If you don't have this information, visit the provider's website and look for information on configuring the account in an email application. You need to have this information to configure the account on the iPhone.

Setting Up an Online Account Manually

With the configuration information for the account in hand, you're ready to set it up:

1. In the Settings app, move to the Mail, Contacts, Calendars screen and tap Add Account.

2. Tap Other.

3. Tap the type of account you want to add. For example, to set up an email account, tap Add Mail Account.

4. Enter the information by filling in the fields you see; various types of information are required for different kinds of accounts. You just need to enter the information you received from the account's provider.

5. Tap Next. If the iPhone can set up the account automatically, its information is verified and it is ready for you to use (if the account supports multiple types of information, you can enable or disable the types with which you want to work on your iPhone). If the iPhone can't set up the account automatically, you're prompted to enter additional information to complete the account configuration. When you're done, the account appears on the list of accounts and is ready for you to use.

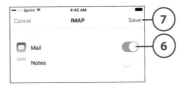

6. Configure the switches for the data sync options you see.

7. Tap Save. The account you configured is available in the related app, such as Mail if you set up an email account.

Multiple Accounts

There is no limit (that I have found so far) on the number of online accounts (even of the same type, such as Gmail) that you can access on your iPhone.

Configuring a Facebook Account

Facebook is one of the most popular social media channels you can use to keep informed about other people and inform them about you. Facebook is integrated into the iOS so you can share photos, messages, and such via your Facebook page, along with using the Facebook app.

To configure Facebook, perform the following steps:

1. Move to the Home screen and tap Settings.

2. Swipe up the screen and tap Facebook. If you see INSTALLED at the top of the screen, the Facebook app is installed on your iPhone and you can get right into your account. If not, tap INSTALL to install the app (download and installing apps is covered in Chapter 6); when the app is done installing, continue with these steps.

No Facebook Account?

If don't have a Facebook account, tap Create New Account and follow the onscreen instructions to create one. When you are done creating the new account, you're signed into it automatically.

---

3. Type your Facebook username.

4. Type your Facebook password.

5. Tap Sign In. Your account information is verified and you are signed into your account.

6. Tap Sign In.

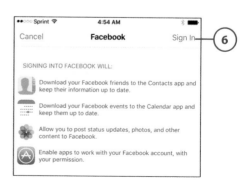

7. To prevent apps from accessing your Facebook information, slide their switches to the off position (white).

8. Tap Update All Contacts. Facebook attempts to match as much of your contact information with your friends as it can. When the process is complete, you are ready to access your Facebook account within the Facebook app or in any number of other apps.

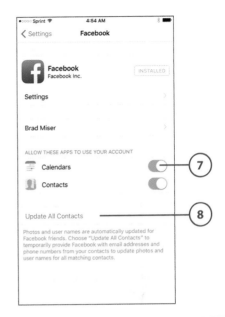

More Facebook Settings

If you tap Settings on the Facebook Settings screen, you can do some additional configuration such as enabling or disabling sound and vibration for Facebook notifications. If you tap your name on that screen, you can change your password (which you might need to do from time to time).

Setting How and When Your Accounts Are Updated

The great thing about online accounts is that their information can be updated any time your iPhone can connect to the Internet. This means you have access to the latest information, such as new emails, changes to your calendars, and so on. There are three basic ways information gets updated:

-   **Push**—When information is updated via Push, the server pushes (thus the name) updated information onto your iPhone whenever that information changes. For example, when you receive a new email, that email is immediately sent (or pushed) to your iPhone. Push provides you with the most current information all the time but uses a lot more battery than the other options.

-   **Fetch**—When information is updated via Fetch, your iPhone connects to the account and retrieves the updated information according to a schedule, such as every 15 minutes. Fetch doesn't keep your information quite as current as Push does, but it uses much less battery than Push does.

• **Manual**—You can cause an app's information to be updated manually. This happens whenever you open or move into an app or by a manual refresh. For example, you can get new email by moving onto the Inboxes screen in the Mail app and swiping down from the top of the screen.

You can configure the update method that is used globally, and you can set the method for specific accounts. Some account types, such as iCloud and Exchange, support all three options while others might support only Fetch and Manual. The global option for updating is used unless you override it for individual accounts. For example, you might want your work account to be updated via Push so your information there is always current, while configuring Fetch on a personal account may be frequent enough.

Configuring How New Data is Retrieved for Your Accounts

To configure how your information is updated, perform the following steps:

1. Move to the Mail, Contacts, Calendars screen of the Settings app.

2. Tap Fetch New Data.

3. To enable data to be pushed to your iPhone, slide the Push switch to on (green). To disable push to extend battery life, set it to off (white). This setting is global, meaning that if you disable Push here, it is disabled for all accounts even though you can still configure Push to be used for individual accounts. For example, if your Exchange account is set to use Push but Push is globally disabled, the Exchange account's setting is ignored and data is fetched instead.

4. To change how an account's information is updated, tap it. The account's screen displays. The options on this screen depend on the kind of account it is. You always have Fetch and Manual; Push is displayed only for accounts that support it.

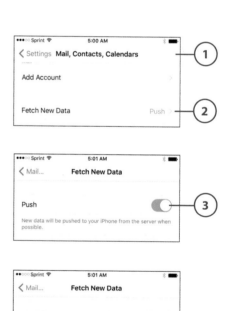

5. Tap the option you want to use for the account: Push, Fetch, or Manual.

   If you choose Manual, information is retrieved only when you manually start the process by opening the related app (such as Mail to fetch your email) or by using the refresh gesture, regardless of the global setting.

   If you choose Fetch, information is updated according to the schedule you set in step 9.

6. If you choose the Push option, choose the mailboxes whose information you want to be pushed by tapping them so they have a check mark; to prevent a mailbox's information from being pushed, tap it so that it doesn't have a check mark. (The Inbox is selected by default and can't be unselected.)

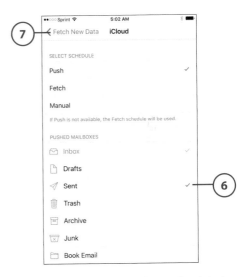

7. Tap Fetch New Data.

8. Repeat steps 5-7 until you have set the update option for each account. (The current option is shown to the right of the account's name.)

9. Tap the amount of time when you want the iPhone to fetch data when Push is turned off globally or for those accounts for which you have selected Fetch or that don't support Push; tap Manually if you want to manually check for information for Fetch accounts or when Push is off. Information for your accounts is updated according to your settings.

How information is being updated for the account

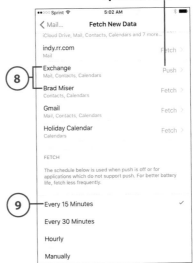

>>>Go Further

TIPS FOR MANAGING YOUR ACCOUNTS

As you add and use accounts on your iPhone, keep the following points in mind:

- You can temporarily disable any data for any account by moving to the Mail, Contacts, Calendars screen and tapping that account. Set the switch for the data you don't want to use to off (white). You might be prompted to keep or delete that information; if you choose to keep it, the data remains on your iPhone but is disconnected from the account and is no longer updated. If you delete it, you can always recover it again by simply turning that data back on. For example, suppose you are going on vacation and don't want to deal with work email, meeting notifications, and so on. Move to your work account and disable all its data. That data disappears from the related apps; for example, the account's mailboxes no longer appear in the Mail app. When you want to start using the account again, simply re-enable its data.

- If you want to completely remove an account from your iPhone, move to its configuration screen, swipe up the screen, and tap Delete Account. Tap Delete in the confirmation dialog box and the account is removed from your iPhone. (You can always sign into the account to start using it again.)

- You can have different notifications for certain aspects of an account, such as email. See Chapter 5, "Customizing How Your iPhone Looks and Sounds," for the details of configuring and using notifications.

- You can change how information is updated at any time, too. If your iPhone is running low on battery, disable Push and set Fetch to Manually so you can control when the updates happen. When your battery is charged again, you can re-enable Push or set a Fetch schedule.

Tap to personalize your
iPhone to make it your own

In this chapter, you learn how to make an iPhone into your iPhone. Topics include the following:

→ Working with the Settings app
→ Setting keyboard, language, and format options
→ Configuring the Control Center
→ Setting Do Not Disturb preferences
→ Setting Privacy and Location Services preferences
→ Setting Passcode, Touch ID, and Auto-Lock preferences
→ Setting restrictions for content and apps

Configuring an iPhone to Suit Your Preferences

As you've seen in previous chapters, the Settings app enables you to configure various aspects of your iPhone, such as connecting your iPhone to a Wi-Fi network and configuring iCloud. The Settings app provides many other configuration tools that you can use to tailor how your iPhone works to suit your preferences. Perhaps the most important of these is the security of your iPhone that you can configure by setting a passcode and fingerprint recognition using Touch ID along with your privacy and location settings. You can also configure the keyboards available to you, the Control Center, Do Not Disturb hours, and how content on your phone can be accessed.

Working with the Settings App

Aptly named, the Settings app is where you configure the many settings that change how your iPhone looks, sounds, and works. Most of the tasks in this chapter involve the Settings app. Rather than repeat the first couple of steps within each task, it is more efficient to show you how the app works so you can easily access the controls you need for each task.

Using the Settings App on Any iPhone

You can work with the Settings app on any iPhone as follows:

1. On the Home screen, tap Settings. The Settings app opens. The app is organized in sections starting at the top with Airplane Mode, Wi-Fi, Bluetooth, and Cellular.

2. Swipe up or down the screen to get to the settings area you want to use.

3. Tap the area you want to config-ure, such as Sounds.

4. Use the resulting controls to con-figure that area. The changes you make take effect immediately.

5. When you're done, you can leave the Settings app where it is or tap the back button, which is always located in the upper-left corner of the screen, until you get back to the main Settings screen to go into other Settings areas.

Searching for Settings

New! You can quickly find settings you need by searching for them:

1. Move into the Settings app.

2. Tap in the Search bar; if you don't see the Search bar, swipe down from the top of the Settings screen until it appears.

3. Type the setting for which you want to search. As you type, potential matches are shown on the list of results. Matches can include a settings area, such as Sounds, and specific settings, such as the ringtone and vibrations used when you receive a call.

4. Tap the setting you want to use.

5. Configure the setting you selected in the previous step.

Using the Settings App on an iPhone 6/6s Plus

When you hold an iPhone 6/6s Plus in the horizontal orientation and use the Settings app, you can take advantage of the iPhone 6/6s Plus' split-screen feature as follows:

1. Hold the iPhone 6/6s Plus so it is horizontal.

2. Tap the Settings app to open it. In the left pane, you see the areas of the Settings app that you can configure. In the right pane, you see tools you can use to configure the selected function. The two panes are independent, making navigation easier than with other iPhones.

3. Swipe up or down on the left pane until you see the function, feature, or app you want to configure.

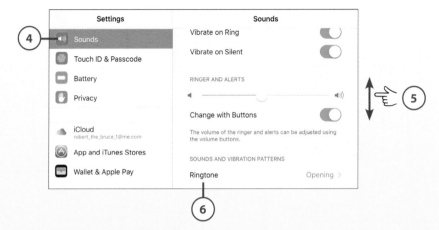

4. Tap the function, feature, or app you want to configure, such as Sounds. Its controls appear in the right pane.

5. Swipe up or down on the right pane until you see the specific setting you want to change.

6. Tap the setting you want to configure, such as Ringtone. Its controls appear in the right pane.

7. Use the tools in the right pane to configure the setting you selected in step 6. These work just as described in the previous task and throughout this chapter except that you move within the right pane instead of changing the entire screen.

8. To move back through the screens in the right pane, use the back button, which is labeled with the name of the screen you came from.

9. Tap another area in the left pane to configure it. As you can see, the split screen makes it very easy to quickly switch between areas in the Settings app.

Setting Keyboard, Language, and Format Options

You'll be working with text in many apps on your iPhone. You can customize a number of keyboard- and format-related options so text appears and behaves the way you want it to.

Setting Keyboard Preferences

You use the iPhone's keyboard to input text in many apps, including Mail, Messages, and so on. A number of settings determine how the keyboard works.

1. On the Settings screen, tap General.

2. Swipe up the screen.

3. Tap Keyboard.

4. Tap Keyboards. This enables you to activate more keyboards so that you can choose a specific language's keyboard when you are entering text. At the top of the screen, you see the keyboards that are available to you.

5. Tap Add New Keyboard.

Fun in Text

The Emoji keyboard allows you to include a huge variety of smiley faces, symbols, and other icons whenever you type. The Emoji keyboard is active by default; however, if you don't see it on the list of active keyboards, you can use these steps to activate it.

Number of active keyboards

Keyboards available when you type

6. Swipe up and down the screen to browse the available keyboards.

7. Tap the keyboard you want to add.

8. Tap the keyboard you added in step 7.

9. Tap the keyboard layout you want to use.

10. Tap Keyboards.

11. Repeat steps 5–10 to add and configure additional keyboards.

12. Tap Keyboards. (Note that the Text Replacement option is explained in the next task.)

Third-party keyboards available

>>>Go Further

THIRD-PARTY KEYBOARDS

You can install and use keyboards that third parties provide (meaning not Apple) on your iPhone. To do this, open the App Store app and search for "keyboards for iPhone" or you can search for a specific keyboard by name if you know of one you want to try. (See Chapter 6, "Downloading Apps, Music, Movies, TV Shows, and More onto Your iPhone," for help using the App Store app.) After you have downloaded the keyboard you want to use, use steps 1 through 5 to move back to the Keyboards Settings screen. When you open the Add New Keyboard screen, you see a section called THIRD-PARTY KEYBOARDS in which you see the additional keyboards you have installed. Tap a keyboard in this section to activate it as you do with the default keyboards. When you move back to the Keyboards screen, you see the keyboard you just activated. Tap it to configure its additional options. Then you can use the new keyboard just like the others you have activated. Make sure you check out the documentation for any keyboards you download so you take advantage of all of their features.

13. To prevent your iPhone from automatically capitalizing as you type, set Auto-Capitalization to off (white).

14. To disable the automatic spell checking/correction, set Auto-Correction to off (white).

15. To disable the Caps Lock function, set the Enable Caps Lock to off (white).

16. To prevent the character you type from being shown in a magnified pop-up as you type it, set the Character Preview switch to off (white).

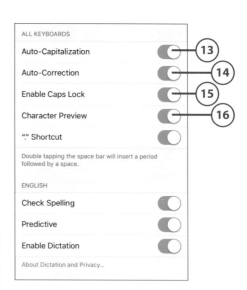

Language Options

The options you see depend on the language being used. For example, if settings apply only to a specific language, you see them in that language's section.

17. To disable the shortcut that types a period followed by a space when you tap the spacebar twice, set the "." Shortcut switch to off (white). You must tap a period and the spacebar to type these characters when you end a sentence.

18. To disable the iPhone's Spell Checker, set the Check Spelling switch to off (white).

19. To disable the iPhone's Predictive Text feature (see Chapter 1), set the Predictive switch to off (white).

20. To disable the iPhone's dictation feature, set the Enable Dictation switch to off (white). The microphone key won't appear on the keyboard and you won't be able to dictate text.

Changing Keyboards

To delete a keyboard, move to the Keyboards Settings screen and swipe to the left on the keyboard you want to remove. Tap Delete. The keyboard is removed from the list of activated keyboards and is no longer available to you when you type. (You can always activate it again later.) To change the order in which keyboards appear, move to the Keyboards screen, tap Edit, and drag the keyboards up and down the screen. When you've finished, tap Done.

Lots More to the Settings App

There's a lot more you can do with the Settings app than is explained in this chapter; here, you learn about some of the "general" iPhone customization/configuration for which you can use the Settings app (more of these are explained in Chapter 5, "Customizing How Your iPhone Looks and Sounds"). You also learn about the Settings app to configure app- or function-specific settings throughout this book. For example, you learn how to use Settings to configure Internet access in Chapter 2, "Connecting Your iPhone to the Internet, Bluetooth Devices, and iPhones/iPods/iPads," and you learn about the email settings in Chapter 9, "Sending, Receiving, and Managing Email."

Creating and Working with Text Replacements

Text replacements are useful because you can use just a few letters to type a series of words. You type the replacement, and it is replaced by the phrase with which it is associated. To configure your text replacements, do the following:

1. Move to the Keyboards screen as described in steps 1–3 in the previous task.

2. Tap Text Replacement.

3. Review the current replacements.

4. To add a replacement, tap Add (+).

5. Type the phrase for which you want to create a replacement.

6. Type the shortcut you want to be replaced by the phrase you created in step 5.

7. Tap Save. If the replacement doesn't contain any disallowed characters, it is created and you move back to the Text Replacement screen where you see your new text replacement. If there is an error, you see an explanation of the error; you must correct it before you can create the replacement.

8. Repeat steps 4–7 to create other text replacements.

9. When you've created all the replacements you want, tap Keyboards.

Shortcuts to Replacements

To change a replacement, tap it. Use the resulting screen to change the phrase or shortcut, and tap Save to update the replacement. To remove a replacement, swipe to the left on it and tap Delete. To search for a replacement, tap in the Search bar at the top of the screen and type the replacements you want to see; you can also use the index along the right side of the screen to find replacements. You can also tap Edit on the Shortcuts screen to change your replacements. And, yes, you can create a phrase without a replacement, but I don't really see much use for that!

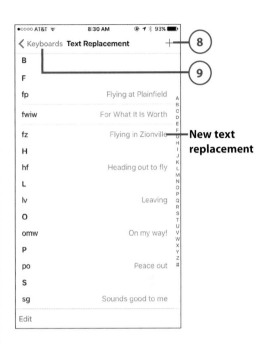

Setting Language and Region Preferences

There are a number of formatting preferences you can set that determine how information is formatted in various apps. For example, you can choose how addresses are formatted by default by choosing the region whose format you want to follow.

1. On the Settings screen, tap General.

2. Swipe up the screen.

3. Tap Language & Region.

4. Tap iPhone Language.

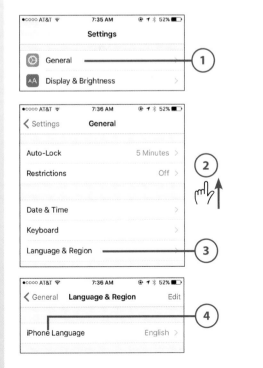

5. Swipe up and down the screen to view the languages with which your iPhone can work or tap in the Search bar and type a language you want to use to find it. The current language is marked with a check mark.

6. Tap the language you want to use.

7. Tap Done.

8. Tap to confirm the change in language you indicated. Your iPhone screen goes dark while the iPhone switches to the new language. When it comes back, you return to the Language & Region screen, and the language you selected starts being used.

9. Tap Add Language.

10. Using steps 5 through 7, find and tap a secondary language. This language is used when your primary language can't be, such as on websites that don't support your primary language.

11. Tap Done.

12. Tap the language you want to be primary to confirm it. The language you selected is configured and you move back to the Language & Region screen. The new language is shown on the list in the center of the screen.

13. To add more languages, tap Add Language and follow steps 10 through 12 to add more languages.

Order, Order!

To change the order of preference for the languages you have configured, tap Edit, drag the languages up or down the screen to set their order, and tap Done to save your changes.

14. Tap Region.

15. Swipe up and down the regions available to you. The current region is marked with a check mark.

16. Tap the region whose formatting you want to use; if there are options within a region, you move to an additional screen and can tap the specific option you want to use.

17. Tap Done. Your iPhone starts using the formatting associated with the region you selected.

18. Tap Calendar.

19. Tap the calendar you want your iPhone to use.

20. Tap Language & Region. You move back to the Language & Region screen. Swipe up until you see the bottom of the screen where there are examples of the format options you have selected, such as the time and date format.

>>>Go Further
ADVANCED FORMATTING

Tapping Advanced on the Language & Region screen enables you to override the format for the region you selected in step 16. On the Advanced screen, set the Automatic switch to off (white). Tap Language and then select the language whose format you want to use. Tap Advanced. At the bottom of the Advanced screen, you see examples of the format associated with the language you have selected and those formats are used. To return to the formats associated with the iPhone's primary language, set the Automatic switch to on (green).

>>>Go Further
THE ACCESSIBLE iPHONE

If you tap the Accessibility option on the General Settings screen, a large number of options you can configure to make your iPhone more accessible appear. For example, you can enable VoiceOver to have the iPhone guide you through screens by speaking their contents. Zoom magnifies the entire screen. Invert Colors changes the screen from dark characters on a light background to light characters on a dark background. Under the Speech option, Speak Selection has the iPhone speak text you have selected, and Speak Auto-text has the iPhone speak corrections it suggests to you, such as auto-capitalizations. There are other options you can configure; explore this screen to find settings of interest to you. If your iPhone starts looking or behaving quite differently, move back to this screen to make sure an Accessibility option hasn't been enabled accidentally. There are many options here, and sometimes one or more of them is turned on accidentally, and it can be confusing if you aren't expecting it.

Configuring the Control Center

As you learned in Chapter 1, the Control Center provides quick access to various settings, app controls, and even apps.

There are a couple of Control Center preferences you can set:

1. On the Settings screen, tap Control Center.

2. To access the Control Center from the Lock screen, set the Access on Lock Screen switch to on (green).

3. To access the Control Center when you are using an app, set the Access Within Apps switch to on (green).

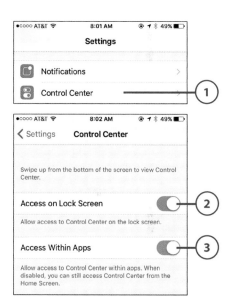

Setting Do Not Disturb Preferences

As you learned in Chapter 1, the Do Not Disturb feature enables you to temporarily silence notifications; you can also configure quiet times during which notifications are automatically silenced.

You can set an automatic Do Not Disturb schedule by performing the following steps:

1. On the Settings screen, tap Do Not Disturb.

2. To activate Do Not Disturb manually, set the Manual switch to on (green). (This does the same thing as activating it from the Control Center.)

3. To configure Do Not Disturb to activate automatically on a schedule, slide the Scheduled switch to on (green).

4. Tap the From and To box.

5. Tap From.

6. Swipe on the time selection wheels to select the hour and minute (AM or PM) when you want the Do Not Disturb period to start.

7. Tap To.

8. Swipe on the time selection wheels to set the hour and minute (AM or PM) when you want the Do Not Disturb period to end.

9. Tap Do Not Disturb.

10. Tap Allow Calls From.

11. Tap the option for whose calls should be allowed during the Do Not Disturb period. The options are Everyone, which doesn't prevent any calls; No One, which sends all calls to voicemail; Favorites, which allows calls from people on your Favorites lists to come through but all others go to voicemail; or one of your contact groups, which allows calls from anyone in the selected group to come through while all others go to voicemail.

12. Tap Do Not Disturb.

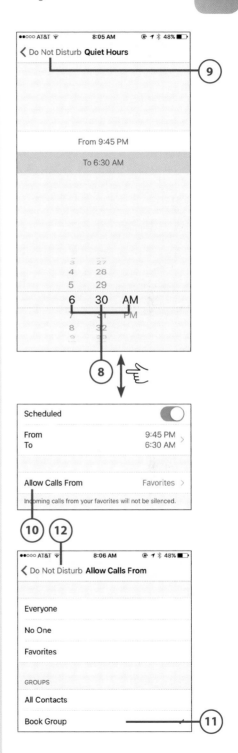

13. Set the Repeated Calls switch to on (green) if you want a second call from the same person within three minutes to be allowed through. This feature is based on the assumption that if a call is really important, someone will try again immediately.

14. If you want notifications to be silenced only when your phone is locked, tap Only while iPhone is locked during the Do Not Disturb period. Tap Always if you want notifications to be silenced regardless of the Lock status.

15. Tap Settings. During the Do Not Disturb period, your iPhone is silent, except for any exceptions you configured. When the scheduled Do Not Disturb period ends, your iPhone resumes its normal notification activity.

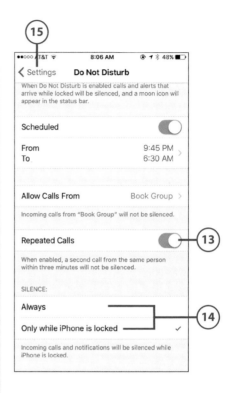

Setting Privacy and Location Services Preferences

Using its GPS or network connection, your iPhone's Location Services feature can determine where the phone is. This is useful in many situations, such as in the Maps app when you want to generate directions. Lots of other apps use this capability, too, such as apps that provide you location-specific information (the Urban Spoon app uses it to determine the restaurants near you, for example). You can configure certain aspects of how these services work. And, if you don't want specific apps to be able to access your iPhone's current location, you can disable this feature for those apps. Of course, if you do, apps that rely on this capability won't work properly (they prompt you to allow access to this service as you try to use them).

You can also determine which apps can access certain kinds of information, such as the apps that are able to access your contact information in the Contacts app.

To configure privacy settings, do the following:

1. Move to the Settings screen and tap Privacy.

2. Tap Location Services.

3. To disable Location Services for all apps, set the Location Services switch to off (white); to leave it enabled, skip to step 6.

4. Tap Turn Off at the prompt. No apps are able to identify your location; skip the rest of these steps because they don't apply when Location Services is disabled.

5. If you have enabled Family Sharing (see Chapter 6 for details), tap Share My Location; if you have not enabled Family Sharing, skip to step 11.

6. To prevent your location from being shared with people configured under your Family Sharing, set the Share My Location switch to off (white) and skip to step 9. If you leave this switch on (green), move to the next step.

7. Tap From.

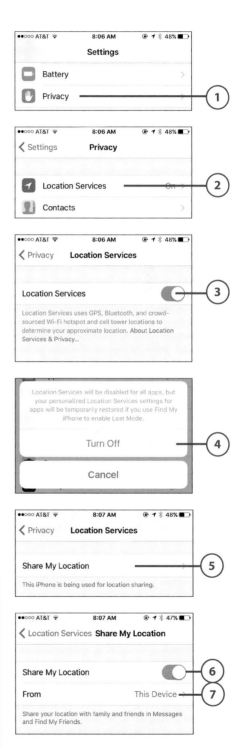

8. Tap the device that should be used to identify your location (this only applies if you have multiple devices configured with your Apple ID and Family Sharing).

9. Tap Share My Location.

10. Tap Location Services.

11. Swipe up and down the list of apps on the Location Services screen. These are all the apps that have requested access to your iPhone's location. Along the right side of the screen, you see the current status of Location Sharing for the app. Always means that the app can always access your location. While Using means the app can only access your location information while you are using it. Never means that using location information for the app has been disabled (some apps won't be able to work properly when set to this status). Apps marked with a purple arrow have recently accessed your location; those that have done so within the past 24 hours are marked with a gray arrow. An outline purple arrow indicates that the app is using a geofence, which is a perimeter around a location that defines an area that is used to trigger some event, such as a reminder.

12. Tap an app to configure its access to Location Services.

13. Tap the status in which you want to place the app's access to your location. Some apps only have the Always or Never options while others also have the While Using the App option.

14. Tap Location Services.

15. Repeat steps 12 through 14 for each app whose access to your location you want to configure.

16. Tap System Services.

17. Enable or disable Location Services for the System Services you see. As with apps, if you disable location services for a system function, it might not work properly.

18. Tap Location Services.

>>>Go Further
MORE ON SYSTEM SERVICES

One of the System Services is Frequent Locations. This service tracks places you visit. This information is used to improve the performance of some apps. If you want to prevent this, tap Frequent Locations and then set the Frequent Locations switch to off (white).

You can use the switches in the PRODUCT IMPROVEMENT section to enable or disable various types of information from being collected, such as what is popular near you.

Use the Status Bar Icon switch to enable or disable the Location Services arrow at the top of the screen when a system service is accessing location information. (This arrow always appears when apps use location information.)

19. Tap Privacy. Next, allow or prevent apps from accessing data stored on your iPhone.

20. Tap the first app on the list; this example shows Contacts. A list of apps that have requested to use the app's data (in this example, contact information) is displayed. If the requesting app is able to use the app's data, its switch is on (green).

21. Prevent a requesting app from accessing the app's data by setting its switch to off (white). That app is no longer able to use the data it requested (which can inhibit some of its functionality).

22. Repeat step 21 for each app you see that you want to prevent from accessing the data.

23. Tap Privacy.

24. Repeat steps 20-23 for each app on the list. Most of time, you can just leave the permissions with the default setting (unless you want to block a specific app from using a certain kind of data).

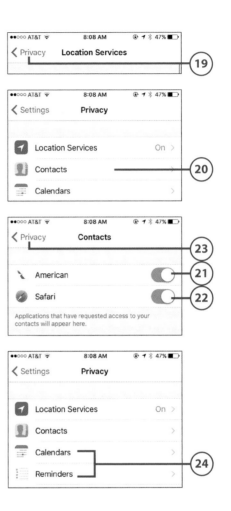

>>>Go Further
MORE ON PRIVACY

Under the list of apps, you see the social accounts section that includes Facebook, Twitter, and other such social media apps. You can control which apps access your social media information similar to how you control which apps can use other types of information (such as your contact information).

Under this is the Diagnostics & Usage section. Using these controls, you can determine if information about performance of apps and your device is communicated back to Apple. You can also determine if information about the performance of apps is shared with app developers.

At the bottom of the Privacy screen, you see the Advertising option. If you tap this, you can limit the tracking of ads you view by setting the Limit Ad Tracking switch to on (green). Typically, this tracking is used by advertisers to present ads that are related to ads you have viewed (the point being to make the ads more effective). You can reset the identifier used to identify you by tapping Reset Advertising Identifier and then tapping Reset.

Setting Passcode, Touch ID, and Auto-Lock Preferences

Your iPhone contains data you probably don't want others to access. You can (and should) require a passcode so your iPhone can't be unlocked without the proper passcode being entered. This gives you a measure of protection should you lose control of your phone. If you have an iPhone 5s or later, you can record your fingerprints so that you can unlock your phone (by automatically entering the passcode) and enter your Apple ID password by touching the Touch ID/Home button. The capability can also be used in other apps and services that require confirmation, such as Apple Pay.

The Auto-Lock feature automatically locks your phone after a specific period of time. This is useful because your iPhone automatically locks and, assuming you require a passcode, the passcode or fingerprint must be provided to be able to unlock your phone.

Securing Your iPhone with Auto-Lock

To configure your phone so it locks automatically, perform the following steps.

1. On the Settings screen, tap General.

2. Swipe up the screen until you see Auto-Lock.

3. Tap Auto-Lock.

4. Tap the amount of idle time you want to pass before the iPhone automatically locks and goes to sleep. You can choose from 1 to 5 minutes; choose Never if you only want to manually lock your iPhone. I recommend that you keep Auto-Lock set to a relatively small value to conserve your iPhone's battery and to make it more secure. Of course, the shorter you set this time to be, the more frequently you have to unlock your iPhone.

5. Tap General. You're ready to configure your passcode and finger-prints (iPhone 5s and later).

Configuring Your Passcode and Fingerprints (iPhone 5s and later)

To configure the passcode you have to enter to unlock your iPhone, perform the following steps (note these steps show an iPhone that has Touch ID; if your model doesn't have this, the steps will be slightly different as you will only be con-figuring a passcode):

1. On the Settings screen, tap Touch ID & Passcode.

Already Have a Passcode?

When you first turned your iPhone on, you were prompted to enter a passcode and to record a fingerprint for Touch ID. If your iPhone already has a passcode set, when you per-form step 1, you're prompted to enter your current passcode. When you enter it correctly, you move to the Touch ID & Passcode (iPhone 5s and later) or Passcode (other models) screen and you can make changes to the current passcode, add new fingerprints, and so on. In this case, you can skip directly to step 5. If you want to change your current passcode, tap Change Passcode and follow steps 3 and 4 to change it. Then continue with step 5.

2. Tap Turn Passcode On.

3. Enter a six-digit passcode.

4. Reenter the passcode. If the two passcodes match, the passcode is set.

5. Tap Require Passcode; when you use Touch ID to unlock your iPhone, you don't have an option for when the passcode is required and can skip to step 8.

Are You Complex?

By default, your passcode is a simple six-digit number. If you want to have a more complex (and more secure) passcode, on the Create or Change Passcode screen, tap Passcode Options. You are prompted to create a new, complex passcode. You can choose Custom Alphanumeric Code, Custom Numeric Code, or 4-Digit Numeric Code. Choose the option you want and then follow the onscreen prompts to create it. The Alphanumeric Code option is the most secure, especially if you use a code that is eight characters or longer that includes both letters and numbers. The steps to set a complex passcode are similar; the difference is that you use the keyboard and numeric keypad to configure the passcode instead of just the numeric keypad.

6. Tap the amount of time the iPhone is locked before the passcode takes effect. The shorter this time is, the more secure your iPhone is, but also the more times you'll have to enter the passcode if your iPhone locks frequently.

7. Tap Touch ID & Passcode.

8. If you have an iPhone 5s or later, tap Add a Fingerprint and continue to step 9; if you have a model that doesn't support Touch ID, skip to step 21.

9. Touch the finger you want to be able to use to unlock your phone and enter your Apple ID password to the Touch ID/Home button, but don't press it. An image of a fingerprint appears.

10. Leave your finger on the Touch ID/Home button until you feel the phone vibrate, which indicates part of your fingerprint has been recorded and you see some segments turn red. The parts of your fingerprint that are recorded are indicated by the red segments, gray segments are not recorded yet.

11. Take your finger off the Touch ID/Home button and touch the button again, adjusting your finger on the button to record other parts that currently show gray lines instead of red ones. Other segments of your fingerprint are recorded.

12. Repeat step 11 until all the segments are red. You are prompted to change your grip so you can record more of your fingerprint.

Gray lines indicate segments to be recorded

Red lines indicate recorded segments

13. Tap Continue.

14. Repeat step 11, again placing other areas of your finger to fill in more gray lines with red ones. When the entire fingerprint is covered in red lines, you see the Complete screen.

15. Tap Continue. The fingerprint is recorded and you move back to the Touch ID & Passcode screen. You see the fingerprint that has been recorded.

16. Repeat steps 8 through 15 to record up to five fingerprints. These can be yours or someone else's if you want to allow another person to access your iPhone.

17. To be able to use Touch ID to unlock your iPhone, ensure the iPhone Unlock switch is set to on (green).

18. To use your fingerprint to make Apple Pay payments, set the Apple Pay switch to on (green).

19. If you want to also be able to enter your Apple ID password by touching your finger to the Touch ID/Home button, set the App and iTunes Store switch to on (green).

20. Enter your Apple ID password and tap OK.

21. Swipe up the screen until you see the Voice Dial switch.

22. To prevent Voice Dial from working, set the Voice Dial switch to off (white). (Voice Dial enables you to make calls by speaking even if you don't use Siri.)

23. Use the switches in the ALLOW ACCESS WHEN LOCKED: section to enable or disable the related functions when your iPhone is locked. The options are Today (the Today tab on the Notifications Center), Notifications View (the Notifications tab of the Notifications Center), Siri, Reply with Message, and Wallet. If you set a switch to off (white), you won't be able to access the corresponding function when your iPhone is locked.

24. If you don't want the iPhone to automatically erase all your data after an incorrect passcode has been entered 10 times, set the Erase Data switch to off (white).

Automatic Erase

When you have enabled the Erase Data function and you enter an incorrect passcode when unlocking your iPhone, you see a counter showing the number of unsuccessful attempts. When this reaches 10, all the data on your iPhone will be erased on the next unsuccessful attempt.

Making Changes

Any time you want to make changes to your passcode and fingerprint (iPhone 5s or later) settings, move back to the Touch ID & Passcode (iPhone 5s or later) or Passcode (other models) screen. Before you can move back to this screen, you must enter your current passcode at the prompt. After you enter your current passcode, you move to the Touch ID & Passcode (iPhone 5s or later) or Passcode (other models) screen. To disable the passcode, tap Turn Passcode Off, tap Turn Off, and enter the passcode. To change your passcode, tap Change Passcode. You then enter your current passcode and enter your new passcode twice. You return to the Passcode Lock screen, and the new passcode takes effect. You can change the other settings similar to how you set them initially as described in these steps. For example, you can add new fingerprints. To remove a fingerprint, move to the Fingerprints screen, swipe to the left on the fingerprint you want to remove, and tap Delete. You can rename a fingerprint by tapping it, editing its name on the resulting screen, and tapping Done (for example, you might want to name the fingerprints so you recognize them, such as My Right Thumb or Jim's Left Thumb).

Setting Restrictions for Content and Apps

You can restrict the access to specific content and apps on your phone. Suppose you let other people borrow your iPhone but don't want them to use certain apps or to see data you'd rather keep to yourself. You can enable a restriction to prevent someone from accessing these areas without entering the restriction code. You can also restrict the use of apps, movies, music, and other content based on the age rating that the app or other content has.

To restrict access to content or apps, perform the following steps:

1. On the Settings screen, tap General.

2. Swipe up the screen until you see Restrictions.

3. Tap Restrictions.

4. Tap Enable Restrictions.

5. Create a Restrictions Passcode. You have to enter this passcode to change the content restrictions or to be able to access restricted content.

6. Reenter your Restrictions Passcode. You return to the Restrictions screen, and the ALLOW switches are enabled.

7. In the ALLOW section, set the switch next to each function you want to disable to off (white). For example, to prevent web browsing, set the Safari switch to off (white); the Safari icon is removed from the Home screen and can't be used. With the other controls, you can prevent access to the Camera, FaceTime, iTunes Store, and so on.

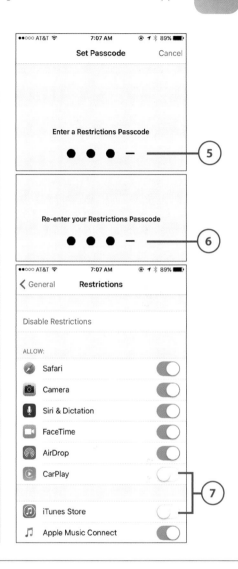

Dueling Passcodes

There are two passcodes: the Lock passcode and the Restrictions passcode. Each controls access to its respective functions. Limiting access to content and apps likely means you will be letting someone else use your phone, so the person who will be using your iPhone might need to be able to unlock it unless you want to have to unlock it for them. If you want to allow them to unlock the phone, but want to restrict access to your Apple Pay information or Apple ID, create a fingerprint for that person, but disable Touch ID for Apple Pay and App and iTunes Stores (see the previous task for details). This enables the person to unlock and use your iPhone, but you can control what they can do by setting a Restrictions passcode and configuring permissions as described in these steps. (You don't want to give the person the passcode to the phone as that defeats the purpose of configuring restrictions.)

In-app Purchases

Some apps, especially games, allow you to make purchases while you are using the app. For example, you can buy additional levels for a game. To prevent in-app purchases, set the In-App Purchases switch to off (white). This is especially important if you let your phone be used by children or others who might inadvertently make purchases you don't want made.

8. Swipe up to see the ALLOWED CONTENT section.

9. Tap Ratings For.

10. Tap the country whose rating system you want to use for content on your iPhone.

Whose Ratings?

The country you select in step 10 determines the options you see in the remaining steps because the restrictions available depend on the location you select. These steps show the United States rating systems; if you select a different country, you see rating options for that country instead.

11. Tap Restrictions.

12. Tap Music, Podcasts, News & iTunes U.

13. To prevent content tagged as explicit from being played, set the EXPLICIT switch to off (white). Explicit content will not be available in the associated apps, such as Music or News.

14. Tap Back.

15. Tap Movies.

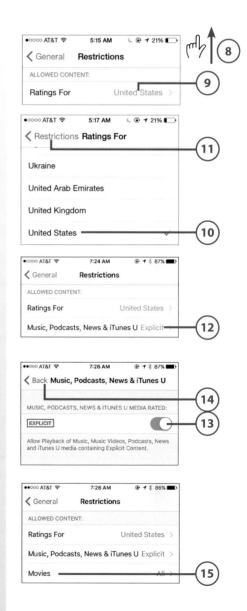

16. Tap the highest rating of movies that you want to be playable (for example, tap PG-13 to prevent R and NC-17 movies from playing); tap Allow All Movies to allow any movie to be played; or tap Don't Allow Movies to prevent any movie content from playing. Prevented movie ratings are highlighted in red.

17. Tap Restrictions.

18. Tap TV Shows and use the resulting screen to set the highest rating of TV shows that you want to be playable (for example, tap TV-14 to prevent TV-MA shows from playing); tap Allow All TV Shows to allow any show to be played; or tap Don't Allow TV Shows to prevent any TV content from playing. Prevented ratings are highlighted in red. Tap Restrictions to return to the Restrictions screen.

19. Use the Books option to enable or disable access to sexually explicit books.

20. Tap Apps and set the highest rating of app that you want to be available (for example, tap 12+ to prevent 17+ applications from working); tap Allow All Apps to allow any application to be used; or tap Don't Allow Apps to prevent all applications. Tap Restrictions to return to the Restrictions screen.

21. Use the Siri option to restrict explicit language for searching the Web.

22. Use the Websites option to control the websites that can be accessed. The options are to limit sites with adult content or to allow only specific websites to be visited. When you select this option, you can create a list of sites and only those sites can be visited.

23. Swipe up the screen until you see the PRIVACY section.

24. Use the settings in the PRIVACY section to determine whether apps can access information stored in each area and whether they should be locked in their current states. For example, you can prevent apps from accessing your calendars or photos. Configuring these is similar to the Privacy settings you read about earlier in this chapter.

25. Swipe up the screen until you see the ALLOW CHANGES section.

26. Tap areas that you want to restrict, such as Cellular Data Use and then tap Don't Allow Changes to prevent changes to that area.

27. To prevent multiplayer games in the Game Center, set the Multiplayer Games switch to off (white). Users will no longer be able to play games against other people.

28. To prevent new friends from being added in the Game Center, set the Adding Friends switch to off (white). Players will be restricted to the friends already allowed.

Removing Restrictions

To remove all restrictions, move to the Restrictions screen (your Restrictions passcode is required) and tap Disable Restrictions. Enter your Restrictions passcode, and the restrictions are removed.

Customize the layout of the icons on your Home screens by placing icons where you want them

Choose the image you want as wallpaper

Tap to configure notifications and sounds

Place icons in folders to keep your Home screens organized

In this chapter, you learn how to make an iPhone look and sound the way you want it to. Topics include the following:

→ Customizing your Home screens
→ Setting the screen's brightness, view, text size, and wallpaper
→ Choosing the sounds your iPhone makes
→ Setting up notifications and the Notification Center

5

Customizing How Your iPhone Looks and Sounds

There are lots of ways that you can customize an iPhone to make it *your* iPhone so that it looks and sounds the way you want it to. You can design your Home screens; set the screen's brightness, text size, and wallpaper; choose the sounds your iPhone makes; and configure the notifications your iPhone displays and plays to keep you informed about what's happening.

Customizing Your Home Screens

The iPhone's Home screens are the starting point for anything you do because these screens contain the icons that you tap to access the apps and web page icons that you want to use; you can also place icons within folders that also have icons on your Home screens. You see and use the Home screens constantly, so it's a good idea to customize them to your preferences.

In the background of the Lock screen and every Home screen is the wallpaper image. In the section called "Customizing the Wallpaper on the Home and Lock Screens," you learn how to configure your iPhone's wallpaper in both locations.

As you know, you can access apps and web page icons on your Home screens by tapping them. The Home screens come configured with icons in default locations. You can change the location of these icons to be more convenient for you. As you install more apps and create your own web page icons, it's a good idea to organize your Home screens so that you can quickly get to the items you use most frequently. You can move icons around the same screen, move icons between the pages of the Home screen, and organize icons within folders. You can even change the icons that appear on the Home screens' Dock. You can also delete icons you no longer need.

Moving Icons Around Your Home Screens

You can move icons around on a Home screen, and you can move icons among screens to change the screen on which they are located.

1. Press the Touch ID/Home button to move to a Home screen if you aren't there already.

2. Swipe to the left or right across the Home screen until the page containing an icon you want to move appears.

3. Tap and hold any icon. After a moment, the icons begin jig-gling and you can then move icons on the Home screens. You also see Delete buttons (an x) in the upper-left corner of some icons, which indicate that you can delete both the icon and app or the web page link (more on this later in this section).

Touch But Don't Press (6s or 6s Plus)

If you are working with an iPhone 6s or 6s Plus, don't press on icons when you want to move them; just touch your finger to the screen. If you apply pressure, you can open the Quick Action menu instead. When you just touch an icon and leave your finger on the screen, the icons will become fuzzy briefly, and then start jiggling indicating you can move them.

4. Tap and hold an icon you want to move; it becomes larger to show that you have selected it.

5. Drag the icon to a new location on the current screen; as you move the icon around the page, other icons separate and are reorganized to enable you to place the icon in its new location.

6. When the icon is in the location you want, lift your finger up. The icon is set in that place.

7. Tap and hold on an icon you want to move to a different page.

8. Drag the icon to the left edge of the screen to move it to a previous page or to the right edge of the screen to move it to a later page. As you reach the edge of the screen, you move to the previous or next page.

9. Drag the icon around on the new screen until it is in the location where you want to place it.

10. Lift your finger up. The icon is set in its new place.

11. Continue moving icons until you've placed them in the locations you want; then press the Touch ID/Home button. The icons are locked in their current positions, they stop jiggling, and the Delete buttons disappear.

Creating Folders to Organize Apps on Your Home Screens

You can place icons into folders to keep them organized and to make more icons available on the same page. To create a folder, do the following:

1. Move to the Home screen containing icons you want to place in a folder.

2. Tap and hold an icon until the icons start jiggling; the Delete buttons appear.

3. Drag one icon on top of another one that you want to be in the new folder together.

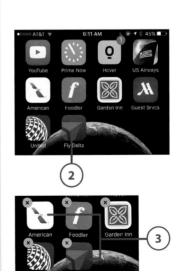

4. When the first icon is on top of the second and a border appears around the second icon, lift your finger. The two icons are placed into a new folder, which is named based on the type of icons you place within it. The folder opens and you see its default name.

5. To edit the name, tap in the name field.

6. Edit the folder's name.

7. Tap Done.

8. Tap outside the folder to close it.

9. If you're done organizing the Home screen, press the Touch ID/Home button. The icons stop jiggling.

Locating Folders

You can move a folder to a new location in the same way you can move any icon. Tap and hold an icon until the icons start jiggling. Drag the folder icon to where you want it to be.

New folder containing two icons

Placing Icons in Existing Folders

You can add icons to an existing folder like so:

1. Move to the Home screen containing an icon you want to place in a folder.

2. Tap and hold an icon until the icons start jiggling and the Delete buttons appear.

3. Drag the icon you want to place into a folder on top of the folder's icon so that the folder's icon enlarges. (The icon doesn't have to be on the same Home screen page; you can drag an icon from one page and drop it on a folder on a different page.)

4. When the folder opens, lift up your finger. The icon is placed within the folder and you see its current location within the folder. (If you don't want to change the icon's location when you place it in the folder, lift up your finger as soon as the folder's icon enlarges; this places the icon in the folder but doesn't cause the folder to open. This is more efficient when you want to place multiple icons within a folder during the same time period.)

5. Drag the new icon to its location within the folder.

6. Tap outside the folder. The folder closes.

7. When you're done adding icons to folders, press the Touch ID/Home button.

Removing Icons from Folders

To remove an icon from a folder, tap the folder from which you want to remove the icon to open it. Tap and hold the icon you want to remove until it starts jiggling. Drag the icon you want to remove from inside the folder to outside the folder. When you cross the border of the folder, the folder closes and you can place the icon on a Home screen.

Folders and Badges

When you place an icon that has a badge (the red circle with a number in it that indicates the number of new items in an app) in a folder, the badge transfers to the folder so that you see it on the folder's icon. When you place more than one app with a badge in the same folder, the badge on the folder becomes the total number of new items for all the apps in the folder. You need to open a folder to see the badges for individual apps it contains.

Configuring the Home Screen Dock

The Dock on the bottom of the Home screen appears on every page. You can place any icons on the Dock that you want, including folder icons.

1. Move to the Home screen containing an icon you want to place on the Dock.

2. Tap and hold an icon until the icons start jiggling and the Delete buttons appear.

3. Drag an icon that is currently on the Dock from the Dock onto the Home screen to create an empty space on the Dock.

4. Drag an icon or folder containing icons from the Home screen onto the Dock.

5. Drag the icons on the Dock around so they are in the order you want them to be.

6. Press the Touch ID/ Home button to set the icons in their current places.

Deleting Icons

You can delete icons from a Home screen to remove them from your iPhone. When you delete an app's icon, its data is also deleted and you won't be able to use the app anymore (of course, you can download it again if you change your mind). When you delete a web page's icon (see Chapter 13, "Surfing the Web," for information on creating web page icons), the bookmark to that web page is deleted.

1. Move to the Home screen containing an icon you want to delete.

2. Tap and hold an icon until the icons start jiggling and the Delete buttons appear (you can delete icons that are inside folders, too).

3. Tap the icon's Delete button.

4. Tap Delete. If the icon was for an app, it and any associated data on your iPhone are deleted. If the icon was for a bookmark, the bookmark is deleted.

Delete "Pastry Panic Free"

Deleting "Pastry Panic Free" will also delete all of its data.

| Delete | Cancel |

>>>Go Further

MORE ON ORGANIZING HOME SCREENS

Organizing your Home screens can make the use of your iPhone more efficient. Here are a few more things to keep in mind:

- You can place many icons in the same folder. When you add more than nine, any additional icons are placed on new pages within the folder. As you keep adding icons, pages keep being added to the folder so that it opens. You can swipe to the left or right within a folder to move among its pages, just as you can to move among your Home screens.

- To change a folder's name, move to a screen showing the folder whose name you want to change. Tap and hold an icon until the icons jiggle. Tap the folder so that it opens, and then tap the current name. Edit the name, tap Done, and tap outside the folder to close it. Press the Touch ID/Home button to complete the process.

- To delete a folder, remove all the icons from it. The folder is deleted as soon as you remove the last icon from within it.

- You can only delete icons for things you've added to your iPhone, which are either apps you've installed or bookmarks to web pages you've added. You can't delete any of the default apps, which is why their icons don't have Delete buttons like apps that you install do. If you don't use some of these default apps, move them to pages of your Home screen that you don't use very often so they don't get in your way, or create a folder for unused icons and store them there, out of your way.

- To return your Home screens to how they were when you first started using your iPhone, open the Settings app, tap General, Reset, Reset Home Screen Layout, and Reset Home Screen. The Home screens return to their default configurations. Icons you've added are moved onto the later pages.

Setting the Screen's Brightness, View, Text Size, and Wallpaper

Because you continually look at your iPhone's screen, it should be the right brightness level for your eyes. However, the screen is also a large user of battery power, so the dimmer an iPhone's screen is, the longer its battery lasts. You should find a good balance between viewing comfort and battery life. Fortunately, your iPhone has an Auto-Brightness feature that automatically adjusts for current lighting conditions.

The iPhone 6, 6s, 6 Plus, and 6s Plus offer two views. The Standard view maximizes screen space and the Zoomed view makes things on the screen larger, making them easier to see but less content fits on the screen. You can choose the view that works best for you.

As you use your iPhone, you'll be constantly working with text so it's also important to configure the text size to meet your preferences.

Although it doesn't affect productivity or usability of the iPhone, choosing your own wallpaper to see in the background of the Home and Lock screens makes your iPhone more personal to you and is just plain fun.

Setting the Screen Brightness, View, and Text Size

To set the screen brightness, perform the following steps:

1. In the Settings app, tap Display & Brightness.

2. Drag the slider to the right to raise the base brightness or to the left to lower it. A brighter screen uses more power but is easier to see.

3. If you don't want to use the Auto-Brightness feature, slide the switch to off (white) to disable this feature. The Auto-Brightness feature adjusts the screen brightness based on the lighting conditions in which you are using the iPhone. You'll get more battery life with Auto-Brightness on, but you might not be comfortable with the brightness of the screen when you use the iPhone where there isn't a lot of ambient light.

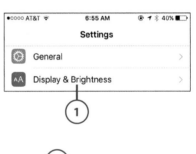

4. Tap View; if you don't see this option, your iPhone doesn't support it and you can skip to step 17. The View settings screen enables you to set the zoom level you want to use.

5. Tap Standard.

6. Look at the sample screen.

7. Swipe to the left or right to see examples of what other screens look like in the Standard view.

8. Look at the next sample screen.

9. Swipe to the left or right to see examples of what other screens look like in the Standard view.

10. Tap Zoomed. The sample screens change to reflect the Zoomed view.

11. Swipe to the left and right to preview the other sample screens in the Zoomed view.

12. If you want to keep the current view, tap Cancel and skip to step 16.

13. To change the view, tap the view you want.

14. Tap Set (if Set is grayed out, the view you selected is already set and you can skip to step 17).

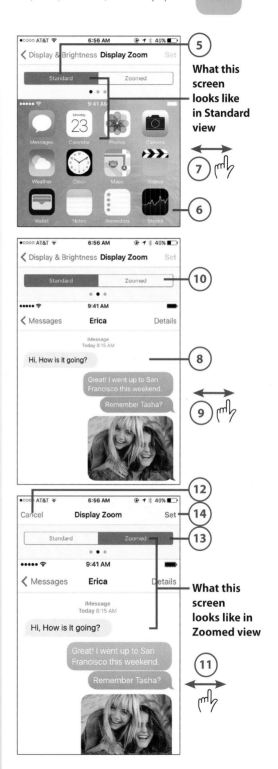

What this screen looks like in Standard view

What this screen looks like in Zoomed view

15. Tap Use Zoomed (this is Use Standard if you are switching to the Standard view). Your iPhone restarts and uses the new view.

16. Move back into the Settings app and then to the Display & Brightness screen.

17. Tap Text Size. This control changes the size of text in all the apps that support the iPhone's Dynamic Type feature.

18. Drag the slider to the right to increase the size of text or to the left to decrease it. As you move the slider, the text at the top of the screen resizes so you can see the impact of the change you are making.

19. When you are happy with the size of the text, tap Display & Brightness.

20. If you want to make all of the text on your iPhone bold, set the Bold Text switch to on (green) and move to step 21. If you don't want to bold the text, skip the next step.

21. Tap Continue. Your iPhone restarts. All the text is in bold, making it easier to read.

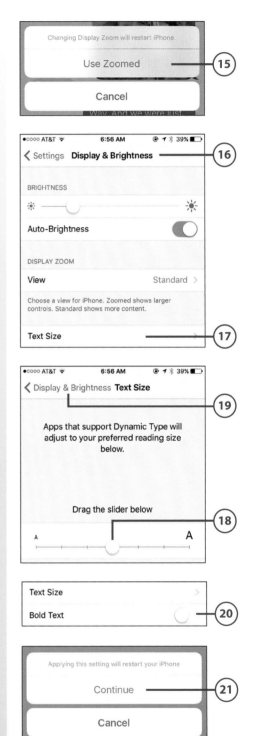

Setting the Wallpaper on the Home and Lock Screens

Wallpaper is the image you see "behind" the icons on your Home screens. Because you see this image so often, you might as well have an image that you want to see or that you believe makes using the Home screens easier and faster. You can use the iPhone's default wallpaper images, or you can use any photo available on your iPhone. You can also set the wallpaper you see on the iPhone's Lock screen (you can use the same image as on the Home screens or a different one). To configure your wallpaper, perform the following steps:

1. In the Settings app, tap Wallpaper. You see the current wallpaper set for the Lock and Home screens.

2. Tap Choose a New Wallpaper. The Choose screen has two sections. The APPLE WALLPAPER section enables you to choose one of the default wallpaper images while the PHOTOS section shows you the photos available on your iPhone. If you don't have any photos stored on your iPhone, you can only choose from the default images. To choose a default image, continue with step 3; to use one of your photos as wallpaper, skip to step 8.

3. Tap Dynamic if you want to use dynamic wallpaper, Stills if you want to use a static image, or Live if you want to use a Live Photo. These steps show selecting a Live Photo, but using a dynamic or still image is similar.

Current wallpaper on your Lock screen   **Current wallpaper on your Home screens**

4. Swipe up and down the screen to browse the images available to you.

5. Tap the image you want to use as wallpaper.

6. Tap Perspective to use the Perspective view of the wallpaper (see the sidebar "More on View Options"), tap Still if you a static version of the image, or tap Live to use a Live Photo.

7. Tap Set and move to step 15.

Wallpaper Options Explained

Dynamic wallpaper has motion (kind of like a screen saver on a computer). Stills are static images. Live Photos show motion when you tap and hold on them. Live Photos are available only on iPhone 6s or iPhone 6s Plus. On other models, you only see the Dynamic and Stills options.

8. To use a photo as wallpaper, swipe up the screen to browse the sources of photos available to you; these include All Photos, Favorites, albums, and so on.

Working with Photos

To learn how to work with the photos on your iPhone, see Chapter 15, "Working with Photos and Video You Take with Your iPhone."

9. Tap the source containing the photo you want to use.

10. Swipe up and down the selected source to browse its photos.

11. Tap the photo you want to use. The photo appears on the Move and Scale screen, which you can use to resize and move the image around.

More on View Options

The Perspective view can be a bit difficult to describe because it is subtle. This view magnifies the wallpaper image when you tilt your iPhone. It is sometimes noticeable and sometimes not, depending on the image you are using for wallpaper. The best thing to do is to enable it to see if you notice any difference or disable it if you prefer not to use it for the specific images you use as wallpaper. You can enable or disable it anytime for your wallpaper on the Lock and Home screens. To change the view without changing the wallpaper, move to the Wallpaper screen and tap the wallpaper (tap the Lock or Home screen) you want to change. Tap Perspective to use the Perspective view or Set if you don't want to use it. To save the view, tap Set or to leave it as it is, tap Cancel.

When you choose a Live Photo as wallpaper, you can touch and hold on the screen to see the image's motion. Note that when you apply a Live Photo to the Home screen wallpaper, it becomes a static image for which you can choose the Still or Perspective view.

12. Use your fingers to unpinch to zoom in or pinch to zoom out, and hold down and drag the photo around the screen until it appears how you want the wallpaper to look.

13. Tap Perspective to use the Perspective view of the wallpaper (see the sidebar "More on View Options"), tap Still if you a static version of the image, or tap Live Photo to use a Live Photo (only available on iPhone 6s or iPhone 6s Plus).

14. Tap Set.

15. Tap Set Lock Screen or Set Home Screen to apply the wallpaper to only one of those screens; tap Set Both to apply the same wallpaper in both locations. The next time you move to the screen you selected, you see the wallpaper you chose.

16. If you set the wallpaper in only one location, tap Choose to move back to the Choose screen and repeat steps 3–15 to set the wallpaper for the other location.

New wallpaper on the Lock screen

New wallpaper on the Home screen

Choosing the Sounds Your iPhone Makes

Sound is one important way your iPhone uses to communicate with you. You can configure the sounds the phone uses in two ways. One is by choosing the general sounds your iPhone makes, which is covered in this section. You can also configure sounds specific apps use to notify you about certain events; this is covered in the next section.

To configure your iPhone's general sounds, do the following:

1. On the Settings screen, tap Sounds.

2. If you want your iPhone to also vibrate when it rings, set the Vibrate on Ring switch to on (green).

3. If you want your iPhone to vibrate when you have it muted, set the Vibrate on Silent switch to on (green).

4. Set the volume of the ringer and alert tones by dragging the slider to the left or right.

5. If you want to also be able to change this volume using the volume buttons on the side of the phone, set the Change with Buttons switch to on (green).

6. Tap Ringtone. On the resulting screen, you can set the sound and vibration your iPhone uses when a call comes in.

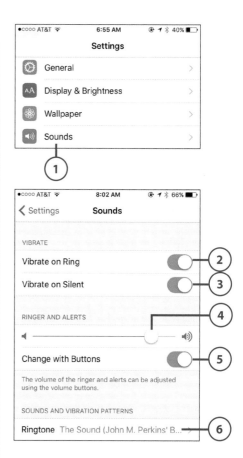

Individual Ringtones and Vibrations

The ringtone and vibration you set in steps 6–14 are the default or general settings. These are used for all callers except for people in your Contacts app for whom you've set specific ringtones or vibrations. In that case, the contact's specific ringtone and vibration are used instead of the defaults. See Chapter 7, "Managing Contacts," to learn how to configure specific ringtones and vibrations for contacts.

7. Swipe up and down the screen to see all the ringtones available to you. There are two sections of sounds on this screen: RINGTONES and ALERT TONES. These work in the same way; alert tones tend to be shorter sounds. At the top of the RINGTONES section, you see any custom ringtones you have configured on your phone; a dark line separates those from the default ringtones that are below the custom ones.

8. Tap a sound, and it plays.

9. Repeat steps 7 and 8 until you have selected the sound you want to have as your general ringtone.

10. If necessary, swipe down the screen so you see the Vibration section at the top.

11. Tap Vibration. A list of Standard and Custom vibrations is displayed.

12. Swipe up and down the screen to see all the vibrations available. The STANDARD section contains the default vibrations while the CUSTOM section shows vibrations you have created.

13. Tap a vibration. It "plays" so you can feel it.

14. Repeat steps 12 and 13 until you've selected the general vibration you want to use; you can tap None at the bottom of the Vibration screen below the CUSTOM section if you don't want to have a general vibration.

15. Tap Ringtone.

16. Tap Sounds. The ringtone you selected is shown on the Sounds screen next to the Ringtone label.

17. Tap Text Tone.

18. Use steps 7–14 and tap Text Tone to set the sound and vibration used when you receive a new text. The process works the same as for ringtones, though the screens look a bit different. For example, the ALERT TONES section is at the top of the screen because you are more likely to want a short sound for new texts.

19. When you're done setting the text tone, tap Sounds.

20. Using the same pattern as you did for ringtones and text tones, set the sound and vibrations for the rest of the events in the list.

21. If you don't want your iPhone to make a sound when you lock it, slide the Lock Sounds switch to off (white). Your iPhone no longer makes this sound when you press the Sleep/Wake button to put it to sleep and lock it.

22. If you don't like the audible feedback when you tap keys on the iPhone's virtual keyboard, slide the Keyboard Clicks switch to off (white) to disable that sound. The keyboard is silent as you type on it.

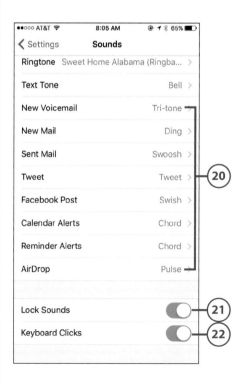

>>>*Go Further*

SOUNDING OFF

Following are some other sound- and vibration-related pointers:

- You can tap the Store button on the Ringtone, Text Tone, and other screens to move to the iTunes Store, where you can download ringtones and other sounds to your iPhone. See Chapter 6, "Downloading Apps, Music, Movies, TV Shows, and More onto Your iPhone," for more information about downloading content from the iTunes Store.

- You can also create your own ringtones using an audio app on a computer, such as GarageBand. GarageBand enables you to move ringtones you create directly into iTunes on a Mac computer. If you use a different app, you need to export the sound from that app and then add it to your iTunes Library. In either case, you can then use iTunes to sync the tones onto your iPhone.

- You can create custom vibration patterns, too. On the Vibration screen, tap Create New Vibration. Tap the vibration pattern you want to create; when you're done tapping, tap Stop. Tap Record to start over if you don't like the one you created. When you're done, tap Save. Name the pattern and tap Save. The patterns you create are available in the CUSTOM section on the Vibration screen, so you can use them just like the iPhone's default vibration patterns. To remove a custom pattern, swipe to the left on it and tap Delete.

Setting Up Notifications and the Notification Center

Many apps use notifications to communicate information to you, such as to inform you about new information, status updates, new email messages, new text messages, and so on. You can use the Notifications settings to enable or disable notifications and to configure them for specific apps. Configuring notifications is one of the most important ways to customize your iPhone so that it keeps you informed as much as you want it to without overwhelming you with too many notifications.

Understanding Notifications and the Notification Center

There are several types of notifications, which include badges, banners, alerts, vibrations, and sounds.

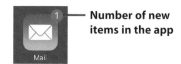

Number of new items in the app

Badges are the counters that appear on an app's or folder's icon to let you know how many new of something you have, such as email messages, texts, event invitations, and so on. You can enable or disable the badge for an app's icon. (Remember that when a badge appears on a folder's icon, it counts all the events for all the apps it contains.)

Banner notification for a new email message

Tap to open the object in the associated app (Mail in this case)

When you swipe down on a Messages banner, you can reply

Type your reply

Swipe up to close the notification

Swipe down to reply (some apps)

Tap Send to send it

Banners are small messages that appear at the top of the screen when something happens, such as when you receive an email message. Banners contain the icon of the app from which they come, and they can show a preview (if you enable the preview setting). Banners are nice because they don't interfere with what you are doing. If you ignore a banner, after a few seconds, it disappears. If you tap a banner, you move into the app producing the banner and can work with whatever the banner is for, such as a new email message.

You can swipe up on a banner to close it. You can swipe down on a banner to reply (for some apps, such as Messages). When you receive a new banner when one is visible on the screen, the first one rotates out of the way so the newest one is displayed. If you receive a lot of notifications at the same time, you see a summary of how many you have received.

Reminder — **Alert notification for a reminder**

Alerts are another means that apps can use to communicate with you. There are alerts for many types of objects, such as texts, emails, reminders, missed call notifications, and so on. The differences between a banner and an alert are that alerts appear in the center of the screen and you must do something to make the alert go away, such as listen to or ignore a voice message. Some alerts have an Options button; tap this button to see and do actions related to the notification. Alerts can contain a variety of other options depending on the app that sent the alert; for example, you can mark a reminder as complete or tap Later to reset the reminder's alert.

Cellular Emergency Notifications

Depending on where you live and which provider you use, you might receive emergency notifications from government agencies for such things as weather emergencies, Amber Alerts (in the United States, these are issued when a child is abducted), and so on. These alerts appear on your iPhone when they are issued to keep you informed of such events. You can enable or disable certain of these notifications.

You should use alerts when you want to be sure to take action on the occurrence about which an alert is sent. For example, you might want to use alerts for calendar events so you have to respond to the notice that the event is coming up, such as the start of a meeting. Banners are better for those notifications that you want to be aware of but that you don't want to interrupt what you are doing, such as email messages. (If an alert appears each time you receive an email message, they can be very disruptive.)

Sounds are audible indicators that something has happened. For example, when something happens in the Game Center, you can be notified via a sound. Earlier in this chapter, you learned how to configure your iPhone's general sounds. You also can configure the sounds used for a specific app's notifications.

Vibrations are a physical indicator that something has happened. Like sounds, you can configure general vibrations, and you can also configure an app's vibration pattern for its notifications.

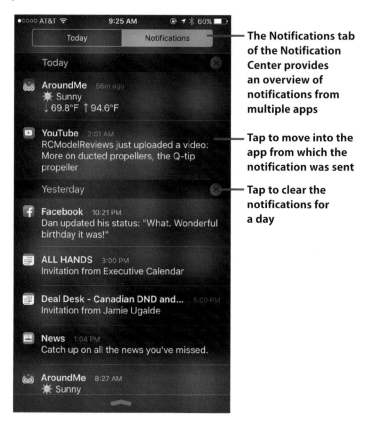

The Notifications tab of the Notification Center provides an overview of notifications from multiple apps

Tap to move into the app from which the notification was sent

Tap to clear the notifications for a day

The Notification Center enables you to access all your notifications on one screen. As you learned in Chapter 1, "Getting Started with Your iPhone," swipe down from the top of the screen to reveal the Notification Center. Tap the Notifications tab, and you see your current notifications grouped by the day on which those notifications occurred. Swipe up and down the screen to review them. Tap the delete (x) button and tap Clear to clear all of the notifications for a day. Tap a notification to move into the app from which the notification was sent. You can configure which apps provide notifications on the Notification Center and how many are allowed.

Setting Global Notification Preferences

Use the following steps to configure general notification settings:

1. On the Settings screen, tap Notifications.

2. In the NOTIFICATIONS VIEW section, tap Sort Order.

3. Tap Recent if you want the notifications shown in the Notification Center to be organized based on the most recent information being toward the top of the screen, and then skip to step 6.

4. Tap Manual if you want to set the order (from top to bottom) of notifications in the Notification Center.

5. Drag apps by their order button up and down to change the order in which their notifications appear in the Notification Center.

6. Tap Notifications.

7. To have notifications on the Notification Center grouped by app instead of by time, set the Group By App switch to on (green); this option is only available if the Sort Order is set to Recent as explained in step 3.

8. Configure each app's notification settings; the details of this are explained in the next task.

9. Swipe up the screen until you see the GOVERNMENT ALERTS section.

More Alerts

Depending on where you live, you might see a different set of alert options in the GOVERNMENT ALERTS section. You can enable or disable any of the alerts you see in this section as explained in steps 8 and 9.

10. If you don't want to receive AMBER alert notifications, set the AMBER Alerts switch to off (white).

11. If you don't want to receive other types of emergency alerts, set the Emergency Alerts switch to off (white).

Configuring Notifications for Specific Apps

You can configure how apps can provide notifications and, if you allow notifications, which type. You can also configure other aspects of notifications, such as whether an app displays in the Notification Center or whether its notifications appear on the Lock screen. Not all apps support all notification options. Some apps, such as Mail, support notification configuration by account (for example, you can set a different alert sound for new mail in each account). You can follow the same general steps to configure notifications for each app; you should explore the options for the apps you use most often to ensure they work the best for you.

The following steps show how to configure Mail's notifications, which is a good example because it supports a lot of notification features; other apps might have fewer features or might be organized slightly differently. But, configuring the notifications for any app follows a similar pattern.

1. Continuing in the Notification Center screen from the previous task, swipe up and down to browse all of the apps installed on your iPhone that support notifications.

2. Tap the app whose notifications you want to configure.

3. If you want the app to provide notifications, set the Allow Notifications switch to on (green) and move to step 4. If you don't want notifications from the app, set the Allow Notifications switch to off (white) and skip the rest of these steps.

4. Tap the account for which you want to configure notifications.

5. To show notifications from the app/account in the Notification Center, set the Show in Notification Center switch to on (green); if you set this to off (white), notifications from the app/account are not shown in the Notification Center.

6. Tap Sounds.

7. Use the resulting Sounds screen to choose the alert sound and vibration for new email messages to the account (refer to the section on setting general sound preferences earlier in this chapter for details on choosing sounds and vibrations).

8. Tap the back button located in the upper-left corner of the screen (it is labeled with the account's name).

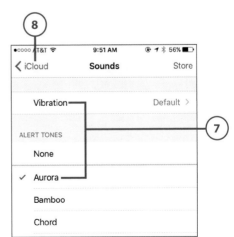

9. To display the app's badge, set the Badge App Icon switch to on (green).

10. If you want the app's notifications for the account to appear on the Lock screen, slide the Show on Lock Screen switch to on (green).

11. Choose the type of notification you want by tapping None, Banners, or Alerts. You know which alert type is currently selected because its name appears in an oblong button.

12. If you don't want a preview to appear in the app's notifications, slide the Show Previews switch to off (white). For example, you might want to keep some types of messages private when you receive a notification; to do so, disable the Show Previews option for that account.

13. Tap the back button, which is located in the upper-left corner of the window and is labeled with the app you are configuring (Mail, in this example).

Installed App Not Shown?

You must have opened an app at least once for it to appear on the Notifications screen.

14. Configure notifications for the other accounts used in the app.

15. Configure notifications for VIP email and threads.

16. Tap Notifications.

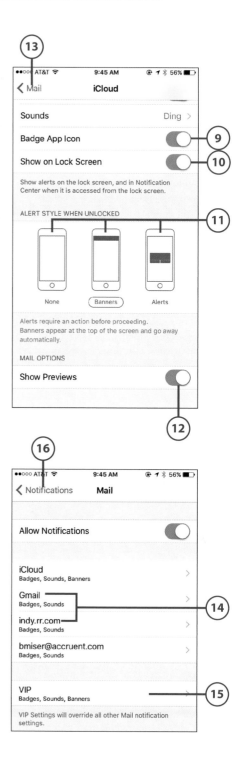

17. Repeat these steps for each app shown on the Notification Center screen. Certain apps might not have all the options shown in these steps, but the process to configure their notifications is similar.

VIPs Are Special

Mail supports VIPs, which are people from whom email messages are treated specially, such as having a dedicated mailbox in the Mail app. You can apply specific notification settings to VIP messages using the VIP option. These override the notification settings for the email account to which messages from VIPs are sent.

Use the App Store
app to download and
install cool and useful
apps on your iPhone

Use the iTunes
Store app to load
up your phone
with great music,
movies, TV shows,
and more

Use the Settings app
to configure your
store preferences

In this chapter, you learn how to add apps, music, TV shows, and other content onto your iPhone, and how to share your goodies with others. Topics include the following:

→ Configuring store settings
→ Using the App Store app to find and install iPhone apps
→ Using the iTunes Store app to download music, ringtones, movies, and TV shows
→ Downloading apps or iTunes Store content you've purchased previously
→ Using Family Sharing to share your store downloads with other people

6

Downloading Apps, Music, Movies, TV Shows, and More onto Your iPhone

One of Apple's past marketing campaigns for the iPhone stated that if you want to do something with an iPhone, there was an app for it. Developers around the world have created many thousands of apps available in the App Store app to download and install on your iPhone.

Along with all these great apps, there is also lots of music, movies, TV shows, ebooks, audiobooks, and much more content available to enjoy on your iPhone. Using the iTunes Store app, you can easily browse and search for content and then download it to your iPhone with just a couple of taps.

A benefit of using the App Store and iTunes Store apps is that anything you download once, can be downloaded again at no cost. If you happen to lose some of your content, you can simply download it again. Or, when you upgrade your iPhone, you can download content you've previously purchased onto it at no cost (you can do the same thing on any of your other iOS devices, too). And, you can use the Family Sharing to share content you purchase with other people.

Another nice thing about using the iTunes and Apps Stores is that you can configure downloads to any of your devices to be automatically downloaded to your iPhone, too, which is where we start this chapter.

Configuring Store Settings

You can configure your iPhone so that music, apps, and books that you download from any of your devices are automatically downloaded to your phone as well. For example, if you purchase an album on your iPad, that same album can be immediately downloaded to your iPhone, too. You can also have any updates to apps installed on your iPhone downloaded and installed automatically.

Configuring Automatic Store Downloads

To have content you purchase from the iTunes Store be automatically downloaded to your iPhone and configure when password entry is required to download content, perform the following steps:

1. Tap Settings.

2. Tap App and iTunes Stores.

3. Tap Password Settings; if you don't see Password settings, Touch ID is configured for the App and iTunes Store and you can skip to step 7. (Touch ID makes it much easier to securely download content from the stores. To learn how to configure Touch ID, see "Setting Passcode, Touch ID, and Auto-Lock Preferences" in Chapter 4, "Configuring an iPhone to Suit Your Preferences.").

4. Tap Always Require if you want your password to be required for every download from either store, or tap Require After 15 Minutes if you want downloads within 15 minutes of the most recent purchase to be allowed without entering your password again. The first option is the most secure, but also requires entering your password more often. The second setting is usually best, unless other people use your phone frequently.

5. If you want to have to enter your password to download free content, set the Require Password switch to on (green); if this switch is off (white), free content can be downloaded without a password. If other people use your phone, it's a good idea to set this to on so they don't load up your phone with content you don't want.

6. Tap App and iTunes Stores.

7. Slide the switches to on (green) for the types of content you want to be downloaded to your iPhone automatically; the options are Music, Apps, Books, and Updates (which causes any updates to the apps installed on your iPhone to be downloaded and installed automatically).

8. If you don't have an unlimited cellular data plan, you might want
   to set the Use Cellular Data to off
   (white) so content is downloaded
   only when you are on a Wi-Fi network. If this is enabled (green), content is downloaded to your iPhone
   when you are using a cellular network, which can consume significant amounts of your data plan.

   After you've completed these
   steps, any new content of the
   types you enabled in step 7 is
   downloaded to your iPhone automatically when it is purchased
   on any of your devices (content
   you've purchased before you configured the Store settings is not
   downloaded automatically, but,
   as you learn at the end of this
   chapter, you can manually download that content at any time).

9. If you want apps that are currently installed on your phone to
   be suggested to you based on
   your current location and app
   use, set the Installed Apps switch
   to on (green). With this enabled,
   as you change locations, apps
   that are relevant to that location
   are suggested on the Lock screen
   and in the App Switcher. Apps are
   also suggested in these locations
   based on the apps that you use.

Apple ID

To work with the Apple ID you use in the App and iTunes Stores, tap the
account shown at the top of the iTunes & App Store screen. On the resulting
prompt, you can view your Apple ID, sign out of your account, or reset your
password (the iForgot option). If you sign out of your account, the Store screen
only has the Sign In button. Tap this and sign into the Apple ID you want to
configure for the stores.

Using the App Store App to Find and Install iPhone Apps

The App Store app enables you to quickly and easily browse and search for apps, view information about them, and then download and install them on your iPhone with just a few taps.

When you use the App Store app, you can find apps to download using any of the following options:

- **Categories**—This link shows you various categories of apps that you can browse.

- **Featured**—This tab takes you to apps featured in the Apps Store. This screen organizes apps in several categories. These categories change from time to time, but they typically include "best new" types of apps (such as games), apps for specific purposes (for example, back-to-school shopping), and so on. Swipe up and down the screen to see all the categories available.

- **Top Charts**—This takes you to lists of the top iPhone apps. This screen has three tabs at the top of the screen: Paid shows you the top apps for which you have to pay a license fee; Free shows you a similar list containing only free apps; and Top Grossing shows the apps that have been downloaded the most (rather than those that have made the most money).

- **Explore**—This option shows apps that are popular or relevant based on your current location. The first time you choose it, you're prompted to allow the App Store app to use your iPhone's Location Services feature to identify your location.

- **Search**—This tool enables you to search for apps. You can search by name, developer, and other keywords.

- **Updates**—Through this option, you can get to the Purchased screen, which enables you to find and download apps you have previously downloaded to your iPhone or other device and shows you the update status of your apps on your iPhone (this topic is covered in the last section of this chapter). If you have automatic updates enabled, you see the list of updates made to the apps on your iPhone along with those that are pending; if you don't have automatic updates enabled, you can use this screen to download and install updates for your apps.

Finding and downloading any kind of app follows this same pattern:

1. **Find the app you are interested in.** You can use the options described in the previous list, find apps by browsing for them, or use the search option to find a specific app quickly and easily.

2. **Evaluate the app.** The information screen for apps provides lots of information that you can use to decide whether you want to download an app (or not). The information available includes a text description, screenshots, ratings and reviews of other users, and so on.

3. **Download and install the app.**

The following tasks provide detailed examples for each of these steps.

Suggestions, Suggestions

If you enabled the App Store setting described in the previous section, when you move around the App Store app, you might see various suggestion screens that present apps that might be of interest to you based on your location or other criteria. You can download and install apps from the suggestion screen, very similarly to the steps you'll find in this chapter for downloading them from other locations. If you don't want to download any of the suggested apps, tap Not Now. None of the tasks in this chapter show the suggestion screens for clarity's sake so to follow the steps as written, just tap Not Now to close a suggestion screen.

Searching for Apps

If you know something about an app, such as its name, its developer, or just about anything else, you can quickly search the App Store to find the app. Here's how to search for an app:

1. Move to the Home screen and tap App Store.

2. Tap Search.

3. Tap in the Search box.

4. Type a search term. This can be the type of app you are looking for based on its purpose (such as travel) or the name of someone associated with the app, its title, its developer, or even a topic. As you type, the app suggests searches that are related to what you are typing.

5. Tap the search you want to perform (to see the full list of search results, tap Search). The apps that meet your search term appear.

6. Swipe up and down on the screen to review the apps that were found by your search.

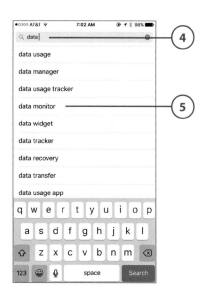

Related Apps

When the search results are on the screen, at the top (just under the Search bar), you see app searches that are related to the one you performed in some way in the Related bar. Tap a related search on this bar to use it to find other apps. As you use related searches, back (<) and forward (>) buttons appear in the Related bar so that you can move back and forth among the searches you have done. For example, tap the back button to get back to a previous search result.

7. If none of the apps are what you are looking for, tap the x in the Search box and repeat steps 4–6 (or use the Related Searches as described in the Related Apps note).

8. When you find an app of interest to you, tap it. You move to the app's information screen.

Related searches

9. Use the app's information on the information screen to evaluate the app and decide if you want to download it. You can read about the app, see screenshots, and read other peoples' reviews to help you decide. If you want to download the app, see "Downloading Apps" later in this chapter for the details.

Follow the Trends?

Before you enter a search term on the Search screen, you see the Trending Searches, which are the searches that are being performed most frequently. You can tap one of these to use it to search for apps.

Browsing for Apps

If you don't know of a specific app you want, you can browse the App Store. To browse, you can tap any graphics or links you see in the App Store app. There are a number of ways to start the browsing process: Categories, Featured, Top Charts, or Explore. When you select one of these options, you can then browse apps associated with or organized by the option you selected. The following steps show you how to browse for apps by category; the other options are similar:

1. Move to the Home screen and tap App Store.

2. Tap Categories.

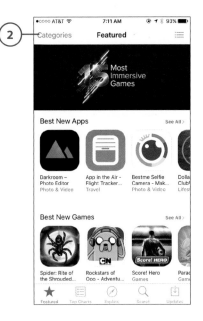

3. Swipe up and down the screen to browse the list until you see a category of interest.

4. Tap a category in which you are interested.

5. If the category has subcategories, swipe up and down the screen to browse the subcategories; if you moved directly to apps, skip to step 7.

6. Tap a subcategory in which you are interested.

7. Swipe up and down to browse the groupings of apps, such as Best New, All-Time Greats, and so on.

8. Swipe left and right on a grouping to browse the apps it contains.

This arrow indicates a category has subcategories

See All, Know All

To browse all the apps in a category, tap the See All option at the top of the category's screen. You see all the apps in that category; swipe up and down the screen to browse the list. Tap an app to see its information.

9. Tap an app in which you are interested. You move to that app's information screen.

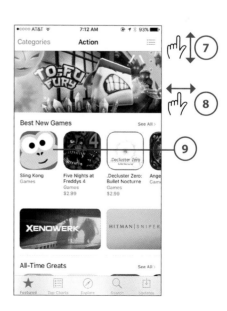

10. Use the information on the information screen to decide whether you want to download this app. You can read about the app, see screenshots, and read other peoples' reviews to help you decide. If you want to download the app, see "Downloading Apps" later in this chapter for the details. Or, you can continue browsing by tapping the name of the category in the top left corner of the screen to return to the category list.

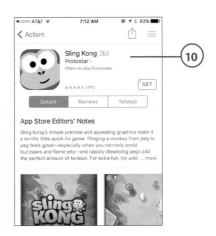

>>>Go Further
MORE ON FINDING APPS

Following are a few pointers to help you use the App Store:

- When you see a "+" inside an app's price or Get button, that means the app is a universal app, which means it runs equally as well on iPhones, iPads, and iPod touches.

- Some apps include video previews. When you see the Play button on an image, it is a video preview. Tap the Play button to watch it. Tap the Done button in the upper left corner of the screen to move back to the screenshots.

- After you have used an app, you can add your own review by moving back to its Reviews tab and tapping Write a Review. You move to the Write a Review screen where you have to enter your iTunes Store account information before you can write and submit a review.

- You can read user reviews of the apps in the App Store. You should take these with a grain of salt. Some people have an issue with the developer, or even the type of app, are viewing an older version of the app, or are commenting on issues unrelated to the app itself, and that causes them to provide low ratings. The most useful individual user reviews are very specific, as in "I wanted the app to do x, but it only does y." It can be more helpful to look at the number of reviews and the average user rating than reading the individual reviews.

Downloading Apps

Downloading and installing apps is about as easy as things get, as you can see:

1. In the App Store, view the app you want to download.

2. Tap GET (for free apps) or the price (for apps that have a license fee). The button then becomes INSTALL, if it is a free app, or BUY, if it has a license fee.

3. Tap INSTALL or BUY. Depending on your App and iTunes Store settings, you might be prompted to sign in with your Apple ID and password to start the download. If you aren't prompted to confirm the download, you can skip the next step because the app starts downloading immediately.

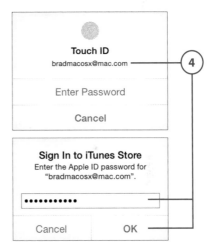

4. If you are prompted to confirm the download, and you are using an iPhone 5s or later and have enabled Touch ID for store downloads, touch the Touch ID/Home button at the prompt; if you are using another model, or you don't use Touch ID for store downloads, type your Apple ID password, and then tap OK.

You see the progress of the process.

When the process is complete, the status information is replaced by the OPEN button.

This app is almost fully downloaded

This app is installed and ready to use

>>>*Go Further*
MORE ON APPS

As you use the App Store app to install apps on your iPhone, keep the following hints handy:

- Like other software, apps are updated regularly to fix problems, add features, or make other changes. If you set the iTunes & App Store AUTOMATIC DOWNLOADS Updates setting to on (green) as described earlier in this chapter, updates to your apps happen automatically in the background. Your apps are always current and so you don't have to update them manually. (More information on updating apps is in Chapter 17, "Maintaining and Protecting Your iPhone and Solving Problems.")

- If you see the Download button (a cloud with a downward-pointing arrow) next to an app rather than Get or Buy, that means you have previously downloaded (and paid for if it isn't free) the app but it is not currently installed on your iPhone. Tap the button to download and install it.

- To let someone else know about an app, tap the Share button and then tap how you want to let him know; the options include AirDrop, Message, Mail, Twitter, and Facebook. To give the app to someone, tap Gift.

- Apps can work in the background to keep their information current, such as Weather and Stocks. To configure this, open the Settings app, tap General, and tap Background App Refresh. Set Background App Refresh to on (green). To enable an app to work in the background, set its switch to on (green). To disable background activity for an app, set its switch to off (white).

- If you want to report a problem you're having with an app, move to the app's Details tab, swipe up the screen, and tap Developer Website. You move to the developer's website and can get information and help with the app.

- Using the Family Sharing feature, you can share apps you download with others. You learn about this in "Using Family Sharing to Share Your Store Downloads with Others," at the end of this chapter.

- After you install an app, move to the Settings screen and look for the app's icon. If it is there, the app has additional settings you can use to configure the way it works. Tap the app's icon in the Settings app and use its settings screen to configure it.

Using the iTunes Store App to Download Music, Ringtones, Movies, and TV Shows

You can use the iPhone's iTunes Store app to download audio and video content from the iTunes Store directly onto your iPhone. You can listen to music you download in the Music app, watch movies and TV shows in the Videos app, and use tones for ringtones and alert tones.

Using the iTunes Store app involves the following general steps:

- **Find the content you are interested in**—Like the App Store app, there are a number of ways to do this. You can search for specific content, or you can browse for content by type, which includes the following (to get to some of these, such as Genius, tap the More button and then tap the item of interest to you):

  - Music enables you to download music.

  - Movies takes you to the movies in the iTunes Store so you can browse, preview, and download them.

  - TV Shows does the same for TV programming.

  - Tones enables you to purchase ringtones and alert tones that you can use as various sounds on your iPhone.

  - Genius shows you recommendations based on content you have previously downloaded that you might also be interested in.

- **Preview the content**—You can sample content before you download it. For example, you can listen to a preview of songs (typically 90 seconds' worth), watch movie trailers, listen to tones, and so on.

- **Download the content**—You can download content with just a couple of taps. After you download content to your iPhone, it immediately becomes available in the related app.

In the following tasks, you see examples of each of these steps.

Searching for iTunes Store Content

When you know something about the content you want, searching is a good way to find it because it is easy and fast. Also, when you search, your results can include multiple types of content. For example, searching on a title can yield an album, a movie, a song, and an audio-book. Here's how to search in the Store:

1. On the iPhone's Home screen, tap iTunes Store. You move to the iTunes Store app. At the bottom of the screen, you choose how you want to look for content by tapping one of the buttons on the iTunes Store toolbar.

2. Tap Search.

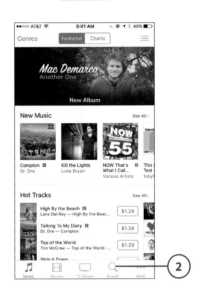

More Trends

Similar to the App Store app, when you haven't entered a search term on the Search screen, you see the searches that are trending. You can tap a trending search to see its results.

3. Tap in the Search box.

Apple Music

In Chapter 14, "Finding and Listening to Music," you learn about Apple Music that allows you to listen to almost all of the music in the iTunes Store for a monthly subscription price, which is about the cost of one album (in the United States). If you use Apple Music, there's no need for you to purchase it from the iTunes Store because you can listen to and, also download, the same music using Apple Music at no additional cost.

4. Type a search criterion, such as an artist's name, a movie title, or even a general topic (for example, a franchise, such as *Star Trek*). As you type, content that matches your search appears under the Search bar.

5. When you see something of interest on the results list, tap it, or to see the entire list of search results, tap Search and then tap the result you want to explore.

6. Swipe up, down, right, and left to browse the search results, which are organized into categories, such as Movies, Albums, Songs, Ringtones, Music Videos, and so on.

7. To limit the results to a specific type of content, tap the related tab. For example, to see the movies related to what you searched for, tap Movies.

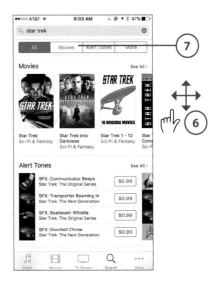

8. Swipe on the screen to browse the list of results for the type of content you selected.

9. When you see something of interest, tap it. You see the Information screen for that content.

10. Use the Information screen to preview and explore the content. Details are provided later in this chapter in the task titled, "Previewing iTunes Store Content."

Stop the Search!

To clear a search, tap the Clear button (x) in the Search bar. Swipe down on the keyboard to close it so that you can see the iTunes toolbar at the bottom of the screen again.

Browsing for iTunes Store Content

Even though browsing isn't as efficient as searching, it is a good way to discover content you might not know about. The details of browsing depend on the type of content for which you are looking. To demonstrate the general process, the task that follows shows browsing music:

1. On the iPhone's Home screen, tap iTunes Store. You move to the iTunes Store app. At the bottom of the screen, you can choose how you want to look for content by tapping one of the buttons on the iTunes Store toolbar.

2. Tap Music. You move to the Music Home page. At the top of the screen, you see options you can use to browse: Genres, Featured (the default), and Charts.

3. Swipe the screen to browse the current contents. The rest of these steps show browsing by genre. The steps for using the other browse options are similar.

4. Tap Genres. You see the list of genres.

5. Swipe up and down the screen to browse the list of genres.

6. Tap the genre you want to explore.

7. Swipe the screen to browse the contents being displayed.

8. Tap something of interest to see more detail. For example, tap the See All link for a category to see all the items in that category.

9. Swipe the results to browse them.

10. Tap an item for which you'd like to see more detail.

11. Use the Information screen to preview and explore the content. Details are provided in the task "Previewing iTunes Store Content."

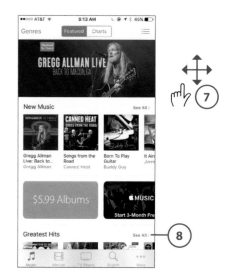

But Wait, There's More

You can access additional categories of content by tapping the More button. On the More screen, you see Tones and Genius. Tap Audiobooks to browse audiobooks you can download and listen to. Tap Tones to download sound snippets from songs or special effects to use as ringtones or alert tones. Tap Genius to see recommended content based on content you have downloaded or content related to content you have downloaded.

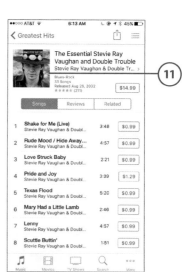

Previewing iTunes Store Content

You can use the Information screen to explore content in which you are interested. This screen looks a bit different for various kinds of content, such as a movie versus an album. However, the general features of this screen are similar, so the following steps showing an album's Information screen will get you started:

1. Move to the Information screen for content you might want to download.

2. Review the summary information at the top of the screen.

3. On the Songs tab (this is called Details for some other types of content), tap More.

4. Read the detailed description/ notes. (Be aware that not all content has notes or other information about it.)

5. Tap the Reviews tab.

6. Swipe up and down the screen to read all the review information. At the top, you see an overview of the reviews, indicated by the star ratings. Toward the bottom of the screen, you can read the individual reviews.

7. Tap Songs.

8. Swipe up the screen to see the list of songs the album or collection contains.

9. To preview a track, tap it. A short preview plays. While it's playing, the track's number is replaced by the Stop button, which you can tap to stop the preview.

10. Continue previewing the content until you are ready to make a decision to download it—or not.

More on Previewing Content

When you are previewing songs and other audio, you can continue to browse around the store; as you do, a preview bar appears at the top of the screen. This bar shows the content currently playing. You can tap its playback button to stop the preview.

When you preview video content, such as watching a trailer for a movie, it plays in a video player. Use the playback controls to watch the video. Tap Done to close the video player.

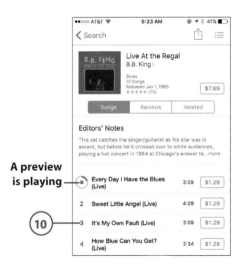

A preview is playing

Downloading iTunes Store Content

Like downloading apps, downloading movies, tones, songs, albums, and so on is just a tap away:

1. Move to the Information screen for content you want to download.

2. Tap the appropriate buy button, which shows the price of the item. For example, to buy an album, tap its price button. To buy a song, tap its price button instead. Likewise, you can buy or rent a movie by tapping its price button (some movies are offered in different formats, and each one has its own price button). The button changes to show what you are buying.

3. Tap the Buy button again, such as BUY ALBUM. If you're prompted to sign into your account, go to step 4. If you recently signed in, the download starts without you signing in and you can skip step 4.

4. If you are using an iPhone 5s or later, at the prompt, touch the Touch ID/Home button. If you are using a different model, enter the password for your Apple ID and tap OK.

   The badge on the More button updates to show you how many items are being downloaded to the iPhone. The download process starts and you can continue to shop in the Store or move into a different app; the download process occurs in the background. If you want to, you can monitor the download process by continuing with these steps.

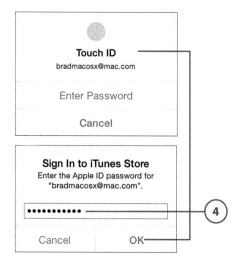

5. Tap More.

Procrastinate If You Want

When you download some content that is large, such as a movie, you have the option to download it later. For example, you might decide you want a movie while you are using your cellular data network but don't want to use a lot of your data plan's monthly allocation to download it. Tap the Later button to defer the download to a later time. You can do the same thing with the Pause button for any content that is downloaded. Tap the Pause button and the download stops where it is. Tap the Resume button to complete the download (for example, when you return to a Wi-Fi network).

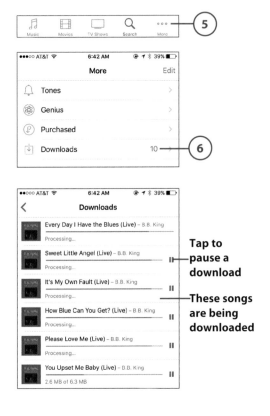

Tap to pause a download

These songs are being downloaded

6. Tap Downloads. You move to the Downloads screen, which displays the progress of the tracks you are purchasing.

When the process is complete, the Downloads screen is empty, indicating that all the content you purchased has been added to the iPhone.

Freebies

Some content (not a lot) in the iTunes Store is free to download. Similar to apps that are free, instead of a button showing the content's price, you see the GET button. Tap GET to start the download process, which works just like that for content you have to pay for, except that you aren't charged for it of course.

Using Your iTunes Store History List

As you are looking at content in the iTunes Store, you'll likely encounter music, movies, and so on that you are interested in but are not sure you want to download. It would be a pain to get back to content via searching or browsing. Fortunately, you can use the History List to go back to content you have previewed.

The History list contains content that you've interacted with in the following ways:

- **Wish List**—To add something to your Wish List, open an item's information screen, tap the Share button, and then tap Add to Wish List.

- **Siri**—When music is playing around you, press and hold the Touch ID/Home button and say "What song is this?" Siri identifies the music playing and adds it to your History List. This is a great way to add music that you hear when you are out and about so you can easily find it again later.

- **Radio**—Songs you listen to via iTunes Radio are added to your History List automatically so that you can purchase them easily. So, if you remember that you heard a great song on iTunes Radio, but don't remember who performed it, you can use this option to easily find it.

- **Preview**—Any content you preview is added to your History List automatically.

You can use your History List to find, preview, and download content similarly to how you do these things from other areas. The following example shows content captured by previewing it, but the other options work in the same way.

When you preview content, such as watching a movie's trailer, it is added to your History List

1. Tap the History List button.

2. Tap the source of content you want to see. For example, tap Previews to see the content you have previewed.

3. Swipe the screen to browse the list of items.

4. To move to an item's Information screen, tap its title.

5. To preview an item, taps its icon.

6. To buy an item, tap its price button and then tap its BUY button.

7. If you've purchased something on this list, tap PLAY to play it.

8. To clear your list, tap Clear and then tap Clear History.

9. To close the list, tap Done.

>>>Go Further

SHOPPING LIKE A PRO

Here are a few more pointers to make your iTunes Store experience even better:

- **Preorder**—You can order content that isn't released yet, such as movies, or a full season of a TV show that is in a current season. When the content you have preordered becomes available, it is downloaded to your iPhone automatically.

- **Renting**—You can rent movies, too. This is less expensive than buying them, but it comes with limitations. You can keep a rented movie for only 30 days. And, after you start watching it, it will play for a 24-hour period (48 hours in some locations). When either of these time periods is up, the rented movie is deleted from your iPhone automatically.

- **Customizing the iTunes Store app toolbar**—You can place any four buttons on the iTunes Store app toolbar by customizing it (the More button is always visible on the toolbar). To change the buttons displayed, tap More and then tap Edit. Drag the buttons you want to place on the bar from the upper part of the screen, and drop them on the toolbar at the location you want them to appear. You can also drag icons around the toolbar to change their locations. When the toolbar is what you want it to be, tap Done.

- **Move from Song to Album**—When you browse a list of songs, tap a song's title twice to move to the Information screen for the album from which the song comes.

- **Share and Share Alike**—Tap the Share button at the top of iTunes screens to share the content you are exploring. You can share by email, message, Twitter, and Facebook. The messages you send contain a link to the item. Tap Gift to give the content to someone else.

- **The Next Time You Sync**—The next time you sync after purchasing audio and video from the iTunes Store on the iPhone, that audio and video is moved into your iTunes Library (if you've configured iTunes to automatically download new content from the iTunes Store, you don't need to sync new content onto your computer). If you've created any smart playlists with live updating enabled and the new audio and video matches that playlist's criteria, the new audio and video become part of those playlists automatically.

- **Clear History**—The Clear button on the History List deletes only the items from the tab you are currently viewing. For example, if you use it on the Previews tab, all the items you have previewed are erased. To clear the other lists, tap the tab for the content you want to clear, tap Clear, and then tap Clear History at the prompt.

- **Automatic Downloads**—If you have other iOS devices or iTunes on your computers configured to automatically download iTunes Store purchases, the content is downloaded to those locations, too.

Downloading Apps or iTunes Store Content You've Purchased Previously

You can download any content you've purchased from the App or iTunes Stores again without paying a fee (rented movies are an exception because you can download those only once and have to pay for them again to download them again). For example, you might download an app, decide that you don't have room for it any more, delete it, and then later want it again. Similarly, you might delete music from your iPhone to free up some memory, and then download it again later when you want to listen to it.

Downloading Previously Purchased App Store Apps

To download apps you previously purchased, perform the following steps:

1. Tap the App Store icon to open the app.

2. Tap Updates.

3. Tap Purchased.

4. If you've configured Family Sharing (see "Using Family Sharing to Share Your Store Downloads with Others" later in this chapter), tap My Purchases to download content you've purchased or tap a person whose content is being shared with you to download content that person has purchased. (The rest of these steps show the My Purchases option.)

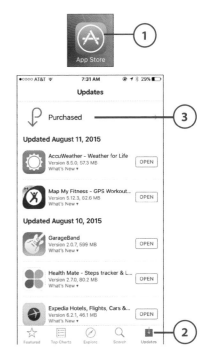

5. Tap Not on This Phone.

6. Swipe up and down the list to browse the apps you've downloaded, but that are not currently installed on your iPhone.

7. Tap the Download button for the app that you want to re-install; if prompted to do so, confirm your Apple ID by tapping the Touch ID button or entering your Apple ID and tapping OK. The app is downloaded and installed on your iPhone. When the process is complete, the OPEN button appears. This indicates that the app has been re-installed on your iPhone and is ready for you to use.

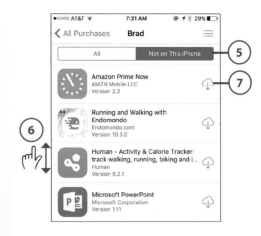

Downloading Previously Purchased iTunes Content

To download music, movies, or other content you previously downloaded, perform the following steps:

1. Open the iTunes Store app.

2. Tap More.

3. Tap Purchased.

4. If you've configured Family Sharing (see "Using Family Sharing to Share Your Store Downloads with Others" later in this chapter), tap Music, Movies, or TV Shows in the MY PURCHASES section to download content you've purchased or tap a person whose content is being shared with you to download content that person has purchased. The rest of these steps show the Music category in the MY PURCHASES section; the other options work similarly.

5. Tap Not on This iPhone. The list shows all the music you've purchased from the iTunes Store but that is not currently stored on your iPhone.

6. Swipe up and down to browse the list.

7. Tap the artist whose music you want to download. A list of content for that artist, organized into categories such as albums or songs, is displayed.

8. Swipe up and down the screen to browse the content you have from the artist (if you have content from only one album, skip to step 12).

9. To download an entire album, tap its Download button and skip to step 15.

10. To download all of the content from that artist, tap Download All and skip to step 15.

11. To download individual songs, tap the album containing the songs you want to download.

12. Browse the contents of the album.

13. Tap a song's Download button to download it and skip to step 15.

14. To download all of the album's songs, tap its Download button.

15. If prompted and you are using an iPhone 5s or later, touch the Touch ID/Home button; if you are using a different model, enter your Apple ID password and tap OK. The content is downloaded to your iPhone. When that process is complete, you can watch or listen to it in the related app , such as the Music app for songs you download.

Using Family Sharing to Share Your Store Downloads with Others

With Family Sharing, you can share your iTunes content with up to six other people. The people with whom you share content don't have to be related to you in any way despite the name of this feature. People with whom you share content can then download content you have purchased to their devices without needing to use your Apple ID or password.

To start using Family Sharing, you need to set it up and then designate the people with whom you will share content.

Setting Up Family Sharing

To set up Family Sharing on your iPhone, do the following:

1. Open the Settings app.

2. Tap iCloud.

3. Tap Set Up Family Sharing.

4. Tap Get Started.

5. If you want to share content under your current iCloud account, tap Continue; if you want to change accounts, tap the link at the bottom of the screen and follow the onscreen instructions to change the account you are configuring.

6. Click Agree to accept the terms and conditions (if you don't accept them, you can't use Family Sharing).

7. Tap Agree to confirm you accept the terms and conditions.

8. To accept changes on the credit card currently associated with your Apple ID, tap Continue; to change the payment method, tap Managing Family Purchases and follow the prompts to make changes.

9. To share your location with the people in your Family Sharing group, tap Share Your Location; if you prefer to not share your location, tap Not Now. You move to the Family screen and are ready to share content with others as described in the next task.

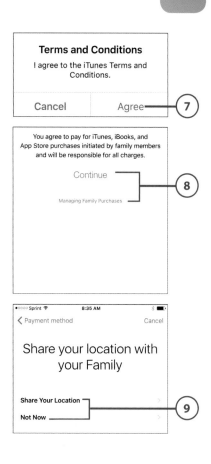

Adding People to Family Sharing

To be able to share content with someone, she must be using a device running iOS 8 or later or a Mac running OS X Yosemite or later. To share your content with someone else, add them to your Family Sharing as follows:

1. If you just completed the previous task and are still on the Family screen, skip to step 4; if this isn't the case, open the Settings app.

2. Tap iCloud.

3. Tap Family.

4. Tap Add Family Member.

5. Enter the email address of the person with whom you are sharing content, and then select the person when he appears on the list. An invitation is sent to the person with whom you are sharing content.

6. Enter your Apple ID password and tap OK.

7. Enter the three-digit security code located on the back of the credit card associated with your account.

8. Tap Next. An invitation is sent to the person you are inviting to share your content.

You return to the Family screen where you see the person whom you invited to share content. You see the Invitation sent status under the person's name. When the person receives your invitation and taps Get Started, he is led through the process of accepting your invitation. Once accepted, the person's status becomes "Adult" or "Child" on your Family screen. This means the person can download content you've purchased from the App or iTunes Stores just like you can download your own content (see "Accessing Shared Content" later in this chapter for details).

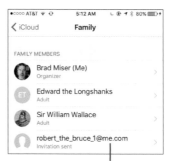

This person will be able to share your content when he accepts your invitation

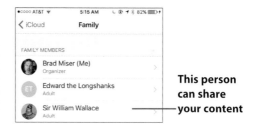

This person can share your content

Your Options Might Be Limited

In some cases, you might not have the option to ask the person you are sharing with to enter the password and only have the invitation option.

Create an Apple ID for a Child

If the person with whom you want to share content doesn't have an account, you can create an Apple ID for that person. Tap Create an Apple ID for a child at the bottom of the Family screen. Tap Next. You then have to indicate you had parental consent, confirm your payment information, enter the child's birthday, enter the child's name, create the Apple ID and password, and configure security questions. (A child is considered to be 13 or under.) You then turn Ask to Buy on or off. If you leave it on, you will have to approve a purchase the child tries to make; if you turn it off, you won't have to approve purchases. Note that any purchases the child makes use the payment information associated with your account. Finally, you accept the terms and conditions. Once the account is created, provide the Apple ID and password to the child, and he will be able to purchase apps and iTunes Store content under your account.

Birthdays

If the person whom you are trying to add to Family Sharing doesn't have a birthday configured in her iCloud settings, you might not be able to complete the process. Ask that person to update their birthday in her iCloud settings, either on her iOS device or via the iCloud website.

Managing Family Sharing

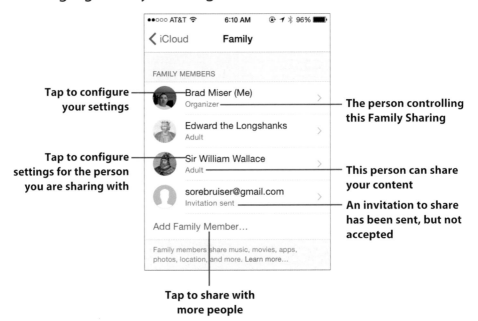

Tap to configure your settings

The person controlling this Family Sharing

Tap to configure settings for the person you are sharing with

This person can share your content

An invitation to share has been sent, but not accepted

Tap to share with more people

You can use the Family screen to manage the people with whom you are sharing content. When you access the Family screen, you see the people with whom you are sharing content and their status.

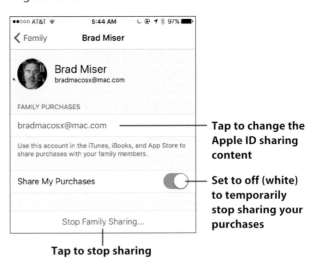

Tap to change the Apple ID sharing content

Set to off (white) to temporarily stop sharing your purchases

Tap to stop sharing

Tap your name (the organizer) to perform the following tasks:

- If you tap the email address, you can change the Apple ID being used to share. People who are currently sharing your content will lose access to your content if you change the account being used to share.

- Set the Share My Purchases switch to off (white) if you don't want those with whom you are sharing to be able to share your content. Set the Share My Purchases switch to on (green) to resume sharing your content.

- Tap Stop Family Sharing and then tap Stop Sharing at the prompt to turn Family Sharing off (see the following It's Not All Good before doing this).

It's Not All Good

You can only stop Family Sharing twice during a year. If you stop it twice, you're unable to use it again until a year passes. If you want to prevent others from sharing your content, set the Share My Purchases switch to off (white) because this doesn't limit your ability to access Family Sharing.

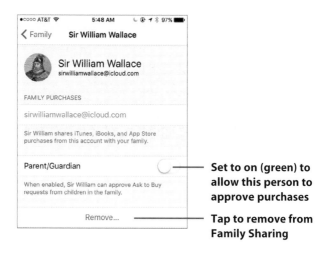

Set to on (green) to allow this person to approve purchases

Tap to remove from Family Sharing

Tap the name of people with whom you are sharing to perform the following tasks:

- Set the Parent/Guardian switch to on (green) to allow the person to approve purchases others make.

- Tap Remove and then tap Remove at the prompt to remove the person from Family Sharing. He is no longer able to access shared content and disappears from the list of people shown on the Family screen.

Accessing Shared Content

Accessing content being shared via Family Sharing is very similar to downloading apps and iTunes Store content previously purchased (see "Downloading Previously Purchased App Store Apps" and "Downloading Previously Purchased iTunes Content"). Following is an example of downloading iTunes content being shared with you (other people can use the same steps to download content you are sharing with them):

1. Using steps 1 through 3 in "Downloading Previously Purchased iTunes Content," move to the Purchased screen of the iTunes app.

2. Tap the person sharing content with you.

3. Tap the type of content you want to download.

4. Tap Not on This iPhone. You see the content being shared with you.

5. Tap the content you want to download.

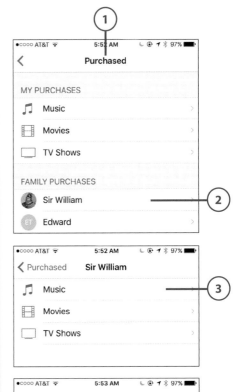

6. Tap Download All to download all the content you see. Tap the download button next to individual items to download specific content, or tap an item (such as album) to explore its content. These options work just like downloading content you purchased from the iTunes Store. When the content is downloaded to your iPhone, you can use the related app to listen to or watch it.

Share and Share Alike

When a person is added to the group shown on the Family tab, any content purchased by any member is immediately available to be shared with all the other members of the group. You should periodically check the Not on This iPhone tab for the people sharing with you to see what new content is available.

Use Settings to configure how contacts are displayed

Tap here to work with your contact information

Use your contact information in many apps

In this chapter, you learn how to ensure that your iPhone has the contact information you need when you need it. Topics include the following:

→ Setting your Contacts preferences
→ Creating contacts on your iPhone
→ Working with contacts on your iPhone
→ Managing contacts on your iPhone

Managing Contacts

Contact information, including names, phone numbers, email addresses, and physical addresses, is useful to have on your iPhone. When you want to contact someone, you don't need to remember an email address or phone number; instead, just tap the name of the person you want to contact. Likewise, you might want to see a contact's address in the Maps app.

The Contacts app enables you to do all these things plus much more. This app makes using your contact information seamless. You can access contact information directly in the Contacts app and take action on it (such as placing a call), or you can use your contact information within other apps, such as Mail, Phone, and Messages.

To use contact information, it first must be stored in the Contacts app. You can add this information to your iPhone via iCloud, Exchange, and other similar accounts; by capturing it when you perform tasks (such as reading email); or by entering information manually. And, you'll need to manage your contact information over time, such as adding to it, or changing it.

Setting Your Contacts Preferences

Using the Settings app, you can determine how contacts are sorted and displayed, if or how names are shortened on various screens, your contact information, and which account should be the default for contact information. You can probably work with your contacts just fine without making any changes to your settings, but if you want to make adjustments, open the Settings app and tap Mail, Contacts, Calendars. Swipe up the screen until you see the CONTACTS section. Use the information in the following table to change your contact settings.

Settings App Explained

To get detailed information on using the Settings app, see "Working with the Settings App" in Chapter 4, "Configuring an iPhone to Suit Your Preferences."

Contacts Settings on the Mail, Contacts, Calendars Screen

Setting	Description
CONTACTS	
Sort Order	Tap First, Last to have contacts sorted by first name and then last name or tap Last, First to have contacts sorted by last name and then first name.
Display Order	To show contacts in the format *first name, last name,* tap First, Last. To show contacts in the format *last name, first name,* tap Last, First.
Short Name	You can choose whether short names are used and, if they are, what form they take. Short names are useful because more contact information can be displayed in a smaller area, and they look "friendlier." To use short names, move the Short Name switch to the on position (green). Tap the format of short name you want to use. You can choose from a combination of initial and name or just first or last name. If you want nicknames for contacts used for the short name when available, set the Prefer Nicknames switch to on (green).
My Info	Use this setting to find and tap your contact information the Contacts app, which it can insert for you in various places and which Siri can use to call you by name; your current contact information is indicated by the label "me" next to the alphabetical index.
Default Account	Tap the account in which you want new contacts to be created by default (which is then marked with a check mark); if you want new contacts to be created on your iPhone instead of under an account, tap On My iPhone. If you have only one account configured for contacts, you don't have this option.
Contacts Found in Mail	If you don't want contact information in the Mail app to be used, such as to automatically complete addresses when you create emails to, or try to identify callers when a number calling you is unknown, set the Contacts Found in Mail switch to off (white). You typically should leave this on (green) unless you find the automatic contact suggestions annoying or not helpful.

Where Contacts Are Stored

You can store your contacts in an online account (for example, iCloud or Google), which is good, because it makes the information accessible on many devices and keeps it backed up. If you don't have an online account, contact information is stored on your iPhone. This is not ideal because, if something happens to your phone, you can lose all of your contacts. You should use at least one online account for storing your contacts (see Chapter 3, "Setting Up and Using iCloud and Other Online Accounts," for detailed information about online accounts).

Creating Contacts on Your iPhone

You can create new contacts on an iPhone in a number of ways. You can start with some information, such as the email address on a message you receive, and create a contact from it, or you can create a contact by manually filling in the contact information. In this section, you learn how to create a new contact starting with information in an email message and how to create a new contact manually.

Creating New Contacts from Email

When you receive an email, you can easily create a contact to capture the email address. (To learn how to work with the Mail app, see Chapter 9, "Sending, Receiving, and Managing Email.")

1. On the Home screen, tap Mail.

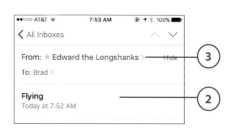

2. Use the Mail app to read an email message (see Chapter 9 for details).

3. Tap the email address from which you want to create a new contact. The Info screen appears—the label of the screen depends on the type of email address you tapped. For example, if you tapped the address from which the email was sent, the screen is labeled Sender. You see as much information as could be gleaned from the email address, which is typically the sender's name and email address.

4. Tap Create New Contact. The New Contact screen appears. The name, email address, and any other information that can be identified is added to the new contact. The email address is labeled with iPhone's best guess, such as other or home.

5. Use the New Contact screen to enter more contact information or update the information that was added (such as the label applied to the email address) and save the new contact. This works just like when you create a new contact manually, except that you already have some information—most likely, a name and an email address. For details on adding and changing more information for the contact, see the next task, which is "Creating Contacts Manually."

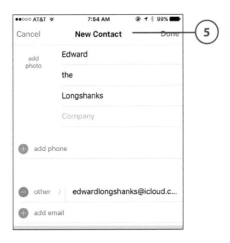

More Information for New Contacts

In some cases, such as when an email comes from an email server that includes full contact information (such as email from an Exchange account), you see a bar at the top of the email message above the From and To section. This bar shows the sender's name and phone number. Under this, you see Ignore and Add to Contacts. Tap Ignore to ignore this additional contact information. Tap Add to Contacts to create a new contact with all of the information available; this does the same thing as steps 3 through 5 except the resulting new contact contains more information with the name and email address; for example, phone numbers.

>>>*Go Further*

MORE ON CREATING CONTACTS FROM APPS

It's useful to be able to create contact information by starting with some information in an app. Keep these points in mind:

- Mail is only one of the apps from which you can create contacts. You can start a contact in just about any app you use to communicate, such as Messages, or get information, such as Maps. The steps to start a contact in these apps are similar to those for Mail. Tap the person or address for which you want to create a contact, and then tap Create New Contact. The Contacts app fills in as much of the information as it can, and you can complete the rest yourself.

- You can also add more contact information to an existing contact from an app you are currently using. You can do this by tapping Add to Existing Contact. You then search for and select the contact to which you want to add the additional information. After it's saved, the additional information is associated with the contact you selected. For example, suppose you have created a contact for a company but all you have is its phone number. You can quickly add the address to the contact by using the Maps app to look it up and then add the address to the company's existing contact information by tapping the location, tapping Add to Existing Contact, and selecting the company in your contacts.

Creating Contacts Manually

Most of the time, you'll want to get the information for a new contact from an app, as the previous task demonstrated, or through an online account, such as contacts stored in your Exchange account. If these aren't available, you can also start a contact from scratch and manually add all the information you need to it. Also, you use the same steps to add information to or change information for an existing contact that you do to create a new one, so even if you don't start from scratch often, you do need to know how to do so.

The Contacts app leads you through creating each type of information you might want to capture. You can choose to enter some or all of the default information on the New Contact screen, or add additional fields as needed. The following steps show creating a new contact containing the most common contact information you are likely to need:

1. On the Home screen, tap Contacts. (If you don't see the Contacts app on the Home screen, tap the Extras folder to open it and you should see the app's icon. You might want to move the Contacts icon from this folder to a more convenient location on your Home screen; see Chapter 5, "Customizing How Your iPhone Looks and Sounds," for the steps to do this.) The All Contacts screen displays.

   If you see the Groups screen instead, tap Done to move to the All Contacts screen.

   If you have only one account that provides contact information, you see its contact list rather than the All Contacts screen, and you are ready to create a new contact.

2. Tap the Add button. The New Contact screen appears with the default fields. (You can add more data fields as needed using the add field command.)

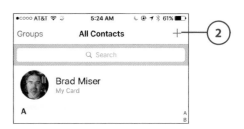

3. To associate a photo with the contact, tap add photo. You can choose a photo already on your phone or take a new photo. These steps show using an existing photo. See the "Taking Photos" note for the steps to take a new photo.

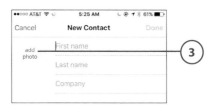

4. Tap Choose Photo.

5. Use the Photos app to move to, select, and configure the photo you want to associate with the contact (see Chapter 15, "Working with Photos and Video You Take with Your iPhone," for help with the Photos app).

6. Tap Choose. You return to the New Contact screen where the photo you selected is displayed.

7. Tap in the First field and enter the contact's first name; if you are creating a contact for an organization only, leave both name fields empty. (The Display Order preference determines whether the First or Last field appears at the top of the screen.)

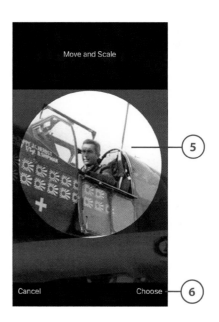

8. Tap in the Last field and enter the contact's last name.

9. Enter the organization, such as a company, with which you want to associate the contact, if any.

10. To add a phone number, tap add phone. A new phone field appears along with the numeric keypad.

Taking Photos

To take a new photo for a contact, tap Take Photo in step 4 instead of Choose Photo. The Camera app's screen appears. Use the iPhone's camera to capture the photo you want to associate with the new contact (taking photos is covered in Chapter 15). Use the Move and Scale screen to adjust the photo so it is what you want to use. Then, tap Use Photo. The photo is pasted into the image icon on the New Contact screen.

11. Use the numeric keypad to enter the contact's phone number. Include any prefixes you need to dial it, such as area code and country code. The app formats the number for you as you enter it.

12. Tap the label for the phone number, such as home, to change it to another label. The Label screen appears.

13. Swipe up and down the Label screen to see all the options available.

14. Tap the label you want to apply to the number, such as iPhone. That label is applied and you move back to the New Contact screen.

15. Repeat steps 10–14 to add more phone numbers to the contact.

16. Swipe up the screen until you see add email.

17. Tap add email. The keyboard appears.

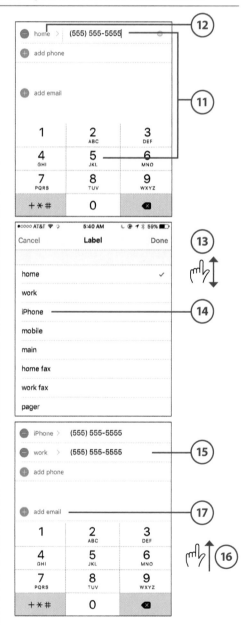

18. Type the contact's email address.

19. Tap the label for the email address to change it.

20. Tap the label you want to apply to the email address. You move back to the New Contact screen.

21. Repeat steps 17–20 to add more email addresses.

22. Swipe up the screen until you see Ringtone.

23. Tap Ringtone. The list of ringtones and alert tones available on your iPhone appears.

24. Swipe up and down the list to see all of the tones available.

25. Tap the ringtone you want to play when the contact calls you. When you tap a ringtone, it plays so you can experiment to find the one that best relates to the contact. Setting a specific ringtone helps you identify a caller without looking at your phone.

26. Tap Done. You return to the New Contact screen, where the tone you selected appears.

27. Using the pattern you have learned in the previous steps, move to the next item you want to set and tap it.

28. Use the resulting screens to enter the information you want to configure for the contact. After you've done a couple of the fields, it is easy to do the rest because the same pattern is used throughout.

29. When you've added all the information you want to capture, tap Done. The New Contact screen closes and the new contact is created and ready for you to use in Contacts and other apps. It is also moved onto other devices with which your contact information is synced. See the "Creating Contacts Expanded" Go Further sidebar for additional information on syncing and maintaining contacts.

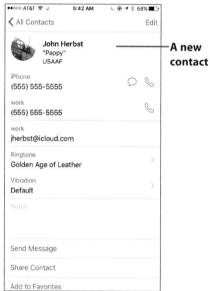

A new contact

>>>Go Further

CREATING CONTACTS EXPANDED

Contacts are useful in many ways so you should make sure you have all the contact information you need. Here are a few points to ponder:

- You can (and should) sync contacts on multiple devices (computers and other iOS devices) by using iCloud, Exchange, Gmail, or other similar accounts to store your contact information on the cloud from where all your devices can access it. Refer to Chapter 3 for the details of setting up an account through which you can sync your contacts.

- By the way, syncing your contacts works in both directions. Any new contacts you create or any changes you make to existing contact information on your iPhone move back to your other devices through the sync process. The bottom line is that you always have the same contact information available no matter which device you are using.

- To remove a field in which you've entered information, tap the red circle with a dash in it next to the field and then tap Delete. If you haven't entered information into a field, just ignore it because empty fields don't appear on a contact's screen.

- The address format on the screens in the Contacts app is determined by the country you associate with the address. If the current country isn't the one you want, tap it and select the country in which the address is located before you enter any information. The fields appropriate for that country's addresses appear on the screen.

- If you want to add a type of information that doesn't appear on the New Contact screen, swipe up the screen and tap add field. A list of additional fields you can add displays. Tap a field to add it; for example, tap Nickname to add a nickname for the contact. Then, enter the information for that new field.

- When you add more fields to contact information, those fields appear in the appropriate context on the Info screen. For example, if you add a nickname, it is placed at the top of the screen with the other "name" information. If you add an address, it appears with the other address information.

- If you have an iPhone 6s or 6s Plus, you can tap and put pressure on the Contacts icon. On the resulting Quick Action menu, you can show your contact info or create a new contact.

Working with Contacts on Your iPhone

There are many ways to use contact information. The first step is always finding the contact information you need, typically by using the Contacts app. Whether you access it directly or through another app (such as Mail), it works the same way. Then, you select the information you want to use or the action you want to perform.

Using the Contacts App

You can access your contact information directly in the Contacts app. For example, you can search or browse for a contact and then view the detailed information for the contact in which you are interested.

1. On the Home screen, tap Contacts. The Contacts screen displays with the contacts listed in the view and sort format determined by the Contacts settings.

The title of the screen depends on what you have selected to view; if All Contacts appears, you are browsing all your contact information. If Contacts appears, you are browsing only some of your contact information based on the contact groups you have elected to view; you learn how to change the groups of contacts you are viewing shortly. (If the Groups screen appears, tap Done. You move back to the All Contacts or Contacts screen.)

You can find a contact to view by browsing (step 2), using the index (step 3), or searching (step 4). You can use combinations of these, too, such as first using the index to get to the right area and then browsing to find the contact in which you are interested.

2. Swipe up or down to scroll the screen to browse for contact information; swipe up or down on the alphabetical index to browse rapidly.

3. Tap the index to jump to contact information organized by the first letter of the format you selected in the Contact Preferences above (last name or first name).

4. Use the Search tool to search for a specific contact; tap in the tool, type the name (you can type last, first, company, and nickname), and then tap the contact you want to view on the results list.

5. To view a contact's information, tap the contact you want to see.

6. Swipe up and down the screen to view all the contact's information.

7. Tap the data or icons on the screen to perform actions, including the following:

   • **Phone numbers**—Tap a phone number or the receiver icon to call it.

   • **Email addresses**—Tap an email address to create a new message to it.

   • **URLs**—Tap a URL to open Safari and move to the associated website.

- **Addresses**—Tap an address to show it in the Maps app.

- **FaceTime**—Tap FaceTime to start a FaceTime call with the contact.

- **Text**—Tap Send Message or the quote bubble icon and choose the phone number or email address to which you want to send a text message.

- **Share Contact**—Tap Share Contact. The Share menu appears. To share the contact via email, tap Mail; to share it via a text, tap Message; or to share it using AirDrop, tap AirDrop. You can also share via Twitter or Facebook. Then, use the associated app to complete the task.

- **Favorites**—Tap Add to Favorites and choose the phone number or email address you want to designate as a favorite. You can use this in the associated app to do something faster. For example, if it's the Phone app, you can tap the Favorites tab to see your favorite contacts and quickly dial one by tapping it. You can add multiple items (such as cell and work phone numbers) as favorites for one contact.

8. To return to the Contacts list without performing an action, tap Contacts.

>>>Go Further

MAKE CONTACT

When working with your contacts, keep the following points in mind:

- **Last known contact**—The Contacts app remembers where you last were and takes you back there whenever you move into the Contacts app. For example, if you view a contact's details and then switch to a different app to send a message, and then back to Contacts, you are returned to the screen you were last viewing. To move back to the main Contacts screen, tap Contacts in the upper-left corner of the screen.

- **Groups**—In a contact app on a computer, such as Contacts on a Mac, contacts can be organized into groups, which in turn can be stored in an online account, such as iCloud. When you sync, the groups of contacts move onto the iPhone. You can limit the contacts you browse or search; tap Groups on the Contacts screen.

The Groups screen displays the accounts (such as iCloud or Exchange) with which you are syncing contact information; under each account are the groups of contacts stored in that account. If a group has a check mark next to it, its contacts are displayed on the Contacts screen. To hide a group's contacts, tap it so that the check mark disappears. To hide or show all of a group's contacts, tap the All *account*, where *account* is the name of the account in which those contacts are stored. To make browsing contacts easier, tap Hide All Contacts to hide all the groups and contacts; then, tap each group whose contacts you want to show on the Contacts screen.

Tap Done to move back to the Contacts screen.

- **Speaking of contacts**—You can use Siri to speak commands to work with contacts, too. You can get information about contacts by asking for it, such as "What is William Wallace's work phone number?" If you want to see all of a contact's information, you can say "Show me William Wallace." When Siri displays contact information, you can tap it to take action, such as tapping a phone number to call it. (See Chapter 12, "Working with Siri," for more on using Siri.)

It's Not All Good

When you create a new contact, it is associated with the account you designated as the default in the Contacts settings and is stored at the account level (not in any of your groups). You can't create groups in the Contacts app, nor can you change the group with which contacts are associated. You have to use a contacts app on a computer to manage groups and then sync your iPhone (which happens automatically when you use an online account, such as iCloud) to see the changes you make to your contact groups.

Accessing Contacts from Other Apps

You can also access contact information while you are using a different app. For example, you can use a contact's email address when you create an email message. When you perform such actions, you use the Contacts app to find and select the information you want to use. The following example shows using contact information to send an email message, and using your contact information in other apps (such as Phone or Messages) is similar.

1. Open the app from which you want to access contact information (this example uses Mail).

2. Tap the New Message button.

3. In the To: field, tap the Add button.

4. Search, browse, or use the index to find the contact whose information you want to use.

5. Tap the contact whose information you want to use. (If a contact doesn't have relevant information, for example, if no email address is configured when you are using the Mail app, that contact is grayed out and can't be selected.)

   If the contact has only one type of the relevant information (such as a single email address, if you started in the Mail app), you immediately move back to the app and the appropriate information is entered, and you can skip to step 7.

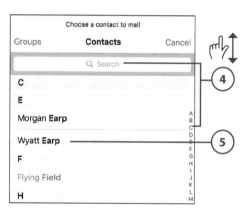

6. If the contact has multiple entries of the type you are trying to use, tap the information you want to use—in this case, the email address. The information is copied into the app and entered in the appropriate location.

7. Complete the task you are doing, such as sending an email message.

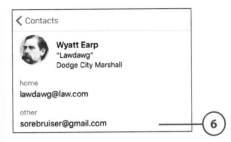

The email address from the Contacts app

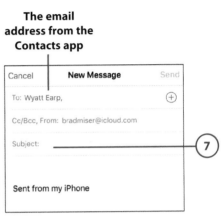

Managing Your Contacts on Your iPhone

When you sync contacts with an iCloud, Exchange, or other accounts, the changes go both ways. For example, when you change a contact on the iPhone, the synced contact manager application, such as Outlook, makes the changes for those contacts on your computer. Likewise, when you change contact information in a contact manager on your computer, those changes move to the iPhone. If you add a new contact in a contact manager, it moves to the iPhone, and vice versa. You can also change contacts manually in the Contacts app.

Updating Contact Information

You can change any information for an existing contact, such as adding new email addresses, deleting outdated information, and changing existing information.

1. View the contact's Info screen.

2. Tap Edit. The Info screen moves into Edit mode, and you see Unlock buttons.

3. Tap current information to change it; you can change a field's label by tapping it, or you can change the data for the field by tapping the information you want to change. Use the resulting tools, such as the phone number entry keypad, to make changes to the information. These tools work just like when you create a new contact (refer to "Creating Contacts Manually," earlier in this chapter).

4. To add more fields, tap add in the related section, such as add phone in the phone number section; then, select a label for the new field and complete its information. This works just like adding a new field to a contact you created manually.

5. To remove a field from the contact, tap its Unlock button.

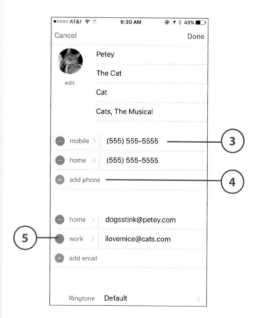

6. Tap Delete. The information is removed from the contact.

7. To change the contact's photo, tap the current photo, or the word *edit* under the current photo, and use the resulting menu and tools to select a new photo, take a new photo, delete the existing photo, or edit the existing one.

8. When you finish making changes, tap Done. Your changes are saved, and you move out of Edit mode.

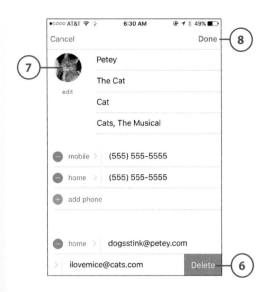

No Tones or Vibes?

If you leave the default tones or vibration patterns set for a contact, you won't see those fields when you view the contact. However, when you edit a contact, all the fields you need to add these to a contact become available.

Adding Information to an Existing Contact While Using Your iPhone

As you use your iPhone, you'll encounter information related to a contact that isn't currently part of that contact's information. For example, a contact might send you an email from a different email address than the one you have stored for her. When this happens, you can easily add the new information to the existing contact. Just tap the information to select it (such as an email address), and then tap Add to Existing Contact. Next, select the existing contact to which you want to add the new information. The new information is added to the contact. Tap Done (or Cancel, if you decide not to keep the new information) to return to the app you were working in.

Deleting Contacts

To get rid of contacts, you can delete them from the Contacts app.

1. Find and view the contact you want to delete.

2. Tap Edit.

3. Swipe to the bottom of the Info screen.

4. Tap Delete Contact.

5. Tap Delete Contact again to confirm the deletion. The app deletes the contact, and you return to the Contacts screen.

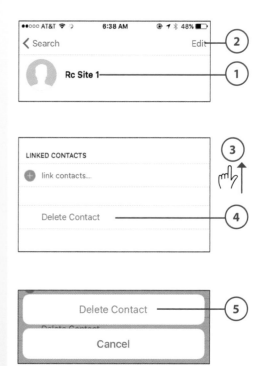

>>>*Go Further*

LINKING CONTACTS

When you enter Edit mode in a contact, the Linked Contacts section appears at the bottom of the screen. You can use this to combine contacts. For example, if you end up with two contacts for the same person, you can link them to combine their information into one contact. Or, you might want to link multiple people to a company. When you link contacts, information from all the linked contacts appears on one contact, which is the contact from which you start the link process.

To link a contact, edit it and tap link contacts. Find and tap the contact you want to link to the one you are editing. That contact's information displays. Tap Link.

The information from the second contact is linked to the first. You can repeat this as many times as you want. (Note that you have to have the group within which a contact is stored displayed to be able to link it.) When you are finished linking contacts, tap Done. The contact to which the others are linked is known as the *unified contact* (or card). It is labeled with the contact from which you started the linking process.

You can change how the information in the unified contact is displayed by viewing the unified contact, and then tapping one of the linked contacts. Tap the command you want to use, such as Use This Photo For Unified Card, which uses the image for the main contact in the unified contact.

To unlink contacts, edit the unified contact, tap the Unlock button next to a linked contact, and tap Unlink. The contact information is separated as it was before you linked them.

Tap to configure
Phone and
FaceTime
settings

Tap to hear *and* see
the person you want
to talk to

Tap to make calls,
listen to voicemail,
and more

In this chapter, you explore all the cell phone and FaceTime functionality that your iPhone has to offer. The topics include the following:

→ Configuring phone settings
→ Making voice calls
→ Managing in-process voice calls
→ Receiving voice calls
→ Managing voice calls
→ Using visual voicemail
→ Communicating with FaceTime

Communicating with the Phone and FaceTime Apps

Although it's also a lot of other great things, such as a music player, web browser, email tool, and such, there's a reason the word *phone* is in *iPhone*. It's a feature-rich cell phone that includes some amazing features, two of which are visual voicemail and FaceTime. Other useful features include a speakerphone, conference calling, and easy-to-use onscreen controls. Plus your iPhone's phone functions are integrated with its other features. For example, when using the Maps application, you might find a location, such as a business, that you're interested in contacting. You can call that location just by tapping the number you want to call directly on the Maps screen.

Configuring Phone Settings

Of course, we all know that your ringtone is the most important phone setting, and you'll want to make sure your iPhone's ringtones are just right. Use the iPhone's Sounds settings to configure custom or standard ringtones and other phone-related sounds, including the new voicemail sound. These are explained in Chapter 5, "Customizing How Your iPhone Looks and Sounds."

You can also have different ringtones for specific people so you can know who is calling just by the ringtone (configuring contacts is explained in Chapter 7, "Managing Contacts").

And you'll want to configure notifications for the Phone app. These include alerts, the app's badge, and sounds. Configuring notifications is also explained in Chapter 5.

It is likely that you can use the Phone app with its default settings just fine. However, you might want to take advantage of some of its features by config- uring the settings described in the following table. To access these settings, open the Settings app and tap Phone.

Provider Differences

The settings for the Phone app depend on the cell phone provider you use. The table lists most, but certainly not all, of the options you may have available. Depending on the provider you use, you may see more, fewer, or different settings than shown in the table. It's a good idea to open your Phone settings to see the options available to you.

Phone Settings

Section	Setting	Description
N/A	My Number	Shows your phone number for reference purposes.
CALLS	Wi-Fi Calling	When enabled, you can place and receive calls via a Wi-Fi network. This is particularly useful when you are in a location with poor cellular reception, but you have access to a Wi-Fi network. When you set the Wi-Fi Calling on This iPhone switch to on (green), you're prompted to confirm your information. When you do, the service starts and you see the Update Emergency Address option; this is used to record your address so if you can place emergency calls via Wi-Fi, your location can be determined. Note that even when you see this option, it might not be supported in your area.
CALLS	Calls on Other Devices	When enabled, and your iPhone is on the same network as other iOS devices (such as iPads) or Macs, you can take incoming calls and place calls from those devices. This can be useful when you aren't near your phone or simply want to use a different device to have a phone conversation. It can also be annoying because when a call comes in, all the devices using this feature start "ringing." When the Allow Calls on Other Devices switch is on (green), you can choose the specific devices calls are allowed on by setting their switches to on (green).

Section	Setting	Description
CALLS	Respond with Text	When calls come in, you have the option to respond with text. For example, you might want to say "Can't talk now, will call later." There are three default text responses or you can use this setting to create your own custom text responses.
CALLS	Call Forwarding	Enables you to forward incoming calls to a different phone number.
CALLS	Call Waiting	Enables or disables the call waiting feature.
CALLS	Show My Caller ID	Shows or hides your caller id information when you place a call.
CALLS	Blocked	Enables you to block incoming calls and text messages. Step-by-step instructions to block calls are in Chapter 17, "Maintaining and Protecting Your iPhone and Solving Problems."
CALLS	TTY	TTY devices enable hearing-impaired people to use a telephone. To use TTY with your iPhone, you need an adapter to connect your iPhone to a TTY device. You also need to turn on TTY support by turning the TTY switch to on (green).
N/A	Change Voicemail Password	Use this option to change your voicemail password.
N/A	Dial Assist	Enable the Dial Assist feature, if you want the correct country code to be added to numbers in your country when dialing those numbers from outside your country or if you want the correct area codes to be added when you dial a local number. For example, if you live in the United States and don't want the correct prefixes added to U.S. phone numbers when you dial them from outside the United States, turn Dial Assist off (white). You then have to add any prefixes manually when dialing a U.S. number from outside the United States.
N/A	SIM PIN	Your iPhone uses a Subscriber Identity Module (SIM) card to store certain data about your phone; the SIM PIN setting enables you to associate a personal ID number (PIN) with the SIM card in an iPhone. To use your account with a different phone, you can remove the SIM card from your iPhone and install it in other phones that support these cards. If you set a PIN, that PIN is required to use the card in a different phone.

Section	Setting	Description
N/A	*Provider Services,* where *Provider* is the name of your provider	This area provides information about your account, such as the numbers you can dial for checking balances, paying bills, and other account management. You can also access your account by tapping the link at the bottom of the screen.

Making Voice Calls

There are a number of ways to make calls with your iPhone; after a call is in progress, you can manage it in the same way no matter how you started it.

Signal strength (more dots equals stronger signal)

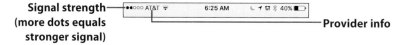

Provider info

You can tell you are able to make a call or receive calls using your cellular network when you see your provider's information at the top of the screen along with strength of the signal your phone is receiving. As long as you see at least one dark dot, you should be able to place and receive calls via the cellular network. More dots are better because they mean you have a stronger signal, meaning the call quality will be better.

Wi-Fi calling is available

If the Wi-Fi calling feature is enabled and your phone is connected to a Wi-Fi network, you see the Wi-Fi calling icon for your provider at the top of the screen.

With a reasonably strong cellular signal or connection to a Wi-Fi network with Wi-Fi calling enabled, you are ready to make calls.

Which Network?

When you leave the coverage area for your provider and move into an area that is covered by another provider that supports roaming, your iPhone automatically connects to the other provider's network. When you are roaming, you see a different provider near the signal strength indicator at the top of the screen. For example, if AT&T is your provider and you travel to Toronto, Canada, the provider might become Rogers instead of AT&T, which indicates you are roaming. (In some cases, your provider might send you a text message explaining the change in networks, including information about roaming charges.) Although the connection is automatic, you need to be very aware of roaming charges, which can be significant depending on where you use your iPhone and what your default network is. Before you travel outside of your default network's coverage, check with your provider to determine the roaming rates that apply to where you are going. Also, see if there is a discounted roaming plan for that location. If you don't do this before you leave, you might get a nasty surprise when the bill arrives showing substantial roaming charges.

Dialing with the Keypad

The most obvious way to make a call is to dial the number.

1. On the Home screen, tap Phone. The Phone apps opens.

2. If you don't see the keypad, tap Keypad.

3. Tap numbers on the keypad to dial the number you want to call. If you dial a number associated with one or more contacts, you see the contact's name and the type of number you've dialed just under the number. (If you make a mistake in the number you are dialing, tap the Delete button located to the right of the number you are dialing at the top of the screen to delete the most recent digit you entered.)

4. Tap the receiver button. The app dials the number, and the Call screen appears.

5. Use the Call screen to manage the call; see "Managing In-Process Voice Calls" later in this chapter for the details.

Number you are calling

Delete

Contact whose number you are dialing

Dialing with Contacts

As you saw in Chapter 7, the Contacts app is a complete contact manager so you can store various kinds of phone numbers for people and organizations. To make a call using a contact, follow these steps.

1. On the Home screen, tap Phone.

2. Tap Contacts.

3. Browse the list, search it, or use the index to find the contact you want to call. (Refer to Chapter 7 for information about using the Contacts app.)

4. Tap the contact you want to call.

5. Tap the number you want to dial. The app dials the number, and the Call screen appears.

6. Use the Call screen to manage the call; see "Managing In-Process Voice Calls" later in this chapter for the details.

Dialing with Favorites

You can save contacts and phone numbers as favorites to make dialing them even simpler. (You learn how to save favorites in various locations later in this chapter. You learn how to make a contact into a favorite in Chapter 7.)

1. On the Home screen, tap Phone.

2. Tap the Favorites button.

3. Browse the list until you see the favorite you want to call. Along the right side of the screen, you see the type of favorite, such as a phone number (identified by the label in the Contacts app, for example, iPhone or mobile) or FaceTime.

4. Tap the favorite you want to call; to place a voice call, tap a phone number (if you tap a FaceTime contact, a FaceTime call is placed instead). The app dials the number, and the Call screen appears.

5. Use the Call screen to manage the call; see "Managing In-Process Voice Calls" later in this chapter for the details.

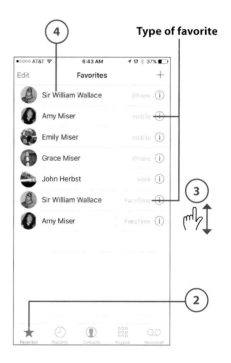

Type of favorite

Nobody's Perfect

If your iPhone can't complete the call for some reason, such as not having a strong enough signal, the Call Failed screen appears. Tap Call Back to try again or tap Done to give up. When you tap Done, you return to the screen from which you came.

Dialing with Recents

As you make, receive, or miss calls, your iPhone keeps tracks of all the numbers for you on the Recents list. You can use the Recents list to make calls.

1. On the Home screen, tap Phone.

2. Tap Recents.

3. Tap All to see all calls.

4. Tap Missed to see only calls you missed.

5. If necessary, browse the list of calls.

6. To call the number associated with a recent call, tap the title of the call, such as a person's name, or the number if no contact is associated with it. The app dials the number, and the Call screen appears. Skip to step 10.

7. To get more information about a recent call, tap its Info button. The Info screen appears.

Info on the Recents Screen

If you have a contact on your iPhone associated with a phone number, you see the person's name and the label for the number (such as mobile). If you don't have a contact for a number, you see the number itself. If a contact or number has more than one call associated with it, you see the number of recent calls in parentheses next to the name or number. If you initiated a call, you see the phone icon next to the contact's name and label.

8. Read the information about the call or calls. For example, if the call is related to someone in your Contacts list, you see detailed information for that contact. If there are multiple recent calls, you see information for each call, such as its status (Canceled Call or Outgoing Call, for example) and time.

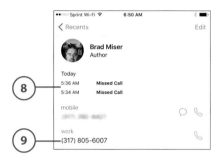

9. Tap a number on the Info screen. The app dials the number, and the Call screen appears.

Going Back

To return to the Recents screen without making a call, tap Recents.

---

10. Use the Call screen to manage the call; see "Managing In-Process Voice Calls" later in this chapter for the details.

Dialing from the Siri Suggestions Screen

Using the SIRI SUGGESTIONS screen, you can quickly call someone you have recently communicated with or someone with whom you communicate regularly. The steps are as follows:

1. On the Home screen, swipe to the right until you see the SIRI SUGGESTIONS screen. At the top of the screen, you see the top four people with whom you have recently communicated.

2. To see the full list, tap Show More. The list expands.

3. Tap the person you want to call. The ways you are able to contact the person appear next to the person's icon at the top of the screen; phone numbers are represented by the receiver icon.

4. Tap the receiver icon.

5. Tap the number you want to call. The app dials the number you tapped.

6. Use the Call screen to manage the call; see the next section for the details.

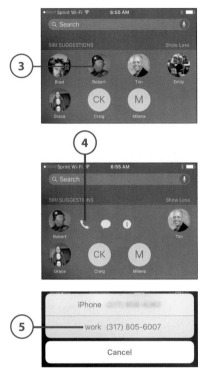

Managing In-Process Voice Calls

When you place a call, there are several ways to manage it. The most obvious is to place your iPhone next to your ear and use your iPhone like any other phone you've ever used. As you place your iPhone next to your ear, the controls on its screen become disabled so you don't accidentally tap onscreen buttons with the side of your face or your ear. When you take your iPhone away from your ear, the Call screen appears again and the Phone app's controls become active again.

When you are on a call, press the Volume buttons on the left side of the iPhone to increase or decrease its volume. Some of the other things you can do while on a call might not be so obvious, as you'll learn in the next few tasks.

Following are some of the buttons on the Call screen that you can use to manage an active call:

Tap to mute your side of the call

Tap to change the call into a FaceTime call

Tap to put the call on speaker

Tap to end the call

- To mute your side of the call, tap mute. You can hear the person on the other side of the call, but he can't hear anything on your side.

- Tap speaker to use the iPhone's speakers to hear the call. You can speak with the phone held away from your face, too.

- Tap FaceTime to convert the voice call into a FaceTime call (more on FaceTime later in this chapter).

- When you're done with the call, tap the receiver button.

Contact Photos on the Call Screen

If someone in your contacts calls you, or you call her, the photo associated with the contact appears on the screen. Depending on how the image was captured, it either appears as a small icon at the top of the screen next to the contact's name or fills the entire screen as the background wallpaper.

Entering Numbers During a Call

You often need to enter numbers during a call, such as to log in to a voicemail system, access an account, or enter a meeting code for an online meeting.

1. Place a call using any of the methods you've learned so far.

2. Tap Keypad.

3. Tap the numbers you want to enter.

4. When you're done, tap Hide. You return to the Call screen.

Making Conference Calls

Your iPhone makes it easy to talk to multiple people at the same time. You can have two separate calls going on at any point in time. You can even create conference calls by merging them together. Not all cell providers support two on-going calls or conference calling, though. If yours doesn't, you won't be able to perform the steps in this section.

1. Place a call using any of the methods you've learned so far.

2. Tap add call.

3. Tap the button you want to use to place the next call. Tap Favorites to call a favorite, tap Recents to use the Recents list, tap Contacts to place the call via contacts, or tap Keypad to dial the number. These work just as they do when you start a new call.

4. Place the call using the option you selected in step 3. Doing so places the first call on hold and moves you back to the Call screen while the Phone app makes the second call. The first call's information appears at the top of the screen, including the word hold so you know the first call is on hold. The app displays the second call just below that, and it is currently the active call.

Similar but Different

If you tap contacts instead of add call, you move directly into the Contacts screen. This might save you one screen tap if the person you want to add to the call is in your Contacts app.

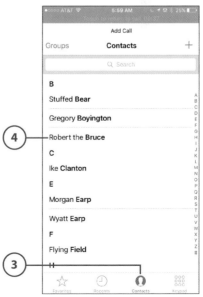

5. Talk to the second person you called; the first remains on hold.

6. To switch to the first call, tap it on the list or tap swap. This places the second call on hold and moves it to the top of the call list, while the first call becomes active again.

7. To join the calls so all parties can hear you and each other, tap merge calls. The iPhone combines the two calls, and you see a single entry at the top of the screen to reflect this.

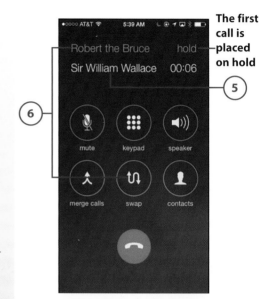

The first call is placed on hold

Merging Calls

As you merge calls, your iPhone attempts to display the names of the callers at the top of the Call screen. As the text increases, your iPhone scrolls it so you can read it. Eventually, the iPhone replaces the names with the word Conference.

Number of Callers

Your provider and the specific technology of the network you use can limit the number of callers you place in a conference call. When you reach the limit, the add call button is disabled.

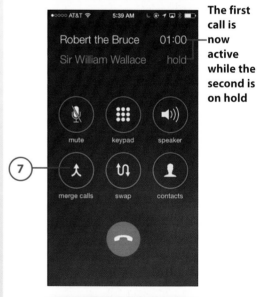

The first call is now active while the second is on hold

8. To add another call, repeat steps 2–7. Each time you merge calls, the second line becomes free so you can add more calls.

9. To manage a conference call, tap the Info button at the top of the screen.

10. To speak with one of the callers privately, tap Private. Doing so places the conference call on hold and returns you to the Call screen showing information about the active call. You can merge the calls again by tapping merge calls.

11. To remove a caller from the call, tap End. The app disconnects that caller from the conference call. You return to the Call screen and see information about the active call.

12. To move back to the Call screen, tap Back. You move to the Call screen and can continue working with the call, such as adding more people to it.

13. To end the call for all callers, tap the receiver button.

It's Not All Good

When you have multiple calls combined into one, depending on your provider, the minutes for each call can continue to count individually. So if you've joined three people into one call, each minute of the call may count as three minutes against your calling plan. Before you use this feature, check with your provider to determine what policies govern conference calling for your account.

Using Another App During a Voice Call

If your provider's technology supports it, you can use your iPhone for other tasks while you are on a call. When you are on a call, press the Touch ID/Home button once to move to the Home screen and then tap a different app (placing the call in speaker mode before you switch to a different app or using the headphones are best for this). Or, you can press the Touch ID/Home button twice and use the App Switcher to move into a different app. The call remains active and you see the active call information in a green bar at the top of the screen. You can perform other tasks, such as looking up information, sending emails, and visiting websites. You can continue to talk to the other person just like when the Call screen is showing. To return to the call, tap the green bar.

Tap to return to the call ———

——— A call is active, and you can use other apps while still talking

Receiving Voice Calls

Receiving calls on your iPhone enables you to access the same great tools you can use when you make calls, plus a few more for good measure.

Answering Calls

When your iPhone rings, it's time to answer the call—or not. If you configured the ringer to ring, you hear your default ringtone or the one associated with the caller's contact information when a call comes in. If vibrate is turned on, your iPhone vibrates whether the ringer is on or not. And if those two ways aren't enough, a message appears on iPhone's screen to show you information about the incoming call. If the number is in your Contacts app, you see the contact with which the number is associated, the label for the number, and the contact's image if there is one. If the number isn't in your contacts, you see the number only.

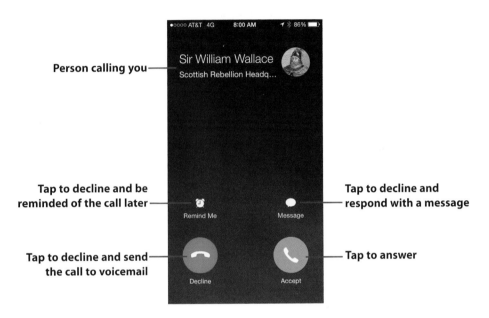

Person calling you

Tap to decline and be reminded of the call later

Tap to decline and respond with a message

Tap to decline and send the call to voicemail

Tap to answer

Wallpaper

If the photo associated with a contact was taken with your iPhone or came from a high-resolution figure, you see the contact's image at full screen when the call comes in, instead of the small icon at the top of the screen.

Calls on Other Devices

By default, when you receive a call on your iPhone, it also comes to any iOS 8 or later devices or Macs running Yosemite or later that are on the same Wi-Fi network, and you can take the call on those devices. To disable this, set the Calls on Other Devices setting to off as described earlier in this chapter.

If your iPhone is locked when a call comes in, swipe the slider to the right to answer it or use the Remind Me and Message icons, which work just like they do when a call comes in when the iPhone isn't locked.

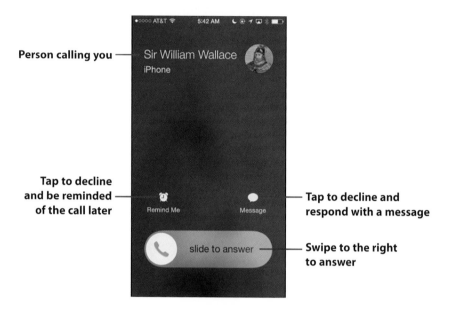

Person calling you ─ Sir William Wallace / iPhone

Tap to decline and be reminded of the call later ─ Remind Me

Tap to decline and respond with a message ─ Message

Swipe to the right to answer ─ slide to answer

When you receive a call, you have the following options:

- **Answer**—Tap Accept (if the iPhone is unlocked) or swipe the slider to the right (if the iPhone is locked) to take the call (you don't have to unlock the phone to answer a call). You move to the Call screen and can work with the call just like calls you place. For example, you can add a call, merge calls, place the call on hold, or end the call.

- **Decline**—If you tap Decline (when the iPhone is unlocked), the Phone app immediately routes the call to voicemail. You can also decline a call by quickly pressing the Sleep/Wake button twice.

- **Silence the ringer**—To silence the ringer without sending the call directly to voicemail, press the Sleep/Wake button once or press either volume button. The call continues to come in, and you can answer it even though you shut off the ringer.

- **Respond with a message**—Tap Message to send the call to voicemail and send a message back in response. You can tap one of the default messages, or you can tap Custom to create a unique message (earlier in the chapter, you learned where you can configure these messages). Of course, the device the caller is using to make the call must be capable of receiving messages for this to be useful.

- **Decline the call but be reminded later**—Tap Remind Me and the call is sent to voicemail. Tap In 1 hour, When I get home, When I get to work, or When I leave to set the timeframe in which you want to be reminded. A reminder is created in the Reminders app to call back the person who called you, and it is set to alert you at the time you select.

Silencio!

To mute your iPhone's ringer, slide the Mute switch located above the Volume switch toward the back so the orange line appears. The Mute icon (a bell with a slash through it) appears on the screen to let you know you turned off the ringer. To turn it back on again, slide the switch forward. The bell icon appears on the screen to show you the ringer is active again. To set the ringer's volume, use the Volume controls (assuming that setting is enabled) when you aren't on a call and aren't listening to an app, such as the Music app.

Answering Calls During a Call

As you saw earlier, your iPhone can manage multiple calls at the same time. If you are on a call and another call comes in, you have a number of ways to respond.

- **Decline incoming call**—Tap Send to Voicemail to send the incoming call directly to voicemail.

- **Place the first call on hold and answer the incoming call**—Tap Hold & Accept to place the current call on hold and answer the incoming one. After you do this, you can manage the two calls just as when you call two numbers from your iPhone. For example, you can place the second call on hold and move back to the first one, merge the calls, and add more calls.

- **End the first call and answer the incoming call**—Tap End & Accept to terminate the active call and answer the incoming call.

- **Respond with message or get reminded later**—These options work just as they do when you are dealing with any incoming phone call.

Auto-Mute

If you are listening to music or video when a call comes in, the app providing the audio, such as the Music app, automatically pauses. When the call ends, that app picks up right where it left off.

Managing Voice Calls

You've already learned most of what you need to know to use your iPhone's cell phone functions. In the following sections, you learn the rest.

Clearing Recent Calls

Previously in this chapter, you learned about the Recents tool that tracks call activity on your iPhone. As you read, this list shows both completed and missed calls; you can view all calls by tapping the All tab or only missed calls by tapping Missed. On either tab, missed calls are always in red, and you see the number of missed calls in the badge on the Recents tab since you last looked at the list. You also see how you can get more detail about a call, whether it was missed or made.

Over time, you'll build a large Recents list, which you can easily clear.

1. Tap Phone.

2. Tap Recents.

3. Tap Edit.

4. To clear the entire list, tap Clear; to delete a specific recent call, skip to step 6.

5. Tap Clear All Recents. The Recents list is reset.

Delete Faster

On the Recents screen, you can delete an individual recent item by swiping to the left on it (starting to the left of the i button) and tapping Delete.

6. Tap a recent item's unlock button.

7. Tap Delete. The recent item is deleted.

8. When you are done managing your recent calls, tap Done.

Adding Calling Information to Favorites

Earlier you learned how simple it is to place calls to someone on your Favorites list. There are a number of ways to add people to this list, including adding someone on your Recents list.

1. Move to the Recents list.

2. Tap the Info button for the person you want to add to your favorites list. The Info screen appears. If the number is associated with a contact, you see that contact's information.

3. Swipe up to move to the bottom of the screen.

4. Tap Add to Favorites. If the person has multiple numbers associated with his contact information, you see each available number. Numbers that are already set as favorites are marked with a blue star. If the contact has email addresses, you can set them as favorites for FaceTime conversations (video or audio only). In other words, you see all the options you can use to communicate with the contact based on his information.

5. Tap the number or email address you want to add as a favorite.

6. Repeat steps 4 and 5 if you want to add the contact's other numbers to the favorites list. Any numbers or email addresses that are set as favorites are highlighted in blue and marked with a blue star. If all the numbers and email addresses are assigned as favorites, the Add to Favorites button doesn't appear on the contact's screen.

Make Contact First

To make someone a favorite, he needs to be a contact in the Contacts app. Refer to Chapter 7 to learn how to make someone who has called you into a contact.

Using the iPhone's Headset for Calls

Your iPhone includes an EarPods headset with a microphone on one of its cords. The mic includes a button in the center of the switch on the right side of the EarPod's cable that you can use to do the following:

- **Answer**—Press the mic button once to answer a call.

- **End a call**—Press the mic button while you are on a call to end it.

- **Decline a call**—Press and hold the mic button for about two seconds. Two beeps sound when you release the button to let you know that your iPhone sent the call to voicemail.

- **Put a current call on hold and switch to an incoming call**—Press the mic button once and then press again.

- **End a current call on hold and switch to an incoming call**—Press the mic button once and hold for about two seconds. Release the button and you hear two beeps to let you know you ended the first call. The incoming call is ready for you.

- **Activate Siri**—Press and hold the mic button until you hear the Siri chime. This is useful when you want to make a call to someone without looking at or touching your phone.

Oh, That Ringing in My Ears

When you have EarPods plugged into your iPhone and you receive a call, the ringtone plays on both the iPhone's speaker (unless the ringer is muted, of course) and through the EarPods.

Using Visual Voicemail

Visual voicemail just might be the best of your iPhone's many great features. No more wading through long, uninteresting voicemails to get to one in which you are interested. You simply jump to the message you want to hear. And because voicemails are stored on your iPhone, you don't need to log in to hear them. If that isn't enough for you, you can also jump to any point within a voicemail to hear just that part, such as to repeat a phone number that you want to write down.

Recording a New Greeting

The first time you access voicemail, you are prompted to record a voicemail greeting. Follow the onscreen instructions to do so.

You can also record a new greeting at any time.

1. Move to the Phone screen and tap Voicemail.

2. Tap Greeting.

3. To use a default greeting that provides only the iPhone's phone number, tap Default and skip to step 10.

4. To record a custom greeting, tap Custom. If you have previously used a custom greeting, it is loaded into the editor. You can replace it by continuing with these steps.

5. Tap Record. Recording begins.

6. Speak your greeting. As you record your message, the red area of the timeline indicates (relatively) how long your message is.

7. When you're done recording, tap Stop.

For the First Time

Some providers require that you dial into your voicemail number the first time you use it. If you tap Voicemail and the phone starts to dial instead of you seeing Visual Voicemail as shown in these figures, this is your situation. You call the provider's voicemail system, and you're prompted to set up your voicemail. When you've completed that process, you can use these steps to record your greeting.

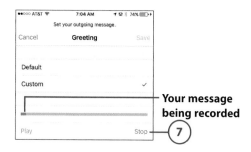

Your message being recorded

8. Tap Play to hear your greeting.

9. If you aren't satisfied, drag the Playhead to the beginning and repeat steps 5–8 to record a new message.

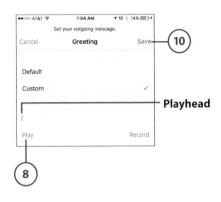

Adding to a Custom Message

To add onto an existing greeting, drag the playhead to where you want to start recording and tap Record. Tap Stop when you're done.

10. When you are happy with your greeting, tap Save. The Phone app saves the greeting as the active greeting and returns you to the Voicemail screen.

No Visual Voicemail?

If your voicemail password isn't stored on your iPhone when you tap Voicemail, your phone dials into your voicemail instead of moving to the Voicemail screen. If that happens, something has gone wrong with your password and you need to reset it. Follow your provider's instructions to reset the password. When you have the new password, open the Phone Settings screen, tap Change Voicemail Password, enter the reset password, create a new password, and re-enter your new password. (You need to tap Done after each time you enter a password.)

Change Greeting

To switch between the default and the current custom greeting, move to the Greeting screen, tap the greeting you want to use (which is marked with a check mark), and tap Save. When you choose Custom, you use the custom greeting you most recently saved.

Listening to and Managing Voicemails

Unless you turned off the voicemail sound, you hear the sound you selected each time a caller leaves a voicemail for you. The number in the badge on the Phone icon and on the Voicemail button on the Phone screen increases by 1 (unless you've disabled the badge). (Note that the badge number on the Phone icon includes both voicemails left for you and missed calls, while the badge number on the Voicemail button indicates only the number of voicemails left for you.) (A new voicemail is one to which you haven't listened, not anything to do with when it was left for you.)

If you receive a voicemail while your iPhone is locked, you see a message on the screen alerting you that your iPhone received a voicemail (unless you have disabled these notifications from appearing on the Lock screen). (It also indicates a missed call, which is always the case when a call ends up in voicemail.) Swipe to the right on the notification to jump to the Voicemail screen so that you can work with your messages.

And in yet another scenario, if you are using your iPhone when a message is left, you see a notification (either a banner or an alert unless you have turned off notifications for the Phone app) that enables you to ignore the new message or to listen to it.

Missing Password

If something happens to the password stored on your iPhone for your voicemail, such as if you restore the iPhone, you are prompted to enter your password before you can access your voicemail. Do so at the prompt and tap OK. The iPhone signs you in to voicemail, and you won't have to enter your password again (unless something happens to it again of course).

Contacts or Numbers?

Like phone calls, if a contact is associated with a number from which you've received a voicemail, you see the contact's name associated with the voicemail message. If no contact exists for the number, you see the number only.

Finding and Listening to Voicemails

Working with voicemails is simple and quick.

1. Move into the Phone app and tap Voicemail (if you tapped a new voicemail banner or the Listen button on an alert, you jump directly to Voicemail screen).

2. Swipe up and down the screen to browse the list of voicemails. Voicemails you haven't listened to are marked with a blue circle.

3. To listen to a voicemail, tap it. You see the timeline bar and controls and the message plays.

4. To pause a message, tap its Pause button.

5. To hear the message on your iPhone's speaker, tap Speaker.

6. To move to a specific point in a message, drag the Playhead to the point at which you want to listen.

Voicemail you haven't listened to

Moving Ahead or Behind

You can also drag the Playhead while a message is playing to rewind or fast-forward it. This is also helpful when you want to listen to specific information without hearing the whole message again.

7. Tap the Play button.

8. To call back the person who left the message, tap Call Back.

9. To delete the message, tap Delete.

10. To share the message, tap the Share button, and then tap how you want to share it, such as Message or Mail. For example, when you tap Mail, you send the voicemail to someone else using the Mail app, so he can listen to it.

Time elapsed in the message   Time remaining in the message

11. To get more information about a message, tap its Info button. The Info screen appears. If the person who left the message is on your contacts list, you see her contact information. The number associated with the message is highlighted in blue.

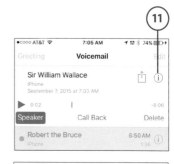

12. Swipe up or down the screen to review the caller's information.

13. Tap Voicemail.

14. To listen to a message you have listened to before (one that doesn't have a blue dot), tap the message and then tap the Play button. It begins to play.

Deleting Messages

To delete a voicemail message that isn't the active message, tap it so it becomes the active message and then tap Delete. Or swipe to the left on the message you want to delete and tap Delete.

Listening to and Managing Deleted Voicemails

When you delete messages, they are moved to the Deleted Message folder. You can work with deleted messages as follows:

1. Move to the Voicemail screen.

2. If necessary, swipe up the screen until you see the Deleted Messages option.

3. Tap Deleted Messages.

Message you've listened to

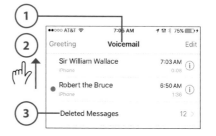

What's Missed?

In case you're wondering, your iPhone considers any call you didn't answer as a missed call. So if someone calls and leaves a message, that call is included in the counts of both missed calls and new voicemails. If the caller leaves a message, you see an alert informing you that you have a new voicemail and showing who it is from (if available). If you don't answer and the caller doesn't leave a message, it's counted only as a missed call and you see an alert showing a missed call along with the caller's identification (if available).

4. Swipe up or down the screen to browse all the deleted messages.

5. Tap a message to listen to it.

6. Tap the Play button. You can use the other playback tools just like you can with undeleted messages.

7. Tap Undelete to restore the deleted message. The iPhone restores the message to the Voicemail screen.

8. To remove all deleted messages permanently, tap Clear All. (If this is disabled, close the open message by tapping it.)

9. Tap Clear All at the prompt. The deleted messages are erased and you return to the Deleted screen.

10. To return to the Voicemail screen, tap Voicemail.

Lost/Forgot Your Password?

If you have to restore your iPhone or it loses your voicemail password for some other reason and you can't remember it, you need to have the password reset to access your voicemail on the iPhone. For most cell phone providers, this involves calling the customer support number and accessing an automated system that sends a new password to you via a text message. For AT&T, which is one of the iPhone providers in the United States, call 611 on your iPhone and follow the prompts to reset your password (which you receive via a text). No matter which provider you use, it's a good idea to know how to reset your voicemail password because it is likely you will need to do so at some point.

Communicating with FaceTime

FaceTime enables you to see, as well as hear, people with whom you want to communicate. This feature exemplifies what's great about the iPhone; it takes complex technology and makes it simple. FaceTime works great, but there are two conditions that have to be true for you and the people you want some FaceTime with. To be able to see each other, both sides have to use a device that has the required cameras (this includes iPhone 4s and newer, iPod touches third generation and newer, iPad 2s and newer, and Macs running Snow Leopard and newer), and have FaceTime enabled (via the settings on an iOS device as you saw earlier or via the FaceTime application on a Mac). And each device has to be able to communicate over a network; an iPhone or cellular iPad can use a cellular data network (if that setting is enabled) or a Wi-Fi network while Macs have to be connected to the Internet through a Wi-Fi or other type of network. When these conditions are true, making and receiving FaceTime calls are simple tasks.

In addition to making video FaceTime calls, you can also make audio-only FaceTime calls. These work similarly to making a voice call except the minutes don't count against your voice plan when you use a Wi-Fi network (if you are making the call over the cellular network, the data does count against your data plan so be careful about this).

Assuming you are in a place where you don't have to pay for the data you use, such as when you use a Wi-Fi network, you don't have to pay for a FaceTime call (video or audio-only) either.

Configuring FaceTime Settings

FaceTime is a great way to use your iPhone to hear and see someone else. There are a few FaceTime settings you need to configure for FaceTime to work. You can connect with other FaceTime users via your phone number, an email address, or your Apple ID.

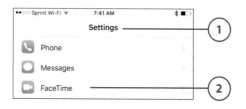

1. Move to the Settings screen.

2. Tap FaceTime.

3. If the FaceTime switch is off (white), tap the FaceTime switch to turn it on (green). If the FaceTime switch is on and you see an Apple ID, you are already signed into an account; in this case, you see the current FaceTime settings and can follow along starting with step 7 to change these settings. You can sign out of the current account by tapping it, and then tapping Sign Out; proceed to step 4 to sign in with a different account.

4. To use your Apple ID for FaceTime calls, tap Use your Apple ID for FaceTime. If you don't sign in to an Apple ID, you can still use FaceTime but it is always via your cellular connection, which isn't ideal because then FaceTime counts under your voice minutes on your calling plan or as data on your data plan.

5. Enter your Apple ID and password. (An Apple ID might be entered already; if so, you can use it or replace it with a different one.)

6. Tap Sign In.

7. Configure the email addresses you want people to use to contact you for FaceTime sessions by tapping them to enable each address (enabled addresses are marked with a check mark) or to disable addresses (these don't have a check mark). (If you don't have any email addresses configured on your iPhone, you are prompted to enter email addresses.)

8. Tap the phone number or email address by which you will be identified to the other caller during a FaceTime call.

Managing Addresses

You can add more email addresses at any time by tapping Add Another Email and following the onscreen prompts to add and confirm the new addresses. To remove an address from FaceTime, tap its Info button (i) and then tap Remove This Email.

Blocking FaceTime

If you tap Blocked at the bottom of the FaceTime Settings screen, you can block people from making calls, sending messages, or making FaceTime requests to your iPhone. Tap Add New and then tap the contact you want to block.

Making FaceTime Calls

FaceTime is a great way to communicate with someone because you can hear and see him (or just hear him if you choose an audio-only FaceTime call). Because iPhones have cameras facing each way, it's also easy to show something to the person you are talking with. You make FaceTime calls starting from the FaceTime, Contacts, or Phone apps and from the SIRI SUGGESTIONS screen. No matter which way you start a FaceTime session, you manage it in the same way.

Careful

If your iPhone is connected to a Wi-Fi network, you can make all the FaceTime calls you want because you have unlimited data. However, if you are using the cellular data network, be aware that FaceTime calls may use data under your data plan. If you have a limited plan, it's a good idea to use FaceTime primarily when you are connected to a Wi-Fi network. (Refer to Chapter 2, "Connecting Your iPhone to the Internet, Bluetooth Devices, and iPhones/iPods/iPads," for information on connecting to Wi-Fi networks.)

To start a FaceTime call from the Contacts app, do the following:

1. Use the Contacts app to open the contact with whom you want to chat (refer to Chapter 7 for information about using the Contacts app).

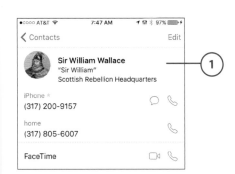

Playing Favorites

If you've set a FaceTime contact as a favorite, you can open the Phone app, tap Favorites, and tap the FaceTime favorite to start the FaceTime session.

2. To place an audio-only FaceTime call, tap the FaceTime audio button. (The rest of these steps show a FaceTime video call, but a FaceTime audio-only is very similar to voice calls described earlier in this chapter.)

3. Tap the contact's FaceTime video button. The iPhone attempts to make a FaceTime connection. You hear the FaceTime "chirping" and see status information on the screen while the call is attempted. When the connection is complete, you hear a different tone and see the other person in the large window and a preview of what he is seeing (whatever your iPhone's front-side camera is pointing at—mostly likely your face) in the small window. If the person you are trying to FaceTime with isn't available for FaceTime for some reason (perhaps he doesn't have a FaceTime-capable device or is not connected to the Internet), you see a message saying that the person you are calling is unavailable for FaceTime and the call terminates.

4. After the call is accepted, manage the call as described in the "Managing FaceTime Calls" task.

Preview window

Failing FaceTime

If a FaceTime request fails, you can't really tell the reason why. It can be a technical issue, such as none of the contact information you have is FaceTime-enabled, the person is not signed into a device, or the person might have declined the request. If you repeatedly have trouble connecting with someone, contact him to make sure he has a FaceTime-capable device and that you are using the correct FaceTime contact information.

No Answer? Leave a Message!

On the FaceTime Unavailable screen, you can tap Leave a Message to send a text or iMessage message to the person with whom you are trying to FaceTime.

Transforming a Call

You can transform a voice call into a FaceTime session by tapping the FaceTime button on the Call screen. When you transform a call into a FaceTime session, the minutes no longer count against the minutes in your calling plan because all communication happens over the Wi-Fi network or your cellular data plan if you enabled that option and aren't connected to a Wi-Fi network. (The voice call you started from automatically terminates when the switch is made.)

Other Ways to FaceTime

To use the FaceTime app to start a call, tap the FaceTime icon on the Home screen. Tap the Video tab to make a video call or the Audio tab to make an audio-only call. Tap the Add (+) button to use your contacts to start the call. You can also enter a name, email address, or phone number in the bar at the top of the screen (if you haven't made or received any FaceTime calls before, you won't see the tabs until you make your first call). Tap a person on the Recents list to place a FaceTime call to that person. Once you've connected, you manage the FaceTime session as described in the rest of this chapter.

You can also place a FaceTime call using Siri by activating Siri and saying "FaceTime *name*" where *name* is the name of the person with whom you want to FaceTime. If there are multiple options for that contact, you must tell Siri which you want to use. After you've made a selection, Siri starts the FaceTime call.

And for yet another option, you can open the SIRI SUGGESTIONS screen, tap the icon for the person you want to FaceTime with, and then tap the FaceTime icon shaped like a video camera to make a FaceTime video call, or tap the FaceTime icon that is shaped like a phone receiver to make an audio-only FaceTime call.

Receiving FaceTime Calls

When someone tries to FaceTime with you, you see the incoming FaceTime request screen message showing who is trying to connect with you and the image you are currently broadcasting. Tap Accept to accept the request and start the FaceTime session. Manage the FaceTime call as described in the "Managing FaceTime Calls" task.

Tap Remind Me to decline the FaceTime request and create a reminder or Message to decline the request and send a message. These options work just as they do for a voice call (you have the same custom message options). You can also press the Sleep/Wake button to decline the request.

However you decline the FaceTime request, the person trying to call you receives a message that you're not available (and a message if you choose that option). She can't tell whether there is a technical issue or if you simply declined to take the call.

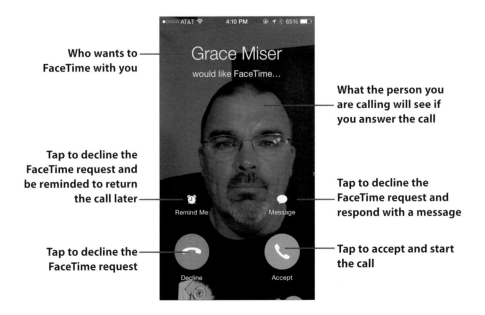

Who wants to FaceTime with you

Grace Miser

What the person you are calling will see if you answer the call

Tap to decline the FaceTime request and be reminded to return the call later

Tap to decline the FaceTime request and respond with a message

Tap to decline the FaceTime request

Tap to accept and start the call

Tracking FaceTime Calls

FaceTime calls are tracked just as voice calls are. Open the FaceTime app and tap Video to see recent video FaceTime calls or Audio to see recent audio FaceTime calls. On the recents list, FaceTime calls are marked with the video camera icon. FaceTime audio-only calls are marked with a telephone receiver icon. FaceTime calls that didn't go through are in red and are treated as missed calls. You can do the same tasks with recent FaceTime calls that you can with recent voice calls.

Managing FaceTime Calls

During a FaceTime call (regardless of who placed the call initially), you can do the following:

Drag to change the location of the preview window

Tap to end the FaceTime session

Tap to mute your side of the call

- Drag the preview window, which shows the image that the other person is seeing, around the screen to change its location. It "snaps" into place in the closest corner when you lift your finger up.

- Move your iPhone and change the angle you are holding it to change the images you are broadcasting to the other person. Use the preview window to see what the other person is seeing.

- Tap Mute to mute your side of the conversation. Your audio is muted and you see the Mute icon in the preview window. Video continues to be broadcast so the other person can still see you.

- To use the camera on the backside of the iPhone, tap the Change Camera button. The other person now sees whatever you have the camera on the back of the iPhone pointed at. If the other person changes her camera, you see what her backside camera is pointing at.

- After a few moments, the controls disappear. Tap the screen to make them reappear.

- Rotate your iPhone to change the orientation to horizontal. This affects what the other person sees (as reflected in your preview), but you continue to see the other person in her iPhone's current orientation.

- Tap the receiver button to end the FaceTime call.

FaceTime Break

Just like when you are in a voice call, you can move into and use other apps (if your provider's technology supports this functionality). You see the green FaceTime in progress bar at the top of the screen. The audio part of the session continues, but the other person sees a still image with a camera icon and the word "Paused." As soon as you move back into the FaceTime session, the video resumes. Likewise, if the other person moves out of the FaceTime app, you'll see the Paused icon.

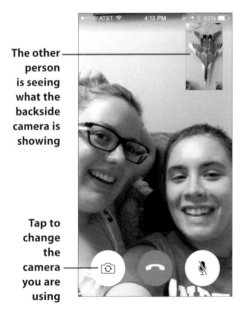

The other person is seeing what the backside camera is showing

Tap to change the camera you are using

Tap the screen to make the controls reappear

Preview shows the landscape orientation

FaceTime works in landscape orientation, too

Tap to configure email settings

Tap to use email

In this chapter, you explore all the email functionality that your iPhone has to offer. Topics include the following:

→ Configuring email accounts
→ Setting Mail app preferences
→ Working with email
→ Managing email

Sending, Receiving, and Managing Email

For most of us, email is an important way we communicate with others, both in our professional and personal lives. Fortunately, your iPhone has great email tools so you can work with email no matter where you are. Of course, you need to be connected to the Internet through a Wi-Fi or cellular data connection to send or receive email—although you can read downloaded messages, reply to messages, and compose messages when you aren't connected.

To use email on your iPhone, you use the Mail app. This app has lots of great features that help you really take advantage of email from all your accounts. Before jumping into the app, you need to have one or more email accounts configured on your iPhone. As you work with your email, there are a number of Mail settings that you might want to configure to tailor how the app works to suit your preferences.

Configuring Email Accounts

Before you can start using an iPhone for email, you have to configure the email accounts you want to access with it. The iPhone supports many kinds of email accounts, including iCloud, Exchange, Gmail, and so on. Setting up the most common types of email accounts is covered in Chapter 3, "Setting Up and Using iCloud and Other Online Accounts," so if you haven't done that already, go back to that chapter and get your accounts set up. Then come back here to start using those accounts for email.

Setting Mail App Preferences

There are a number of settings that impact how the Mail app works. The good news is that you can use the Mail app with its default settings just fine. However, you might want to tweak how it works for you by making changes using the Settings app; you can use the information in the table that follows to understand the options available to you.

To access the settings in the table, first tap the Settings icon on the Home screen, open the Settings area listed in the table, and then move to the location to make changes to the setting (e.g., to change the amount of text shown in email previews, open the Settings app; tap Mail, Contacts, Calendars; and then tap Preview). For each setting, you see a description of what it does along with options (if applicable).

Settings App Explained

To get detailed information on using the Settings app, see "Working with the Settings App" in Chapter 4, "Configuring an iPhone to Suit Your Preferences."

Mail and Related Settings

Settings Area	Location	Setting	Description
Mail, Contacts, Calendars	ACCOUNTS	Email accounts	You can configure the accounts used in the Mail app to determine which account can receive or send email on your iPhone (see Chapter 3 for details).
Mail, Contacts, Calendars	N/A	Fetch New Data	Determines when new email is downloaded to your iPhone (see Chapter 3 for a complete explanation of the options).

Settings Area	Location	Setting	Description
Mail, Contacts, Calendars	MAIL	Preview	Determines the number of lines you want to display for each email when you view the Inbox and in other locations, such as alerts. This preview enables you to get the gist of an email without opening it. More lines give you more of the message, but take up more space on the screen.
Mail, Contacts, Calendars	MAIL	Show To/ Cc Label	Slide the switch to on (green) to always see the To and Cc labels in email headers. (With this disabled, you can still view this information for an email by tapping Details on a message screen.)
Mail, Contacts, Calendars	MAIL	Swipe Options	Change what happens when you swipe to the left or right on email when you are viewing an Inbox. You can set the Swipe Right motion to be None, Mark as Read, Flag, Move Message, or Archive. When you swipe all the way to the right on a message, the action you configure for the Swipe Right is performed. When you do a partial swipe, you see a button that you can tap to perform the action. You can set the Swipe Left motion to be None, Mark as Read, Flag, or Move Message. When you do a partial swipe to the left, you see the More button, which leads to a menu of actions, and the option you configure for the Left Swipe setting. When you do a full swipe to the left, a message is deleted. Note that you can't have the same option configured for both directions.
Mail, Contacts, Calendars	MAIL	Flag Style	Determines how messages you flag are marked; you can choose a colored circle or a flag icon. Flagging messages marks messages that you want to know are important or that need your attention.
Mail, Contacts, Calendars	MAIL	Ask Before Deleting	When this switch is on (green), you're prompted to confirm when you delete or archive messages. When this switch is off (white), deleting or archiving messages happens without the confirmation prompt.
Mail, Contacts, Calendars	MAIL	Load Remote Images	When this switch is on (green), images in HTML email messages are displayed automatically. When this switch is off (white), you have to manually load images in a message. (If you receive a lot of spam, you should turn this off so that you won't see images in which you might not be interested.)

Settings Area	Location	Setting	Description
Mail, Contacts, Calendars	MAIL	Organize By Thread	When this switch is on (green), messages in a conversation are grouped together as a "thread" on one screen. This makes it easier to read all the messages in a thread. When this switch is off (white), messages are listed individually. (You learn more about working with threads in the "Working with Email" task later in this chapter.)
Mail, Contacts, Calendars	MAIL	Always Bcc Myself	When this switch is on (green), you receive a blind copy of each email you send; this means that you receive the message, but you are hidden on the list of recipients. When this switch is off (white), you don't receive a blind copy.
Mail, Contacts, Calendars	MAIL	Mark Addresses	This feature highlights addresses in red that are not from domains that you specify. You enter the domains (everything after the @ in email addresses, such as icloud.com) from which you do not want addresses to be marked (highlighted in red) when you create email. You can add multiple domains to the list by separating them with commas. All addresses from domains not listed will be marked in red. To disable this feature, delete all the domains from the list.
Mail, Contacts, Calendars	MAIL	Increase Quote Level	When this option is enabled (green), the text of an email you are replying to or forwarding (quoted content) is automatically indented. Generally, you should leave this enabled so it is easier for the recipients to tell when you have added text to an email, versus what is from the previous email messages' quoted content.
Mail, Contacts, Calendars	MAIL	Signature	Signatures are text that is automatically added to the bottom of new email messages that you create. For example, you might want your name and email address added to every email you create.
			You can configure the same signature for all your email accounts or have a different signature for each account.
			If you don't want to use a signature, delete any signatures that are currently configured. (Note that the default signature is "Sent from my iPhone.")

Settings Area	Location	Setting	Description
Mail, Contacts, Calendars	MAIL	Default Account	Determines which email account is the default one used when you send an email (this setting isn't shown if you only have one email account). You can override the default email account for an email you are sending by choosing one of your other email addresses in the From field.
Display & Brightness	N/A	Text Size	Changes the size of text in all apps that support Dynamic Type (Mail does). Drag the slider to the right to make text larger or to the left to make it smaller.
Display & Brightness	N/A	Bold Text	Changes text to be bold when the Bold Text switch is set to on (green).

More on Marking Addresses

When you configure at least one address on the Mark Addresses screen, all addresses except those listed on the Mark Addresses screen are in red text on the New Message screen. This is useful to prevent accidental email going to places where you don't want it to go. For example, you might want to leave domains associated with your workplace off this list so that whenever you send email to addresses associated with your workplace, the addresses appear in red to remind you to pay close attention to the messages you are sending.

Email Notifications and Sounds

If you want to be alerted whenever new email is received and when email you create is sent, be sure to configure notifications for the Mail app. These include whether unread messages are shown in the Notification Center, the type of alerts, whether the badge appears on the Mail icon, whether the preview is shown, the alert sound, and whether new messages are shown on the Lock screen. For a detailed explanation of configuring notifications, refer to Chapter 4.

Working with Email

The iPhone's Mail app offers lots of great features and is ideally suited for working with email on your iPhone. The Mail app offers a consolidated Inbox, so you can view email from all your accounts at the same time. Also, the Mail app organizes your email into threads (assuming you didn't disable this feature), which makes following a conversation convenient.

You've got email

When you move to a Home screen, you see the number of new email messages you have in the badge on the Mail app's icon (assuming you haven't disabled this); tap the icon to move to the app. Even if you don't have any new email, the Mail icon still leads you to the Mail app. Other ways Mail notifies you of new messages include by displaying alerts and the new mail sound. (You determine which of these options is used for each email account by configuring its notifications as explained in the "Email Notifications and Sounds" note.)

Tap a command on the Quick Action menu to use it

New! If you are using an iPhone 6s or 6s Plus, you can press on the Mail icon to open the Quick Actions menu and choose an action you want to perform. For example, you can start a new email message by tapping New Message or move directly to your VIP email by tapping VIP.

About Assumptions

The steps and figures in this section assume you have more than one email account configured and are actively receiving email from those accounts on your iPhone. If you have only one email account active, your Mailboxes screen contains that account's folders instead of mailboxes from multiple accounts and the Accounts sections that appear in these figures and steps. Similarly, if you disable the Organize by Thread setting, you won't see messages in threads as these figures show. Instead, you work with each message individually.

The Mail app enables you to receive and read email for all the email accounts configured on your iPhone. The Mailboxes screen is the top-level screen in the app and is organized into two sections.

The Inboxes section shows the Inbox for each account along with folders for email from people designated as VIPs (more on this later), your unread messages, and your draft messages (you've started but haven't sent yet). Next to each Inbox or folder the number of new emails in that Inbox or folder is shown. (A new message is simply one you haven't viewed yet.) At the top of the section is All Inboxes, which shows the total number of new messages to all accounts; when you tap this, the integrated Inbox containing email from all your accounts is displayed.

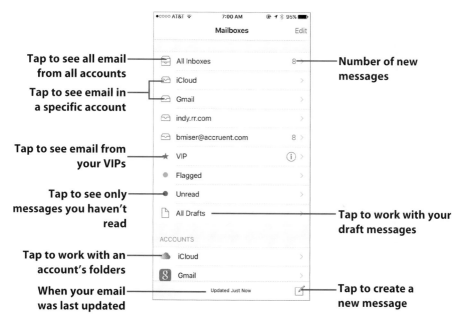

The Accounts section shows each email account with another counter for new messages. The difference between these sections is that the Inbox options take you to just the Inbox for one or all of your accounts, whereas the Account options take you to all the folders under each account.

Receiving and Reading Email

To read email you have received, perform the following steps:

1. On the Home screen, tap Mail. Mail opens. If the Mailboxes screen isn't showing, tap the back button in the upper-left corner of the screen until you reach the Mailboxes screen.

2. To read messages, tap the Inbox that contains messages you want to read, or tap All Inboxes to see the messages from all your email accounts. Various icons indicate the status of each message, if it is part of a thread, if it has attachments, if it is from a VIP, and so on.

3. Swipe up or down the screen to browse the messages. You can read the preview of each message to get an idea of its contents.

4. If a message you are interested in is in a thread, tap it. You can tell a message is part of a thread by double right-facing arrows along the right side of the screen—single messages have only one arrow. (If it isn't part of a thread, skip to step 6.) A thread is a group of emails that are related to the same subject. For example, if someone sends an email to you saying how wonderful the *My iPhone* book is, and you reply with a message saying how much you agree, those two messages would be grouped into one thread. Other messages with the same subject are also placed in the thread.

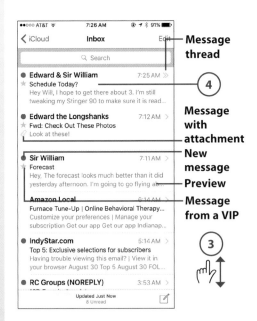

Message thread

Message with attachment

New message

Preview

Message from a VIP

5. Swipe up or down the screen to browse the messages in the thread.

6. To read a message (whether in a thread or not), tap it. As soon as you open a message, it's marked as read and the new mail counter reduces by one. You see the message screen with the address information at the top, including whom the message is from and whom it was sent to. Under that the message's subject along with time and date it was sent are displayed. Below that is the body of the message. If the message has an attachment or is a reply to another message, the attachment or quoted text appears toward the bottom of the screen.

7. Swipe up and down the screen to read the entire message.

Standard Motions Apply

You can use the standard finger motions on email messages, such as unpinching or tapping to zoom, swiping directions to scroll, and so on. You can also rotate the phone to change the orientation of messages from vertical to horizontal; this makes it easier to type.

Number of messages in the thread

Message thread

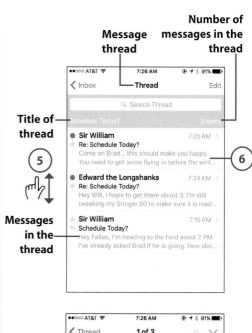

Title of thread

Messages in the thread

Quoted message

8. If the message contains an attachment, swipe up the screen to get to the end of the message. If an attachment hasn't been downloaded yet, it starts to download automatically (unless it is a large file). If the attachment hasn't been downloaded yet, which is indicated by a downward-facing arrow in the attachment icon, tap it to download it into the message. When an attachment finishes downloading, its icon changes to represent the type of file it is. If the icon remains generic, it might be of a type the iPhone can't display and you would need to open it on a computer or other device.

Attachment downloading

9. Tap the attachment icon to view it.

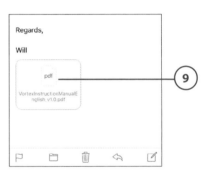

10. Scroll the document by swiping up, down, left, or right on the screen.

11. Unpinch or double-tap to zoom in.

12. Pinch or double-tap to zoom out.

13. To see the available actions for the attachment, tap the Share button.

14. Swipe to the left or right to see all the available options.

15. Tap the action you want to take, such as opening the attachment in a different app, printing it, sharing it via email, and so on. Tap Cancel to return to the attachment if you don't want to do any of these. If you open the attachment in an app, work with the attachment in that app. To return to the email, tap the Back to Mail link in the top-left corner of the screen.

16. Tap Done (depending on the type of attachment you were viewing, you tap the Back button instead).

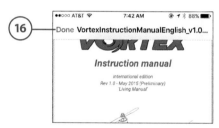

17. To view information for an email address, such as who sent the message, tap it. The Info screen appears; its title tells you how the person relates to the message. For example, if you tapped the email address in the From field, the screen title is Sender. You see the person's email address along with actions you might want to perform, such as placing a call or FaceTime invitation. You can also add him to your Favorites list or designate him as a VIP (if he isn't one already), and you can create a contact for him or add new information to an existing contact.

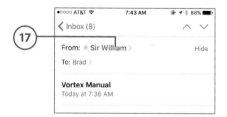

18. Tap Message to return to the message.

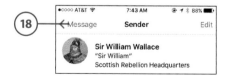

19. To read the next message in the current Inbox, tap the down arrow.

20. To move to a previous message in the current Inbox, tap the up arrow.

21. To move back to see the entire Inbox, tap Inbox.

Two Other Ways to Open New Email

You can view a preview of email messages in notifications you receive and tap the notification to get to the full message. You can also use Siri to get and read new email.

Receiving and Reading Email on an iPhone 6 Plus or 6s Plus

The iPhone 6 Plus' and 6s Plus' larger screen provides some additional functionality that is unique to it. You can access this by holding the iPhone 6 Plus or 6s Plus horizontally when you use the Mail app.

1. Open the Mail app and hold the iPhone so it is oriented horizontally. The mail window splits into two panes. On the left is the Navigation pane, where you can move to and select items you want to view. When you select something in the left pane, it appears in the Content pane on the right, which shows the email message you were most recently reading.

2. In the left pane, navigate to the Mailboxes screen by tapping the back button until it disappears.

3. Swipe up or down the Navigation pane to browse the mailboxes and accounts available to you. Notice that the two panes are independent. When you browse the left pane, the right pane doesn't change.

4. Tap the mailbox or account whose contents you want to view.

5. Tap the message or thread that you want to read. If you tapped a message, its content appears in the right pane and you can skip to step 8.

6. Swipe up and down the messages to browse all of them in the thread.

7. Tap the message you want to read. It appears in the Content pane.

8. Read the message.

9. Use the other tools to work with it; these work just like they do on other models and when you hold the iPhone vertically. For example, tap the up arrow to move to the previous message in the current Inbox.

10. To read the message in full screen, tap the Full Screen View button. The Content pane uses the entire screen.

11. Work with the message.

12. When you're done, tap the back button, which is labeled with the name of the mailbox or folder containing the message you are reading. The screen splits into two panes again.

13. Select and read other messages.

14. When you're done, tap the back button, which is labeled with the name of the mailbox or folder whose contents you are browsing.

Using 3D Touch for Email (iPhone 6s and 6s Plus)

You can use the 3D Touch feature on an iPhone 6s or 6s Plus for email as follows:

1. Browse a list of email messages.

2. Tap and hold on an email in which you are interested. A Peek of that email appears.

3. Review the preview of the email that appears in the Peek.

4. To open the email so you can read all of it, press down slightly harder until it pops open and use the steps in the earlier task to read it (skip the rest of these steps).

5. To see actions you can perform on the email, swipe up on the Peek.

6. Tap the action you want to perform, such as Reply, to reply to the email.

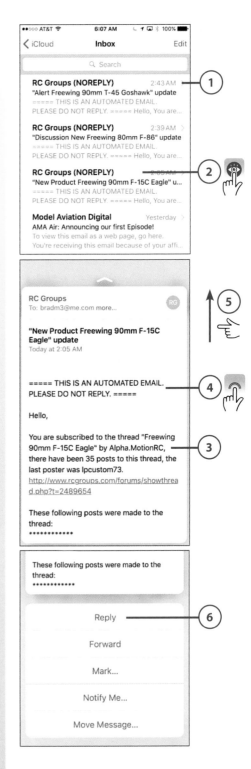

MORE ON RECEIVING AND READING EMAIL

Check out these additional pointers for working with email you receive:

- If more messages are available than are downloaded, tap the Load More Messages link. The additional messages download to the inbox you are viewing.

- You can change the amount of detail you see at the top of the message screen by tapping More to show all of the detail, such as the entire list of recipients, or Hide to collapse that information.

- The Mail app identifies a thread by its subject and sender. As replies are made, the messages continue to be categorized by subject because Re: is appended to it. It even remains in the thread if the initial subject continues to be in the message but other words are added.

- If a message includes a photo, Mail displays the photo in the body of the email message if it can. You can zoom in or out and scroll to view it just as you can for photos in other apps.

- If you tap a PDF attachment in a message and the iBooks app is installed on your iPhone, you're prompted to select Quick Look or Open in iBooks. If you select Open in iBooks, the document opens in the iBooks app where you can read it using the powerful features it offers for reading ebooks and other documents.

- Some emails, especially HTML messages, are large and don't immediately download in their entirety. When you open a message that hasn't been fully downloaded, you see a message stating that this is the case. Tap the link to download the rest of the message.

- If you have other apps with which an attachment is compatible, you can open the attachment in that app. For example, if you have Pages installed on your iPhone and are viewing a Word document attachment, you can tap the Share button and tap Open in Pages to open the document in the Pages app. You can get the same options by tapping and holding down on the attachment's icon in the body of a message until the Action menu appears.

Sending Email

You can send email from any of your accounts. Follow these steps for a basic walk-through of composing and sending a new email message:

1. Tap the Compose button at the bottom of any Mail screen (if you are using an iPhone 6s or 6s Plus, you can press down on the Mail app's icon and choose New Message to create a new email from a Home page). A new email message containing your signature is created.

2. Tap the To field and type in the first recipient's email address. As you type, Mail attempts to find matching addresses in your Contacts list, or in emails you've sent or received, and displays the matches it finds. To select one of those addresses, tap it. Mail enters the rest of the address for you. Or, just keep entering information until the address is complete.

3. To address the email using your Contacts app, tap the Add button.

4. Use the Contacts app to find and select the contact to whom you want to address the message. (Refer to Chapter 7 for the details about working with contacts.) When you tap a contact who has only one email address, that address is pasted into the To field and you return to the New Message window. When you tap a contact with more than one email address, you move to the Info screen, which shows all available addresses; tap the address to which you want to send the message.

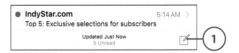

Have Multiple Email Accounts?

If you have more than one email account, it's important to know from which account you are sending a new message. If you tap the Compose button while you are on the Mailboxes screen or the Inboxes screen, the From address is the one for the account you set as your default; otherwise, the From address is the email account associated with the Inbox you are in.

5. Repeat steps 2–4 to add other recipients to the message.

6. Tap the Cc/Bcc, From line. The Cc and Bcc lines expand.

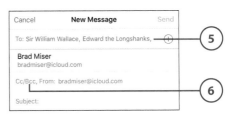

Removing Addresses

To remove an address, tap it so it is highlighted in a darker shade of blue; then tap the Delete button on the iPhone's keyboard.

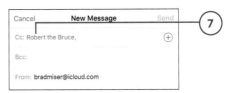

7. Follow the same procedures from steps 2–4 to add recipients to the Cc field.

8. Follow the same procedures from steps 2–4 to add recipients to the Bcc field.

9. If the correct account is shown, skip to step 11; to change the account from which the email is sent, tap the From field. The account wheel appears at the bottom of the screen.

10. Swipe up or down the wheel until the From address you want to use is shown between the lines.

11. Tap in the Subject line. The account selection wheel closes.

12. Type the subject of the message.

13. If you want to be notified when someone replies to the message you are creating, tap the bell; if not, skip to step 16.

14. Tap Notify Me. When anyone replies to the message, you are notified.

15. If you don't see the body of the message, swipe up the screen and it appears.

16. Tap in the body of the message, and type the message above your signature. Mail uses the iOS's text tools, attempts to correct spelling, provides Predictive Text, and makes suggestions to complete words. To accept a proposed change, tap the spacebar when the suggestion appears on the screen; to ignore a correction, tap the x in the suggestion box. If the Predictive Text feature is enabled, you can tap the words shown above the keyboard that you want to enter. You can also use the copy and paste feature to move text around, and you can edit text using the spell checker and other text tools. (Refer to Chapter 1, "Getting Started with Your iPhone," for the details of working with text.)

17. To make the keyboard larger, rotate the iPhone so that it is horizontal.

18. When you finish the message, tap Send. The progress of the send process is shown at the bottom of the screen; when the message has been sent, you hear the send mail sound you configured, which confirms that the message has been sent. If you enabled the reply notification for the message, you are notified when anyone replies to it.

Write Now, Send Later

If you want to save a message you are creating without sending it, tap Cancel. A prompt appears; select Save Draft to save the message; if you don't want the message, tap Delete Draft instead. When you want to work on a draft message again, tap and hold down the New Message button. After a moment, you see your most recent draft messages; tap the draft message you want to work on. You can make changes to the message and then send it or save it as a draft again. (You can also move into the Drafts folder to select and work with draft messages; moving to this folder is covered later in this chapter.)

Using Mail's Suggested Recipients

As you create messages, Mail suggests recipients based on the new message's current recipients. For example, if you regularly send emails to a group of people, when you add two or more people from that group, Mail suggests others you may want to include. As you add others to the message, Mail continues suggesting recipients based on the current recipient list. You can use these suggestions to quickly add more recipients to a new message.

Mail's suggestions for more recipients for the new message

1. Create a new message.

2. Add at least two recipients. Just below the To line, Mail suggests additional recipients for the new message based on other messages you have created.

3. Tap the additional recipients you want to add to the new message. As you select these recipients, Mail keeps making suggestions and new people appear in the gray bars.

4. When you're done adding To recipients, tap in the next field you want to complete and continue creating the new message.

Replying to Email

Email is all about communication, and Mail makes it simple to reply to messages.

1. Open the message you want to reply to.

2. Tap the Share button.

3. Tap Reply to reply to only the sender or, if there was more than one recipient, tap Reply All to reply to everyone who received the original message. The Re: screen appears showing a new message. Mail pastes the contents of the original message at the bottom of the body of the new message below your signature. The original content is in blue and is marked with a vertical line along the left side of the screen.

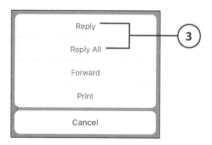

Including a Photo or Video in a Message

To add a photo or video to a message, tap twice in the body. Swipe to the left on the resulting toolbar (if you don't see it immediately) until you see the Insert Photo or Video command, and then tap it. Use the Photos app (see Chapter 15, "Working with Photos and Video You Take with Your iPhone," for information about this app) to move to and select the photo or video you want to attach. Tap Choose. The photo or video you selected is attached to the message.

4. Use the message tools to add or change the To, Cc, or Bcc recipients.

5. Write your response.

6. Tap Send. Mail sends your reply.

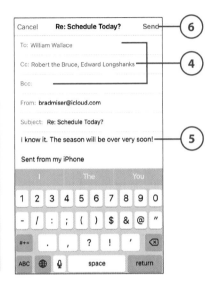

Sending Email from All the Right Places

You can send email from a number of places on your iPhone. For example, you can share a photo with someone by viewing the photo, tapping the Share button, and then tapping Mail. Or you can tap a contact's email address to send an email from your contacts list. For yet another example, you can share a YouTube video. In all cases, the iPhone uses Mail to create a new message that includes the appropriate content, such as a photo or link; you use Mail's tools to complete and send the email.

Print from Your iPhone

If you need to print a message, tap the Share button and tap Print. To learn about printing from your iPhone, refer to Chapter 1.

Forwarding Emails

When you receive an email you think others should see, you can forward it to them.

1. Read the message you want to forward.

2. If you want to include only part of the current content in the message you forward, tap where you want the forwarded content to start. This is useful (and considerate!) when only a part of the message applies to the people to whom you are forwarding it. If you want to forward the entire content, skip to step 4.

3. Use the text selection tools to select the content you want to include in your forwarded message.

4. Tap the Share button.

5. Tap Forward.

6. If the message includes attachments, tap Include at the prompt if you also want to forward the attachments, or tap Don't Include if you don't want them included. The Forward screen appears. Mail pastes the contents of the message that you selected, or the entire content if you didn't select anything, at the bottom of the message below your signature. It you included attachments, they are added to the new message as well.

7. Address the forwarded message using the same tools you use when you create a new message.

8. Type your commentary about the message above your signature.

9. Tap Send. Mail forwards the message.

Large Messages

Some emails, especially HTML messages, are so large that they don't immediately download in their entirety. When you forward a message whose content or attachments haven't fully downloaded, Mail prompts you to download the "missing" content before forwarding. If you choose not to download the content or attachments, Mail forwards only the downloaded part of the message.

Managing Email

Following are some ways you can manage your email. You can check for new messages, see the status of messages, delete messages, and organize messages using the folders associated with your email accounts.

Checking for New Email

To manually retrieve messages, swipe down from the top of any Inbox or the Mailboxes screen. The screen "stretches" down and when you lift your finger, the Mail app checks for and downloads new messages.

Swipe down to update your email

Mail also retrieves messages whenever you move into the app or into any Inbox or all your Inboxes. Of course, it also retrieves messages according to the Fetch New Data option you selected. It downloads new messages immediately when they arrive in your account if Push is enabled or automatically at defined intervals if you've set Fetch to get new email periodically. (Refer to Chapter 3, "Setting Up and Using iCloud and Other Online Accounts," for an explanation of these options and how to set them.)

How many unread messages you have in the current Inbox

When your email was last updated

The bottom of the Mailboxes or Inbox screen always shows when email was most recently downloaded to your iPhone; on the bottom of Inbox screens, you also see the number of new email messages (if there are any unread messages).

Understanding the Status of Email

When you view an Inbox or a message thread, you see icons next to each message to indicate its status (except for messages that you've read but not done anything else with, which aren't marked with any icon).

When the message is replied to you receive a notification

Message you've flagged

Message with attachments

Message to which you've replied

Unread message

Message you've forwarded

Message from a VIP

Managing Email from the Message Screen

Tap to delete a message

To delete a message while reading it, tap the Trash button. If you enabled the warning preference, confirm the deletion and the message is deleted. If you disabled the confirmation prompt, the message is deleted immediately.

Dumpster Diving

As long as an account's trash hasn't been emptied (Chapter 3 has tasks to show how to configure when this happens), you can work with a message you've deleted by moving to the account's screen and opening its Trash folder.

Tap to manage a message

Tap to mark a message as unread (or read)

Tap to flag a message

Tap to mark a message as junk and move it to the Junk folder

Tap to receive a notification when a reply is made or stop notifications if they are active

To take other action on a message you are reading, tap the Flag icon. On the menu that opens, you can do the following:

- Tap Flag to flag the message or Unflag to unflag it.

- Tap Mark as Unread or Mark as Read to change its read status.

- Tap Move to Junk to mark the message as junk and move it to the Junk folder.

- Tap Notify Me to receive a notification when there is a reply to the message or Stop Notifying to remove the notification.

Where Has My Email Gone?

When you send an email to the Archive folder, it isn't deleted. To access messages you've archived, tap the back button in the upper-left corner of the screen until you get to the Mailboxes screen. Tap the account to which email you've archived was sent. Then tap the Archive folder.

Managing Email from an Inbox

Previously in this chapter, you saw the settings options for swipe actions for email. You can use those to configure how right and left swipes affect your email from an Inbox screen, such as flagging a message with a left swipe. (Depending on the choices you set for the swipe preferences, the results you see when you swipe might be different than shown here. However, the swipe right or swipe left actions still reveal commands you can use unless you chose None in the settings, in which case nothing happens when you swipe on a message.)

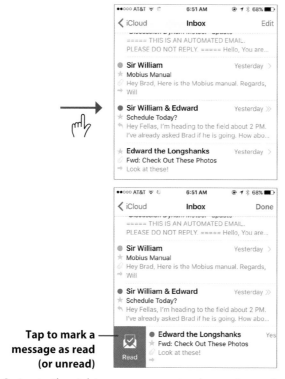

Tap to mark a message as read (or unread)

Swipe to the right on a message to change its read status. If the message has been read, you can reset its status to unread or if it hasn't been read, you can mark it as read.

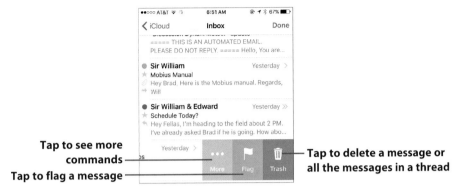

Tap to see more commands

Tap to flag a message

Tap to delete a message or all the messages in a thread

Swipe to the left on a message to see several options. Tap Trash to delete the message or messages if you swiped on a thread (the number of messages that will be deleted is shown in parentheses). Tap Flag to flag the message or Unflag to remove the flag. Tap More to open a menu of additional commands.

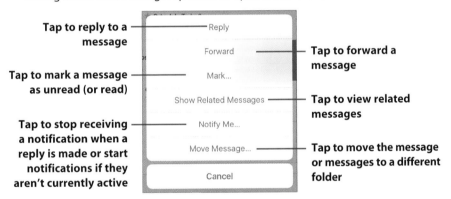

Tap to reply to a message

Tap to mark a message as unread (or read)

Tap to stop receiving a notification when a reply is made or start notifications if they aren't currently active

Tap to forward a message

Tap to view related messages

Tap to move the message or messages to a different folder

When you tap More, you see other commands for actions you can take on the message. These include:

- Tap Reply to reply to a message.
- Tap Forward to forward a message.
- Tap Mark as Unread or Mark as Read to change its read status.
- Tap Show Related Messages to show messages related to the one on which you swiped.
- Tap Notify Me to receive a notification when there is a reply to the message or Stop Notifying to remove the notification.
- Tap Move Messages to move one or more messages to a different folder.

No Stop Swiping to Delete

If you quickly swipe all the way to the left on a message on an Inbox screen, the message is deleted in one fell swipe.

Managing Multiple Emails at the Same Time

You can also manage email by selecting multiple messages on an Inbox screen, which is more efficient because you can take action on multiple messages at the same time.

1. Move to an Inbox screen showing messages you want to manage.

2. Tap Edit. A selection circle appears next to each message, and actions appear at the bottom of the screen.

3. Select the message(s) you want to manage by tapping their selection circles. As you select each message, its selection circle is marked with a check mark. At the top of the screen, you see how many messages you have selected.

   When you use an iPhone 6 Plus or 6s Plus in the horizontal orientation, you see the selection screen on the left and a preview of what you have selected in the right pane. Even though it looks a bit different, it works in the same way.

4. To delete the selected messages, tap Trash. Mail deletes the selected messages and exits Edit mode. (If you enabled the warning prompt, you have to confirm the deletion.)

5. To change the status of the selected messages, tap Mark. (On an iPhone 6 Plus or 6s Plus held horizontally, the menu options appear as buttons across the bottom of the screen instead of as a menu as shown here.)

6. Tap the action you want to take on the selected messages. You return to the Inbox screen and exit Edit mode.

Selected messages

Tap to flag (or unflag) the selected messages

Tap to mark the selected messages as unread (or read)

Tap to mark the selected messages as junk and move them to the Junk folder

Organizing Email from the Message Screen

You can have various folders to organize email, and you can move messages among these folders. For example, you can recover a message from the Trash by moving it from the Trash folder back to the Inbox.

1. Open a message you want to move to a different folder.
2. Tap the Mailboxes button. The Mailboxes screen appears. At the top of this screen is the message you are moving. Under that are the mailboxes available under the current account.

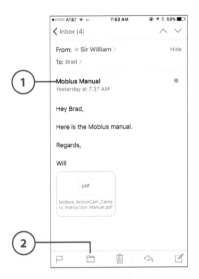

Move to Other Accounts

If you want to move a message to a folder under a different account, tap Accounts in the upper-left corner of the screen. Tap the account to which you want to move the message (not all accounts will be available; if an account is grayed out, you can't move a message to it). Then tap the mailbox into which you want to move the message.

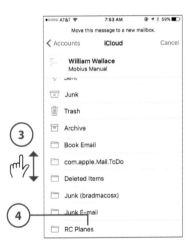

3. Swipe up and down the screen to browse the mailboxes available in the current account.
4. Tap the mailbox to which you want to move the message. The message moves to that mailbox, and you move to the next message in the list you were viewing.

   When you use an iPhone 6 Plus or 6s Plus in the horizontal orientation, you see the list of folders you are navigating in the left pane and a preview of the messages you have selected in the right pane.

Makin' Mailboxes

You can create a new mailbox to organize your email. Move to the Mailboxes screen and tap the account under which you want to create a new mailbox. Tap Edit, and then tap New Mailbox. Type the name of the new mailbox. Tap the Mailbox Location and then choose where you want the new mailbox located (for example, you can place the new mailbox inside an existing one). Tap Save. You can then store messages in the new mailbox.

Organizing Email from the Inbox

Like deleting messages, organizing email from the Inbox can be made more efficient because you can move multiple messages at the same time.

1. Move to an Inbox screen showing messages you want to move to a folder.

2. Tap Edit. A selection circle appears next to each message. Actions appear at the bottom of the screen.

3. Select the messages you want to move by tapping their selection circles. As you select each message, its selection circle is marked with a check mark.

4. Tap Move.

5. Swipe up and down the screen to browse the mailboxes available in the current account.

   On an iPhone 6 Plus or 6s Plus held horizontally, you see the list of folders in the left pane and a preview of the selected messages in the right pane.

6. Tap the mailbox to which you want to move the selected messages. They are moved into that folder, and you return to the previous screen, which is no longer in Edit mode.

Picking at Threads

When you select a thread, you select all the messages in that thread. Whatever action you select is taken on all the thread's messages at the same time.

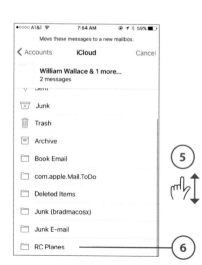

Viewing Messages in a Mailbox

You can open a mailbox within an account to work with the message it contains. For example, you might want to open the Trash mailbox to recover a deleted message.

1. Move to the Mailboxes screen.

2. If necessary, swipe up the screen to see the ACCOUNTS section.

3. Tap the account containing the folders and messages you want to view. You see all of that account's mailboxes and folders. Like with other tasks, when you hold an iPhone 6 Plus or 6s Plus horizontally, you can navigate folders in the left pane and read messages you select in the right pane.

4. Tap the folder or mailbox containing the messages you want to view. You see the messages it contains. In some cases, this can take a few moments for the messages to be downloaded if that folder or mailbox hasn't been accessed recently.

5. Tap a message or thread to view it. (If you want to move messages, such as to recover messages that are in the Trash, see "Organizing Email from the Inbox.")

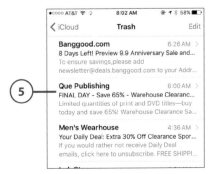

Changing Mailboxes

You can change the mailboxes that appear on the Mailboxes screen. Move to the Mailboxes screen and tap Edit. To cause a mailbox to appear, tap it so that it has a check mark in its circle. To hide a mailbox, tap its check mark so that it just shows an empty circle. For example, you can show the Attachments mailbox to make messages with attachments easier to get to. Drag the Order button for mailboxes up or down the screen to change the order in which mailboxes appear. Tap Add Mailbox to add a mailbox not shown to the list. Tap Done to save your changes.

Saving Images Attached to Email

Email is a great way to share photos. When you receive a message that includes photos, you can save them on your iPhone.

1. Move to the message screen of an email that contains one or more photos or images.

2. Tap the Share button.

3. Tap Save X Images, where X is the number of images attached to the message. (If there is only one image, the command is just Save Image.) The images are saved in the Photos app on your iPhone. (See Chapter 15 for help working with the Photos app.)

Searching Your Email

As you accumulate email, you might want to find specific messages. For example, suppose you want to retrieve an email message that was sent to a specific person, but you can't remember where you stored it. Mail's Search tool can help you find messages like this quite easily.

1. Move to the screen you want to search, such as an account's Inbox or a folder's screen.

2. Swipe down to move to the top of the screen.

3. Tap in the Search tool.

4. Enter the text for which you want to search. As you type, Mail makes suggestions about what you might be searching for. These appear in different sections based on the type of search Mail thinks you are doing, such as People, Subjects, and more.

5. To use one of Mail's suggestions to search, such as a person, tap their name; or continue typing your search term and when you are done, tap Search. Mail searches for messages based on your search criterion and you see the results.

6. Work with the messages you found, such as tapping a message to read it. Tap the back button in the upper-left corner of the screen to return to the search results.

7. To clear a search and exit Search mode, tap Cancel.

8. To clear a search but remain in Search mode, tap the Clear button.

   When you use an iPhone 6 Plus or 6s Plus horizontally, searching is even better, because you can select a found message in the search results in the right pane and ready it in the right pane.

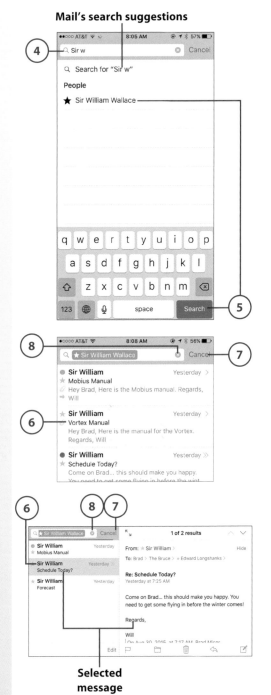

Mail's search suggestions

Selected message

Working with VIPs

The VIP feature enables you to indicate specific people as your VIPs. When a VIP sends you email, it is marked with a star icon and goes into the special VIP mailbox so you can access these important messages easily. You can also create specific notifications for your VIPs, such as a unique sound when you receive email from a VIP (see Chapter 5, "Customizing How Your iPhone Looks and Sounds").

Designating VIPs

To designate someone as a VIP, perform the following steps:

1. View information about the person you want to be a VIP by tapping his name in the From or Cc fields as you learned earlier in the chapter.

2. On the Info screen, tap Add to VIP. The person is designated as a VIP and any email from that person receives the VIP treatment.

Accessing VIP Email

To work with VIP email, do the following:

1. Move to the Mailboxes screen.

2. Tap VIP.

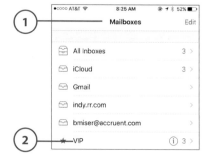

3. Work with the VIP messages you see.

>>>Go Further

MORE ON VIPS

Here are a few more tidbits on VIPs:

- Messages from VIPs are marked with the star icon no matter in which mail-box you see the messages. If you haven't read a VIP message, the star is blue. If you have read it, the star is gray.

- To see the list of your current VIPs, move to the Mailboxes screen and tap the Info button (i) for the VIP mailbox. You see everyone currently desig-nated as a VIP. Tap Add VIP to add more people to the list. Tap VIP Alerts to create special notifications for VIPs.

- To return a VIP to normal status, view his information and tap Remove from VIP.

Managing Junk Email

Junk email, also known as spam, is an unfortunate reality of email. No matter what precautions you take, you are going to receive some spam emails. Of course, it is good practice to be careful about where you provide your email address to limit the amount of spam you receive.

Consider using a "sacrificial" email account when you shop, post messages, and in the other places where you're likely to get spammed. If you do get spammed, you can stop using the sacrificial account and create another one to take its place. Or you can delete the sacrificial account from your iPhone and continue to use it on your computer where you likely have better spam tools in place. If you have an iCloud account, you can set up and use email aliases for this purpose.

The Mail app on the iPhone doesn't include any spam or filtering tools. However, if you use an account or an email application on a computer that features a junk mail/spam tool, it acts on mail sent to your iPhone, too. For example, if you configure spam tools for a Gmail account, those tools act on email before it reaches your iPhone. Similarly, if you use the Mail app on a Mac, its rules and junk filter work on email as you receive it; the results of this are also reflected on your iPhone.

To change how you deal with junk email on your iPhone, change the junk email settings for your account online (such as for Gmail) or by changing how an email app on a computer deals with junk mail. The results of these changes are reflected in the Mail app on your iPhone.

Many email accounts, including iCloud and Google, have Junk folders; these folders are available in the Mail app on your iPhone. You can open the Junk folder under an account to see the messages that are placed there. As you saw earlier, you can also move a message to the Junk folder by swiping to the left on it, tapping More, and then tapping Move to Junk.

It's Not All Good

Unfortunately, while you can move email to a Junk folder in the Mail app, this really doesn't do any good, because the Mail app doesn't use that action to be able to mark similar future emails as junk like email apps on computers do. On an iPhone, there's really no difference between moving a message to a Junk folder and deleting it. Because it is faster to delete a message, that is a better way to get rid of junk email than moving it to a Junk folder.

Tap to send and receive
text messages, photos,
video, and more

Send messages
from other apps
too, such as to
share photos

Tap to configure
Messages

In this chapter, you'll explore the texting and messaging functionality your iPhone has to offer. The topics include the following:

→ Preparing Messages for messaging
→ Sending messages
→ Receiving, reading, and replying to messages
→ Working with messages

10

Sending, Receiving, and Managing Texts and iMessages

You can use the iPhone's Messages app to send, receive, and converse; you can also send and receive images, videos, and links with this app. You can maintain any number of conversations with other people at the same time, and your iPhone lets you know whenever you receive a new message via audible and visible notifications that you can configure. In addition to conversations with other people, many organizations use text messaging to send important updates, such as airlines communicating flight status changes.

The Messages app can send and receive text messages via your cell network based on telephone numbers—this is the texting function that almost all cell phones support. Using this option, you can send text messages to and receive messages from anyone who has a cell phone capable of text messaging.

You can also use iMessage within the Messages app to send and receive messages via an email account to and from other iOS devices (iOS 5 or newer) or Macs (running OS X Lion or newer). This is especially useful when your cell phone account has a limit on the number of texts you can send via your cell account; when you use iMessage for texting, there is no limit on the amount of data you can send and so you incur no additional costs for your messages. The iMessages option is also really useful because you can send messages to and receive messages from iPod touch, iPad, and Mac users even though these devices don't have cell phone capability.

Preparing Messages for Messaging

Like most of the apps described in this book, there are settings for the Messages app you can configure to choose how the app works for you. For example, you can configure iMessage so you can communicate via email addresses, configure how standard text messages are managed, and so on. You can also choose to block messages from specific people.

Setting Your Text and iMessage Preferences

Perform the following steps to set up Messages on your iPhone:

1. Move to the Settings app and tap Messages.

2. Set the iMessage switch to on (green).

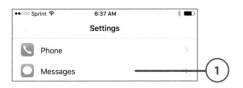

3. Tap Use your Apple ID for iMessage.

Already Signed In to an Apple ID?

If you have already signed into an Apple ID for Messages, you can start with step 5 to configure the settings being used for your messages. If you want to change the Apple ID currently being used for iMessage, tap Send & Receive, tap the Apple ID shown at the top of the iMessage screen, and then tap Sign Out. You can then use these steps to sign into a different Apple ID for Messages.

---

4. Type your Apple ID and associated password, and then tap Sign In.

5. Tap Text Messaging Forwarding; if you don't see this option, your cell phone carrier doesn't support it and you can skip to step 11.

6. Set the switch to on (green) for a device on which you want to be able to receive and send text messages using your iPhone's cell phone function (this doesn't impact messages sent via iMessages). A code appears on the device for which you turned on the switch (in this case, Brad's Mac Mini).

7. Type the code into the Text Message Forwarding box on the iPhone.

8. Tap Allow.

9. Repeat steps 6 through 8 to enable other devices to receive text messages via your iPhone's cell phone function.

10. Tap Messages.

11. To notify others when you read their messages, slide the Send Read Receipts switch to on (green). Be aware that receipts apply only to iMessages (not texts sent over a cellular network).

12. To send texts via your cellular network when iMessage is unavailable, slide the Send as SMS switch to on (green). If your cellular account has a limit on the number of texts you can send, you might want to leave this set to off (white) so you use only iMessage when you are texting. If your account has unlimited texting, you should set this to on (green).

13. Tap Send & Receive. At the top of the iMessage screen, you see the Apple ID via which you'll send and receive iMessages. On the rest of the screen are the phone number and email addresses that can be used with the Messages app.

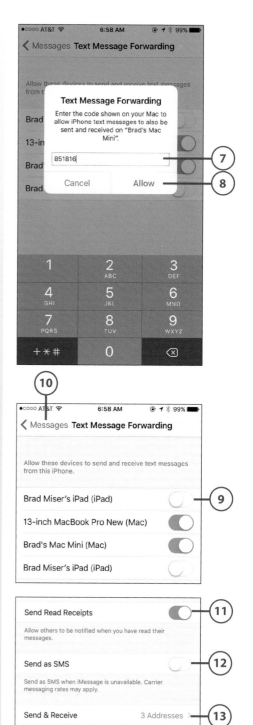

14. To prevent an email address from being available for messages, tap it so it doesn't have a check mark; to enable an address so it can be used for messages, tap it so it does have a check mark.

15. Tap the phone number or email address you want to use by default when you start a new text conversation. Each number or email address becomes a separate conversation in the Messages app so choose the number or address you want to use most frequently to start new conversations.

16. Tap Messages.

17. Swipe up the screen so you see the SMS/MMS section.

18. If you don't want to allow photos and videos to be included in messages sent via your phone's cellular network, set the MMS Messaging switch to off (white). You might want to disable this option if your provider charges more for these types of messages—or if you simply don't want to deal with anything but text in your messages.

19. To keep messages you send to a group of people organized by the group, set the Group Messaging switch to on (green). When enabled, replies you receive to messages you send to groups (meaning more than one person on a single message) are shown on a group message screen where each reply from anyone in the group is included on the same screen. If this is off (white), when someone replies to a message sent to a group, the message is separated out as if the original message was just to that person. (The steps in this chapter assume Group Messaging is on.)

20. To add a subject field to your messages, set the Show Subject Field switch to on (green). This divides text messages into two sections; the upper section is for a subject, and you type your message in the lower section. This is not commonly used, and the steps in this chapter assume this setting is off.

21. To display the number of characters you've written compared to the number allowed (such as 59/160), set the Character Count switch to on (green). When it is off, you don't see a character count for messages you send. Technically, text messages you send via the cellular network are limited to 160 characters, so showing the character count helps you see where you are relative to this limit (iMessages don't have a limit).

22. Use the Blocked option to block people from texting you (see the next task).

23. Tap Keep Messages.

24. Tap the length of time for which you want to keep messages.

25. If you tap something other than Forever, tap Delete. The messages on your iPhone older than the length of time you selected in step 21 are deleted.

26. Tap Messages.

27. Set the Filter Unknown Senders switch to on (green) if you want messages from people or organizations not in the Contacts app to be put on a separate list. Notifications for those messages are also disabled. This can be useful if you receive a lot of messages from people you don't know and don't want to be annoyed by notifications about those messages.

28. Tap Expire in the AUDIO MESSAGES section.

29. Tap Never if you want to keep audio messages until you delete them or After 2 Minutes to have them deleted after two minutes. If you selected After 2 Minutes, audio messages are automatically deleted two minutes after you listen to them. This is good because audio messages require a lot of storage space and deleting them keeps that space available for other things.

30. Tap Messages.

31. If you want to be able to listen to audio messages by lifting the phone to your ear, set the Raise to Listen switch to on (green). If you set this to off (white), you need to manually start audio messages.

32. Tap Expire in the VIDEO MESSAGES section.

33. Tap Never if you want video messages included in an iMessage to be kept on your phone or After 2 Minutes to have them automatically deleted after two minutes. Video messages can take up a lot of storage space so it's usually a good idea to choose After 2 Minutes.

34. Tap Messages. You're ready to send and receive messages.

Removing and Adding Addresses

To remove an address from iMessage, tap its Info button (i) and then tap Remove This Email. Tap Remove Email Address at the prompt, and you are no longer able to use that address for iMessage. You can add more email addresses for iMessage messages by tapping Add Another Email. Enter the email address you want to add. If you use an email that is not associated with your Apple ID, a verification email is sent to that address. You need to click the link in that email to be able to use the address with the Messages app. When the address is verified, you see it on the list of options for messaging. You also receive notifications on other devices on which the same Apple ID is configured informing you that the addresses have been enabled for iMessage on your iPhone.

Avoiding Scam Email

When you enable email addresses for iMessage, the resulting confirmation message should only contain a link you click to verify the address you provided. If you receive an email asking for your Apple ID or other identifying information, this is not from Apple and you should delete it without responding to it.

Audio and Video Messages

There are two types of audio and video messages you can send via the Messages app. Instant audio and video messages are included as part of the message itself. Audio and videos can also be attached to messages. The Expire settings only affect instant audio or video messages. Audio or videos that are attached to messages are not deleted automatically.

Blocking People from Messaging or Texting You

To block a phone number or email address from sending you a message, you need to have a contact configured with that information. Refer to Chapter 7, "Managing Contacts," for the steps to create contacts. Creating a contact from a message you receive is especially useful for this purpose. When you start receiving messages from someone you want to block, use a message to create a contact. Then use the following steps to block that contact from sending messages to you:

1. Move to the Messages screen in the Settings app.

2. Swipe up the Messages screen.

3. Tap Blocked.

4. Tap Add New.

5. Use the Contacts app to find and tap the contact you want to block. (Note that contacts without email addresses or phone numbers that don't have the potential to send messages to you are grayed out and cannot be selected.) You return to the Blocked screen and see the contact on your Blocked list. Any messages from the contact, as long as they come from an email address or phone number included in his contact information, won't be sent to your iPhone.

6. Repeat steps 4 and 5 to block other addresses or phone numbers for the person you are blocking or to block other people.

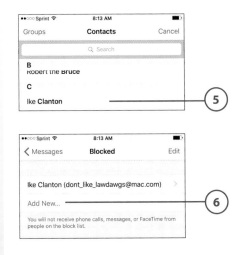

>>>Go Further

MORE ON MESSAGES CONFIGURATION

Following are a few more Messages configuration tidbits for your consideration:

- You can use only one Apple ID for iMessage at a time. To change the account you are using, move to the iMessage screen by tapping Send & Receive on the Messages Settings screen. Then tap the Apple ID shown. Tap Sign Out. You can then sign in to a different Apple ID.

- SMS stands for Short Message Service, which is what text messages use. MMS stands for Multimedia Messaging Service, which adds the ability to include multimedia elements (photos, video, sound, and so on) in text messages. All text devices and accounts support SMS, but they don't all support MMS.

- You should also configure the notifications the Messages app uses to communicate with you. You can configure the alert styles (none, banners, or alerts), badges on the icon to show you the number of new messages, sounds and vibrations when you receive messages, and so on. Messages also supports repeated alerts, which by default is to send you two notifications for each message you receive but don't read. Configuring notifications is explained in detail in Chapter 5, "Customizing How Your iPhone Looks and Sounds."

• To unblock someone so you can receive messages from them again, move to the Messages screen in the Settings app, tap Blocked, swipe to the left across the contact you want to unblock, and tap Unblock.

Sending Messages

You can use the Messages app to send messages to people using a cell phone number (as long as the device receiving it can receive text messages) or an email address that has been registered for iMessage. If the recipient has both a cell number and iMessage-enabled email address, the Messages app assumes you want to use iMessage for the message.

When you send a message to more than one person and at least one of those people can use only the cellular network, all the messages are sent via the cellular network and not as an iMessage.

More on Mixed Recipients

If one of a message's recipients has an email address that isn't iMessage-enabled (and doesn't have a phone number), the Messages app attempts to send the message to that recipient as an email message. The recipient receives the email message in an email app on his phone or computer instead of through the Messages app.

Whether messages are sent via a cellular network or iMessage isn't terribly important, but there are some differences. If your cellular account has a limit on the number of texts you can send, you should use iMessage when you can because those messages won't count against your limit. Also, when you use iMessage, you don't have to worry about a limit on the number of characters in a message. When you send a message via a cellular network, your messages might be limited to 160 characters.

Creating and Sending Messages

You can send text messages by entering a number or email address manually or by selecting a contact from your contacts list.

1. On the Home screen, tap Messages.

2. Tap New Message (if you don't see this, tap the back button in the upper-left corner of the screen until you do). If you haven't used the Messages app before, you skip this step and move directly to the compose message screen in the next step.

3. Type the recipient's name, email address, or phone number. As you type, the app attempts to match what you type with a saved contact or to someone you have messaged with before and shows you a list of suggested recipients. You see phone numbers or email addresses for each recipient on the list. Phone numbers or addresses in blue indicate the recipient is registered for iMessages and your message will be sent via that means. When you see a phone number in green, the message will be sent as a text message over the cellular network. If a number or email address is gray, you haven't sent any messages to it yet; you can tap it to attempt to send a message. You also see groups you have previously messaged.

4. Tap the phone number, email address, or group to which you want to send the message. The recipients' names are inserted into the To field. Or, if the information you want to use doesn't appear, just type the complete phone number (as you would dial it to make a call to that number) or email address.

Tap to select a recipient from your contacts

iMessage-enabled email address

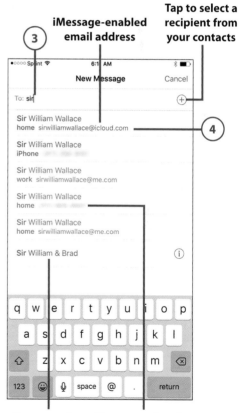

Group you've previously messaged

Phone number that hasn't been used for messaging

Straight to the Source

You can tap the Add button (+) in the To field to use the Contacts app to select a contact to whom you want to address the message.

Go to the Group

You can tap the Info button (i) next to a group on the suggested recipients list to see the people that are part of that group.

5. If you want to send the message to more than one recipient, tap in the space between the current recipient and the + button and use steps 3 and 4 to enter the other recipients' information, either by selecting contacts, or by entering phone numbers or email addresses. As you add recipients, they appear in the To field. (If you addressed the message to a number or email address that matches a number in your contacts, the contact's name replaces the number in the To field. If not, the number or email address remains as you entered it.)

Change Your Mind?

To remove a contact or phone number from the To box, tap it once so it becomes highlighted in blue and then tap the Delete key on the keyboard.

6. Tap in the Message bar, which is labeled iMessage if you entered iMessage addresses or Text Message if you entered a phone number. The cursor moves into the Message bar and you are ready to type your message.

7. Type the message you want to send in the Message bar.

8. Tap Send, which is blue if you are sending the message via iMessage or green if you are sending it via the cellular network. The Send status bar appears as the message is sent; when the process is complete, you hear the message sent sound and the status bar disappears.

If the message is addressed to iMessage recipients, your message appears in a blue bubble in a section labeled iMessage. If the person to whom you sent the message enabled his read receipt setting, you see when he reads your message.

If you sent the message via the cellular network instead of iMessage, you see your message in a green bubble in a section labeled Text Message.

When you send a message, you see a new conversation screen if the message was not sent to someone or a group of people with whom you were previously messaging. If you have previously sent messages to the same recipient or recipients, you move back to the existing conversation screen and your new message is added to that conversation instead.

If you've addressed the message to only one person, that person's name appears at the top of the screen. If the message is going to more than one recipient, the title of the screen is Group MMS (assuming MMS is enabled) or just Group if it is an iMessage conversation.

Recipients of the message

Message sent to more than one person

When the message was sent

This message has been sent via iMessage

Recipient of the message

This message has been sent via a cellular network

When the message was sent

>>>Go Further
TEXT ON

Following are some additional points to help you take your texting to the next level (where is the next level, anyway?):

- **iMessage or Cell**—If the recipient has an iOS device or Mac that has been enabled for iMessage, text messages are sent via iMessage when possible even if you choose the recipient's phone number.

- **Group Messaging**—If you've enabled the Group Messaging setting, when you include more than one recipient, the title of the new screen becomes Group. If all the recipients use the current version of the Messages app and have also enabled this setting, any messages sent in reply are grouped on one screen. If that isn't true, the messages are treated as if the Group Messaging setting is off.

- **No Group Messaging**—When you address a message to more than one person with Group Messaging disabled, it is sent to each person but becomes a separate conversation from that point on. If one or more of the recipients replies to the message, only you see the responses. In other words, replies to your messages are sent only to you, not to all the people to whom you sent the original message.

- **Larger Keyboard**—Like other areas where you type, you can rotate the iPhone to be horizontal where the keyboard is larger as is each key. This can make texting easier, faster, and more accurate.

- **Recents**—When you enter To information for a new message, included on the list of potential recipients are people being suggested to you by your iPhone. When a suggested recipient has an Info button (i), tap that button, tap Ignore Contact, and then tap Ignore at the prompt to prevent that person from being suggested in the future.

Receiving, Reading, and Replying to Messages

Text messaging is about communication, so when you send messages you expect to receive responses. People can also send new messages to you. The Messages app keeps messages grouped as a conversation consisting of messages you send and replies you receive to the same person or group of people.

Receiving Messages

Swipe to the right on the notification to move into the Messages app to read the entire message

Message alert notification on the Lock screen

When you aren't currently using the Messages screen in the Messages app and receive a new message (as a new conversation or as a new message in an ongoing conversation), you see, hear, and feel the notifications you have configured for the Messages app. (Refer to Chapter 5, "Customizing How Your iPhone Looks and Sounds" to configure your message notifications.)

If you are on the Messages screen in the Messages app when a new message comes in, you hear and feel the new message notification sound and/or vibration, but a notification alert box does not appear. The conversation containing a new message is marked with a blue circle.

Your new messages

Tap a message to move into the Messages app

Swipe down to open the Notification Center and tap the Notifications tab to see your messages

You can also access your new messages using the Notification Center. Swipe down from the top of the screen to open the Notification Center and tap the Notifications tab. In the Messages section, you see the new messages with the newest message being at the top of the screen and older messages shown toward the bottom. You can swipe up and down the screen to browse the messages or tap a message to read it in the Messages app.

If a new message is from someone with whom you have previously sent or received a message, and you haven't deleted all the messages to or from those recipients (no matter how long it has been since a message was added to that conversation), the new message is appended to an ongoing conversation. That conversation then moves to the top of the list of conversations on the Messages screen. If there isn't an existing message to or from the people involved in a new message, a new conversation is started and the message appears at the top of that list.

Speaking of Texting

Using Siri to hear and speak text messages is extremely useful. Check out Chapter 12, "Working with Siri," for examples showing how you can take advantage of this great feature.

Reading Messages

You can get to new messages you receive by doing any of the following:

Tap an alert to read a new message in the Messages app

- Tap a banner alert notification from Messages. You move into the message's conversation in the Messages app.

- Open the Messages app and tap the conversation containing a new message; these conversations appear at the top of the Messages list and are marked with a blue circle. The conversation opens and you see the new message.

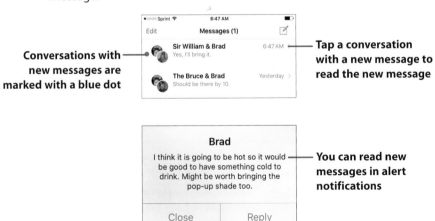

Conversations with new messages are marked with a blue dot

Tap a conversation with a new message to read the new message

You can read new messages in alert notifications

- Read a message in its alert notification.

- Swipe to the right on a message notification when it appears on the Lock screen.

- Open the Notifications tab of the Notification Center and tap a message.

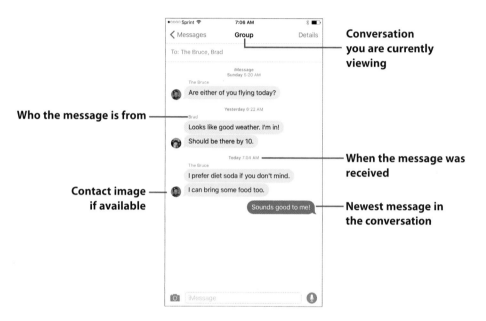

- If you receive a new message in a conversation that you are currently viewing, you immediately see the new message.

However you get to a message, you see the new message in either an existing conversation or a new conversation. The newest messages appear at the bottom of the screen. You can swipe up and down the screen to see all of the messages in the conversation. As you move up the screen, you move back in time.

Messages sent to you are on the left side of the screen and appear in a gray bubble. Just above the bubble is the name of the person sending the message; if you have an image for the contact, that image appears next to the bubble. The color of your bubbles indicates how the message is sent: blue indicates an iMessage while green indicates a cellular message.

Viewing Images or Video You Receive in Messages

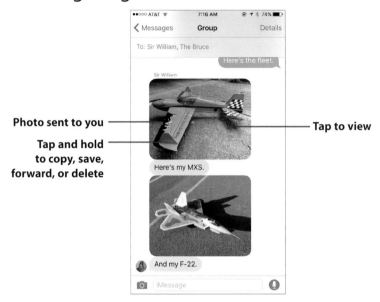

Photo sent to you — *Tap to view*

Tap and hold
to copy, save,
forward, or delete

When you receive a photo or video as an attachment, it appears in a thumbnail along with the accompanying message. (Video can also be embedded in a message as you'll see shortly.)

Tap to copy —

Tap to delete or
forward in another
message

Tap to save on
your iPhone

To copy the photo or video and paste it into another app, tap and hold on it; when the Copy command appears, tap it. To save the image on your iPhone, tap and hold on it until the menu appears; then tap Save. To forward it to someone else, tap and hold on the image. On the resulting menu, tap More. Tap the Share button located in the bottom-right corner of the screen. Complete the New Message that appears to send the photo along with a message. To delete the photo, tap and hold on the image. On the resulting menu, tap More. Then tap the Trash button.

To view a photo or video attachment, tap it. You see the photo or video at a larger size.

Number of photos in the conversation

Tap to return to the conversation

Tap to share

Tap to bring up a list of recent photos in the conversation

Swipe to see other photos or videos in the conversation

If there is more than one photo or video in the conversation, you see the number of them at the top of the screen. Swipe to the left or right to move through the available photos. You can rotate the phone, zoom, and swipe around the photo just like viewing photos in the Photos app. You can watch a video in the same way, too.

Tap the List button to see a list of the recent photos in the conversation (this only appears if there is more than one photo in the conversation). Tap a photo on the list to view it.

Tap the Share button to share the photo with others via a message, email, tweet, Facebook, and so on. (When you hold an iPhone 6 Plus or 6s Plus horizontally, all the buttons are at the top of the screen.)

To move back to the conversation, tap Done.

Listening to Audio in Messages You Receive in Messages

Messages can include embedded audio that is recorded and added to a conversation so you can hear it (you learn how to send your own audio shortly).

Audio message

Tap to play

Tap and hold to see more options

Tap to listen via the speakerphone

When you receive an audio message, you can tap the Play button to play it or if you enabled the Raise to Listen option, lift the phone to your ear and the message plays automatically. Tap the Speaker icon to hear the message via the iPhone's speakerphone.

Tap to pause

Tap and hold to see more options

While the message is playing you see its status along with the Pause button that you can tap to pause it. After the message finishes, you see a message saying that it expires in 2 minutes or 1 year, depending on your settings earlier. That message is quickly replaced by Keep.

Tap to show the Trash button so you can delete the audio

Speakerphone is on

Tap to save the audio message

Tap Keep to save the message on your phone. (Keep disappears indicating the audio is saved.) To delete a message you have kept, tap and hold on it until you see More. Tap More and then tap the Trash. (If you have chosen the setting to have the audio messages expire in 2 minutes in the Settings app, then you can just let it expire rather than deleting it. See, "Setting Your Text and iMessage Preferences," earlier in this chapter.)

Kept Audio Messages

When one or more of the recipients of an audio message that you sent keeps it, a status message is added to the conversation on your phone. So, you know who keeps audio messages you have sent. And, others know when you keep their messages, too.

Watching Video in Messages You Receive in Messages

Messages can include embedded video that is recorded and added to a conversation so you can watch it.

Video message ——

Tap and hold to see more options

Tap to watch ——

When you receive video in a message, you can tap the Play button to watch it. The video plays. Tap it to stop the playback.

Video is playing ——
Tap to stop the video ——

Assuming you left the Expire setting for videos at After 2 Minutes, the video is deleted automatically after two minutes. Like an audio message, you see a brief message saying when the video will be deleted that is replaced by the Keep button. To keep the video in the conversation, tap Keep.

Tap to save the video 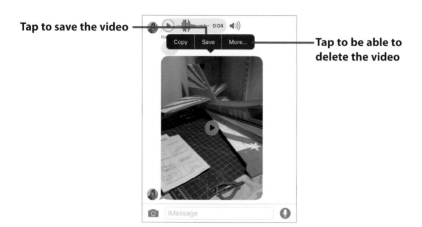 **Tap to be able to delete the video**

To save a video message on your phone, tap and hold on it until the menu appears, and then tap Save. It is saved in the Photos app (see Chapter 15, "Working with Photos and Video You Take with Your iPhone," for information about using the Photos app).

If you want to delete a video before it expires or if you have the Expire setting on the Never option, tap and hold on the video to open the menu and then tap More. Tap the Trash and tap Delete Message at the prompt.

Replying to Messages from the Messages App

To reply to a message, read the message and do the following:

1. Read, watch, or listen to the most recent message.

2. Tap in the Message bar.

3. Type your reply or use the Dictation feature to speak your reply (this is translated to text unlike recording and embedding an audio message).

4. Tap Send. (If the message will be sent via the cellular network, the Send button is green; if it will be sent via iMessage, it is blue.) The message is sent, and your message is added to the conversation. Messages you send are on the right side of the screen in a blue bubble if they were sent via iMessage or a green bubble if they were sent via the cellular network.

Message you've sent and added to the conversation

Blue indicates this is an iMessage

Mix and Match

The Messages app can switch between types of messages. For example, if you have an iMessage conversation going but can't access the iMessage service for some reason, the app can send messages as a cellular text. It can switch the other way, too. The app tries to send iMessages first if it can but chooses whichever method it can to get the messages through. (If you disabled the Send as SMS option, messages are only sent via iMessage.)

More Tricks of the Messaging Trade

My Acquisitions Editor Extraordinaire pointed out that when people have cellular data turned off, they can't receive messages. You don't see a warning in this
case; you can only tell the message wasn't delivered because the "Delivered"
status doesn't appear under the message. The message is delivered as soon as
the other person's phone is connected to the Internet again, and its status is
updated accordingly on your phone. Also, when an iMessage can't be delivered,
you can tap and hold on it; then tap Send as Text Message. The app tries to
send the message via SMS instead of iMessage.

Replying to Messages from a Banner Alert

If you have banner alerts configured
for your messages, you can reply
directly from the alert:

1. Swipe down on the center of the
   banner alert notification. The
   reply box opens.

2. Type your reply.

3. Tap Send. Your message is added
   to the conversation.

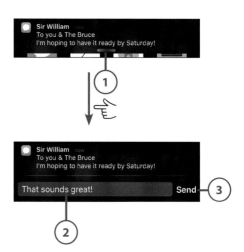

Using Quick Actions to Send Messages (iPhone 6s and 6s Plus)

You can use the Quick Actions feature on an iPhone 6s or 6s Plus with the Messages app as follows:

1. Press on the Messages icon. The Quick Actions menu appears.

2. Tap the person to whom you want to send a message or tap New Message to send a new message to someone not shown on the list. If you choose a person, you move into an existing conversation with that person or a new conversation is started. If you choose New Message, you move to the New Message screen.

3. Complete and send the message.

Having a Messages Conversation

Messaging is all about the back-and-forth communication with one or more people. You've already learned the skills you need, so put them all together. You can start a new conversation by sending a message to one or more people with whom you don't have an ongoing conversation; or you can add to a conversation already underway.

1. Send a new message to a person or add a new message to an existing conversation. You see when your message has been delivered. If you sent the message to an individual person via iMessages and he has enabled his Read Receipt setting, you see when he has read your message and you see a bubble as he is composing a response. (If you are conversing with more than one person, the person doesn't have her Read Receipt setting enabled, or the conversation is happening via the cellular network, you don't see either of these.)

Your message has been delivered

Your message has been read

Seen But Not Read

Don't take the Read status too literally. All it means is that the conversation to which your message was added has been viewed. Of course, the Messages app can't know whether the recipient actually read the message.

As the recipient composes a response, you see a bubble on the screen where the new message will appear when it is received (again, only if it is an iMessage with a single individual). Of course, you don't have to remain on the conversation's screen waiting for a response. You can move to a different conversation or a different app. When the response comes in, you are notified per your notification settings.

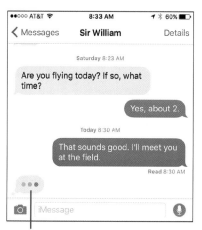

The recipient is composing a response

2. Read the response.

3. Send your next message.

4. Repeat these steps as long as you want. Conversations remain in the Messages app until you remove them. Messages within conversations remain forever (unless you delete them, for one year, or for 30 days depending on your Keep Messages setting as shown earlier in this chapter).

The iMessage Will Be With You…Always

Messages that are sent with iMessage move with you from device to device, so they appear on every device configured to use your iMessage account. Because of this, you can start a conversation on your iPhone while you are on the move and pick it up on your iPad or Mac later.

Working with Messages

As you send and receive messages, the interaction you have with each person or group becomes a separate conversation. A conversation consists of all the messages that have gone back and forth. You manage your conversations from the Messages screen.

Multiple Conversations with the Same People

The Messages app manages conversations based on the phone number or email address associated with the messages in that conversation rather than the people (contacts) involved in the conversation. So, you may have multiple conversations with the same person if that person used a different means, such as a phone number and an email address, to send messages to you.

Managing Messages Conversations

Use the Messages screen to manage your messages.

1. On the Home screen, tap Messages.

   The Messages screen showing conversations you have going appears. Conversations containing new messages appear at the top of the list. The name of the conversation is the name of the person or people associated with it, or it might be labeled as Group if the app can't display the names. If a contact can't be associated with the person, you see the phone number or email address you are conversing with instead of a name.

If you have the badge enabled, you see the number of new messages on the Messages icon

Information Messages

Many organizations use messages to keep you informed. Examples are airlines that send flight status information, retailers that use messages to keep you informed about shipping, and so on. These messages are identified by a set of numbers that don't look like a phone number. You can't send a response to most of these messages; they are one-way only. In some cases, you can issue commands related to the texts from that organization, such as "Stop" to stop further texts from being sent.

2. Swipe up and down the list to see all the conversations.

3. Tap a conversation you want to read or reply to. The conversation screen appears; the name of the screen is the person with whom you are conversing, her number if she isn't in your contacts list, or Group if the message includes multiple recipients.

See the Time of Every Message

To see the time or date associated with every message in the conversation being displayed, swipe to the left and hold your finger down on the screen. The messages shift to the left and the time of each message appears along the right side of the screen. The date associated with each message appears right before the first message on that date.

4. Read the new messages in the conversation. Your messages are on the right side of the screen in green (cell network) or blue (iMessage), whereas the other people's messages are on the left in gray. Messages are organized so the newest message is at the bottom of the screen.

5. Swipe up and down the conversation screen to see all the messages it contains.

6. To add a new message to the conversation, tap in the Message bar, type your message, and tap Send.

7. Swipe down the screen. As the screen scrolls down, you move back in time in the conversation.

8. To see details about the conversation, tap Details. The Details screen appears. At the top of the screen, you see location information for the people with whom you are texting if it is available (you learn more about locations in messages later in this chapter).

Number of new messages in all conversations   Day or time of most recent message

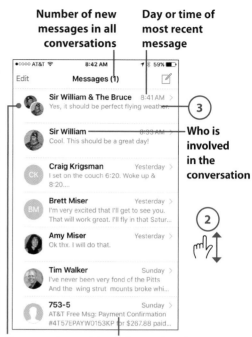

Who is involved in the conversation

Conversations with new messages   Informational text (not a conversation)

If a conversation involves only one other person, you see that person's name here instead of Group and the To field is hidden

9. If you are working with a group message and want to give it a more meaningful name, swipe down the screen to reveal the Group Name field at the top of the screen. If you are working with a conversation involving one other person, skip to step 11.

10. Tap in the Group Name field, enter the name of the group, and tap Done. The conversation is renamed with the name you entered.

11. To place a voice call or audio-only FaceTime call to one of the participants in the conversation, tap the phone icon. If the person has a phone number configured, you're prompted to choose Voice Call or FaceTime Audio. When you make a choice, that call is placed. If the person only has an email address, an audio-only FaceTime call is placed over the Internet. You move into the Phone or FaceTime app and use that app to complete the call. (See Chapter 8, "Communicating with the Phone and FaceTime Apps," for the details about those apps.) Move to the Home screen and tap Messages or use the App Switcher to return to the Messages app.

12. To place a FaceTime video call, tap the video camera icon. You move into the FaceTime app to complete the call. When you're done, move to the Home screen and tap Messages or use the App Switcher to return to the Messages app.

13. To view a participant's contact information or send an email, tap the Info button.

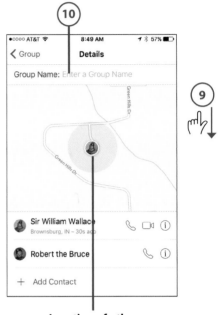

Location of other participants (if available)

New conversation name

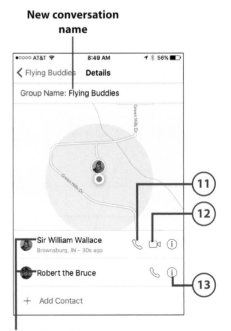

List of participants in the conversation

14. View the contact's information. The information highlighted in blue is what is being used in the conversation. For example, an email address shown in blue is being used for an iMessage message.

15. Tap an email address and use the Mail app to send an email message (details are in Chapter 9, "Sending, Receiving, and Managing Email").

Receiving and Reading Messages on an iPhone 6 Plus or 6s Plus

The iPhone 6 Plus' or 6s Plus' larger screen provides some additional functionality that is unique to it. You can access this by holding the iPhone 6 Plus or 6s Plus horizontally when you use the Messages app.

1. Open the Mail app and hold the iPhone so it is oriented horizontally. The window splits into two panes. On the left is the Navigation pane, where you can move to and select conversations you want to view. When you select a conversation in the left pane, its messages appear in the Content pane on the right.

2. Swipe up or down the Navigation pane to browse the conversations available to you. Notice that the two panes are in-dependent. When you browse the left pane, the right pane doesn't change.

3. Tap the conversation containing messages you want to read. The messages in that conversation appear in the Content pane on the right.

4. Swipe up and down the Content pane to read the messages in the conversation.

5. Listen to embedded audio, watch embedded video, or work with attachments just like when you hold the iPhone vertically.

List of conversations   **Messages in selected conversation**

Selected conversation

6. To add a message to the conversation, tap in the send bar, type your message, and tap Send. Of course, you can embed audio or video, attach photos or video, or send your location just as you can when using Messages when you hold the iPhone vertically.

7. To work with the conversation's details, tap Details.

8. To change conversations, tap the conversation you want to view.

Using 3D Touch for Messages (iPhone 6s and 6s Plus)

You can use the 3D Touch feature on an iPhone 6s or 6s Plus with the Messages app as follows:

1. Browse your messages.

2. Tap and hold on a message in which you are interested. A Peek of that message appears.

3. Review the preview of the message that appears in the Peek.

4. To open the message so you can read the conversation of which it is a part, press down slightly harder until it pops open and use the steps in the earlier task to read it (skip the rest of these steps).

5. To see actions you can perform on the message, swipe up on the Peek.

6. Tap the action you want to perform, such as Ok, to reply to the message with that message. If you tap the Custom command, you can create a custom reply to the message as you can when you view the conversation.

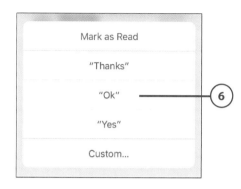

Adding Images and Video to Conversations

You can include any image, photo, or video stored on your iPhone in a text conversation, or you can take a photo or video to include in a message. This is a great way to share photos and videos.

1. Move into the conversation with the person to whom you want to send a photo, or start a new conversation with that person.

2. Tap the Camera button. A dialog appears that allows you to add photos or videos in three ways. Perform steps 3 through 6 to send a photo you've recently taken. Perform steps 7 through 11 to send any photo or video stored on your iPhone. Start with step 12 to take a new photo or video and send it.

3. If you have taken the photo recently, swipe to the left or right on the thumbnails you see above Photo Library to view the photos available to send.

4. Tap the photo you want to send. The photo is enlarged and marked with a check mark to show it is selected.

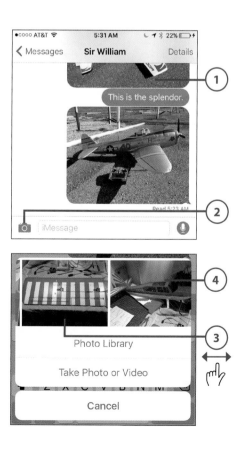

Limitations, Limitations

Not all cell carriers support MMS messages (the type that can contain images and video), and the size of messages can be limited. Check with your carrier for more information about what is supported and whether there are additional charges for using MMS messages. If you're using iMessage, you don't have this potential limit and are always able to include images and video in your texts. Also be sure your recipient can receive MMS messages before sending one.

5. To send more photos, swipe to the left and right on the photo to browse the others, and then tap the photo you want to send.

6. To send the photos without comment, tap Send *X* Photos, where *X* is the number of photos you selected; the photos send and you go back to the conversation and can skip the rest of these steps. To send the photos and make a comment about them, tap Add Comment; the photos are added to the conversation and you are ready to type your comment; skip to step 15.

7. Tap Photo Library.

8. Browse the source containing the photos you want to send. (For more information about viewing sources of photos, see Chapter 15.)

9. Swipe up or down the screen until you see the photo you want to send.

10. Tap the photo you want to send.

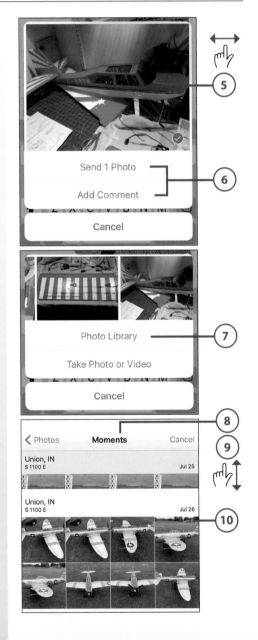

11. Tap Choose. You move back to the conversation and see the image in the Send box; move to step 16.

12. Tap Take Photo or Video.

13. Choose VIDEO to take video or PHOTO to take a photo.

14. Take the photo or video you want to send. (For more information about taking photos or videos, see Chapter 15.)

15. Tap Use Photo or Use Video or tap Retake to redo the photo or video you are sending.

16. Type the message you want to send with the photo or video; if you want to just send the photo or video, skip this step.

17. Tap Send. The message, and photo or video, is sent.

This Isn't Houston, but There Is a Problem

If a message you try to send is undeliverable or has some other problem, it is marked with an exclamation point inside a red circle. Tap that icon and tap Try Again to attempt to resend the message.

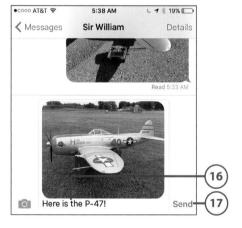

Sharing with Messages

You can share all sorts of information via Messages from many apps, such as Safari, Contacts, Maps, and so on. From the app containing the information you want to share, tap the Share button. Then tap Messages. The information with which you are working is automatically added to a new message. Use the Messages app to complete and send the message.

Adding Audio Recordings to Conversations

In a previous task you learned how to listen to embedded audio messages. Here's how to send your own embedded audio messages:

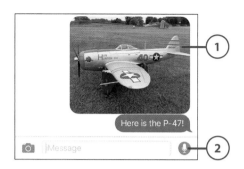

1. Move to the conversation to which you want to add an audio message, or start a new conversation.

2. Tap and hold on the Microphone at the right edge of the screen (not the one on the keyboard). Recording starts.

3. Speak your message; keep your finger touching the Microphone while you speak.

4. When you are done recording, take your finger off the screen.

5. To replay your message, tap the Play button.

6. To delete your message, tap Delete (x).

7. To send the message, tap the upward-facing arrow. The audio message is added to the conversation and the recipients are able to listen to it.

Your message is being recorded

Embedded vs. Attachments

When you record audio or video for a message, it is embedded in the message. When you use the steps in "Adding Images and Video to Conversations," the images or video are attachments to the conversation. You can view or watch these similarly, but attachments are not affected by the Expire settings, and you can do more actions with attachments than you can with embedded items, such as forwarding to others and viewing all the attachments to a conversation.

Adding Video and Photos to Conversations

Here's how to add embedded video and photos to your conversations:

1. Move to the conversation to which you want to add video or photos, or start a new conversation.

2. Tap and hold the Camera icon until the video and photo tool appears and the Messages screen is replaced by the video camera screen.

3. If you don't want to take a "selfie" video or photo, tap the Switch Camera button to change to the backside camera.

4. Adjust the image to what you want it to be when you start the video or take a photo.

5. To take a photo, tap the white Shutter button. The photo is taken and added to the conversation; skip to step 8.

6. To take a video, tap the red Record button. The video starts recording.

7. When you're done recording, tap the Stop button. The video is added to the message.

8. To send the photo or video, add your commentary and tap the Send button. The photo or video is added to the conversation and the recipients are able to view it.

Adding Locations to Conversations

Location information can be available for the participants in a conversation. You can add your location information to a conversation as follows:

1. Move to the conversation to which you want to add your location information.

2. Tap Details.

3. To share your current location as a snapshot, tap Send My Current Location. Your current location is captured and sent to the recipients of the message.

Current Locations

When a current location is added to a conversation, it is static, meaning it is only the location at that point in time. It appears as a map thumbnail in the conversation. Recipients can tap it to zoom in on the location, and then tap Directions to Here to generate directions from their location to the one sent as the current location.

4. To dynamically share your location so that it updates as you move around, tap Share My Location.

5. Tap how long you want your location information to be shared.

6. Tap Use to share your location or Not Now if you change your mind and don't want to share it. If you choose Use, your location is shared with the participants in the conversation and can be viewed on the Details screen on their devices. A notification that you are sharing your location is added to the conversation.

Who you are sharing your location with

Use This Device When Sharing Your Location?

You are currently using "Brad M Miser's iPhone" to share your location in Find My Friends and Messages.

Not Now   Use

7. To stop sharing your location, tap Stop Sharing My Location. If you selected to share it for one hour or until the end of the day, location sharing stops automatically at the time you selected.

Time until your location information expires

Browsing Attachments to Conversations

As photos and videos are added to a conversation, they are collected so you can browse and view them at any time:

1. Move to the conversation in which you want to browse attachments.

2. Tap Details.

3. Swipe up until you see the ATTACHMENTS section.

4. Swipe up and down on the attachments until you see one you want to view.

5. Tap the attachment you want to view.

6. View the attachment, such as watching a video.

7. Tap the attachment.

8. Tap the list button to see a list of all the attachments; tap an attachment to view it.

9. Tap the Share button to share the attachment via messages, email, and so on or to save it to your iPhone, add it to a contact, or take one of other available actions on it.

10. Tap Done to return to the Details screen.

Stop Bugging Me!

You can disable notifications for a specific conversation by moving to its Details screen and setting the Do Not Disturb switch to on (green). You no longer are notified when new messages arrive in that conversation. Set the switch to off (white) to have notifications resume.

Deleting Messages and Conversations

Old text conversations never die, nor do they fade away. All the messages you receive from a person or that involve the same group of people stay in the conversation. Over time, you can build up a lot of messages in one conversation, and you can end up with lots of conversations. (If you set the Keep Messages setting to be 30 Days or 1 Year, messages older than the time you set are deleted automatically.)

Long Conversation?

When a conversation gets very long, the Messages app won't display all its messages. It keeps the more current messages visible on the conversation screen. To see earlier messages, swipe down on the screen to move to the top and tap Load Earlier Messages.

When a conversation gets too long or if you just want to remove specific messages from a conversation, take these steps:

1. Move to a conversation containing an abundance of messages.

2. Tap and hold on a message you want to delete.

3. Tap More. The message on which you tapped is marked with a check mark to show it is selected.

Delete Them All!

To delete the whole conversation, instead of performing step 4, tap Delete All, which appears in the upper-left corner of the screen. Tap Delete Conversation. The conversation and all its messages are deleted.

---

4. Tap other messages you want to delete. They are marked with a check mark to show you have selected them.

5. Tap the Trash can icon.

6. Tap Delete X Messages, where X is the number of messages you have selected. The messages are deleted and you return to the conversation.

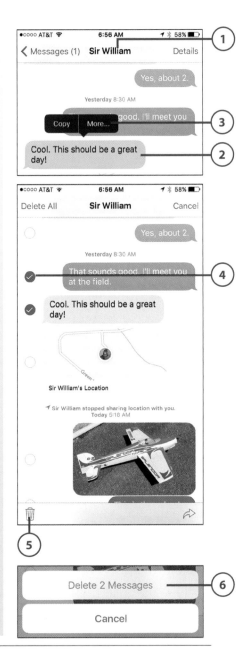

Pass It On

If you want to send one or more messages to someone else, perform steps 1–3. Tap the Forward button that appears in the lower-right corner of the screen. A new message is created and the messages you selected are pasted into it. Select or enter the recipients to whom you want to send the messages, and tap Send.

Deleting Conversations

If a conversation's time has come, you can delete it.

1. Move to the Messages screen.

2. Swipe to the left on the conversation you want to delete.

3. Tap Delete. The conversation and all the messages it contains are deleted.

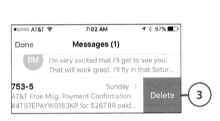

>>>Go Further
TEXTING LINGO

People frequently use shorthand when they text. Here is some of the more common shorthand you might see. This list is extremely short, but there are many websites dedicated to providing this type of information if you are interested. One that boasts of being the largest list of text message acronyms is www.netlingo.com/acronyms.php.

- FWIW—For What It's Worth
- LOL—Laughing Out Loud
- ROTFL—Rolling On the Floor Laughing
- CU—See You (later)
- PO—Peace Out
- IMHO—In My Humble Opinion
- TY—Thank You
- RU—Are You
- BRB—Be Right Back
- CM—Call Me

- DND—Do Not Disturb
- EOM—End of Message
- FSR—For Some Reason
- G2G—Got to Go
- IDK—I Don't Know
- IKR—I Know, Right?
- ILU—I Love You
- NM or NVM—Never Mind
- OMG—Oh My God
- OTP—On the Phone
- P911—Parent Alert
- PLZ—Please

Go here to figure
out where and when
you're supposed to be

Use this app
to remind
yourself of…
anything

Tap here to
configure your
date, time,
and reminder
preferences

In this chapter, you explore all the calendar and reminder functionality your iPhone has to offer. Topics include the following:

→ Setting calendar, reminder, and time preferences
→ Working with calendars
→ Working with reminders

Managing Calendars and Reminders

When it comes to time management, your iPhone is definitely your friend. Using the iPhone's Calendar app, you can view calendars that are available on all your devices. You can also make changes to your calendars on your iPhone, and they appear on the calendars on your other devices so you have consistent information no matter which device you happen to be using at any time. The Reminders app ensures you don't forget tasks or anything else you want to remember.

Setting Calendar, Reminder, and Time Preferences

There are a number of time, date, reminders, and calendar settings that impact how you use your iPhone to manage your calendars and time. In most cases, you can leave these settings in their default positions and start using the apps right away (beginning with "Working with Calendars" later in this chapter).

If you decide you want to make changes in these apps, you can use the information in the table that follows to understand the options available to you.

To access the settings in the table, first tap the Settings icon on the Home screen, open the Settings area, and then move to the location shown (e.g., to change the 24-Hour Time setting, open the Settings app, tap General, and then tap Date & Time). For each setting, you see a description of what it does along with options (if applicable).

Settings App Explained

To get detailed information on using the Settings app, see "Working with the Settings App" in Chapter 4, "Configuring an iPhone to Suit Your Preferences."

Calendar, Reminder, and Time Settings

Settings Area	Location	Setting	Description
Mail, Contacts, Calendars	CALENDARS	Time Zone Override	When disabled, the time for events is based on your current time zone. When enabled, the time zone for events on the calendars is overridden with the time zone for a city you select. This is useful if you always want event times to be based on a specific time zone. (See the Go Further sidebar at the end of this task for a more in-depth explanation of Time Zone Override.)
Mail, Contacts, Calendars	CALENDARS	Alternate Calendars	You can choose among different types of calendars, such as Chinese or Hebrew.
Mail, Contacts, Calendars	CALENDARS	Week Numbers	When on (green), week numbers appear on your calendars in the Month view.

Settings Area	Location	Setting	Description
Mail, Contacts, Calendars	CALENDARS	Show Invitee Declines	When on (green) and someone declines a meeting, they are shown on the Invitee list as having declined. When off (white), they are removed from the list.
Mail, Contacts, Calendars	CALENDARS	Sync	Determines how far back events are synced onto your calendars. You can choose 2 weeks, 1 month, 3 months, 6 months, or all events.
Mail, Contacts, Calendars	CALENDARS	Default Alert Times	Determines the default alert times for birthdays, events, and all-day events. When you set the Time To Leave switch to on (green), the Calendar app can use your travel time to configure an event's alert.
Mail, Contacts, Calendars	CALENDARS	Start Week On	Determines the first day of the week.
Mail, Contacts, Calendars	CALENDARS	Default Calendar	Determines which calendar is used for new events by default (you can override this setting for any events you create).
Mail, Contacts, Calendars	CALENDARS	Events Found in Mail	When on (green) and the Mail app detects event information in an email, it presents a prompt that enables you to add the event to a calendar.
General	Date & Time	24-Hour Time	Causes the iPhone to display 24-hour instead of 12-hour time.
General	Date & Time	Set Automatically	When on (green), the iPhone sets the time and date automatically based on the current network it is using. When off (white), you can manually set the time zone, time, and date.
N/A	Reminders	Sync	Determines how far back reminders are synced onto your calendars. You can choose 2 weeks, 1 month, 3 months, 6 months, or all reminders.
N/A	Reminders	Default List	Determines which reminder list new reminders are placed on when you create them. You can override this for any new reminder you create.

>>>Go Further

MORE ON TIME ZONE OVERRIDE

The Time Zone Override feature can be a bit confusing. If Time Zone Override is on, the iPhone displays event times according to the time zone you select on the Time Zone Override screen. When Time Zone Override is off, the time zone used for calendars is the iPhone's current time zone, which is set automatically based on your location or your manual setting. This means that when you change time zones (automatically or manually), the times for calendar events shift accordingly. For example, if an event starts at 3 P.M. when you are in the Eastern time zone, its start time becomes 12 P.M. if you move into the Pacific time zone.

When Time Zone Override is on, the dates and times for events become fixed based on the time zone you select for Time Zone Override. If you change the time zone the iPhone is in, no change to the dates and times for events is shown on the calendar because they remain set according to the time zone you selected for the Time Zone Override. Therefore, an event's actual start time might not be accurately reflected for the iPhone's current time zone because it is based on the fixed Time Zone Override city.

Notifications

The Calendar and Reminders apps can communicate with you in various ways, such as displaying alerts or banners when something happens that you might want to know about; for example, you can be alerted with a banner when you receive an invitation to an event. Configuring notifications for these apps will make them even more valuable. The information you need to configure notifications is explained in the section called "Setting Up Notifications and the Notification Center" in Chapter 4.

Working with Calendars

The Calendar app helps you manage your calendars; you'll notice I wrote *calendars* rather than *calendar*. That's because you can have multiple calendars in the app at the same time. To use the most cliché example, you might have a calendar for work and one for your personal life. Or, you might want a calendar for your travel plans, and then share that calendar with people who care about your location.

In most cases, you start by adding existing calendar information from an Exchange, iCloud, Google, or similar account. From there, you can use the Calendar app to view your calendars, add or change events, and much more. Any changes you make in the Calendar app are automatically made in all the locations that use calendars from the same account, or you can manually sync calendar information via iTunes on your computer.

The best option for storing your calendar information is an online account (such as iCloud, Exchange, or Google) because you can easily access your calendar information from many devices, and your calendars are kept in sync automatically. To learn how to configure an online account for calendar information, refer to Chapter 3, "Setting Up and Using iCloud and Other Online Accounts."

Viewing Calendars and Events

You use the Calendar app to view and work with your calendars, and you can choose how you view them, such as by month, week, or day.

To get into your calendars, move to the Home screen and tap the Calendar app (which shows the current day and date in its icon and a badge if you have at least one new invitation). The most recent screen you were viewing appears.

There are three viewing modes you use in the app. The mode in which you'll spend most of your time is the one that displays your calendars in various views, such as showing a month, week, or day. Another mode is the Calendars tool that enables you to choose and edit the calendar information that is displayed. The third mode is your Inbox, which you use to work with event invitations you receive.

The badge indicates how many invitations to events you have received

Configuring Calendars

To configure the calendar information you see in the app, perform the following steps:

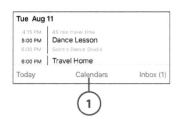

1. If you only have one calendar, skip to step 2. Tap Calendars to see all of your synced calendars. If you don't see this at the bottom of the screen, you are already on the Calendars screen (look for "Calendars" at the top of the screen).

   The Calendars screen displays the calendars available, organized by the account from which they come, such as ICLOUD, EXCHANGE, or GMAIL. By default, all your calendars are displayed, which is indicated by the check marks next to the calendars' names. Any calendars that don't have a check mark next to their names are not displayed when you view your calendars.

2. Tap a calendar with a check mark to hide it. The check mark disappears and the calendar is hidden. (The calendar is still there, you just won't see it when you are viewing your calendars.)

3. To show a calendar again, tap its name. It is marked with a check mark and appears when you are viewing calendars.

4. Tap the info button to see or change a calendar's information settings. Not all types of calendars support this function, and those that do can offer different settings. The following steps show an iCloud calendar; if you are working with a calendar of a different type, such as an Exchange calendar, you might not have all or the same options as those shown here. In any case, the steps to make changes are similar across all available types of calendars.

Calendars with check marks are displayed

Calendars without check marks are hidden

5. Change the name of the calendar by tapping it and then making changes on the keyboard; when you're done making changes, swipe down the screen to close the keyboard.

6. To share the calendar with someone, tap Add Person, enter the email address of the person with whom you are sharing it, and tap Add. (Sharing calendars is explained in more detail later in this chapter.)

7. If the calendar is shared and you don't want to be notified when shared events are changed, added, or deleted, set the Show Changes switch to off (white). When this switch is enabled and a change is made to a shared calendar, you receive notifications about the changes that were made. If the calendar is not shared, you won't see this switch.

8. Swipe up the screen.

9. Tap the color you want events on the calendar to appear in.

10. If you want alerts to be enabled (active) for the calendar, set the Event Alerts switch to on (green). (Not all types of calendars support this setting.)

11. To make the calendar public so that others can subscribe to a read-only version of it, set the Public Calendar switch to on (green), tap Share Link, and then use the resulting Share tools to invite others to subscribe to the calendar (more on this later in this chapter).

12. To remove the calendar entirely (instead of hiding it from view), tap Delete Calendar and then tap Delete Calendar at the prompt. The calendar and all its events are deleted. (It's usually better just to hide a calendar as described in step 2 so you don't lose its information.)

13. Assuming that you didn't delete the calendar, tap Done.

14. Edit other calendars as needed.

15. Tap Done. The app moves into viewing mode, and the calendars you enabled are displayed.

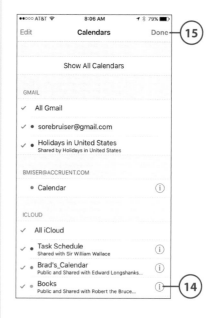

>>>Go Further

ALL OR NOTHING

You can make all your calendars visible by tapping the Show All Calendars button at the top of the screen; tap Hide All Calendars to do the opposite. After all the calendars are shown or hidden, you can tap individual calendars to show or hide them. You can show all the calendars from the same account by tapping the All command at the top of each account's calendar list, such as All iCloud to show all your iCloud calendars. Tap this again to hide all the account's calendars.

Another Way to Edit

You can also edit a calendar by tapping Edit at the upper-left of the Calendars screen and then tapping the calendar you want to edit. When you are done editing calendars, tap Done.

Navigating Calendars

The Calendar app uses a hierarchy of detail to display your calendars. The lowest level of detail, but longest timeframe displayed, is the year view. Next is the month view, which shows more detail but covers a shorter timeframe. This is followed by the week/day view; showing the highest level of detail is the event view.

Viewing Calendars

You can view your calendars from the year level all the way down to the day/week view. It's easy to move among the levels to get to the time period you want to see. Here's how:

1. Starting at the year view, swipe up and down until you see the year in which you are interested. (If you aren't in the year view, keep tapping the back button located in the upper-left corner of the screen until the back button disappears.)

2. Tap the month in which you are interested. The days in that month display, and days with events are marked with a dot.

3. Swipe up and down the screen to view different months.

4. To see the detail for a date, tap it. There are two ways to view the daily details: the Calendar view or the List view. Steps 5 through 8 show the Calendar view while steps 9 though 11 show the List view. Each of these views has benefits and as you can see, it is easy to switch between them.

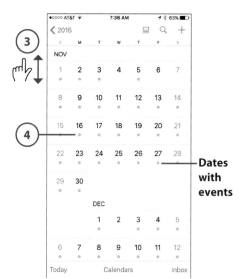

Today Is the Day

To quickly move to the current day, tap Today, located at the bottom of the screen.

5. To see the Calendar view, ensure the List button is not selected (isn't highlighted). On the resulting screen are the days of the week you are viewing. The date in focus is highlighted with a red circle when that day is today and a black circle for any other day. Below this area is the detail for the selected day showing the events on that day.

6. Swipe to the left or right on the dates or date being displayed to change the date for which detailed information is being shown.

7. Swipe up or down on the date detail to browse all its events.

8. Tap an event to view its detail and skip to step 12.

9. To see the events in List view, tap the List button so it is highlighted.

10. Swipe up and down to see the events for each day.

11. Tap on an event to view its detail.

12. Swipe up and down the screen to see all of the event's information.

13. Read information about the event.

14. **Tap the Calendar or Alert fields to change these settings.**

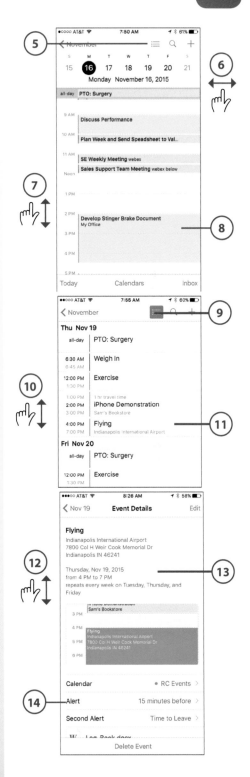

15. Tap attachments to view them.

16. Tap any links to move to information related to the event.

17. Read notes associated with the event.

18. See the event's location on a map.

19. Tap the date to move back to the week/day view.

Red Line

The red line stretching horizontally across the screen indicates the current time, which is shown at the left end of that line.

20. Tap the back button (labeled with the month you are viewing) to move back to the month view.

21. To view your calendars in the multiday view, rotate your iPhone so it is horizontal. You can do this while in the week/day view or the month view.

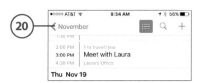

22. Swipe left or right to change the dates being displayed.

23. Swipe up or down to change the time of day being displayed.

24. Tap an event to see its detail.

Using 3D Touch for Events (iPhone 6s and 6s Plus Only)

You can use the 3D Touch feature on an iPhone 6s or 6s Plus with the Calendar app as follows:

1. Browse events, such as when you use the List view.

2. Tap and hold on an event in which you are interested. A Peek of that event appears.

3. Review the preview of the event that appears in the Peek.

4. To open the event so you can see all of its detail, press down slightly harder until it pops open and use the steps in the earlier task to work with it (skip the rest of these steps).

5. To see actions you can perform on the event, swipe up on the Peek.

6. Tap the action you want to perform, such as Delete Event, to delete the event from your calendar.

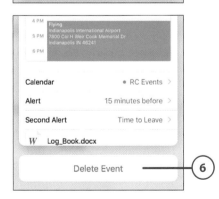

Adding Events to a Calendar

There are a number of ways you can add events to your calendar. You can create an event in an app on a computer, website, or other device and sync that event onto the iPhone through an online account. You can also manually create events in the Calendar app on the iPhone. Your events can include a lot of detail. You can choose to just create the basic information on your iPhone while you are on the move and complete it later from a computer or other device, or you can fill in all the details directly in the Calendar app.

1. Tap the Add button, which appears in the upper-right corner of any of the views when your phone is vertical (except when you are viewing an event's details). The initial date information is taken from the date currently being displayed, so you can save a little time if you view the date of the event before tapping the Add button.

2. Tap in the Title field and type the title of the event.

3. Tap the Location bar and type the location of the event; if you allowed the app to use Location Services, you're prompted to find and select a location; if not, just type the location and skip to step 6.

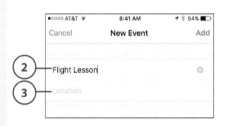

Location Prompt

The first time you create an event, you might be prompted to allow the Calendar app to access your location information. When you allow the app to use Location Services, you can search for and select event locations. The app can use this information to include an estimate of travel time for the event and to display events on a map when you view their detail.

4. Type the location in the Search bar. Sites that meet your search are shown below.

5. Tap the location for the event.

6. To set the event to last all day, set the All-day switch to the on position (green); when you select the All-day option, you provide only the start and end dates (you don't input times as described in the next several steps). To set a specific start and end time, leave this in the off (white) position; you'll set both the dates and times as described in the following steps.

7. To set a timeframe for the event, tap Starts. The date and time tool appears.

8. Swipe up or down on the date wheel until the date on which the event starts appears in the center.

9. Swipe up or down on the hour wheel until the event's starting hour is shown.

10. Scroll and select the starting minute in the same way.

11. Swipe up or down on the hour wheel to select AM or PM.

12. If you want to associate the event with a specific time zone, tap Time Zone; if not, don't tap it and skip to step 14.

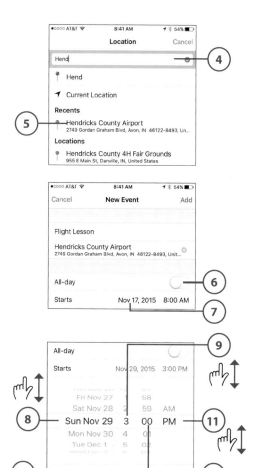

Your Results Might Vary

The fields and options available when you create a new event are based on the calendar with which the event is associated. For example, an iCloud calendar offers different options than an Exchange calendar does. If you aren't creating an event on your default calendar, it's a good idea to associate the event with a calendar before you fill in its details (to do that, perform step 31 before you do step 2).

13. Search for and select the time zone with which the event should be associated.

14. Tap Ends.

15. Use the date and time tool to set the ending date and time (if applicable) for the event; these work the same way as for the start date and time.

16. Tap Ends. The date and time tool closes.

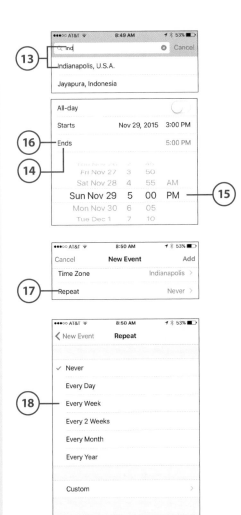

No Changes?

When you change a selection on most of the screens you see, you automatically return to the previous screen. If you don't make a change, you can return to the previous screen by tapping the back button that always appears in the upper-left corner of the screen (it can have different labels depending on the context of the current screen).

17. To make the event repeat, tap Repeat and follow steps 18–23. (For a nonrepeating event, skip to step 24.)

18. Tap the frequency with which you want the event repeated, such as Every Day, Every Week, and so on; if you want to use a repeat cycle not shown, tap Custom and create the frequency with which you want the event to repeat.

Custom Repeat

To configure a custom repeat cycle for an event, such as the first Monday of every month, tap Custom on the Repeat screen. Then use the Frequency (Monthly for the example) and Every (for example, On the first Monday) settings to configure the repeat cycle. Tap Repeat to return to the Repeat screen and then New Event to get back to the event you are creating.

19. Tap End Repeat to set a time at which the event stops repeating.

20. To have the event repeat ad infinitum, tap Never and skip to step 23.

21. To set an end to the repetition, tap On Date.

22. Use the date tool to set the date for the last repeated event.

23. Tap New Event.

24. To configure travel time for the event, tap Travel Time; if you don't want to configure this, skip to step 31.

25. Set the Travel Time switch to on (green).

26. To manually add a travel time to the event, tap it and skip to step 30.

27. To build a travel time based on a starting location, tap Starting Location.

No Change Needed

If you don't make a change to one of the settings, such as on the Repeat screen, you need to tap the Add Event link to get back to the Add Event screen.

28. To use your current location as the starting point, tap Current Location. Alternatively, use the search tool to find a starting location, and then tap it to select that location.

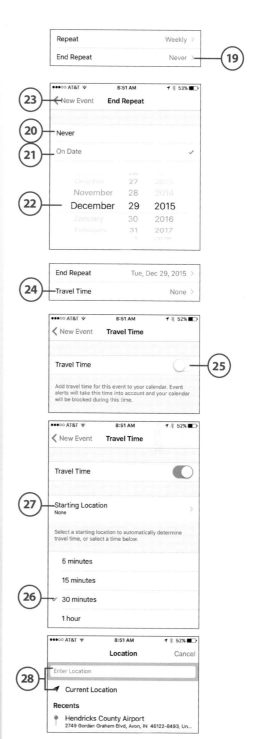

29. Tap the method you will use to travel to the location.

30. Tap New Event.

31. To change the calendar with which the event is associated, tap Calendar (to leave the current calendar selected, skip to step 33).

32. Tap the calendar with which the event should be associated.

33. To invite others to the event, tap Invitees; if you don't want to invite someone else, skip to step 38.

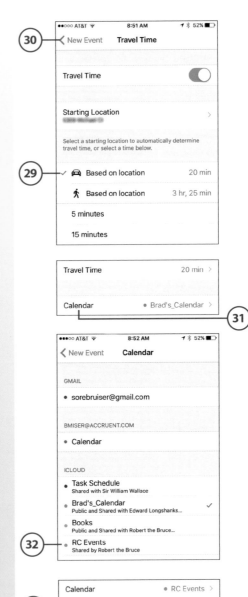

34. Enter the email addresses for each person you want to invite; as you type, the app tries to identify people who match what you are typing. You can tap a person to add him to the event. You can also use the Add button to choose people from your Contacts.

35. Repeat step 34 until you've added everyone you want to invite.

36. Tap Done. You move to the Invitees screen and see those whom you invited.

Automatic Sharing

When you add an event to a calendar that is shared with others, the people with whom the calendar is shared are invited to the event automatically.

37. Tap New Event.

38. To set an alert for the event that is different than the default, tap Alert; if you want to use the default alert, skip to step 40.

39. Tap when you want to see an alert for the event.

40. To set a second alert that is different than the default, tap Second Alert; to use the default, skip to step 42.

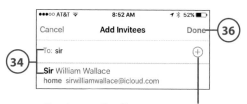

Tap to use the Contacts app to select a contact's email address

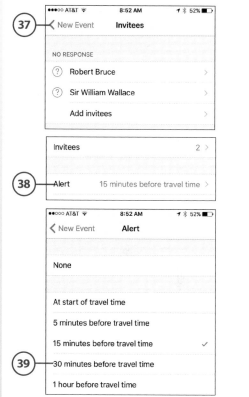

41. Tap when you want to see a second alert for the event. If you have included travel time in the event, the At start of travel time option is useful because it alerts you when your journey should begin.

42. To indicate your availability during this event, tap Show As.

43. Tap the availability status you want to indicate during the event.

44. To enter a URL associated with the event, tap in the URL field.

45. Type the URL.

46. Tap Done.

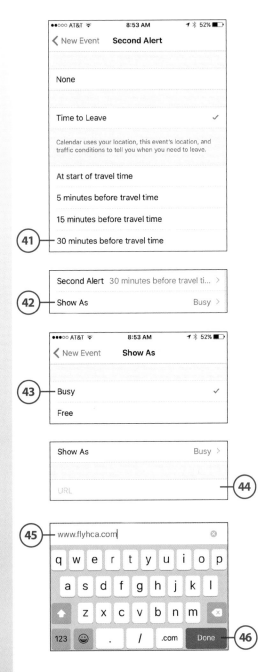

47. Tap Notes and type information you want to associate with the event.

48. Tap Add. The event is added to the calendar you selected, and invitations are sent to its invitees. Alerts trigger according to the event's settings.

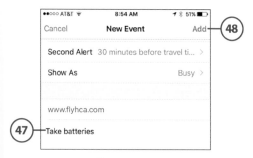

New event on the calendar

A Better Way to Create Events

Adding a lot of detail to an event in the Calendar app can be challenging. One effective and easy way to create events is to start with Siri. You can activate Siri and say something like "Create meeting with William Wallace in my office on November 15 at 10 AM." Siri creates the event with as much detail as you provided (and might prompt you to provide additional information, such as which email address to use to send invitations). When you get to a computer or iPad, edit the event to add more information, such as website links. When your calendar is updated on the iPhone, via syncing, the additional detail for the event appears in the Calendar app, too. (See Chapter 12, "Working with Siri," for detailed information about using Siri.)

Using Quick Actions the with Calendar App (iPhone 6s and 6s Plus Only)

You can use the Quick Actions feature on an iPhone 6s or 6s Plus with the Calendar app as follows:

1. Press on the Calendar icon. The Quick Actions menu appears.

2. To add a new event, choose Add Event and use the steps in the previous task to create the event.

3. To view an event, choose the event you want to see. You move to the event and can see all of its information.

Searching Calendars

You can search for events to locate specific ones quickly and easily. Here's how:

1. Tap the Search tool. A list of all your events displays.

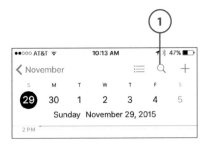

2. Tap in the Search box.

3. Type your search term. The events shown below the Search bar are those that contain your search term.

4. Swipe up or down the list to review the results.

5. Tap an event to see its detail.

6. Swipe up or down the event's screen to review its information.

7. Tap Back to return to the results.

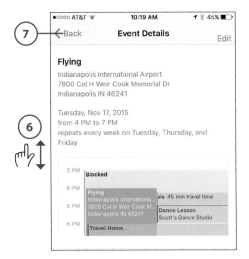

8. Continue reviewing the results until you get the information for which you were searching.

9. Tap Cancel to exit the search mode or the Clear button (x) to clear the search but remain in search mode.

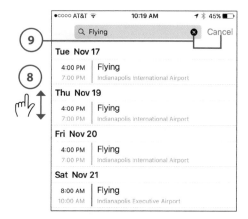

Working with Invitations

When someone invites you to an event, you receive an invitation notification in the Calendar app. You can accept these invitations, at which point the event is added to your calendar. You can tentatively accept, in which case the event is added to your calendar with a tentative status, or you can decline the event if you don't want it added to your calendar.

1. Tap the Calendar app icon when you see the badge on the app's icon indicating how many invitations you've received but not dealt with.

2. Tap Inbox (the number in parentheses is the number of invitations you have received).

3. If you have multiple invitations, swipe up and down the screen to browse them.

4. If you see enough information about the event to be able to make a decision about it, tap Accept, Maybe, or Decline. The event is added to your calendar if you tap Accept or Maybe. If you tap Decline, it is not added.

5. Tap an invitation to see its detail.

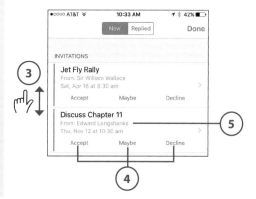

Invitation Notifications

You can use Notification settings to configure how the Calendar app informs you about invitations you receive. Refer to Chapter 4 for details. You can move to an invitation directly from its notification; for example, when a banner alert for an invitation appears on the screen, tap it to move the invitation's details.

6. Swipe up and down the Event Details screen to see all its information.

7. To see how the proposed event relates to other events on the same date, look at the section of the calendar during which the event is being proposed. You see any events that might conflict with the one to which you have been invited.

8. To choose the calendar on which the event should be shown, tap Calendar, and on the resulting screen, tap the calendar on which you want to store the event. Tap the back button located in the upper-left corner of the screen to return to the Event Details screen.

9. To view details about whom the invitation is from, tap the Invitation from bar. You move to the person's contact information (from Contacts if her information is stored there or as much as can be gleaned from the invitation if it isn't). Tap the back button located in the upper-left corner of those screens to return to the Event Details screen.

10. Tap the Reply section to see the status for each invitee to the event. You see a list of each person to whom the invitation was sent along with their current status. Tap Back to return to the Event Details screen.

11. If you want to change the event's alert, tap Alert and use the resulting Alert screen to choose an alert.

12. Use the Travel Time option to configure your travel time to the event. This works just like when you create an event (see "Adding Events to a Calendar" earlier in this chapter).

What You See Depends

Like when you create an event, the fields and options you see for an event to which you've been invited depend on the type of calendar the event is being sent from (for example, Exchange events have different options than iCloud events have). Although the details for each type of calendar are slightly different, these steps will help you deal with any invitations you receive.

13. To set your availability during the event, tap Show As and then tap your status during the event; in most cases, you tap Busy so others who want to schedule time with you will see that you aren't available.

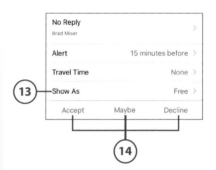

14. Indicate what you want to do with the event by tapping Accept, Maybe, or Decline. If you tap Accept or Maybe, the event is added to the calendar with the status you indicated. If you tap Decline, the event is not placed on a calendar, and the recipient receives a notice that you have declined.

After you make a decision, you move back to the Inbox. Any events you have accepted, indicated maybe, or declined disappear from the list of events. Events that you have accepted from another device, such as from a computer, are shown with an OK button, which you can tap to remove the invitation from the list.

Tap Back to move back to the Event Details screen.

15. Use steps 5 through 14 to take action on other invitations you have received or tap OK to clear events you've dealt with on other devices.

16. To review the invitations to which you've responded, tap Replied.

17. Swipe up and down the screen to review all the invitations to which you have responded. The highlight box indicates your status for each event, such as Accept for those you have accepted or Decline for those you declined (these are also marked with a strikeout through their titles).

18. Tap an event to see its details.

19. To change your current status, tap one of the other status states. For example, to accept a meeting you previously declined, tap Accept. The status changes immediately.

20. When you are done reviewing invitations, tap Done to close the Inbox. You move back to the calendar. If you accepted or indicated maybe for any events, they are added to your calendar.

Event you declined

Event you accepted

Sharing Calendars

You can share your calendars with other people to enable them to both see and change your calendar, according to the permissions you provide. If you set the View & Edit permission, the person is able to both see and change the calendar. If you set someone's permission to View Only, she can see, but not change, the calendar.

1. Move to the Calendars screen. Calendars you are sharing are indicated by the Shared with name, text just under the calendar name, where *name* is the name of the person with whom you are sharing the calendar.

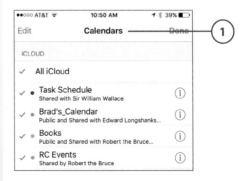

2. To see who is currently sharing a calendar, or to share a calendar, tap the Info button (i) for the calendar to be shared. If the calendar is currently being shared, the SHARED WITH section appears on the Edit Calendar screen, which contains the names of and permissions granted to the people who are sharing the calendar. The status of each person's acceptance is shown under his name (Accepted, Pending, or Declined).

3. To share a calendar with someone else (whether it is currently shared or not), tap Add Person.

4. Type and select the person's email address, and then tap Add. You return to the Edit Calendar screen, and see the person you added on the SHARED WITH list. The person you invited receives an invitation to join the calendar you are sharing. If he accepts, the shared calendar becomes available in the calendar app he uses. As people make decisions about the calendar you are sharing, the status below each invitee's name changes to reflect the current status. You also see notifications when an invitee responds if you allow the app to provide notifications to you.

5. If you don't want the person to be able to change the calendar, tap View & Edit.

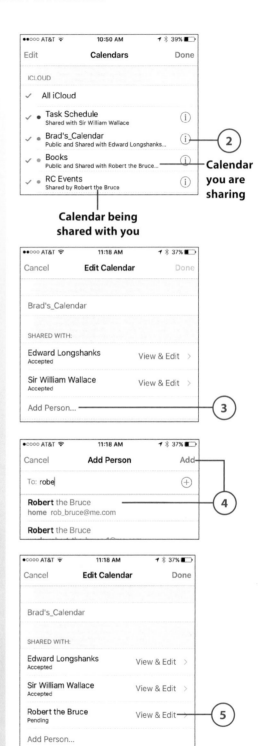

6. Slide the Allow Editing switch to off (white); the person will be able to view but not change the calendar.

7. Tap Edit Calendar.

8. When you're done sharing the calendar, tap Done.

9. When you are finished configuring calendar sharing, tap Done.

It's All in the Family

If you configure Family Sharing (see Chapter 6, "Downloading Apps, Music, Movies, TV Shows, and More onto Your iPhone"), a Family calendar is created automatically and shared with everyone who is in the group you are sharing with. By default, everyone in the group has View & Edit permissions.

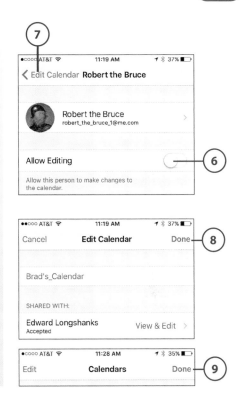

Managing Calendars, Events, and Invitations

Following are some more points about the Calendar app you might find helpful:

*   You can also use the List view when you are viewing the calendar in month view. Tap the List button (just to the left of the Search button). The list opens at the bottom of the screen and shows the events on the day currently selected (indicated in the black circle unless the day selected is today in which case the circle is red).

Swipe down to open the Notification Center

Swipe to see your events

- You can see today's events at any time by swiping down from the top of the screen to open the Notification Center. On the Today tab is a summary of your events for the day; your next event is shown just under the date at the top of the screen. Swipe up and down on the Calendar section to see the entire day's events.

Alert style event notification

Banner style event notification

- When an event's alarm goes off, an onscreen notification appears (according to the notification settings for the Calendar app) and the calendar event sound you've selected plays. When an alert notification appears, the event's title, location (if one is set), and time appear. You have to take some action. You can tap Close to dismiss the alert or tap Options to see additional choices. On the Options dialog box, tap Snooze to snooze the alarm, View Event to see its details, or Close to dismiss the alarm. When a banner notification appears, you see the event's name and location. You can tap the event to view its details or ignore it and it moves off the screen after a few moments. You can also swipe up from the bottom of the notification to manually close it.

- If an event gets canceled after you accept it or indicated maybe, you receive a notification in your Inbox that displays a strikethrough through the event's title. Tap Delete to remove the event from your calendar.

- When you receive an invitation, the event is tentatively added to your calendar until you make a decision about it. The status changes as you accept, tentatively accept, or decline invitations.

- Siri is useful for working with calendars, especially for creating events. See Chapter 12 for detailed information about using Siri.

- You can publish a calendar by making it public. When you do this, anyone who can access the shared calendar on the Web can view, but not change, the published calendar. To make a calendar public, move to its Edit Calendar screen and slide the Public Calendar switch to on (green). Tap Share Link. Then tap Mail to send the link via email, tap Message to send it via the Messages app, or tap Copy to copy the link so you can paste elsewhere. Tap AirDrop, Twitter, or Facebook to share the link in those ways. The link can be clicked to view your calendar or, if the person uses a compatible application, to subscribe to it so it appears in her calendar application.

Working with Reminders

The Reminders app does just what it sounds like it does, which is to remind you about things. The things it reminds you about are up to you; these might be to-do items/tasks, thoughts you want to be reminded to follow up on later, or anything else you can think of. Reminders are also useful for lists of things you need to get or want to remember to think about later. Just as you can have multiple calendars to manage your events, you can have multiple lists for your reminders.

Tap to see what you want to be reminded about

The badge indicates how many items you are currently being reminded of

Open the Reminders app by tapping its icon on the Home screen. Tap the list you want to view. If a list is already open, swipe down the screen to view the area showing all the reminder lists.

You can see how easily you can move between these two views. There are a couple of other views you can use, too (as you learn in a bit), but you'll likely spend most of your time on these two.

Creating Reminders

You can manually create reminders by performing the following steps:

1. Tap the Reminders icon on the Home screen.

2. If you see a reminder list instead of the list of reminder lists, skip this step. If you see the list of your reminder lists, tap the list on which you want to create a new reminder.

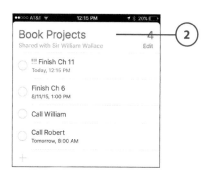

3. Tap in an open reminder space that contains the +. The keyboard appears.

4. Type the reminder.

5. To create more reminders, tap the return button on the keyboard.

6. Create the next reminder.

7. Repeat steps 5 and 6 until you've created all the reminders you want.

8. Tap Done. You can stop here if you only want basic information in the reminder, which is just the reminder's text (the app won't actually remind you unless you configure the reminder for a specific date and time). Continue these steps to fully configure a reminder.

9. Tap the reminder you want to configure for an alert.

10. Tap the info button.

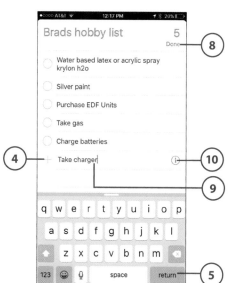

11. Slide the Remind me on a day switch to on (green) to set a specific date and time on which you want to be reminded; if you don't want the reminder to be time based, skip to step 16 instead.

12. Tap Alarm to open the date and time tool.

13. Use the date and time tool to set a time for the reminder; these work by scrolling to the desired day and time, just like when you create an event (see "Adding Events to a Calendar," earlier in this chapter).

14. To have the reminder repeated, tap Repeat, and on the resulting screen tap the repeat interval. This also works just like it does when you create an event.

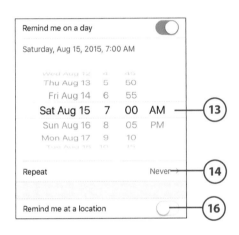

15. If you configured the reminder to repeat, tap End Repeat (this appears only when you have set a reminder to repeat). Use the tools on the End Repeat screen to set the end of the repeating event, and tap Done (this works just like setting the Repeat).

16. Slide the Remind me at a location switch to on (green) to set the reminder to be activated based on you leaving or arriving at a location; if you don't want to set this, skip to step 20.

Location Services Required

If you haven't enabled Location Services on your iPhone and for the Reminders app specifically, you're prompted to do so the first time you enable the Remind me at a location feature. You only have to do this the first time or after you disable the required Location Services.

17. Tap Location.

18. Tap Current Location, tap one of the addresses that appear on the list, or enter an address to associate the reminder with one of those locations, and then select it on the list.

19. Tap When I Arrive to be reminded when you arrive at the location you selected, or tap When I Leave to be reminded when you leave the location you selected.

20. Drag the circle to be larger or smaller to change the distance from the location at which the reminder is triggered. As you drag, the distance appears.

21. Tap Details.

Location and Time Interactions

If you set both a date/time reminder and a location reminder, you're reminded at the earliest event, such as the time passing or the change in location you set.

22. Tap the priority you want to associate with the reminder.

23. Tap List.

It's Not All Good

It Turns Out That Priorities Really Don't Matter

Note that the priority rating is just a visual indication of the reminder's importance. Currently, there are no automatic actions that happen based on priority, such as the reminder list for a given day being sorted by priority by default or getting automatic alerts for high priority items. Hopefully, the priority setting will become more useful in future versions of the iOS software.

24. Tap the list on which you want to store the reminder (reminder lists are organized by the accounts from which they come).

25. Tap Notes.

26. Type notes you want to associate with the reminder.

27. Tap Done. The reminder is complete and you return to the reminder list, where you see the reminder you created including the alert time and location and notes.

The Ultimate Assistant

Siri can handle reminders really well. Activate Siri and say something like "Remind me to take batteries to the field at 10 A.M. today." Siri creates the reminder for you. You can move to it in the Reminders app to add more detail if you want, but using Siri makes creating reminders really fast and easy. See Chapter 12 for more on Siri.

Organizing Reminders with Lists

You can keep multiple lists of reminders for different purposes. Following are some tips to help you with your lists:

- The title of the current list is shown at the top of the list screen.

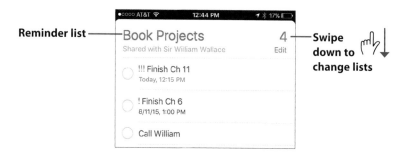

Reminder list ——— Book Projects ——— Swipe down to change lists

- To move between your lists, swipe down on the list title at the top of the screen. The list of your lists appears. Tap the list you want to view; the list and the reminders it contains appear.

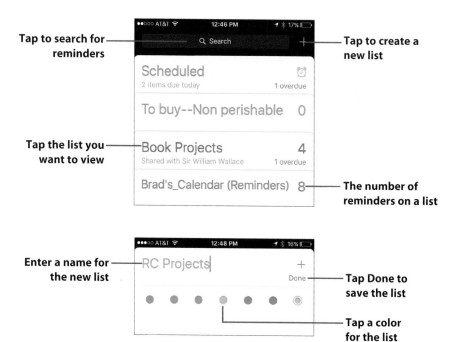

Tap to search for reminders — Tap to create a new list

Tap the list you want to view

The number of reminders on a list

Enter a name for the new list — Tap Done to save the list

Tap a color for the list

- To create a new list, tap the Add button (+), and then tap List at the prompt. Type the new list's name. Tap the color you want to associate with the list, and then tap Done. You can then assign reminders to the new list.

- To change a list, move to its screen and tap Edit. Change the list's name and tap color to change the list's color. Tap Done to save your changes.

- You can share reminder lists just like sharing calendars. Tap Edit while viewing a list, and then tap Sharing. Tap Add person, configure the people with whom you want to share the list, and then tap Add. Tap Done. After the people you invite accept the invitation, they see the list in the Reminders app on their device.

- If you enable Family Sharing, a list called "Family" is created automatically and shared with everyone on your Family Sharing list. Family Sharing is covered in "Using Family Share to Share your iTunes Store Content," in Chapter 6, "Downloading Apps, Music, Movies, TV Shows, and More onto Your iPhone."

- To delete a list, tap Edit while viewing that list. Tap Delete List and confirm this is what you want to do at the prompt. The list and all the reminders it contains are deleted.

Managing Reminders

When you have reminders set up, you can manage them using some of the tips in the following list:

- When a reminder's Remind Me time or location event occurs, you see an alert according to the notification setting for the Reminders app. If it is a banner, you can tap it to view the reminder's details or ignore it. If it is an alert, you must dismiss it or view the reminder's details.

- To mark a reminder as complete, tap its radio button. The next time you move back to the list, the reminder doesn't appear (it is moved onto your Completed list).

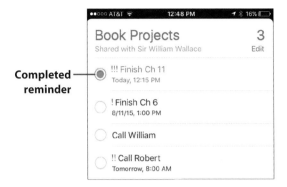

Completed reminder

- To see your completed reminders, tap Show Completed, located at the bottom of the screen. All the reminders on the list appear. Those whose radio buttons are filled with the list's color are complete. Tap Hide Completed, also located at the bottom of the screen, to show only active reminders again.

- To see your reminders organized by date instead of by list, move to the Lists screen and tap the Scheduled list (which is marked with the alarm clock icon). The Scheduled list shows your reminders based on the time and date with which they are associated. Swipe down on the word "Scheduled" to return to the List screen.

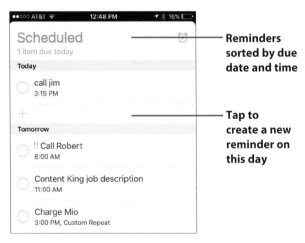

Reminders sorted by due date and time

Tap to create a new reminder on this day

- To change or delete a reminder, tap it. Edit its text if needed. Tap the Information button to change its other details. Tap Done when you've made all the changes you want to make.

- To search for reminders, move to the list of reminder lists, swipe down to open the Search bar, and type your search term in the Search bar. As you type, reminders that match your search term are shown. Tap a reminder to view it.

- To delete a reminder, swipe across it to the left and tap Delete.

Speak to Siri to send and hear messages, create events and reminders, make calls, and much more

Go here to set up Siri

Dictate text input instead of typing

In this chapter, you'll learn about all the great things you can do with your iPhone by speaking to it. Topics include the following:

→ Setting up Siri
→ Understanding Siri's personality
→ Learning how to use Siri by example
→ Getting suggestions from Siri

Working with Siri

Siri gives you the ability to talk to your iPhone to control it, get information, and to dictate text. Siri also works with lots of iPhone apps—this feature enables you to accomplish many tasks by speaking instead of using your fingers on the iPhone's screen. For example, you can hear, create, and send text messages; reply to emails; make phone and FaceTime calls; create and manage events and reminders; and much more. Using dictation, you can speak text into any supported app instead of typing. The SIRI SUGGESTIONS page presents people you communicate with, apps you use, and news you might be interested in so you do tasks very easily and quickly. The Siri Search bar is amazingly powerful and you can get to all sorts of information from one quick query.

In fact, Siri does so many things, it's impossible to list them all in a short chapter like this one; you should give Siri a try for the tasks you perform and to get the information you need, and in many cases, Siri can handle what you want to do.

Think of Siri as your own personal, digital assistant to help you do what you want to do more quickly and easily (especially when you are working in handsfree mode).

You don't have to train Siri to work with your voice either; you can speak to it normally and Siri does a great job understanding what you say. Also, you don't have to use any specific kind of phrases when you have Siri do your bidding. Simply talk to Siri like you talk to people (well, you probably won't be ordering other people around like you do Siri, but you get the idea).

Your iPhone has to be connected to the Internet for Siri and dictation to work. That's because the words you speak are sent over the Internet, transcribed into text, and then sent back to your iPhone. If your iPhone isn't connected to the Internet, this can't happen, and if you try to use it, Siri reports that it can't complete its tasks.

Because your iPhone is likely to be connected to the Internet most of the time (via Wi-Fi or a cellular network when you have cellular data enabled), this really isn't much of a limitation—but it is one you need to be aware of.

Just start speaking to your phone and be prepared to be amazed by how well it listens! You'll find many examples in this chapter to get you going with specific tasks; from there, you can explore to learn what else Siri can do for you.

Setting Up Siri

There are several settings that impact how Siri works. In most cases, you can leave these settings in their default positions (including those you selected the first time your turned your iPhone on) and start using Siri right away (beginning with "Understanding Siri's Personality" later in this chapter).

If you decide you want to make changes to Siri's settings, you can use the information in the table that follows to understand the options available to you.

To access Siri's settings, first tap the Settings icon on the Home screen, tap General, and then tap Siri. To use Siri when your iPhone isn't connected to a Wi-Fi network, you need to ensure that Cellular Data is turned on. For each of these settings, you see a description of what it does along with options (if applicable).

Settings App Explained

To get detailed information on using the Settings app, see "Working with the Settings App" in Chapter 4, "Configuring an iPhone to Suit Your Preferences."

Siri Settings

Settings Area	Location	Setting	Description
General	Siri	Siri	When on (green), Siri is ready to do your bidding. When off (white), Siri is disabled.
General	Siri	Allow "Hey Siri"	When this switch is on (green), you can activate Siri by saying, "Hey Siri" (along with the other options). The first time you turned your iPhone on, you were prompted to speak the phrases Siri uses to recognize when you want its attention. When this switch is off (white), you can only activate Siri with the other options.
General	Siri	Language	Set the language you want Siri to use to speak to you.
General	Siri	Siri Voice	Choose the accent and gender of the voice that Siri uses to speak to you (the options you see depend on the language you have selected).
General	Siri	Voice Feedback	Choose when Siri provides verbal feedback as it works for you. When Always On is selected, Siri provides verbal feedback at all times. If you want to control Siri's voice feedback with the ring (Mute) switch, choose Control with Ring Switch. If you only want voice feedback when you are operating in handsfree mode, such as when you are using the iPhone's EarPods or a Bluetooth headset, tap Handsfree Only. Regardless of this setting, you always see Siri's feedback on the screen.
General	Siri	My Info	Choose your contact information in the Contacts app, which Siri uses to address you by name, take you to your home address, etc.
General	Keyboard	Enable Dictation	When on (green), you can tap the Microphone key on the keyboard to dictate text. When off (white), the Microphone key is hidden and you can't dictate text.
Cellular	Cellular Data		When Cellular Data is on (green), your iPhone can access its cellular data network to connect to the Internet. This must be turned on for Siri to work when you aren't connected to the Internet via a Wi-Fi network.

Understanding Siri's Personality

Siri's personality is pretty simple because it follows a consistent pattern when you use it, and it always prompts you for input and direction when needed.

Siri is ready for a task

Siri is listening to you speak

If Siri is already active, tap the Microphone icon at the bottom of the screen. If not, activate Siri using one of the following methods:

- Pressing and holding the Touch ID/Home button until the Siri screen appears and you feel the phone vibrate.

- Pressing and holding the center part of the buttons on the EarPods until the Siri screen appears and you hear the Siri tone.

- Saying "Hey Siri" (if you've enabled this setting) until the Siri screen appears and you hear the Siri tone.

This puts Siri in "listening" mode and the "What can I help you with?" text appears along with a line at the bottom of the screen that shows when Siri is hearing you. This screen indicates Siri is ready for your command. If you don't speak within a second or two, Siri starts prompting you for a request and presents examples of what you can do.

Speak your command or ask a question. As you speak, the line at the bottom of the screen oscillates to show you that Siri is hearing your input, and Siri displays what it is hearing you say at the top of the screen. When you stop speaking, Siri goes into processing mode.

"Hey Siri show me my —— **What Siri heard**
appointments today"   **you say**
tap to edit

After Siri interprets what you've said, it provides two kinds of feedback to confirm what it heard: it displays what it heard on the screen and provides audible feedback to you (unless it's disabled through the settings you learned about earlier). Siri then tries to do what it thinks you've asked and shows you the outcome.

If it needs more input from you, you're prompted to provide it and Siri moves into "listening" mode automatically. If Siri asks you to confirm what it is doing or to make a selection, do so. Siri completes the action and displays what it has done; it also audibly confirms the result (again unless audible feedback is disabled as described earlier). If you want Siri to do more for you, tap the

Microphone icon at the bottom of the screen and speak your command. If you want to work with the object Siri created for you in its associated app, tap the object Siri presents.

Also, how Siri interacts with you can depend on how it was activated. For example, if you started the interaction using the verbal "Hey Siri" option, Siri assumes you want to interact verbally and may respond with other options than you would see or hear when you activate Siri manually. When you ask Siri to show you your appointments for the day in this mode, you see the summary, but then Siri asks if you want to hear the details; if you say yes, Siri reads each event to you. When you activate Siri by using the Touch ID/Home button with the same request, Siri stops after showing you the summary.

When you're done with Siri, you can lock the iPhone or tap the Touch ID/Home button to move back to the Home screen or to the app you were using.

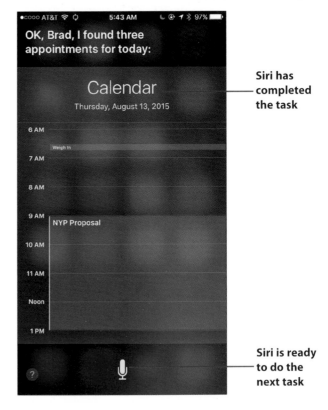

Siri has completed the task

Siri is ready to do the next task

Siri uses this pattern for all the tasks it does, but often Siri needs to get more information from you, such as when there are multiple contacts that match the command you've given. Siri prompts you for what it needs to complete the work. Generally, the more specific you make your initial command, the fewer steps you have to work through to complete it. For example, if you say "Meet Will at the park," Siri may require several prompts to get you to tell it who Will is and what time you want to meet him at the park. If you say "Meet William Wallace at the park on 10/17 at 10 am," Siri will likely be able to complete the task in one step.

The best way to learn how and when Siri can help you is to try it—a lot. You find a number of examples in the rest of this chapter to get started.

Following are some other Siri tidbits:

- If Siri doesn't automatically quit "listening" mode after you've finished speaking, tap the oscillating line. This stops "listening" mode and Siri starts processing your request. You need to do this more often when you are in a noisy environment because Siri might not be able to accurately discern the sound of you speaking versus the ambient background noise.

- If you are having trouble with Siri understanding commands, speak a bit more slowly and make sure you firmly enunciate and end your words. If you tend to have a very short pause between words, Siri might run them all together, making them into something that doesn't make sense or that you didn't intend.

- However, you can't pause too long between words or sentences because Siri interprets pauses of a certain length to mean that you are done speaking and goes into processing mode. Practicing with Siri will help you develop a good balance between speed and clarity.

- If Siri doesn't understand what you want, or if you ask it a general question, it will often perform a web search for you. Siri takes what it thinks you are looking for and does a search. You then see the results page for the search Siri performed and you might have to manually open and read the results by tapping the listing you want to see. It opens in the Safari app. In some cases, Siri reads the results to you.

- When Siri presents information to you on the screen, you can often tap that information to move into the app with which it is associated. For example, when you tap an event that Siri has created, you move into the Calendar app, where you can add more detail using that app's tools, such as inviting people to an event, changing the calendar it's associated with, and so on.

- When Siri needs direction from you, it presents your options on the screen, such as Yes, Cancel, Confirm, lists of names, and so on. You can speak these items or tap them to select them.

- Siri is very useful for some tasks, such as creating reminders, responding to text messages, and so on, but not so useful for others, such as inputting search criteria, because it can take longer to use Siri than to just type your input.

- Siri is not so good at editing text you dictate. In many cases, your only option is to replace the text you've dictated. For short text blocks, such as text messages or tweets, this can be fine, but for longer blocks of text, you have to use the virtual keyboard to make changes to just portions of text. You can use Siri to quickly dictate blocks of text and then edit the text using the iPhone's text editing tools.

- To use Siri effectively, you should experiment with it by trying to say different commands or similar commands in different ways. For example, when creating events, you can include more information in your initial command to reduce the number of steps because Siri doesn't have to ask you for more information. Saying "Meet with Wyatt Earp at 10am on 11/3 in my office" requires fewer steps than saying "Meet with Wyatt Earp" because you've given Siri all the information it needs to complete the task.

- When Siri can't complete a task that it thinks it should be able to do, it usually responds with the "I can't connect to the network right now," or "Sorry, I don't know what you mean." This indicates that your iPhone isn't connected to the Internet, the Siri server is not responding, or Siri just isn't able to complete the command for some other reason. If your iPhone is connected to the Internet, try the command again.

- When Siri can't complete a task that it knows it can't do, it will respond by telling you so. Occasionally, you can get Siri to complete the task by rephrasing it, but typically you have to use an app directly to get it done.

- If you have a passcode set to protect your iPhone's data (which you should), Siri might not be able to complete some tasks because the phone is locked. If that happens, simply unlock your phone and continue with what you were doing.

- Siri is really good at retrieving all sorts of information for you. This can include schedules, weather, directions, unit conversions, and so on. When you need something, try Siri first, as trying it is really the best way to learn how Siri can work for you.

- Siri sees all and knows all (well, not really, but it sometimes seems that way). If you want to be enlightened, try asking Siri questions. Some examples are "What is the best phone?," "Will you marry me?," "What is the meaning of life?," "Tell me a joke," etc. Some of the answers are pretty funny, and you don't always get the same ones so Siri can keep amusing you. I've heard it even has responses if you curse at it, though I haven't tried that particular option.

Learning How to Use Siri by Example

As mentioned earlier in this chapter, the best way to learn about Siri is to use it. Following are a number of tasks for which Siri is really helpful. Try these to get some experience with Siri and then explore on your own to make Siri work at its best for you.

Using Siri to Make Voice Calls

You can use Siri to make calls by speaking. This is especially useful when you are using your iPhone in handsfree mode.

1. Activate Siri (such as by pressing and holding the Touch ID/Home button).

2. Say "Call *name numberlabel*," where *name* is the person you want to call and *numberlabel* is the label of the specific number you want to call, such as Home, Work, iPhone, and so on. Siri identifies the contact you named. If the contact has only one number or you were specific about which number you want to call, Siri places the call and you move into the Phone app. If you weren't specific about the number you want to call (you simply said "Call *name*") and the person has multiple numbers, Siri lists the numbers available and asks you which number to use.

Siri has found multiple numbers for William

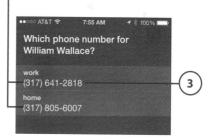

3. Speak the label for the number you want to call, or tap it. Siri dials the number for you and you move to the Phone app as if you had dialed the number yourself.

Placing FaceTime Calls

You can also use Siri to make FaceTime calls by saying "FaceTime *name*."

Composing New Email with Siri

To create email with Siri, do the following:

1. Activate Siri.

2. Say "Send email to *name*," where *name* is the person you want to email. Siri creates a new email addressed to the name you spoke. (If the recipient has more than one email address, Siri prompts you to choose the address you want to use.) Next, Siri asks you for the subject of the email.

More Than One Recipient?

To send an email to more than one recipient, say "and" between each name as in, "Send email to William Wallace and Edward Longshanks." Siri adds each address before and after the "and."

3. Speak the subject of the email. Siri inserts the subject, and then prompts you for the body of the message.

4. Speak the body of the email. As you speak, you can include punctuation; for example, to end a sentence, say the word "period" or to end a question, say the words "question mark." When Siri completes the email, it displays the message on the screen and prompts you to send it.

5. Say "send" to send the email or "cancel" to delete it. If you say "send," Siri sends the message, confirms it will be sent, and plays the sent mail sound when it is.

Replying to Emails with Siri

You can also use Siri to speak replies to emails you've read. Here's how:

1. Open the message to which you want to reply.

2. Activate Siri.

3. Say "reply to this email." Siri prompts you for what you want your reply to say.

4. Complete and send the reply; this works just like when you create a new message.

>>>Go Further

DOING MORE IN EMAIL WITH SIRI

Following are some other ways to use Siri for email:

- If you tell Siri to "Read email," Siri tells you how many emails are in your Inboxes and starts reading the time and date of the most recent email message followed by the subject and sender of the message. Siri then does the same for the next email until it has read a number of them. When it gets to the last message it reads, it prompts you to ask if you want to hear the entire list. On the screen, Siri lists the emails; you can tap an email message to read it yourself.

- Siri can read the content of email messages to you when you speak commands that tell it which email you want it to read, such as "Read most recent email," or "Read last email from William Wallace." Siri reads the entire message to you.

- To edit an email Siri created, say "Change." Siri prompts you to change the subject, change the message, cancel it, or send it. If you choose one of the change options, you can replace the subject or the body of the message. To change just some of the subject or body or to change the recipients, tap the message and edit it in the Mail app.

- You can start a new and completely blank email by saying "New email." Siri prompts you for the recipients, subject, and body.

- You can address a new email and add the subject with one statement, such as "Send email to William Wallace about flying."

- You can retrieve your email at any time by activating Siri and saying "Check email." Siri checks for new email and then announces how many emails you have received since the oldest message in your Inboxes was received. If you don't have any new email messages. Siri announces how many emails you have received.

- You can determine if you have emails from a specific person by asking something like, "Any email from William Wallace?" Siri's reply includes the number of emails in your Inboxes from William and displays them on the screen. Tap an email to read it.

- You can forward an email you are reading by saying "Forward this email" and then following Siri's lead to complete the process.

Having Messages Read to You

The Messages app is among the best to use with Siri because you can speak just about any task you would normally do with messages. Especially useful is Siri's ability to read new messages to you. When you receive new text messages, do the following to have Siri read them to you:

1. When you receive a text notification, activate Siri.

2. Speak the command "Read new text messages." Siri reads all the new text messages you've received, announcing the sender before reading each message. You have the option to reply (covered in the next task) or have Siri read the message again.

Siri is reading a text message

Siri reads each new message in turn until it has read all of them and then announces, "That's it" to let you know it has read all of them.

Siri only reads new text messages to you when you aren't on the Messages screen. If you've already read all your messages and you aren't in the Messages app, when you speak the command "Read text messages," Siri tells you that you have no new messages.

Reading Old Messages

To read an old message, move back to the conversation containing the message you want to hear. Activate Siri and say the command "Read text message." Siri reads the most recent text message to you.

Replying to Messages with Siri

You can also use Siri to speak replies to messages you've received. Here's how:

1. Listen to a message.

2. At the prompt, say "Reply." Siri prepares a reply to the message.

3. Speak your reply. Siri displays your reply.

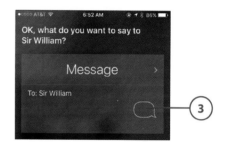

4. At the prompt, say "Send" to send it, "Cancel" to delete it, or "Change" to replace it. If you tell Siri that you want to send the message, Siri sends it and then confirms that it was sent.

Sending New Messages with Siri

To send a new message to someone, do the following:

1. Activate Siri.

2. Say "Send text to *name*," where *name* is the person you want to text. Siri confirms your command and prepares to hear your text message.

3. Speak your message. Siri listens and then prepares your message.

4. If you want to send the message, say "Send." Siri sends the message.

>>>*Go Further*
DOING MORE MESSAGING WITH SIRI

Following are some other ways to use Siri with messaging:

- If you say "Change" after you have created a new message, Siri prompts you to replace the message with a different one. If you say "Review" after creating a new message, Siri reads your message back to you. If you say "Cancel," Siri stops the process and deletes the message.

- To send a text message to more than one recipient, say "and" between each name, as in, "Send text to William Wallace and Edward Longshanks."

- You can speak punctuation, such as "period" or "question mark" to add it to your message.

- You can tap buttons that Siri presents on the screen, such as Send or Cancel, to take those actions on the message you are working on.

- Messages you receive or send via Siri are stored in the Messages app just like messages you receive or send by tapping and typing.

- You can dictate into a text message you start in the Messages app (you learn about dictating later in this chapter).

Using Siri to Create Events

Siri is useful for capturing meetings and other events you want to add to your calendars. To create an event by speaking, do the following steps:

1. Activate Siri.

2. Speak the event you want to create. There are a number of variations in what you can say. Examples include "Set up a meeting with William Wallace on Friday at 10 am," "Doctor appt on Thursday at 1 pm," and so on. If you have any conflicts with the event you are setting up, Siri lets you know about them.

Invitees

If you include the name of someone for whom you have an email address, Siri automatically sends invitations. If you include a name that matches more than one contact, Siri prompts you to choose the contact you want to invite. If the name doesn't match a contact, Siri enters the name but doesn't send an invitation.

3. Say "Confirm" if you don't have any conflicts or "Yes" if you do and you still want to have the appointment confirmed; you can also tap Confirm. Siri adds the event to your calendar. Say "Cancel" to cancel the event.

4. To add more information to an event Siri has created for you, tap it on the confirmation screen. You move into the Calendar app and can edit the event just like events you create within that app.

Using Siri to Create Reminders

Using Siri to create reminders is one of the more useful things you can do with Siri, assuming you find reminders useful of course. Here's how:

1. Activate Siri.

2. Speak the reminder you want to create. Examples include "Remind me to buy the A-10 at Motion RC," "Remind me to finish Chapter 10 at 10 a.m. on Saturday," "Remind me to buy milk when I leave work," and so on. Siri provides a confirmation of what you asked. If you didn't mention a time or date when you want to be reminded, Siri prompts you to provide the details of when you want to be reminded.

3. Speak the date and time when you want to be reminded. If you included a date and time in your original reminder request, you skip this step. Unlike some of the other tasks, Siri creates the reminder without confirming it with you.

4. If you don't want to keep the reminder, activate Siri and say "Remove."

5. To add detail to the reminder, tap it. You move into the Reminders app and can add more information to the reminder as you can when you create one manually.

>>>Go Further

GOING FURTHER WITH SIRI TO MANAGE TIME

Following are some other ways to use Siri with the Calendar, Reminders, and Clock apps:

- You can change events with Siri, too. For example, if you have a meeting at 3 p.m., you can move it by saying something like "Move my 3 pm meeting to Friday at 6 pm."

- You can get information about your events with Siri by saying things such as "Show me today's appointments," "Do I have meetings on November 3?," "What time is my first appointment tomorrow?," "What are my appointments tomorrow?," and so on. Siri tells you about the events and shows you what they are on the screen. You can tap any event to view it in the Calendar app.

- You can speak to your iPhone to set alarms. Tell Siri what you want and when you want the alarm to be set. For example, you can say something like "New alarm *alarmname* 6 am tomorrow," where *alarmname* is the label of the alarm. Siri sets an alarm to go off at that time and gives it the label you speak. It displays the alarm on the screen along with a status button so you can turn it off if you change your mind. You don't have to label alarms, and you can just say something like "Set alarm 6 am tomorrow." However, a label can be useful to issue other commands. For example, if an alarm has a name, you can turn off an alarm by saying "Turn off *alarmname*." Any alarms you create with Siri can be managed just like alarms you create directly in the Clock app.

- To set a countdown timer, tell Siri to "Set timer for x minutes," where x is a number of minutes (you can do the same to set a timer for seconds or hours, too). Siri starts a countdown for you and presents it on the screen. You can continue to use the iPhone however you want. When the timer ends, you see and hear an alert. You can also reset the time, pause it, and so on by speaking.

- You can get information about time by asking questions, such as "What time is it?," "What is the date?," and so on. You can add location information to the time information, too, as in "What time is it in London, England?"

- Tapping any confirmation Siri displays takes you back into the related app. For example, if you tap a clock that results from your asking what time it is, you can tap that clock to move into the Clock app. If you ask about your schedule today, you can tap any of the events Siri presents to move back into the Calendar app to work with them.

- When you use Siri to create events and reminders, they are created on your default calendar (events) or reminder list (reminders).

Using Siri to Get Information

Siri is a great way to get information about lots of different topics in many different areas. You can ask Siri for information about a subject, places in your area, unit conversion (such as inches to centimeters), and so on. Just try speaking what you want to learn to best get the information you need. Here's an example looking for pizza places in my area:

1. Activate Siri.

2. Say something like, "Show me pizza restaurants close to me." Siri presents a list of results that match your query and even provides a summary of reviews at the top of the screen. (You must have Location Services enabled for this to work. Refer to Chapter 4 for information about configuring Location Services.)

Siri is also useful for getting information about topics. Siri responds by conducting a web search and showing you the result. For example, suppose you want to learn about William Wallace. Activate Siri and say, "Tell me about William Wallace." Siri responds with information about your topic. You can have Siri read the information by activating Siri and saying "Read." Siri reads the results (this doesn't always work; it works best when the results are presented via Wikipedia or something similar).

If you like pizza (or just about anything else), Siri can help you find it.

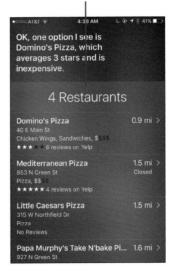

Want to learn about something? Just ask Siri.

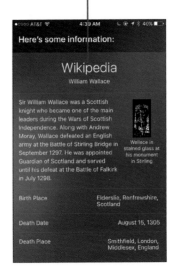

Using Siri to Play Music

You can also play music by telling Siri which music you want to hear.

1. Activate Siri.

2. Tell Siri the music you want to hear. There are a number of variations in what you can say. Examples include "Play album Time of My Life," "Play song Gone by Switchfoot," "Play playlist Jon McLaughlin," and so on. Siri provides a confirmation of what you asked and begins playing the music.

3. To move into the Music app to control the music with your fingers, tap Open Music.

>>>Go Further

MORE SPOKEN COMMANDS FOR MUSIC

There are a number of commands you can speak to find, play, and control music (and other audio). "Play *artist*" plays music by the artist you speak. "Play *album*" plays the album you name. In both cases, if the name includes the word "the," you need to include "the" when you speak the command. "Shuffle" plays a random song. "Play more like this" uses the Genius to find songs similar to the one playing and plays them. "Previous track" or "next track" does exactly what they sound like they do. To hear the name of the artist for the song currently playing, say "Who sings this song?" You can shuffle music in an album or playlist by saying "Shuffle playlist *playlistname*." You can stop the music, pause it, or play it by speaking those commands.

Using Siri to Get Directions

With Siri, it's easy to get directions—you don't even have to stop at a gas station to ask.

1. Activate Siri.

2. Speak something like "Show me directions from Indianapolis Motor Speedway to Lucas Oil Stadium." If you don't include the "from" part, Siri assumes you want directions from your current location (as in "Show me directions to Lucas Oil Stadium").

3. If Siri needs you to confirm one or more of the locations, tap the correct one. Siri uses the Maps app to generate directions.

4. To start turn-by-turn instructions, tap Start.

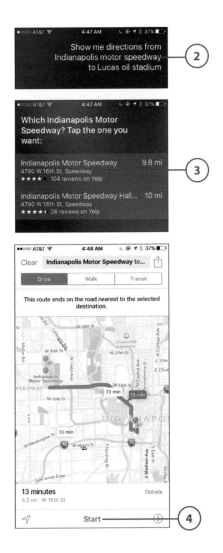

It's Not All Good

Voice commands to Siri work very well, but they aren't perfect. Make sure you confirm your commands by listening to the feedback Siri provides when it repeats them or reviewing the feedback Siri provides on the screen. Sometimes, a spoken command can have unexpected results, which can include making a phone call to someone in the Contacts app. If you don't catch such a mistake before the call is started, you might be surprised to hear someone answering your call instead of hearing music you intended to play. You can put Siri in listening mode by tapping the Microphone button, and then saying "no" or "stop" to stop Siri should a verbal command go awry.

Using Dictation to Speak Text Instead of Typing

You can use the iPhone's dictation capability to speak text into any app, such as Mail, Messages, and so on. In fact, any time you see the Microphone button on the keyboard, dictation is available to you. Here's how this works:

1. In the app you are using, put the cursor where you want the text you will dictate to start. For example, if you are creating an email, tap in the body.

2. Tap the Microphone key on the virtual keyboard.

3. Speak the text you want to add. For instance, when you create a new message, you can speak punctuation, but in this mode, you can create a new paragraph by saying "new paragraph." While you are speaking, you see the line that oscillates as you speak and the text you are speaking at the location of the cursor.

4. Tap Done when you finish your dictation. The Dictation box closes, and the keyboard reappears. The text you spoke is part of the message. From there, you can edit it just like text you've typed.

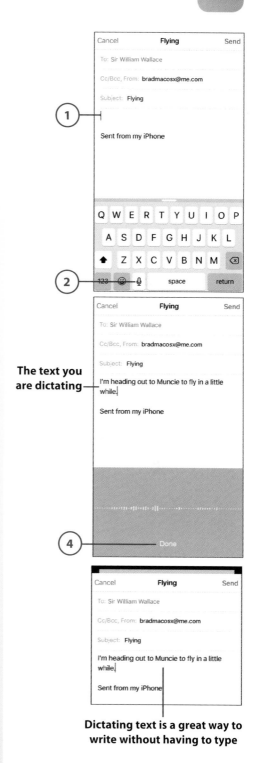

The text you are dictating

Dictating text is a great way to write without having to type

Using Siri to Open Apps

As you accumulate apps on your iPhone, it can take several taps and swipes to get to a specific app, such as one that is stored in a folder that isn't on the page of the Home screen you are viewing. With Siri, you can open any app on your phone with a simple command.

1. Activate Siri.

2. Say "Open *appname*," where *appname* is the name of the app you want to open. Siri opens the app for you, and you move to the last screen in that app you were using.

Getting Suggestions from Siri

New! This chapter has focused on speaking to Siri and having it perform your command, but Siri has a few more tricks up its digital sleeve. In addition to its amazing ability to respond to your voice, Siri also provides the very useful SIRI SUGGESTIONS screen. This screen shows you the people you've interacted with recently and makes it easy to contact them again. It also shows apps you have used recently. In the NEARBY section, you see locations that might be of interest to you based on your current location. At the bottom of the screen, you see news that might be of interest to you.

No Siri Suggestions?

If you don't see the SIRI SUGGESTIONS screen, open the Settings app, tap General, tap Spotlight Search, and set the Siri Suggestions switch to on (green).

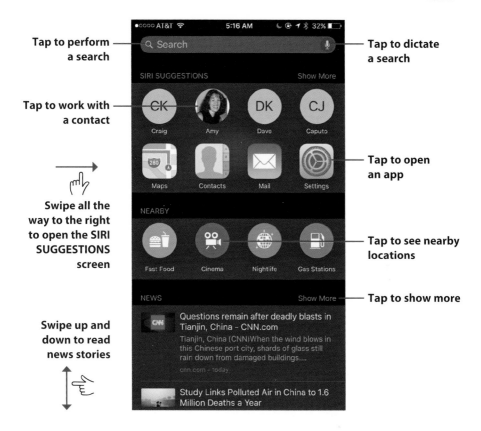

Tap to perform a search

Tap to dictate a search

Tap to work with a contact

Tap to open an app

Swipe all the way to the right to open the SIRI SUGGESTIONS screen

Tap to see nearby locations

Tap to show more

Swipe up and down to read news stories

To access Siri suggestions, move to the Home screen and swipe all the way to the right. The SIRI SUGGESTIONS screen appears. On this screen you can do the following:

Search term

Search results

- Tap in the Search bar to type a search or tap the Microphone to dictate a search. Siri presents the results of the search to you based on the source of information, such as Wikipedia, a web search, YouTube, and so on. You can tap a result to move to it. You can also tap the commands at the bottom of the screen, such as Search App Store, to search in other places.

- Tap Show More to expand any of the sections you see, such as SIRI SUGGESTIONS. The section opens so you see more of its information.

Tap to see the contact's information

Tap to communicate with the contact

- Tap a contact to reveal options you can use to communicate with her via a phone call, message, or FaceTime; tap the Info button (i) to move to the contact's information in the Contacts app.

- Tap an app you've used recently to return to it.

- Tap a category of location shown in the NEARBY section to move to the Maps app and see a list of places of that type. You can use the Maps app to quickly get directions to a specific location.

- Swipe up and down in the NEWS section to browse news stories. Tap a story to read its detail in the News app.

Tap to configure Safari

Tap to have the World Wide Web in the palm in your hand

In this chapter, you explore the amazing web browsing functionality your iPhone has to offer. Topics include the following:

→ Setting Safari preferences
→ Visiting websites
→ Viewing websites
→ Working with multiple websites at the same time
→ Searching the Web
→ Saving and organizing bookmarks
→ Using 3D Touch with Safari
→ Sharing web pages
→ Completing forms on the Web
→ Signing in to websites automatically

Surfing the Web

The Web has become an integral part of most of our lives. It is often the first step to search for information, make plans (such as travel arrangements), conduct financial transactions, shop, and so much more. Safari on the iPhone puts the entire Web in the palm of your hand. Safari is a full-featured web browser; anything you can do on a website in a browser on a computer can be done with Safari on your iPhone.

Setting Safari Preferences

Like most apps, Safari offers settings you can use to adjust the way it works. You can likely use Safari with its default settings just fine; when the time comes that you want to tweak how Safari works for you, use the following table as a reference for the settings available to you. To access these settings, tap the Settings icon on the Home screen, and then tap Safari.

Safari Settings

Settings Area	Location	Setting	Description
SEARCH	Search Engine	Search Engine	Enables you to choose your default search tool; the options are Google (default), Yahoo, Bing, or DuckDuckGo.
SEARCH	N/A	Search Engine Suggestions	When this switch is on (green), Safari asks your default search engine for suggestions related to what you type in the Address/Search bar. This makes search easier because you can type your search term in the bar instead of first moving to the search web page.
SEARCH	N/A	Safari Suggestions	When this switch is on (green), Safari makes suggestions related to what you type in the Address/Search bar. This makes search easier because you can type your search term in the bar instead of first moving to the search webpage.
SEARCH	Quick Website Search	Quick Website Search	When this switch is on (green), you can perform a search at a specific website by typing its name before your search term. For example, you can type "wiki william wallace" in the Address/Search box and the first section of the results will be entries in the Wikipedia related to William Wallace; this saves you the steps of moving to the search engine results, and then tapping the articles you want to read because you can do this directly from the Search screen instead.
SEARCH	N/A	Preload Top Hit	When this switch is on (green), the sites you move to or find more frequently are loaded while you search, making accessing them faster.
GENERAL	Passwords	Passwords	When you tap this setting and confirm your security (with Touch ID or a passcode), you see the list of passwords stored on your iPhone. Tap a password to see its details or edit it. Swipe to the left on a password, and then tap Delete to remove it.
GENERAL	Autofill	Autofill	These settings enable you to automatically log in to websites and to quickly complete forms on the Web by automatically filling in key information for you. Set the Use Contact Info switch to on (green), and then tap your contact information in the Contacts app. You can determine what data is saved on your iPhone by setting the following switches on (green) or off (white): Names and Passwords or Credit Cards. Tap Saved Credit Cards to view or change existing credit card information or to add new credit cards to Safari.

Settings Area	Location	Setting	Description
GENERAL	N/A	Frequently Visited Sites	When this switch is on (green) and you move into the Address/Search bar, Safari shows a section of sites that you visit frequently, making them easier to return to.
GENERAL	Favorites	Favorites	Use this option to choose the folder of bookmarks for sites that you use most frequently. The bookmarks in the folder you select appear at the top of the screen when you move into the Address/Search bar, making them fast and easy to use.
GENERAL	Open Links	Open Links	This tells Safari the option you want to see when you tap and hold a link on a current web page to open a new web page. The In New Tab option causes Safari to open and immediately take you to a new tab displaying the web page with which a link is associated. The In Background option causes Safari to open pages in the background for links you tap so you can view them later.
GENERAL	N/A	Block Pop-ups	Some websites won't work properly with pop-ups blocked, so you can use this setting to temporarily enable pop-ups by sliding the switch to off (white). When the Block Pop-ups switch is on (green), pop-ups are blocked.
PRIVACY & SECURITY	N/A	Do Not Track	To enable private browsing, which means Safari doesn't track and keep a list of the sites you visit, set the Do Not Track switch to on (green). With this setting on, you won't be able to use the History list to return to sites you visited.
PRIVACY & SECURITY	Block Cookies	Block Cookies	Enables you to choose the kind of cookies you want to allow to be stored on your iPhone. The Always Block option blocks all cookies. The Allow from Current Website Only setting allows cookies only from the website you are currently viewing to be stored on your phone. Allow from Websites I Visit blocks cookies from sites you didn't visit directly. This is the setting I recommend you choose because it enables websites you visit to store information on your iPhone while blocking cookies from sites you didn't visit. The Always Allow option accepts all cookies (not recommended).
PRIVACY & SECURITY	N/A	Fraudulent Website Warning	If you don't want Safari to warn you when you visit websites that appear to be fraudulent, set the Fraudulent Website Warning switch to off (white).

Settings Area	Location	Setting	Description
PRIVACY & SECURITY	N/A	Clear History and Website Data	When you tap this command and confirm it by tapping Clear History and Data at the prompt, Safari removes the websites you have visited from your history list. The list starts over, so the next site you visit is added to your history list again—unless you have enabled private browsing. It also removes all cookies and other website data that have been stored on your iPhone.
READING LIST	N/A	Use Cellular Data	The Reading List enables you to store web pages on your iPhone for offline reading. If you want to allow pages to be saved to your iPhone when you are using its cellular data connection, slide the Use Cellular Data switch to the on (green) position. When it is off (white) you can only use this feature when connected to Wi-Fi.
Advanced	Website Data	Website Data	Website Data displays the amount of data associated with websites you have visited; swipe up on the screen and tap Remove All Website Data to clear this data.
Advanced	N/A	JavaScript	Set this switch to off (white) to disable JavaScript functionality (however, some sites won't work properly without JavaScript).
Advanced	N/A	Web Inspector	This switch controls a feature that is used by website developers to see how their sites work on an iPhone.

Making Cookies

Cookies are data that websites store on the device you use to browse them. Cookies can contain data about you, such as areas you last visited or things in which you are interested. Cookies are typically used to direct you back to these areas or point you to related areas. Most of the time, cookies are harmless and can even be helpful to you, at least from legitimate sites you intentionally visit.

Visiting Websites

If you've used a web browser on a computer before, using Safari on an iPhone is a familiar experience. If you've not used a web browser before, don't worry because using Safari on an iPhone is simple and intuitive.

Syncing Bookmarks

Using iCloud, you can synchronize your Internet Explorer favorites or Safari bookmarks on a Windows PC—or Safari bookmarks on a Mac—to your iPhone so you have the same set of bookmarks available available on your phone that you do on your computer and other devices, and vice versa (refer to Chapter 3, "Setting Up and Using iCloud and Other Online Accounts"). You should enable iCloud's Safari switch before you start browsing on your iPhone, so you avoid typing URLs or re-creating bookmarks. When you enable Safari syncing via iCloud, you can also view tabs open in Safari on other devices, such as a Mac or an iPad.

Using Bookmarks to Move to Websites

Using bookmarks you've synced via iCloud onto your iPhone makes it easy to get to websites that are of interest to you. You can also create bookmarks on your iPhone (you learn how later in this chapter) and use them just like bookmarks you've synced onto the iPhone.

1. On the iPhone Home screen, tap Safari.

2. Tap the Bookmarks button.

Back to the Bookmarks

The most recent Bookmarks screen is retained when you move away from Bookmarks and then come back. Each time you open your Bookmarks, you're at the same place you were when you left it.

3. Tap the Bookmarks tab (the open book) if it isn't selected already. (If you don't see this tab, tap the back button in the upper-left corner of the screen until you do.)

4. Swipe up or down the list of bookmarks to browse the bookmarks and other folders of bookmarks available to you.

5. To move to a bookmark, skip to step 10; to open a folder of bookmarks, tap it.

Your Favorites bookmark folder

Bookmark

Folder containing bookmarks

6. Swipe up or down the folder's screen to browse the folders and bookmarks it contains.

7. You can tap a folder to see the bookmarks it contains.

Change Your Mind?

If you decide not to visit a bookmark, tap Done. You return to the page you were previously viewing.

---

8. To return to a previous screen, tap the back button in the upper-left corner of the screen, which is labeled with the name of the folder you previously visited (the parent folder); this disappears when you are at the top-level Bookmarks screen

9. Repeat steps 5–8 until you see a bookmark you want to visit.

10. Tap the bookmark you want to visit. Safari moves to that website.

11. Use the information in the section "Viewing Websites" later in this chapter to get information on viewing the web page.

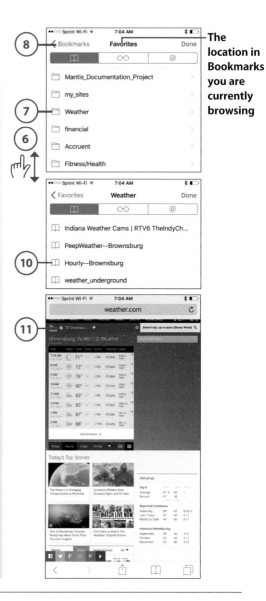

The location in Bookmarks you are currently browsing

Playing Favorites

You might see two Favorites folders on the Bookmarks screen. The folder marked with a star is the folder you designated, using the Safari settings described previously in this chapter, as the place to store Favorites on your iPhone. If you use Safari on a computer, you can also configure bookmarks and folders of bookmarks on its Bookmarks bar. When these bookmarks are synced from your computer to the iPhone, they might be stored in a folder of bookmarks also called Favorites and shown with the standard folder icon. If you set this synced folder in your iPhone's Safari settings to also be its Favorites folder, you won't have to deal with this potentially confusing situation of having two Favorites folders.

iPhone Web Pages

Some websites have been specially formatted for mobile devices. These typically have less complex information on each page, so they load faster. When you move to a site like this, you might be redirected to the mobile version automatically, or you might be prompted to choose which version of the site you want to visit. On the mobile version, there is typically a link that takes you to the "regular" version, too. (It's sometimes called the Desktop, Full, or Classic version.) Sometimes the version formatted for handheld devices offers less information or fewer tools than the regular version. Because Safari is a full-featured browser, you can use either version.

Using Your Favorites to Move to Websites

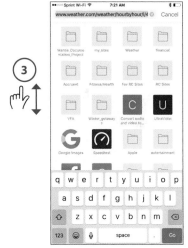

Using the Safari settings described earlier, you can designate a folder of bookmarks as your Favorites. You can get to the folders and bookmarks in your Favorites folder more quickly and easily than navigating to it as described in the previous section. Here's how to use your Favorites:

1. On the Home screen, tap Safari. (If you are in Safari and have the Bookmarks screen open, tap Done to close it.)

2. Tap in the Address/Search bar (if you don't see the Address/Search bar, tap at the top of the screen to show it). Just below the Address/Search bar are your Favorites (bookmarks and folders of bookmarks). The keyboard opens at the bottom of the screen.

3. Swipe up and down on your Favorites. The keyboard closes to give you more room to browse.

More Commands

At the top of the Favorites screen, you might see two more commands. Tap Add to Favorites to add a bookmark to the current site to your Favorites folder. Tap Request Desktop Site if you are currently viewing the mobile version of a site and want to see the "full" version; you move to that version after you tap the command.

4. To move to a bookmark, tap it and skip to step 8.

5. To move into a folder, tap it.

6. Continue browsing your Favorites until you find the bookmark you want to use. Like using the Bookmarks screen, you can tap a folder to move into it, tap a bookmark to move to its website, or tap the back button to move to the previous screen.

7. Tap the bookmark for the site you want to visit.

8. Use the information in the section "Viewing Websites" later in this chapter to view the web page.

Folder of bookmarks

Bookmark

Typing URLs to Move to Websites

A Uniform Resource Locator (URL) is the Internet address of a web page. URLs can be relatively simple, such as www.apple.com, or they can be quite long and convoluted. The good news is that by using bookmarks, you can save a URL in Safari so you can get back to it using its bookmark (as you learned in the previous two tasks) and thus avoid typing URLs. To use a URL to move to a website, do the following:

1. On the Home screen, tap Safari. (If you are in Safari and have the Bookmarks screen open, tap Done to close it.)

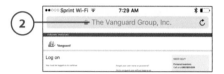

2. Tap in the Address/Search bar (if you don't see the Address/Search bar, tap at the top of the screen). The URL of the current page becomes highlighted, or if you haven't visited a page, the Address/Search bar is empty. Just below the Address/Search bar, your Favorites are displayed. The keyboard appears at the bottom of the screen.

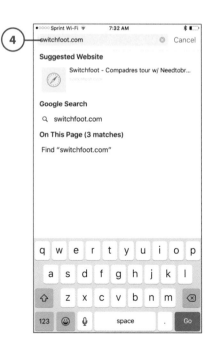

3. If an address appears in the Address/Search bar, tap the clear button (x) to remove it.

4. Type the URL you want to visit. If it starts with www (which almost all URLs do), you don't have to type "www". As you type, Safari attempts to match what you are typing to a site you have visited previously and completes the URL for you if it can. Just below the Address/Search bar, Safari presents a list of sites that might be what you are looking for, organized into groups, such as Suggested Websites.

Shortcut for Typing URLs

URLs include a top-level domain code that represents the type of site (theoretically anyway) that URL leads to. Common examples are .com (commercial sites), and .edu (educational sites). To quickly enter a URL's code, tap and hold the period key to see a menu from which you can select other options, such as .net, or .edu. Select the code you want on the keyboard, and it is entered in the Address/Search bar.

5. If one of the sites shown is the one you want to visit, tap it. You move to that web page; skip to step 8.

6. If Safari doesn't find a match, continue typing until you enter the entire URL.

7. Tap Go. You move to the web page.

8. Use the information in the section "Viewing Websites" to view the web page.

Using Your Browsing History to Move to Websites

As you move about the Web, Safari tracks the sites you visit and builds a history list (unless you enabled the Do Not Track option, in which case this doesn't happen and you can't use History to return to previous sites). You can use your browsing history list to return to sites you've visited.

1. Tap the Bookmarks button.

2. If you aren't on the Bookmarks screen, tap the back button until you move to the Bookmarks screen. (Safari remembers your last location, so if you were last on the Bookmarks screen, you don't need to tap any buttons to get back there.)

3. If necessary, swipe down the Bookmarks page until you see the History folder.

4. Tap History.

5. Swipe up and down the page to browse all the sites you've visited. The more recent sites appear at the top of the screen; the further you move down the screen, the further back in time you go. Earlier sites are collected in folders for various times, such as This Morning, or Monday Afternoon.

6. Tap the site you want to visit. The site opens and you can use the information in the section "Viewing Websites" to view the web page.

Erasing the Past

To clear your browsing history, tap the Clear button at the bottom of the History screen. At the prompt, tap the timeframe that you want to clear; the options are The last hour, Today, Today and yesterday, or All time. Your browsing history for the period of time you selected is erased. (Don't you wish it was this easy to erase the past in real life?)

Viewing Websites

Even though your iPhone is a small device, you'll be amazed at how well it displays web pages designed for larger screens.

1. Use Safari to move to a web page as described in the previous tasks.

Where Did the URL Go?

When you first move to a URL, you see that URL in the Address/Search bar. After you work with a site, the URL is replaced with the high-level domain name for the site (such as sitename.com, sitename.edu, etc.). To see the full URL again, tap the Address/Search bar.

2. To browse around a web page, swipe your finger right or left, or up or down.

3. To zoom in manually, unpinch your fingers.

4. To zoom in automatically, tap your finger on the screen twice.

5. To zoom out manually, pinch your fingers.

6. To zoom on a column or a figure, tap it twice.

7. To move to a link, tap it once. Links can come in many forms including text (most text that is a link is in color and underlined) or graphics. The web page to which the link points opens and replaces the page currently being displayed.

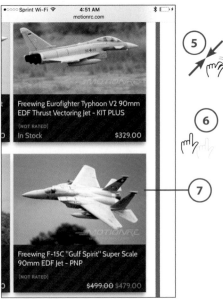

Do More with Links

To see options for a link, tap and hold your finger down for a second or so. When you lift your finger, a menu appears. Tap Open to open the page to replace the current page at which the link points (this is the same as tapping a link once). Tap Open in Background to open the page in a new Safari window that opens in the background, or tap Open in New Tab to open the new page in the new tab. The command that appears depends on the Open Links Safari setting. Tap Add to Reading List to add the page to your Reading List. If the link is an image, tap Save Image to save the image on your phone. Tap Copy to copy the link's URL so that you can paste it elsewhere, such as in an email message. Tap Cancel to return to the current page and take no action.

8. To view the web page in landscape orientation, rotate the iPhone so that it is horizontal.

9. Scroll, zoom in, and zoom out on the page to read it, as described in steps 2–7.

10. To refresh a page, tap Refresh. (Note: while a page is loading, this is the "x" button; tap it to stop the rest of the page from loading.)

11. To move to a previous page you've visited, tap the back button (left-facing arrow).

12. To move to a subsequent page, tap the forward button (right-facing arrow).

13. As you move around, the Address/Search bar at the top of the page and the toolbar at the bottom of the page are hidden automatically; to show them again, tap the top or bottom of the screen (on the iPhone 6 and 6s Plus, tap the top of the screen when the phone is horizontal).

Different Phones Different Look

The type of iPhone you are using to browse the Web affects how pages look and where controls are located. For example, when you use an iPhone 5s, you see black at the top and bottom of the screen while you see white there on an iPhone 6. Also, when you rotate an iPhone 5s, the tools are at the top and bottom of the screen, while on an iPhone 6, the controls are at all the top of the screen.

Working with Multiple Websites at the Same Time

When you move to a web page by using a bookmark, typing a URL, or tapping a link on the current web page, the new web page replaces the current one. However, you can also open and work with multiple web pages at the same time so that a new web page doesn't replace the current one.

When you work with multiple web pages, each open page appears in its own tab. You can use the tab view to easily move to and manage your open web pages. You can also close open tabs, and you can even open web pages that are open on other devices on which your iCloud account has been configured and Safari syncing enabled.

There are two ways to open a new web page in a new tab. One is to tap and hold on a link on the current web page; you can use the resulting Open command to open the new page. There are two options for this approach; the one you use is determined by the Open Links preference set as described earlier in this chapter. The In Background option causes the new page to open and move to the background. This is most useful when you want to read the new page at a later time, such as when you are done with the current one. The In New Tab option causes the new page to open and move to the front so you see it instantly while moving the current page and its tab to the background.

The second way to open a new web page in a new tab is by using the Tab Manager.

All these options are described in the following tasks.

Tapping without Holding

When you tap, but don't hold down a link on a web page, the web page to which the link points opens and replaces the current web page—no new tab is created. When you tap and hold a link, the behavior is determined by the setting you chose in the preferences as covered in a task earlier in this chapter ("Setting Safari Preferences").

Opening New Pages in the Background

If you enabled the In Background option for the Open Links preference, you can open new web pages by doing the following:

1. Tap and hold on the link you want to open in the background.

2. Tap Open in Background. The page to which the link points opens. The only result you see is the page "jumping" down to the Tab Manager button in the lower-right corner of the screen.

3. Continue opening pages in the background; see "Using Tab View to Manage Open Web Pages" to learn how to use the tab view to move to pages that are open in the background.

Opening New Pages in a New Tab

If you enabled the In New Tab option for the Open Links preference, you can open new pages by doing the following:

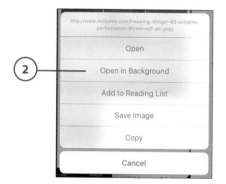

1. Tap and hold on the link you want to open in the background.

2. Tap Open in New Tab. A new tab opens and displays the page to which the link points. The web page from which you started moves into the background.

3. Continue opening pages; see "Using Tab View to Manage Open Web Pages" to learn how to use the tab view to manage your open pages.

Just Open It

If you tap the Open command on the menu in step 2 of the previous tasks, the new web page replaces the one you were viewing on the current tab. This is the same as just tapping a link on the page rather than tapping and holding on it.

Using Tab View to Manage Open Web Pages

As you open new pages, whether in the background or not, new tabs are opened. Safari's tab view enables you to view and work with your open pages/tabs. Here's how:

1. Tap the tab view button. Each open page appears on its own tab.

2. Swipe up or down on the open tabs to browse them.

3. Tap a tab/page to move into it. The page opens and fills the Safari window.

4. Work with the web page.

5. Tap the tab view button.

Open web pages/tabs

6. To close a tab, click its close button or swipe to the left on the tab you want to close. That page/tab closes.

7. To open a new tab, tap the Add button to create new tab that shows your Favorites screen; navigate to a new page in that tab using the tools you've already learned in other tasks (tapping bookmarks or typing a URL).

8. To close the tab view, tap Done. The tab view closes, and the page you were most recently viewing is shown.

Tabs Are Independent

Each tab is independent. So, when you are working with a tab and use the back/forward buttons to move among its pages, you are just moving among the pages open under that tab. Pages open in other tabs are not affected.

Opening Web Pages That Are Open on Other Devices

When you enable iCloud Safari syncing, iCloud tracks the websites you have open on all the devices on which you have Safari syncing enabled, including your iPhone, iPads, and Macs. This is really handy when you have pages open on another device and want to view them on your iPhone. (Pages open on your iPhone are available on your other devices, too.) To view a page you have open on another device, do the following:

1. Open the tab view.

2. Swipe up the screen until you see the pages open on other devices. There is a section for each device; sections are labeled with the device's name. In each device's section, you see the pages open in Safari on those devices.

3. Tap the page you want to view. The page opens on the iPhone and becomes a new tab.

A Mac with open web pages

Keep Private Things Private

If you aren't browsing in Private mode and tap the Private button at the bottom of the tab view, Safari moves into Private mode and stops tracking the sites you visit. Tap the button again to return to the previous state. If you are browsing in Private mode, tapping the Private button shows or hides the tabs in the tab view.

Searching the Web

In the first task of this chapter, you learned that you can set Safari to search the Web using Google, Yahoo!, Bing, or DuckDuckGo. No matter which search engine you chose, you search the Web in the same way.

1. Tap in the Address/Search bar. The keyboard appears along with your Favorites.

2. If there is any text in the Address/Search bar, tap the clear button.

3. Type your search word(s). As you type, Safari attempts to find a search that matches what you typed. The list of suggestions is organized in sections, which depend on what you are searching for and the search options you configured through Safari settings. One section, labeled with the search engine you are using (such as Google Search), contains the search results from that source. Other sections can include Bookmarks and History, or Apps (from the App Store). At the bottom of the list is the On This Page section, which shows the terms that match your search on the page you are browsing.

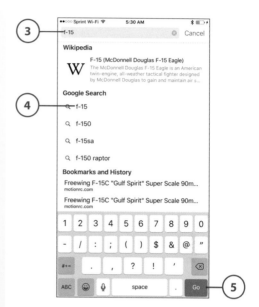

Quick Website Search

If you enabled the Quick Website Search feature, you can include the site you want to search in the Address/Search bar, such as "Wiki F-15." When you do this, the results from the site you entered appear at the top of the list and you can access them directly by tapping the information that appears (as opposed to having to move to the search engine site first as in these steps).

4. To perform the search using one of the suggestions provided, tap the suggestion you want to use. The search is performed and you can skip to step 6.

5. If none of the suggestions are what you want, keep typing until you have entered the entire search term, and then tap Go. The search engine you use performs the search and displays the results on the search results page.

6. Use the search results page to view the results of your search. These pages work just like other web pages. You can zoom, scroll, and tap links to explore results.

Searching on a Web Page

To search for words or phrases on a web page you are viewing, perform these steps, except in step 4, tap the word or phrase for which you want to search in the On This Page section (you may have to swipe up the screen to see this section). You return to the page you are browsing and each occurrence of your search term on the page is highlighted.

Saving and Organizing Bookmarks

In addition to moving bookmarks from a computer or iCloud onto your iPhone, you can save new bookmarks directly in your iPhone (they are synced onto other devices, too). You can also organize bookmarks on your iPhone to make them easier and faster to access.

Creating Bookmarks

When you want to make it easy to return to a website, create a bookmark. Do the following to create a new bookmark:

1. Move to a web page for which you want to save a bookmark.

2. Tap the Share button.

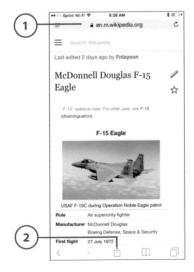

3. Tap Add Bookmark. The Add Bookmark screen appears, showing the title of the web page you are viewing; which will also be the name of the bookmark initially; its URL; and the Location field, which shows where the bookmark will be stored when you create it.

4. Edit the bookmark's name as needed, or tap the Clear button (x) to erase the current name, and then type the new name of the bookmark. The titles of some web pages are quite long, so it's a good idea to shorten them so the bookmark's name is easier to read on the iPhone's screen and you can fit more bookmarks on the screen.

5. Tap Location. The Location section expands and you see all of the folders of bookmarks on your phone. The folder that is currently selected is marked with a check mark.

6. Swipe up and down the screen to find the folder in which you want to place the new bookmark. You can choose any folder on the screen; folders are indented when they are contained within other folders.

7. To choose a folder in which to store the new bookmark, tap it. You return to the Add Bookmark screen, which shows the location you selected.

Name of web page/bookmark

URL of web page

Current bookmark location

8. Tap Save. The bookmark is created and saved in the location you
   specified. You can use the bookmark to return to the website at
   any time.

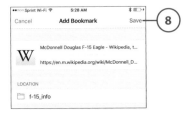

It's Not All Good

Unfortunately, bookmarks that you create on the iPhone are useful on the
computer to which they are synced only if you use Internet Explorer or Safari
(Windows PC) or Safari (Mac). If you use Firefox, Chrome, or another web browser, the bookmarks moved onto the computer from the iPhone are of little value
to you because they appear in only one of the supported browsers (Internet
Explorer or Safari). You can make them available in other browsers, but that
requires going through extra gyrations, which can negate the value of syncing.

Organizing Bookmarks

You've seen how bookmarks can be contained in folders, which is a good thing
because you're likely to have a lot of them.
You can change the names and locations
of your existing bookmarks and folders as
follows:

1. Move to the Bookmarks screen
   showing the bookmarks and
   folders you want to change. (You
   can't move among the Bookmarks
   screens while you are in Edit
   mode so you need to start at the
   location where the items you want
   to change are located.)

2. Tap Edit. Unlock buttons appear
   next to the folders and bookmarks
   you can change; some folders,
   such as the History folder, can't
   be changed. The order icons also
   appear on the right side of the
   screen, again only for folders or
   bookmarks you can change.

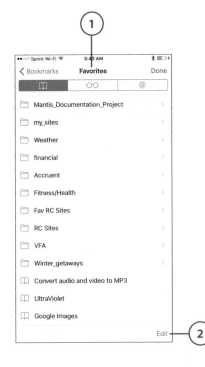

3. Touch the order icon next to the bookmark or folder you want to move and drag it up or down the screen to change the order in which it appears on the screen. When you drag a folder or bookmark between other items, they slide apart to make room for the folder or bookmark you are dragging. The order of the items in the list is the order in which they appear on the Bookmarks screen.

4. To change the name or location of a folder, tap it.

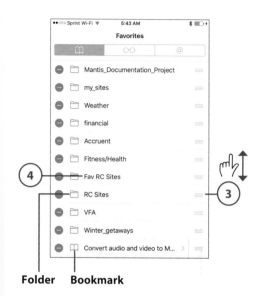

Folder **Bookmark**

Can't Move?

If you have only one bookmark you've added, you can't move them around as described here because Safari won't let you "disturb" the default bookmarks and folders (such as Favorites and History). You can only delete default bookmarks.

---

5. Change the name in the name bar.

6. To change the location of the folder, tap the Location bar, which shows the folder's current location.

7. Swipe up and down the list of folders until you see the folder in which you want to place the folder you are working with.

8. Tap the folder into which you want to move the folder you are editing.

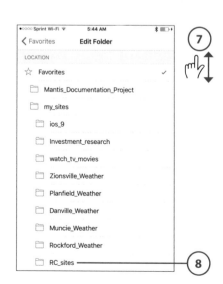

9. Tap the back button. You move back to the prior Bookmarks screen, which reflects any changes you made.

10. Tap a bookmark you want to change.

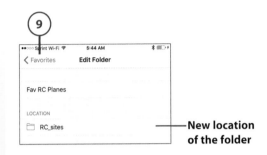

New location of the folder

Editing a Bookmark

If the bookmark you want to change isn't on the Bookmarks screen you are currently viewing, tap Done to exit Edit mode. Then open the folder containing the bookmark you want to change and tap Edit. You are able to change the bookmark.

11. Change the bookmark's name in the name bar.

12. If you want to change a bookmark's URL, tap the URL bar and make changes to the current URL. For example, you might want to change it to have the bookmark point to a site's home page rather than the page you are viewing.

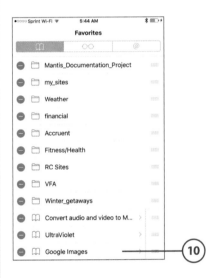

13. To change the location of the folder or bookmark, tap the Location bar and follow steps 7 and 8.

14. Tap Done. You move back to the previous screen, and any changes you made—such as changing the name or location of a bookmark—are reflected.

Can't Change?

You can't change default bookmarks, you can only delete them.

15. To create a new folder, tap New Folder.

16. Enter the name of the folder.

17. Follow steps 6–8 to choose the location in which you want to save the new folder.

18. Tap Done. The new folder is created in the location you selected. You can place folders and bookmarks into it by using the Location bar to navigate to it.

19. Tap Done. Your changes are saved and you exit Edit mode.

Browsing Both Ways

As you browse, make sure you try both the horizontal and vertical orientations. Safari sometimes offers different features in the two orientations on different models. For example, when you open the Bookmarks screen and rotate an iPhone 6 Plus or 6s Plus, the screen is divided into two panes. On the left is the Bookmarks pane you are viewing while the right pane shows the web page you were browsing. If you tap a bookmark, the web page in the right pane becomes the page at which the bookmark points.

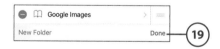

Deleting Bookmarks or Folders of Bookmarks

You can get rid of bookmarks or folders of bookmarks you don't want any more by deleting them:

1. Move to the screen containing the folder or bookmark you want to delete.

2. Swipe to the left on the folder or bookmark you want to delete.

3. Tap Delete. The folder or bookmark is deleted. Note that when you delete a folder, all the bookmarks it contains are deleted, too.

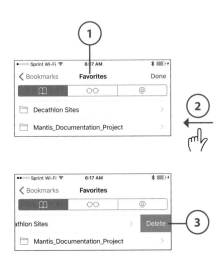

Creating Bookmarks on the Home Screen

You can add a bookmark icon to a Home screen so that you can visit a web page from there; this handy trick saves you several navigation moves that would be required to move into Safari and type the URL or use a bookmark to get the page you want to see.

1. Use Safari to move to a web page to which you want to have easy access from the Home screen.

2. Tap the Share button.

3. Tap Add to Home Screen.

4. If needed, edit the name of the icon that will appear on the Home screen. The default name is the name of the web page. It's best to edit it to a shorter name because it has a small amount of room on its icon on the Home screen.

5. Tap Add. You move to the Home screen and see the icon you added (it is added to the last page of your Home screen). You can return to the site at any time by tapping this button.

Tap to open the web page

Location Is Everything

You can organize the buttons on the pages of the Home Screen so that you can place your web page buttons in convenient locations, and you can create folders on your Home screens to keep your web page icons neat and tidy there, too. Refer to Chapter 5, "Customizing How Your iPhone Looks and Sounds," for details.

Using 3D Touch with Safari (iPhone 6s and iPhone 6s Plus Only)

Like other default iPhone apps, Safari supports 3D Touch, which you can use in a couple of ways.

Perform a Peek to see the Quick Actions menu

Move to the Reading List

Open a new tab in which the sites won't be tracked

Open the Bookmarks screen

Open a new tab and allow the sites to be tracked

When you press on the Safari app's icon, you see the Quick Actions menu. You can select from among its options to quickly perform actions in Safari. For example, choose New Tab to open a new tab in which you can navigate to a web page, or choose Show Bookmarks to jump to the Bookmarks page.

 Perform a Peek on links you are browsing

When you see this, you can swipe up the screen to see options

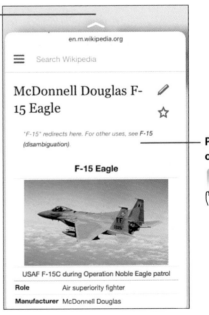

Perform a pop to open the web page

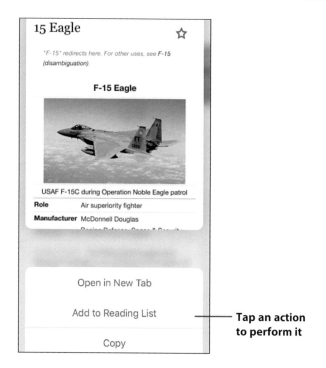

Tap an action to perform it

When you are browsing links, such as when you have performed a search, or your bookmarks, press on a link or a bookmark in which you are interested to perform a Peek on it. In the Peek window, you see the web page for the link or web page on which you peeked. If you continue to press on the Peek, it pops open, so you can view the web page in Safari. When you perform a Peek on some screens, such the links resulting from a search, you see an upward-facing arrow at the top of the screen; this indicates you can swipe up the screen to reveal a menu of commands. Tap a command to perform it. For example, tap Open in New Tab to open the web page in a new tab in Safari.

Sharing Web Pages

Safari makes it easy to share web pages that you think will be valuable to others. There are many ways to share, including AirDrop, Message, Mail, Twitter, and Facebook. A couple of examples will prepare you to use any of them.

Emailing a Link to a Web Page

You can quickly email links to web pages you visit.

1. Use Safari to navigate to a web page whose link you want to email to someone.

2. Tap the Share button.

3. Tap Mail. A new email message is created, and the link to the web page is inserted into the body. The subject of the message is the title of the web page.

4. Complete and send the email message. (Refer to Chapter 9, "Sending, Receiving, and Managing Email," for information about the Mail app.) When the recipient receives your message, he can visit the website by tapping the link included in the email message.

Messaging a Web Page

If you come across a page that you want to share with someone via Messages, Safari makes it easy.

1. Use Safari to navigate to a web page whose link you want to message to someone.

2. Tap the Share button.

3. Tap Message. A new message is created, and the link to the web page is inserted.

4. Address the message.

5. Enter text you want to send along with the link to the web page.

6. Tap Send. Your message is sent. The recipients can visit the web page by tapping the link included in the message.

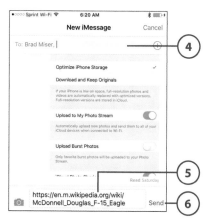

>>>Go Further
MORE WAYS TO SHARE THE WEB

If you want to share a web page in the old-fashioned way, you can print it by opening the Action menu and tapping Print (assuming you have your iPhone set up to print, as explained in Chapter 1, "Getting Started with Your iPhone"). If you tap Copy, the web page's address is copied to the clipboard, so you can paste into documents, emails, notes, or messages. You can also share via Twitter and Facebook.

Completing Forms on the Web

Just like web browsers on a computer, you often have to complete forms on your iPhone, such as to log in to your account on a website or request information about something. You can manually enter information or use AutoFill to have Safari add the information for you. (AutoFill must be enabled using Safari settings, as explained at the beginning of this chapter.)

Manually Completing Forms

To manually fill in a form, do the following:

1. Open Safari and move to a website containing a form.

2. Zoom in on the fields you need to complete.

3. Tap in a field. If you tapped a text field, the keyboard appears.

4. Enter the information in the field. (If the site suggests information you want to enter, just tap it to enter it. You might have to tap Done to temporarily hide the keyboard to see all the suggestions. If a suggestion isn't the information you want to enter, just keep typing.)

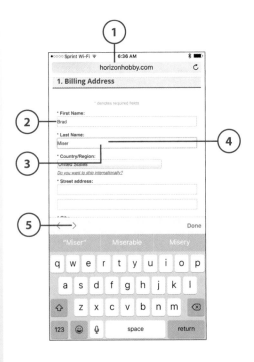

5. Tap the next button. If there isn't another field on the form, this button is disabled, so skip this step. If it is enabled, you move to the next field on the form.

Selecting Data

You can select, instead of type, some types of information. For example, when you are entering an address, you usually choose a state or province from a list. And you often choose dates rather than typing them. When you see a downward-facing arrow in a field, tap it to choose that information or just move into a field that you select like any other. The selection tool replaces the keyboard at the bottom of the screen. Swipe on the wheels or use the other tools in this area to select the data you want to enter.

6. Repeat steps 4 and 5 to complete all the fields on the form.

7. Tap Done. If it's open, the keyboard closes and you move back to the web page.

8. Tap Next, Continue, Submit, Go, Login, or whatever button is provided to send the form's information to the website.

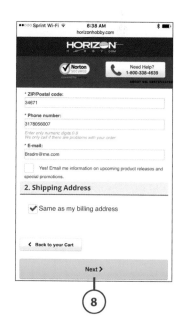

Using AutoFill to Complete Forms

AutoFill makes completing forms faster and easier because Safari can enter information for you with the tap of a button.

1. Open Safari and move to a website containing a form. Zoom in on the fields you need to complete, and tap in a field. If you tapped a text field, the keyboard appears.

2. Tap AutoFill. Safari fills any fields it can, based on the information you designate when you configure AutoFill to use your contact information. Any fields that Safari completes are highlighted in yellow.

3. Use the steps shown in the preceding task to review all the fields and to type in what AutoFill wasn't able to complete or edit those that AutoFill completed but that need to be changed.

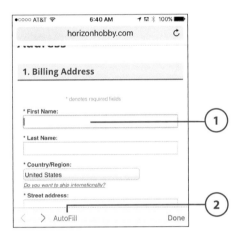

AutoFillin'

For AutoFill to work, it must be enabled in the Safari settings as described at the beginning of the chapter. If the data AutoFill enters is not correct, use the Safari settings to choose your correct contact info.

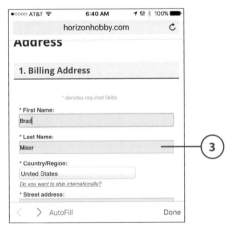

Signing In to Websites Automatically

If you enable Safari to remember usernames and passwords, it can enter this information for you automatically. When Safari encounters a site for which it recognizes and can save login information, you are prompted to allow Safari to save that information. This doesn't work with all sites; if you aren't prompted to allow Safari to save login information, you can't use this feature with that site. When saved, this information can be entered for you automatically.

1. Move to a web page that requires you to log in to an account.

2. Enter your account's username and password.

3. Tap the button to log in to your account, such as Continue, Sign In, Submit, Login, and such. You are prompted to save the login information.

4. To save the information, tap Save Password. The next time you move to the login page, your username and password are entered for you automatically. Tap Never for This Website if you don't want the information to be saved and you don't want to be prompted again. Tap Not Now if you don't want the information saved but do want to be prompted again later to save it.

>>>*Go Further*

LETTING SAFARI CREATE PASSWORDS FOR YOU

If you have enabled the Names and Passwords setting, Safari can create passwords for you. Go to a website that requires you to create a password, such as when you register for a new account. When you tap in a field that Safari recognizes as requiring a password, tap Suggest Password. Safari presents a password for you; most of these are not easy to remember, but that doesn't matter because it is saved for you automatically so you won't have to enter it manually. If you want to use the recommended password, tap Use Suggested Password; Safari enters the password in the password and verify password fields. When syncing is enabled, the password is stored on the synced devices, too, so you are able to sign in from those devices just as easily.

Tap here to download
music from the iTunes
Store onto your phone

Tap here to configure
your iPhone for music

Tap here to enjoy
musical bliss

In this chapter, you explore how you can use the Music app to enjoy all sorts of music. Topics include the following:

→ Understanding sources of music
→ Setting up and finding music with My Music
→ Setting up and finding music with Apple Music
→ Finding music with iTunes Radio
→ Playing music
→ Using AirPlay to listen to your iPhone's music on other devices

Finding and Listening to Music

Apple's very first portable "i" device, the original iPod, did only one thing—though it did that one thing better than any other device ever—which was to enable people to take their music with them and enjoy it anywhere. While the iPhone has evolved way beyond anything the first iPod could do, one of the best reasons to have an iPhone is that they continue to be amazing devices for listening to all kinds of music. The Music app enables you to quickly move to and play any music in your personal music library, or you can access Apple's enormous music library through Apple Music and iTunes Radio.

Understanding Sources of Music

There are different sources of music that you can listen to using the Music app. It's important to understand the types of music to which you want to listen because what you can do with that music depends on where the music comes from. In the Music app, you can listen to music from the following sources:

- **My Music**. This source contains music that you own. You can store and listen to music that you own or that you've added through using Apple Music on your phone for no additional cost, and you don't need to connect to the Internet to listen to your music that is stored on the phone.

The benefit of this source is that once you've paid for the music or as long as you keep your Apple Music subscription current, you can listen to it for no additional cost (unless you also use iTunes Match, which requires an annual subscription fee). If you don't use Apple Music, don't have a large music collection already, or aren't willing to spend quite a lot of money to build up a music collection, the selection of music available to you is likely a bit limited.

This source is best if you tend to listen to a limited variety of music, and you already own most of the music you want to listen to.

- **Apple Music.** This subscription service from Apple enables you to access its huge music library. You use Apple Music to stream music onto your phone. You can also download it to the phone so that you can listen to it when your phone isn't connected to the Internet or if you want to avoid using cellular data to stream music.

  The benefit of Apple Music is that the amount of music available to you is both enormous and extremely diverse. Unless you have very niche musical tastes, you are likely to find any music you want to listen to in Apple Music. And, you can stream that music directly onto your phone or download it there. And, you can add Apple Music to the My Music source (however, if you let your Apple Music subscription expire, you won't be able to listen to that music anymore).

  As you listen to music, and indicate you like it by tapping the Heart button while you listen to it, Apple Music presents other music you might enjoy so that you can constantly explore and discover more music to which you want to listen.

  The downside of Apple Music is that it requires a monthly subscription fee.

  If you enjoy exploring music and like listening to different music frequently, Apple Music may be a great source for you.

- **iTunes Radio.** This source, which is free to use, consists of streamed music that "goes together" and is organized in stations. You can listen to existing stations or you can create your own stations based on songs or playlists that you like. Your phone must be connected to the Internet to be able to listen to iTunes Radio.

  iTunes Radio is nice because it is free to use and you can choose from a broad range of existing stations as well as create your own.

The downside of iTunes Radio is that you must be connected to the Internet to listen to it, but more significantly, the selection of music you listen to is largely not in your control. When you choose a station, you hear the music in that station as it is. Even when you create a station based on a song or playlist, the songs you hear are determined by the iTunes Radio feature.

iTunes Radio is nice when you want to discover new music based on specific songs you like and when you don't really care about the specific music you want to hear.

Of course, you can mix and match these sources. For example, you may already own music and also use Apple Music and iTunes Radio to expand the music available to you.

To listen to music in the Music app, you must first find the music to which you want to listen. How you do that depends on the source of that music. For example, finding music from Apple Music is a bit different than finding music already stored on your phone, such as music you have downloaded from the iTunes Store. Once you've selected the music you want to listen to, the tools you use to control the music are similar.

Following are three sections on configuring your Phone for the different music sources described in the previous list and using those sources to find music. The section found later in this chapter, titled "Playing Music," covers listening to music from any of these sources.

Setting Up and Finding Music with My Music

To listen to music you own, you first add your music to the Music app. Then, you can find the music you want to listen to in a number of ways.

Adding Your Music to the Music App

You can add your music to the Music app in two primary ways:

- You own music that you purchase from the iTunes Store using the iTunes app. The steps to find and download music from the iTunes Store are provided in Chapter 6, "Downloading Apps, Music, Movies, TV Shows, and More onto Your iPhone." Once downloaded, you can access that music using the My Music source.

- You also own music you've added to the iTunes app on a computer, either by downloading it from the iTunes Store or importing it from audio CDs into iTunes. You copy music from the iTunes app onto your phone by syncing music onto the phone. Connect the iPhone to your computer and open iTunes. Select your iPhone on the menu at the top of the iTunes window. Then, click Music on the toolbar along the left side of the iTunes window. Check the Sync Music check box, and then configure the music you want to copy onto the phone, such as picking specific albums or songs to copy. Click the Sync button and the music you selected is copied onto the phone. You use the My Music source to find and play it.

>>>Go Further
MORE ON MY MUSIC

Here are a couple of other ways you can work with music you own:

- **Importing audio CDs.** You can add music you own on audio CDs to the iTunes app on a computer by importing it. First, open the iTunes preferences dialog box and move to the General tab. Configure how you want CDs to be imported, such as when you insert a CD into your computer. Second, insert an audio CD into your computer and start the import process; iTunes starts it for you automatically if you configured it to do so. Once imported, you can sync that music onto your iPhone.

- **iTunes Match.** This is Apple's online music storage service for music that you own. All your music is copied onto the cloud, so that you can stream or download it to any of your devices. This makes accessing your music library convenient. To use iTunes Match, you pay a fee and subscribe to it. You then configure each device to use iTunes Match. If you don't use Apple Music, iTunes Match may be a good option to make your own music available on the cloud.

Using My Music to Find Music

Before you can listen to music, you need to find the music you want to listen to by using one of the many browsing and searching features the Music app offers. These include browsing your music by artist, searching, and so on.

Finding Music by Artist

You can find music by browsing artists in the My Music source. You can then see all the music by a specific artist and select the music you want to play.

1. On the Home screen, tap Music.

2. Tap My Music

3. Tap Library; if Apple Music isn't enabled, you don't need to perform this step. You move directly into your library.

4. Tap the browse category shown just above the list of songs.

5. Tap Artists. The list of all artists whose music is available in the My Music source appears. Artists are grouped by the first letter of their first name or by the first letter of the group's name (not counting the as the first word in a name).

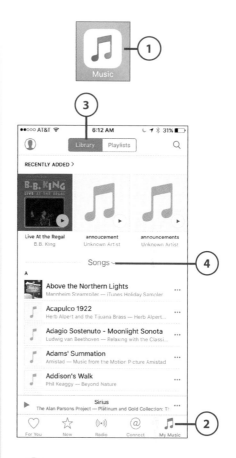

6. Swipe up and down the list to browse all available artists. As you swipe, the index appears along the right side of the screen.

7. To jump to a specific artist, tap the letter along the right side of the screen for the artist's or group's first name; to jump to an artist or a group whose name starts with a number, tap # at the bottom of the screen. For each artist, you see album art associated with the artist's music along with the number of albums and songs available to you.

Browse with Speed

If you swipe on top of the index, you can browse screens at a very fast speed. This is especially useful when you are browsing very long lists though it can be a bit hard to control. You can use it to quickly get to the general area of the index close to the artist's name and then tap a letter to see that letter's section.

8. Tap an artist whose music you'd like to explore. A list of albums by that artist appears. The artist's home page appears. Here, you see all of the albums and songs in your My Music source by that artist.

9. Swipe your finger up and down the screen to browse the artist's songs and albums.

10. Tap an album. You see the songs in that album.

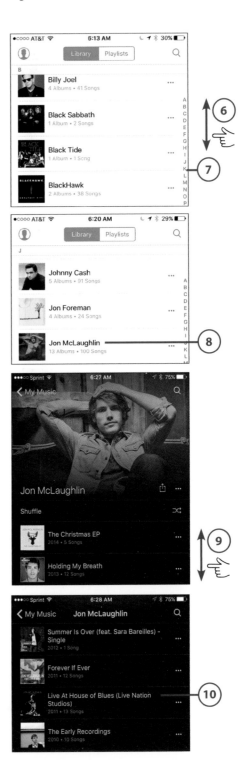

11. Swipe up and down the screen to browse the songs in the album.

12. Tap the play button for the album to play it or tap a song to play that song. The music plays.

13. Use the Music app to control the music (covered in detail in the "Playing Music" section).

Finding My Music in Other Ways

When you open the category menu by tapping the current category, you can browse music to find what you want to play with the following options:

- **Albums**—This view shows your music organized by album. You can browse albums. Tap an album whose music you want to listen to. You see a list of songs on that album and can tap a song to play it.

- **Songs**—This option shows you a list of all the songs available to you. The list is organized alphabetically; you can browse it or tap a letter on the index to jump to songs starting with that letter. Tap a song to play it.

- **Music Videos**—This takes you to a list of your music videos so you can watch and listen to them.

Straight to the Top

If you don't see the category currently selected, swipe down the screen until you get to the top and you'll see it.

- **Genres**—This list shows you music by the genre with which it is associated, such as Rock, Country, and so on.

- **Composers**—Songs can have composers associated with them (composers are responsible for writing the music while the artist is responsible for playing it). Sometimes these are the same people, but sometimes they aren't, especially for classical music. This shows you music organized by composer rather than artist.

- **Compilations**—This is similar to albums except a compilation can contain songs from multiple artists, such as greatest hits of the '70s, or a collection of songs grouped in other ways.

- **Home Sharing**—The Shared source shows you music being shared via the Home Sharing feature that enables you to share content in the iTunes app on a computer with other computers and iOS devices on the same network. When you tap this, you see a list of all the iTunes Libraries being shared. Tap a library to see the music available to you. Browse, select, and play shared music as you do with music in your iPhone's music library. (If a shared library requires a password, you have to enter that to be able to access its music.)

You can also find music using playlists, which are collections of music that you create in iTunes on a computer or directly on the iPhone. A playlist can include music grouped for any reason, such as being from the same artist, your favorite songs, and so on. You access playlists in the My Music source by tapping the Playlists tab at the top of the screen if Apple Music is enabled, or by tapping Playlists on the Dock at the bottom of the screen if Apple Music is not enabled.

After you've made a selection on the category menu or selected a playlist, you can browse the resulting music similarly to the steps shown in the previous task. You can swipe up and down screens to browse their content, and then tap on the item you want to explore in more detail, such as a genre. Then, you can play the entire contents of the grouping you selected, or you can play individual songs as described in the "Playing Music" task later in this chapter.

>>>*Go Further*

ROLL YOUR OWN PLAYLISTS

You can manually create new playlists in the Music app. Open the Playlists source and tap New. Type the name of the playlist and tap Add Songs. On the resulting screen, choose how you want to select songs such as by Artists. Browse the resulting source of songs. Tap a song's Add button (+) to add it to the new playlist. Tap the back button in the upper-left corner of the screen to move back to the source. Repeat these steps to add as many songs as you want in the same way. Tap Done. You move to the playlist's screen. Change the order of songs in the playlist by dragging the Order button on the right edge of the screen up or down. Tap a song's Unlock button, and then tap Delete to delete it from the playlist. When you've completed all the songs in the new playlist, tap Done. The new playlist is available in the Playlists source.

Finding Music in My Music by Searching

Browsing is a useful way to find music, but it can be faster to search for specific music in which you are interested. You can search most of the screens you browse. When a category, such as Songs, contains many items, searching can get you where you want to go more quickly than browsing. Here's how:

1. Tap the Search tool at the top of the screen.

2. Tap My Music to search your music.

3. Type the song title, artist, album, or other criteria for which you want to search. As you type, the items that meet your search criterion are shown; the more you type, the more specific your search becomes. Below the Search tool, the results are organized into categories, such as ARTISTS, ALBUMS, and SONGS.

4. When you think you've typed enough to find what you're looking for, tap Search. The keyboard disappears.

5. Browse the results.

6. Tap a song to play it (see "Playing Music" later in this chapter for details).

7. Tap an artist or album to browse and play the music in that group.

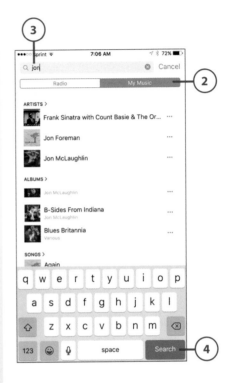

Clearing a Search

You can clear a search by tapping the "x" that appears on the right end of the Search tool. Tapping Cancel clears the search, and also closes the Search screen.

>>>Go Further

MUSIC SETTINGS

If you open the Music Settings screen, you see several settings that impact how you can view and listen to music:

- **PLAYBACK & DOWNLOADS.** Use these controls to determine how music is downloaded via your cellular network. If you want music to be downloaded or streamed only when you are connected to Wi-Fi, set the Use Cellular Data switch to off (white). If you want the highest quality music to be available via your cellular data connection, set the High Quality on Cellular switch to on (green).

- **LIBRARY.** Use the Sort Albums option to determine if albums are sorted by the artist or title. Set the Genius switch to on (green) if you want to be able to use the Genius feature to create playlists based on the music you have in your library.

- **PLAYBACK.** Use the EQ control to configure the Equalizer to adjust how music sounds, such as increasing the bass. Use the Volume Limit control to set an upper limit on the volume level of music. Set the Sound Check switch to on (green) if you want the Music app to attempt to "level out" the volume of different music you play.

- **HOME SHARING.** If you have more than one computer with iTunes on a local network, use this area to sign into your Apple ID; the music in iTunes on each computer can be accessed and played on all the others on the network.

Setting Up and Finding Music with Apple Music

Apple Music is Apple's subscription music service. For a monthly fee (currently $9.99 per month for a single membership or $14.99 per month for a family membership in the United States), you can listen to any music in Apple's music library. This library is huge and you are likely to find and listen to any music of interest to you. You can stream music to listen to it via the Internet or you can download it to your phone so that you don't have to be connected to the Internet to listen to it.

Apple Music provides suggestions to you for music you might enjoy based on the music you listen to, or search for, and based on music you indicate that you like by tapping the Heart button while you view or listen to it. Over time, these suggestions get more specific to your musical tastes so that Apple Music's recommendations should help you discover and enjoy new music.

Apple Music is accessible on your iPhone, other iOS devices (such as an iPad), and any computer with the iTunes software on it. (Note that with a single membership, you can play Apple Music on only one device at a time.)

Like My Music, you can browse and search for music in the Apple Music collection and then listen to the music you find.

Subscribing to Apple Music

You can subscribe to Apple Music as follows:

1. Open the Music app and tap the Account icon in the upper-left corner of the screen.

2. Tap Join Apple Music.

3. Tap the type of account you want: Individual enables you to access Apple Music on one device at a time while Family enables Apple Music for up to six accounts at a time. (At press time, Apple Music was available for a free three-month trial period.)

4. Follow the onscreen instructions to complete the process. The specific screens you see depend on the current status of your Apple ID. You are prompted to indicate the kind of music you like by choosing favorite bands, genres, and so on; Apple Music starts recommending music for you using the choices you make. (Apple Music changes its recommendations over time based on what you listen to and what you manually like by tapping the Heart button.) When the process is complete, Apple Music is enabled in the Music app and you see its options on the Dock at the bottom of the screen.

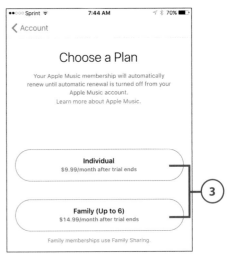

Sign In Please

If you aren't signed into an Apple ID, you need to do so by entering your Apple ID and password and tapping Sign In in order to join Apple Music.

Apple Music and Family Sharing

When you choose a Family plan for Apple Music, the group of people you have set up under Family Sharing can access Apple Music. See Chapter 6 for the details of setting up and managing Family Sharing.

Searching Apple Music

You can search for music in Apple Music by song title, artist, type (for example, classical guitar) similarly to how you search My Music.

1. Tap the Search tool.

2. Tap Apple Music. On the results list, you see the searches that are currently trending; you can tap one of these to perform that search.

3. Type your search term. This can be very specific, such as a song title or artist's name, or more broad, such as a type of music. As you type, you see searches that match your term on the results list. Because the collection of music available in Apple Music is so large, you might need to be more specific with your search term than when you search My Music.

4. Tap the search you want to perform.

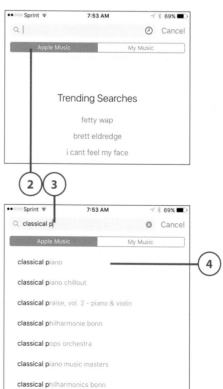

5. Browse the results.

6. Tap a song to play it (see "Playing Music" later in this chapter for details).

7. Tap an artist, album, or playlist to browse and play the music in that group.

Browsing Apple Music for You

For You music is music that Apple Music has selected for you (hence the name) based on what you have listened to, what is already in your music library, and what you indicate that you like (you learn how to do this later). To browse music Apple Music has selected, perform the following steps:

1. Tap For You. On the For You screen, you see a collection of playlists, albums, and songs that Apple Music recommends.

2. Swipe up and down the screen to browse the selected music.

3. To play music in an album or playlist, tap its Play button (see "Playing Music" later in this chapter for details).

4. To explore the contents of a playlist or album, tap its artwork. You see the list of songs in the collection you tapped.

5. Review and play the music you see (see "Playing Music" later in this chapter for details).

6. Tap For You to return to the For You screen to browse for other music.

Browsing New Apple Music

The New music category leads you to music that is new to Apple Music. You can browse new music similarly to how you browse For You Music.

1. Tap New. On the New screen, you see a collection of playlists, albums, and songs that are new to Apple Music.

2. Swipe up and down the screen to browse the selected music.

3. To browse a specific genre of music, tap All Genres.

4. Browse the genres.

5. Tap a genre for which you want to see new music.

6. Swipe up and down the screen to browse the new music in the selected genre.

7. To play music in an album or playlist, tap its Play button (see "Playing Music" later in this chapter for details).

8. To explore the contents of a playlist, collection of playlists, or album, tap its artwork. For example, when you tap a collection of playlists, you see the specific playlists in the collection, based on genre, artist, or other factors.

9. Swipe up and down the screen to browse the contents of the item you selected.

10. Tap an item of interest, such as a collection of playlists.

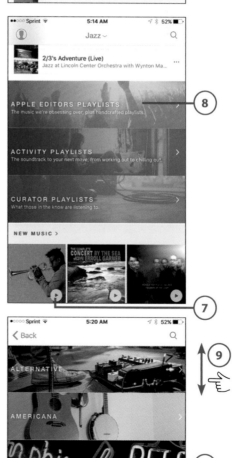

11. To see the contents of an album or playlist, taps its artwork.

12. To play an album or playlist, tap its Play button (see "Playing Music" later in this chapter for details).

13. Tap Back to return to the previous screen.

Downloading Songs from Apple Music

You can download Apple Music songs onto your phone so that you can listen to them when the phone isn't connected to the Internet. Here's how:

1. Open the Settings app, tap Music, and set the iCloud Music Library switch to on (green).

2. If you have music on your phone, tap Merge to merge that music with the music on the cloud or Replace to replace the music on the phone with that stored on the cloud. You only need to perform steps 1 and 2 once. With iCloud Music Library enabled, you can save music on your phone.

3. Move to a song in Apple Music you want to download.

4. Tap the ellipsis.

All at Once

Tap the ellipsis next to an album and then tap Make Available Offline to download the entire album to your phone.

5. Tap Make Available Offline. The song is downloaded to your iPhone and is marked with the iPhone icon indicating it is stored on your phone so you don't need to be connected to the Internet to listen to it.

This song has been downloaded

Monitoring Downloads

When you are downloading songs, the Downloads banner appears at the top of some screens. Tap this to move to the Downloads screen. Here, you see the progress of downloads and pause them, if you want to. When all the songs have been downloaded, the list empties. Tap Done to close the Downloads screen. Downloads occur in the background so you don't have to view the Downloads screen, but it's there if you are interested.

Adding Apple Music to My Music

You can add Apple Music to your My Music collection to make it easier to return to. For example, suppose you find an album on Apple Music that you really like. Adding it to My Music makes it part of the My Music source, which makes it easier to find than going back and searching Apple Music for it. To add music to your My Music, do the following:

1. Perform steps 1 and 2 in the previous task if you haven't done so.

2. Find an album or playlist you want to add to My Music.

3. Tap the Add button (+). The music is added to your My Music source and is marked with a check mark.

This Apple Music is also in My Music

Downloading is Optional

Note that adding music to My Music does not download that music to your iPhone and you must still be connected to the Internet to listen to it (see the previous task to download music).

Finding Music with iTunes Radio

iTunes Radio streams music from the Internet onto your iPhone. iTunes Radio "stations" are collections of songs based on the same artist, similar artists, genres, similar songs, or other criteria. You can use the default iTunes stations to find music, or you can create your own stations based on music you like.

iTunes Radio is similar to Apple Music in that you can choose from a large variety of music. However, you can't choose the specific music you listen to with iTunes Radio as you can with Apple Music. You can only choose a default station or base a new station on a song or artist. iTunes Radio selects the music you hear. Also, you can't save iTunes Radio music on your iPhone to listen to when your phone isn't connected to the Internet.

Playing Music with an iTunes Radio Station

To find music in iTunes Radio, do the following:

1. Tap Radio.

2. Browse the screen to view the available stations.

3. Tap the station you want to hear. The first song starts to play (see "Playing Music" later in this chapter for details).

Creating Your Own iTunes Radio Stations Based on an Artist, a Genre, or a Song

To create your own stations, do the following:

1. Find music you want to base a station on; you can do this in any of the ways described in previous tasks, such as searching by artist or title.

2. Tap the ellipsis for the music you want to base the station on. This can be for a song, an album, or for other items.

3. On the resulting menu, tap the radio icon. The station is created and begins to play (see "Playing Music" later in this chapter for details).

Returning to iTunes Radio Stations You Created

You can go back to radio stations you created as follows:

1. Tap Radio.

2. Tap Recently Played. You see the list of stations you have played recently, including default stations and those you created.

3. Browse the list of stations.

4. Tap a station to play it.

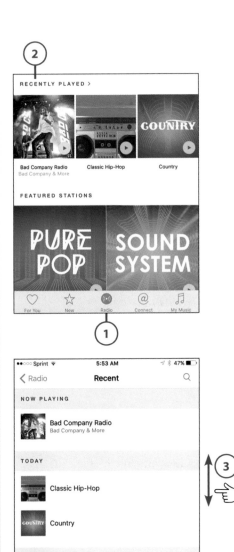

Playing Music

After you find and select what you want to hear, use the Music app's playback controls to listen to your heart's content. You can control music playback from a number of places. You have different options for your music based on the type of music you are listening to; for example, when you listen to Apple Music, you can download that music onto your phone.

Playing Music on the Miniplayer

Tap to open the Now Playing screen

Miniplayer

Pause

Song currently playing

Ellipsis

Amount of song played

When you play music, the Miniplayer appears at the bottom of the screen. On this bar, you see the song currently playing, the artist, and album (when you start a radio station, you first see the name of that station, which is replaced by the music details). You also see the Pause/Play button that you can tap to stop or start the music. You can tap the ellipsis to open a menu of commands (see "Understanding the Music App's Icons and Commands" later in this chapter).

While the Miniplayer appears, you can use the upper part of the Music app's screen to find other music to listen to, to download more music, and so on. The Miniplayer remains on the screen as long as music plays so you can control what is playing while you are doing other things with the app.

To have more control over the music and to see other options, tap the song information. The Now Playing screen opens.

Chapter 14

Playing Music on the Now Playing Screen

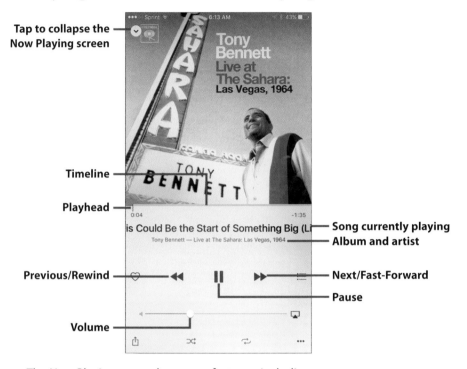

Tap to collapse the Now Playing screen

Timeline

Playhead

Previous/Rewind

Volume

Song currently playing

Album and artist

Next/Fast-Forward

Pause

The Now Playing screen has many features, including:

- **Timeline**—Just below the art, you see the timeline. The elapsed time is on the left side, and the remaining time is on the right. The red line is the Playhead that shows you where you are in the song. You can drag this to the left to move back in the song or to the right to move ahead.

- **Song information**—Below the timeline is the song's name (in larger, bold font). Under that is the artist and album title. If any of this information is too large to fit on the screen, it scrolls across the screen to display it all.

- **Previous/Rewind**—If the current song has been playing for more than a second or two, tap this button once to move to the beginning of the current song. If you are at the beginning of the current song, tap it to move to the previous song in the current source (album, artist, and so on). Tap and hold to rewind in the current song.

- **Pause/Play**—Tap Pause to pause the song. Tap Play to play it again.

- **Next/Fast-Forward**—Tap once to move to the next song on the list (or the next randomly selected song, if you are shuffling). Tap and hold to fast-forward in the current song.

- **Volume**—Drag the slider to the left to lower the volume or to the right to increase it.

The Now Playing screen has a number of other icons you can use; these are explained in "Understanding the Music App's Icons and Commands."

To collapse the Now Playing screen, tap the downward-facing arrow at the top of the screen. You return to the Miniplayer.

Turn It Up! (Or Down!)

No matter which technique you use to find and play music, you can control the volume using the Volume buttons on the left side of your iPhone. Press the upper button to increase volume or the lower one to decrease it. While you are pressing a button, a volume indicator appears on the screen to show you the relative volume level as you press the buttons. When you are on the Now Playing screen or viewing the Music control bar (covered later in this chapter), you can also use the Volume slider to set the sound level. And, if you listen with the EarPods included with your iPhone, you can use the buttons on the right EarPod's wire to crank it up (press and hold the top button) or down (press and hold the bottom button).

Playing Music from an Album's or Playlist's Screen

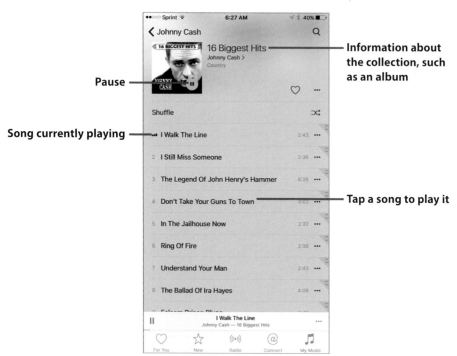

You can also play music from any album's, playlist's, or other music collection's screen. When you browse a collection, you see the list of songs it contains. You can play the entire collection by tapping the Play button in its graphic at the top of the screen or tap a song to play it.

Like the Miniplayer and Now Playing screen, you can use the various icons on the screen to control the music and perform specific actions (see the next section for details).

Understanding the Music App's Icons and Commands

As you listen to music from different sources and in different ways (such as the Now Playing screen or an album's screen), you see various icons that perform actions or lead you commands you can use. The following table provides an explanation of these icons and commands.

Music App Icons and Commands

Icon	Explanation
•••	The ellipsis opens a menu containing contextual commands, meaning the options you see depend on the type of music you are working with. For example, you see different options when using Apple Music than you do with Your Music.
♡	Tap this to indicate you like music. This tells Apple Music to identify more music that is similar to (or "goes with") music that you like. You see this music in Apple Music's For You collection.
⤭	Tap this to shuffle music in the current source so it plays in random order instead of the order in which it is listed on the screen.
▯	This indicates a song has been downloaded to the phone can be played when the iPhone isn't connected to the Internet.
+	Tap to add the music to your My Music collection.
((•))	Tap to create a radio station based on the music.
⬆	Tap to share the music.

Icon	Explanation
Play Next	Tap to the play the music after the music currently playing finishes.
Add to Up Next	Tap to add the music to the Up Next list (see "Playing Music from the Up Next List").
Add to a Playlist...	Tap to add the music to a current playlist.
Make Available Offline	Tap to download the music to your iPhone.
Remove Downloads	Tap to remove downloaded music from your phone.
Remove from My Music	Tap to remove the music from your My Music collection.
♥	Tap to indicate you don't like the music and Apple Music avoids including similar music in the For You collection.
☰	Tap to open the Up Next list (see "Playing Music from the Up Next List").
▱	Tap to play the music via AirPlay (see "Using AirPlay to Listen to Your iPhone's Music on Other Devices").
↻	Tap to repeat the current music once. Tap it again to repeat the current music twice. Tap it a third time to turn repeat off.
Delete	Tap to delete music you own from the iPhone.

Sleep Timer

Here's a tip courtesy of my Acquisitions Editor. To cause your music to stop playing after a specific period of time, open the Control Center (by swiping up from the bottom of the screen) and tap the Clock icon. Use the wheels to set the amount of time that you want the music to play. Tap When Timer Ends. Swipe up the screen and tap Stop Playing. When the timer expires, the music stops.

Playing Music from the Up Next List

The Up Next list contains the music that plays next. You can use this list to create a specific collection of music you want to play in a specific order, and to play specific songs. When you play music on an album or in a playlist, all the songs in the collection are added to the Up Next list automatically.

Tap to open the Up Next list

Tap to close the list

Browse past and upcoming music

Tap to add more songs

Song currently playing

Tap to remove a song

Tap a song to play it

Drag songs up or down to change the order in which they play

To open the Up Next list, tap the Up Next button on the Now Playing screen. Swipe up and down the screen to browse the music shown, which is grouped into HISTORY, which shows songs you've already played; NOW PLAYING, which shows the song currently playing; UP NEXT, which shows upcoming songs; and RESUME, which shows radio stations that are paused and that you can resume. You can tap a song to play it. You can drag songs up and down the list to change the order in which they play. You can tap Add and then choose songs to add to the list. Tap Clear to remove a song from the list. Tap Done to close the list.

Playing Music from the Control Center

Swipe up
to open the
Control Center

Use these controls in
the Control Center
to control music

To get to some of the music controls quickly, swipe up from the bottom of the screen to open the Control Center. Just above the AirDrop and AirPlay buttons is the Audio section. Here you see some of the controls you can use for music playback; the controls here work the same as they do in the Music app.

Use the controls you see; then, close the Control Center by swiping down from its top and continue what you were doing. Or, tap the artist—title information to jump to the Now Playing screen (the Control Center closes when you do this).

More Than Just Music

The controls in the Audio section change based on the app you are using to play audio. For example, when you are using the Podcasts app to play a podcast, these tools control the podcast's playback. Likewise, if you play audio with a different app, these controls work for that app.

Playing Music from the Lock Screen

When audio is playing and your iPhone is locked, you can control music playback right from the Lock screen.

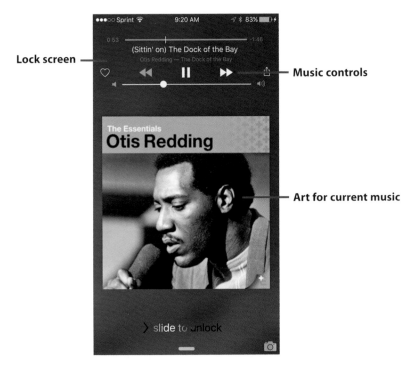

Lock screen

Music controls

Art for current music

Press the Sleep/Wake or Touch ID/Home button. Your iPhone wakes up and you see the Lock screen, which displays information about and controls for the music currently playing. Use the controls you see; these work like they do in the Music app.

When you're done controlling the tunes, press the Sleep/Wake button again to prevent the controls from being on the screen (so that they don't accidentally get activated if you put your iPhone back in your pocket, for example).

Controlling Music from the EarPods

You have basic controls over music by using the switch on the EarPods that came with your iPhone. Press the upper part of the switch to increase volume or the lower part to decrease it. Press the center part to play or pause music.

Siri and Music

You can use Siri to select, play, and control music, too. For example, you can activate Siri and say "Play album Frank Sinatra's Greatest Hits" to play that album or "Play Song Free Bird" to play that song. You can say, "Show me music by Switchfoot" to see music by that group. Refer to Chapter 12, "Working with Siri," for details.

Using 3D Touch with the Music App (iPhone 6s and iPhone 6s Plus Only)

Like other default iPhone apps, the Music app supports 3D Touch, which you can use in a couple of ways.

Perform a Peek to see the Quick Actions menu

Select to play the Beats 1 station

The song currently playing; select to jump to the Now Playing screen

Select to search for music

When you press on the Music app's icon, you see the Quick Actions menu. At the bottom of this menu, you see the song currently playing. You can select Play Beats 1 to play that music, select Search to jump to the search screen, or select the current song to jump to the Now Playing screen.

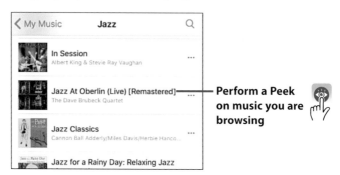

Perform a Peek on music you are browsing

When you see this,
you can swipe up the
screen to see option

Perform a pop to
open the music

Tap an action
to perform it

When you are browsing music, press on music in which you are interested to perform a Peek on it. In the Peek window, you view the music on which you pressed. If you continue to press on the Peek, it pops open, so you can browse and play the music. When you perform a Peek on some types of music, you see an upward-facing arrow at the top of the screen; this indicates you can swipe up the screen to reveal a menu of commands. Tap a command to perform it. For example, tap Play to play the music you are viewing.

Using AirPlay to Listen to Your iPhone's Music on Other Devices

With AirPlay, you can stream your music and other audio to other devices so you can hear it using a sound system instead of the iPhone's speakers or EarPods. For example, if you have an Apple TV connected to a home theater system, you can stream your audio to the Apple TV so it plays via the home theater's audio system. You can also stream to an AirPort Express base station to which you've connected speakers. Or, you can stream to AirPlay-compatible speakers that are designed to receive AirPlay signals directly.

Bluetooth Speakers

You can also use Bluetooth to stream music from your iPhone to Bluetooth speakers. Just pair and connect the iPhone to the speakers; the music plays through the speakers. This is a great way to make your music sound better when you are out and about because there are lots of great Bluetooth speakers that you can carry with you. See Chapter 2, "Connecting Your iPhone to the Internet, Bluetooth Devices, and iPhones/iPods/iPads," for the details about using Bluetooth devices.

To use AirPlay, your iPhone needs to be on the same Wi-Fi network as the devices to which you are going to stream the music. Or, if you are streaming to Bluetooth speakers, your iPhone needs to be paired to the speakers you want to use.

Tap to open the AirPlay menu

After you have set up the devices you are going to use, such as an AirPort Express base station and speakers, you can stream by tapping the AirPlay button located on screens in the Music app or in the Control Center.

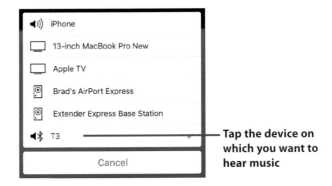

Tap the device on which you want to hear music

On the AirPlay menu, tap the device to which you want to stream music. The music plays on the device.

To return music playback to your iPhone, open the AirPlay menu and tap iPhone.

>>>Go Further
CONNECTING WITH ARTISTS

The Music app enables you to connect with artists who have music in Apple's Music library. This works sort of like Twitter or other social networks. When you add music to your library, you automatically follow artists; tap the Connect button and browse the screen to see information posted by the artists you are following. You can tap posts to move to other locations, such as larger posts or to the artist's page. Some posts include URLs that take you to locations on the Web, such as the artist's tour dates.

In addition to artists, you can follow playlists (when you listen to a playlist, you also automatically follow that playlist). When new information about a playlist you are following is added, it appears on the Connect screen, too.

You can manually follow an artist or playlist by tapping the Follow button.

View, edit, and share photos, slideshows, and video

Take photos and video

Configure photo and camera settings

In this chapter, you'll explore all the photo and video functionality that your iPhone has to offer. Topics include the following:

→ Setting your Photos & Camera preferences
→ Taking photos and video with your iPhone
→ Viewing, editing, and working with photos on your iPhone
→ Viewing, editing, and working with video on your iPhone
→ Using AirPlay to view photos and videos on a TV
→ Using iCloud with your photos

Working with Photos and Video You Take with Your iPhone

The iPhone's cameras and Camera app capture high quality photos and video. Because you'll likely have your iPhone with you at all times, it's handy to capture photos with it whenever and wherever you are. And, you can capture video just as easily.

Whether you've taken photos and video on your iPhone or added them from another source, the Photos app enables you to edit, view, organize, and share your photos. You'll likely find that taking and working with photos and videos are among the most useful things your iPhone can do.

Each generation of iPhone has had different photo and video capabilities and features. The current versions sport high-quality cameras, and in fact, there is a camera on each side of the iPhone. One takes photos of what you are looking at while one takes photos of what the screen is facing (usually for taking selfies). Current generations also have a flash; the ability to zoom; take burst, panoramic, and time-lapse photos; and other features you expect from a quality digital camera. The iPhone 6s and 6s Plus models can also take Live Photos, which capture a small amount of video along with the photo.

The iPhone's photo and video capabilities and features are probably the largest area of differences between the various models. Because of the fairly large variation in capabilities of iPhone models that can run iOS 9, it's impossible to cover all the differences in this chapter; because the iPhone 6s and iPhone 6s Plus are the most advanced models, they are the focus of this chapter. If you have a different model, some of the tasks described might not be applicable to you, or some of the details in this chapter might be different than what you see on your iPhone if it is an older model.

Additionally, the iPhone's photo and video capabilities have been increasingly tied into iCloud. For example, you can store your entire photo library under your iCloud account; this offers many benefits including backing up all your photos, making it easy to access your photos from any device, and being able to quickly share your photos with others. Therefore, I've assumed you are using iCloud and have configured it to work with photos as described in Chapter 3, "Setting Up and Using iCloud and Other Online Accounts." Like differences in iPhone camera capabilities, if you don't use iCloud with your photos, some of the information in this chapter doesn't apply to you and what you see on your phone might look different than what you see in this chapter.

Setting Your Photos & Camera Preferences

The following table describes options in the Settings app that you can access by tapping Settings, and then tapping Photos & Camera. The default settings allow you to take photos and video without making any changes to these settings, but it's good to know where they are and what they do if you decide to change how your apps work.

Settings App Explained

To get detailed information on using the Settings app, see "Working with the Settings App" in Chapter 4, "Configuring an iPhone to Suit Your Preferences."

Photos & Camera Settings

Section	Setting	Description
N/A	iCloud Photo Library	When enabled, all your photos are stored in the cloud so that you can access them from multiple devices. Additionally, this ensures that your photos are backed up in the event something happens to your iPhone. I recommend you enable this option to protect your photos, even if you only use your iPhone for photos and video. The only downside is that photos can require large amounts of storage. You might need to upgrade your iCloud storage space at some point to store all of your photos there.
N/A	Optimize iPhone Storage	If you select this option, only versions of your photos that are optimized for the iPhone are stored on your phone; this saves space so that you can keep more photos and videos on your iPhone, while providing images with quality perfect for displaying on the iPhone's screen. Full resolution photos are uploaded to the cloud so you can still use them with devices that are capable of displaying them in all their glory.
N/A	Download and Keep Originals	This option downloads full resolution versions of your photos and videos on your iPhone. They consume more space than optimized versions, and you aren't likely to be able to tell the difference when viewing them on your iPhone, so Optimize iPhone Storage is the better option.
N/A	Upload to My Photo Stream	When enabled, all your photos are automatically uploaded to your iCloud Photo Stream when you are connected to the Internet with Wi-Fi. New photos are also downloaded from the cloud to your iPhone and other devices with this setting enabled.
N/A	Upload Burst Photos	Later in this chapter, you learn about Burst photos, which are a series of photos taken rapidly. This setting determines if all of the photos in a burst are uploaded to the cloud or only photos you tag as favorites are uploaded. Because burst photos can take up a lot of space, it's usually better to leave this disabled. If you leave this disabled, when you select favorite photos in a burst series, only those photos are uploaded.
N/A	iCloud Photo Sharing	When enabled, you can share your photos with others and subscribe to other people's Photo Streams to share their photos.
PHOTOS TAB	Summarize Photos	When this switch is on (green), you see thumbnails for only some of the photos in a collection and the timeframe of each group is larger. If you set this to off (white), you see a thumbnail of every photo in your collections, which takes up much more screen space and you have to scroll more to move among your collections. This setting impacts how you see Collections view and Years view only.
CAMERA	Grid	When this switch is on, you see a grid on the screen when you are taking photos with the Camera app. This grid can help you align the subject of your photos in the image you are capturing.

Section	Setting	Description
CAMERA	Record Video	Use the options under this menu to determine how video is recorded. The options available depend on the model of iPhone you have. You can choose from among different combinations of resolution and frame rate. Higher resolution and frame rates mean better quality video, but also larger files.
CAMERA	Record Slo-mo	The selections under this menu determine the resolution and frame rate for slow-motion video. Like regular video, the higher the resolution and frame rate, the better quality the resulting video is and the file sizes are larger.
HDR (High Dynamic Range)	Keep Normal Photo	When this switch is on (green) the HDR (you'll learn more about this in a later sidebar) and the normal version of photos are stored. When this switch is off (white), only the HDR version of the photo is stored.

Taking Photos and Video with Your iPhone

You use the Camera app to take photos and video with your iPhone. This app has a number of controls and features. Some features are easy to spot while others aren't so obvious. By the end of this section, you'll know how to use these features to take great photos and video with your iPhone.

The general process for capturing photos or video is:

1. Choose the type of photo or video you want to capture.

2. Set the options for the type of photo or video you selected.

3. Take the photos or video.

4. View and edit the photos or video you captured.

The information you need to accomplish this process is provided in tables and tasks throughout this chapter.

Type of photo or video being taken

TIME-LAPSE   SLO-MO   VIDEO   PHOTO   S

Swipe to the left or right to choose the type of photo or video you want to take

The first step in taking photos or video is to choose the type of photo or video that you want to capture. You do this by swiping to the left or right on the selection bar just above the large shutter button at the bottom of the Camera app's screen, as shown in the previous figure. The option shown in yellow at the center of the screen is the current type of photo or video you will capture. The options available in the Camera app are explained in the following table.

Types of Photo and Video iPhones Can Capture

Type of Photo or Video	Description
TIME-LAPSE	This captures a video with compressed time so that the time displayed in the video occurs much more rapidly than "real time." This is what is often used to show a process that takes a long time, such as a plant growing, in just a few seconds.
SLO-MO	This takes slow motion video so that you can slow down something that happens quickly.
VIDEO	The VIDEO option captures video at a real-time speed. The steps to take video are provided in the task "Taking Video," later in this chapter.
PHOTO	The PHOTO tool captures still photos (or Live Photos on iPhone 6s or 6s Plus). Step-by-step instructions showing how to use this option are provided in the task "Taking Photos," later in this chapter.
SQUARE	Takes "square" photos in which the height and width are the same.
PANO	This one takes panoramic photos that enable you to capture very wide images. An example of capturing a panoramic photo is provided in the task "Taking Panoramic Photos," later in this chapter.

When you choose the type of photo or video you want to take, there are quite a few options you can select (the options available to you depend on the specific model of iPhone you are using). When you select options, the icons you see on the screen change to reflect your selection. For example, when you choose a self-timed photo, the Self-Timer icon changes to show the time delay you have selected. And, not all options are available at the same time. For example, you can't set the flash and HDR to on at the same time because you can't take HDR images with the flash.

The following table describes the icons and tools available on the Camera app's screen. (Remember that the specific icons and tools you see depend on the type of photo or video you are capturing and the model of iPhone you are using.)

Photo and Video Options and Icons

Icon	Description
⚡	**Flash**. When you tap this icon, you see a menu with the flash options, which are Auto (the app uses the flash when required), On (flash is always used), or Off (flash is never used). Tap the option you want to use and the menu closes. When the flash is set to on, the icon is yellow.
⚡	**Flash Being Used**. When this icon appears on the screen, it indicates the flash will be used when taking a photo or video.
HDR	**High Dynamic Range (HDR)**. Tap this to set the HDR options. (You learn more about HDR in the "More on Taking Photos and Video" Go Further sidebar later in this chapter.) The options are Auto, On, or Off. When the flash is set to on, this is disabled and you see a line through the HDR icon because you can't use the flash with HDR images.
◎	**Live Photo on**. When enabled, you take Live Photos (see the "Live Photos" note following this table) and the Live Photos icon is yellow. To turn Live Photos off, tap this icon. This is only available on 6s and 6s Plus.
◎	**Live Photo off**. When disabled, you take static photos and the Live icon is white. To turn Live Photos on, tap this icon. This is available only on 6s and 6s Plus.
⏱	**Self-timer**. When you tap this icon, a menu appears on which you can choose a 3- or 10-second delay for photos. When you choose a delay, the icon is replaced with one showing the delay you set.
📷	**Change Camera**. When you tap this icon, you toggle between the back side and front side camera (front camera is typically used for selfies).
◯	**Shutter**. This button changes based on the type of photo or video you are taking. For example, when you are taking a photo, this button is white as shown. When you take a video, it becomes red. It looks a bit different for other types as well, such as TIME-LAPSE. Regardless of what the button looks like, its function is the same. Tap it to start the process, such as to take a photo or start capturing video. If applicable, tap it again to stop the process, such as stopping video capture. To take burst photos, you tap and hold it to capture the burst.
◕	**Filter**. When you tap this button, a palette of filters appears. You can tap a filter to apply it to the photo or video you are capturing. For example, you can apply the Instant filter to make a photo look like it was taken on an old instant camera. When you apply a filter, you see the image with the filter applied. Generally, it's better to apply filters after you take a photo so that you have an original, unfiltered version of the photo (this is covered in the task "Applying Filters to Photos" later in this chapter).
◕	**Filter applied**. When the Filter icon is in color, you know a filter is currently applied. Tap the icon, and then tap the None option in the center of the screen to remove the filter.

Icon	Description
00:00:08	**Timer**. When you capture video, the timer shows the elapsed time of the video you are capturing.
	Focus/exposure box. When you frame an image, the camera uses a specific part of the image to set the focus, exposure, and other attributes. The yellow box that appears on the screen indicates the focus/exposure area. You can manually set the location of this box by tapping on the part of the image that you want the app to use to set the image's attributes. The box moves to the area on which you tapped and sets the attributes of the image based on that area.
	Exposure slider. When you tap in an image you are framing, the sun icon appears. If you tap on this icon, you see the exposure slider. Drag the sun up to increase the exposure or down to decrease it. The image changes as you move the slider so you can see its impact immediately.
AE/AF LOCK	**AE/AF lock**. When you tap an image to set the location of the focus/exposure box and keep your finger on the screen after a second or so, the focus and exposure becomes locked based on the area you selected. This icon indicates that the exposure and focus are locked so you can move the camera without changing the focus or exposure that will be used when you capture the image. Tap the screen to release the lock and refocus on another area.
	Faces found. When your iPhone detects faces, it puts this box around them and identifies the area as a face. You can use faces to organize photos by applying names to the faces in your photos.
	Zoom slider. You can unpinch on an image to zoom in or pinch on an image to zoom out. When you do, the Zoom slider appears on the screen. This indicates the relative level of zoom you are applying. You can also drag the slider toward the - to zoom out or drag it toward the + to zoom in to change the level of zoom you are using.

And Now a Few Words on Live Photos (iPhone 6s and 6s Plus)

The iPhone 6s and 6s Plus can capture Live Photos. A Live Photo is a static image, but it also has a few of what Apple calls "moments" of video around the static image that you take. To capture a Live Photo, you set the Live function to be on (the icon is yellow) and take the photo as you normally would. When you are viewing a Live Photo you have taken, tap and hold on the photo to see the motion associated with that photo. When you aren't tapping and holding on a Live Photo, it looks like any other photo you've taken.

Taking Photos

You can use the Camera app to capture photos, like so:

1. On the Home screen, tap Camera.

2. To capture a horizontal photo, rotate your iPhone so that it's horizontal; of course, you can use either orientation to take photos just as you can with any other camera.

3. Swipe up or down (right or left if the phone is vertical) on the selection bar until PHOTO is in the center and in yellow.

4. If you want to change the camera you are using, tap the Change Camera button. When you change the camera, the image briefly freezes, and then the view changes to the other camera. On some iPhone models, the front camera (the one facing you when you look at the screen) has fewer features than the back camera. For example, you can't zoom when using the front camera on all models except the iPhone 6s and 6s Plus.

5. Set the Flash, HDR, Live, and Self-timer options you want to use for the photo; see the previous table for an explanation of these options you can use and how they work.

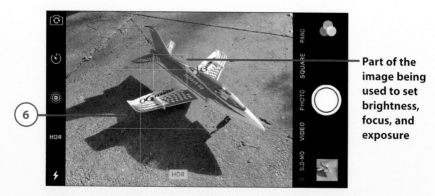

Part of the image being used to set brightness, focus, and exposure

6. Frame the image by moving and adjusting the iPhone's distance and angle to the object you are photographing; if you have the Grid turned on, you can use its lines to help you frame the image the way you want it. When you stop moving the phone, the Camera app indicates the part of the image that is used to set focus, brightness, and exposure with the yellow box. If this is the most important part of the image, you are good to go. If not, you can set this point manually by tapping where you want the focus to be (see step 9).

7. To zoom in, unpinch on the image. The camera zooms in on the subject and the Zoom slider appears.

8. Unpinch on the image or drag the slider toward the + to zoom in or pinch on the image or drag the slider toward the – to zoom out to change the level of zoom until it's what you want to use.

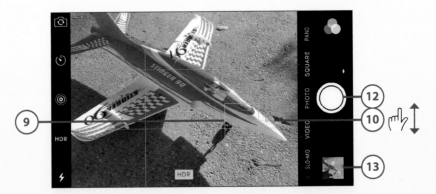

9. Tap the screen to manually set the area of the image to be used for setting the focus and exposure. The yellow focus box appears where you tapped.

10. To change the exposure, swipe up on the sun icon to increase the brightness or down to decrease it.

11. Continue making adjustments in the framing of the image, the zoom, focus point, and brightness until it is the image you want to take.

12. Tap the Shutter button on the screen, or either Volume button on the side of the iPhone. The Photo app captures the photo, and the shutter closes briefly while the photo is recorded. When the shutter opens again, you're ready to take the next photo.

13. To see the photo you most recently captured, tap the Thumbnail button to view it.

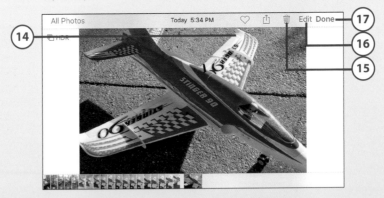

14. Use the photo-viewing tools to view the photo (see "Viewing, Editing, and Working with Photos on Your iPhone" later in this chapter for the details).

15. To delete a photo, tap the Trash Can button, and then tap Delete Photo.

16. To Edit the photo, tap the Edit button and use the resulting editing tools to make changes to it (see "Viewing, Editing, and Working with Photos on Your iPhone" later in this chapter for the details).

17. Tap Done. You move back into the Camera app, and can take more photos.

Taking Panoramic Photos

The Camera app can take panoramic photos by capturing a series of images as you pan the camera across a scene, and then "stitching" those images together into one panoramic image. To take a panoramic photo, perform the following steps:

1. Open the Camera app.

2. Swipe on the selection bar until PANO is selected. On the screen, you see a bar representing the entire image that contains a smaller box representing the current part of the image that will be captured.

3. Tap the Shutter button. The app begins capturing the image.

4. Slowly sweep the iPhone to the right while keeping the arrow centered on the line on the screen (if you move the phone too fast, you see a message on the screen telling you to slow down). The better you keep the tip of the arrow aligned with the line, the more consistent the center line of the resulting image will be.

5. When you've moved to the "end" of the image you are capturing or the limit of what you can capture in the photo, tap the Shutter button. You move back to the starting point and the panoramic photo is created. You can tap the image's thumbnail to view, delete, or edit it as described in the previous task.

Current position in the image

The shaded bar indicates the total possible area that can be included in the image

As you move the iPhone from the start of the image to the end, keep the arrow centered on the line

Taking Video

You can capture video as easily as you can still images. Here's how.

1. Move into the Camera app.

2. To capture horizontal video, rotate the iPhone so that it's horizontal; of course, you can use either orientation to take video just as you can with any other video camera.

3. Swipe on the selection bar until VIDEO is selected.

4. Choose the camera on the back of the iPhone or the one facing you, configure the flash, or zoom in, just like setting up a still image. (The Self-timer, grid, and HDR mode are not available when taking video.)

5. Tap on the screen where you want to focus.

6. If needed, adjust the exposure by sliding the "sun" icon up or down.

7. To start recording, tap the Shutter button. You hear the start/stop recording tone and the app starts capturing video; you see the timer on the screen showing how long you've been recording.

Length of video

9

8

8. To take still images while you take video, tap the white Shutter button.

9. To stop recording, tap the red Shutter button again. Also, like still images, you can then tap the video's thumbnail to preview it. You can use the Photos app's video tools to view or edit the clip. (See "Viewing, Editing, and Working with Video on Your iPhone" later in this chapter for the details.)

Taking Photos and Video from the Lock Screen

Because it is likely to be with you constantly, your iPhone is a great camera of opportunity. You can use its Quick Access feature to quickly take photos when your iPhone is asleep/locked. Here's how:

1. When the iPhone is locked, press the Touch ID/Home button. The Lock screen appears.

2. Swipe up on the camera icon. The Camera app opens. (If you don't swipe far enough up the screen, the Lock screen "drops" down again. Swipe almost all the way up the screen to open the Camera app. It also opens more easily if you give the icon a quick flick up.)

3. Use the Camera app to take the photo or video as described in the previous tasks. You can only view the most recent photos or videos you captured from within the Camera app. Move to the Photos app to see more.

Taking Photos and Video from the Control Center

You can get to the camera quickly using the Control Center, too.

1. Swipe up from the bottom of the screen to open the Control Center.

2. Tap the Camera button. The Camera app opens.

3. Use the Camera app to take photos or video as you've learned in the previous tasks.

Taking Photos with Quick Actions (iPhone 6s, 6s Plus Only)

New! On an iPhone 6s or 6s Plus, the Quick Access menu offers a selection of photos and video commands that you can choose right from a Home screen.

1.   Tap and hold on the Camera icon until the Quick Actions menu opens.

2.   Tap the type of photo or video you want to take. The Camera app opens and is set up for the type you selected.

3.   Use the Camera app to capture the photo or video.

>>>Go Further
MORE ON TAKING PHOTOS AND VIDEO

The Photos app enables you to do all sorts of interesting and fun things with photos and video. Following are some additional pointers that help you make the most of this great app:

- **Set once**. You only need to set the Flash, HDR, and other options when you want to change the current settings because these settings are retained even after you move out of the Camera app and back into it.

- **HDR.** The High Dynamic Range (HDR) feature causes the iPhone to take three shots of each image with each shot having a different exposure level. It then combines the three images into one higher-quality image. HDR works best for photos that don't have motion and where there is good lighting. (You can't use the iPhone's flash with HDR images.) Also, HDR photos take longer to capture.

  When the Keep Normal Photo switch in the Photos & Camera Settings is on, you see two versions of each HDR photo in the Photos app: One is the HDR version, and the other is the normal version. If you prefer the HDR versions, set the Keep Normal Photo switch to off so that your photos don't use as much space on your iPhone, and you don't have twice as many photos to deal with.

- **Location.** The first time you use the Camera app, you are prompted to decide whether or not you allow it to use Location Services. If you allow the Camera app to use Location Services, the app uses the iPhone's GPS to tag the location where photos and video were captured. Some apps can use this information, such as the Photos app on your iPhone, to locate your photos on maps, find photos by their locations, and so on.

- **Sensitivity.** The iPhone's camera is sensitive to movement, so if your hand moves while you are taking a photo, it's likely to be blurry. Sometimes, part of the image will be in focus while part of it isn't, so be sure to check the view before you capture a photo. This is especially true when you zoom in. If you are getting blurry photos, the problem is probably your hand moving while you are taking them. Of course, since it's digital, you can take as many photos as you need to get it right; you'll want to delete the rejects (you learn how later) periodically, so you don't have to waste storage room or clutter up the Photos app with them.

- **Burst photos.** When you press and hold on the Shutter button while taking photos, a series of images is captured rapidly and you see a counter showing the number being taken. When you release the Shutter button, a burst photo is created; the burst photo contains all of the images you captured, but appears as a single image in the Photos app. You can review the images in the burst and choose to keep only the images you want to save (this task is covered later in this chapter).

- **Self-timer.** When you set the Self-timer option, you choose either a 3- or 10-second delay between when you tap the Shutter button and when the image is captured. Like the other settings, the Self-timer is persistent so you need to turn it off again when you want to stop using it.

- **Self-timer and burst**. If you set the timer, and then tap and hold on the Shutter button for a second or so, a burst of ten photos is captured when the timer expires.

- **Slow-motion video**. You can also take slow-motion video. Choose SLO-MO on the selection bar. Set up the shot and take the video as you do with normal speed video. When you play it back, the video plays in slow motion except for the very beginning and ending. (The speed of the video is determined by the Record Slo-mo setting, described earlier.)

- **Time-lapse video**. When you choose the TIME-LAPSE option, you can set the focus and exposure level and choose the camera you want to use. You record the video just like "real time" video. When you play it back, the video plays back rapidly so you seemingly compress time.

- **Screenshots**. You can take screenshots of your iPhone's screen by pressing and holding the Home and Sleep/Wake buttons at the same time. The screen flashes white and the shutter sound plays to indicate the screen has been captured. The resulting image is stored in the All Photos (or Camera Roll if you don't use the iCloud Photo Library) album. You can view the screen captures you take, email them, send them via Messages, or other tasks as you can with photos you take with the iPhone's camera.

Viewing, Editing, and Working with Photos on Your iPhone

After you've loaded your iPhone with photos, you can use the Photos app to view them individually and as slideshows. You can also edit your photos and use them in a number of tasks, such as sharing your photos via AirDrop or email.

Finding Photos to Work With by Browsing

The first step in viewing, editing, or doing other tasks with photos is finding the photos you want to work with. When you open the Photos app, you see three ways to access your photos: Photos, Shared, and Albums. You can browse these sources to find photos in which you are interested.

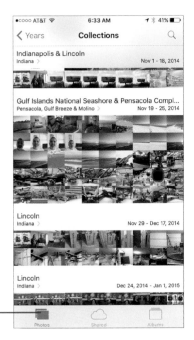

Your photos in groups by date and location

The Photos source organizes your photos with groupings of photos by date and location. (This is done automatically based on the data associated with your photos.) The top level is Years, which shows your photos grouped by the year in which they were taken. You can then "drill down" into a year where you find collections, under which photos are organized by location and date ranges, which are determined according to the time, date, and location information on your photos. When you tap one of these collections, you drill down and see moments, which show you the detail of a collection. At the moment level, you see and can work with the individual photos in the collection.

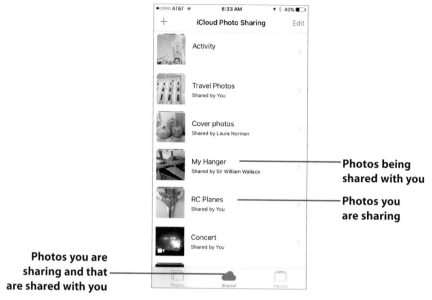

Photos being shared with you

Photos you are sharing

Photos you are sharing and that are shared with you

Shared shows photos you are sharing with other people and photos other people are sharing with you. For each group of photos being shared, you see the name of the group and who is sharing it (you, for photos you are sharing, or the name of the person sharing with you). When you tap a shared group, you see the photos it contains and can work with them. (Working with photo sharing is covered in detail in "Using iCloud with Your Photos" later in this chapter.)

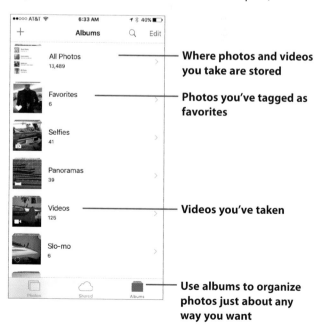

Where photos and videos you take are stored

Photos you've tagged as favorites

Videos you've taken

Use albums to organize photos just about any way you want

Albums allow you to organize your photos in a number of ways. Following are some of the albums or types of albums you might see:

- **All Photos or Camera Roll**. When you see the All Photos album, you have the iCloud Photo Library enabled so that you can use this album to see all the photos in your library. When this is not enabled, you see Camera Roll instead. When you use the iCloud Photo Library, all your photos are stored here. If you don't use it, this album contains photos and videos you've taken with the iPhone's camera or saved from other apps, such as attachments to email in Mail.

- **Favorites**. This folder contains images you have tagged as a favorite by tapping its Heart button.

- **Selfies**. Photos you take with the front-facing camera are stored here.

- **Panoramas**, **Videos, Slo-mo, Time-lapse, Bursts, and Screenshots**. These folders contain photos and videos of the types for which they are named. For example, to get to the videos you have taken, open the Videos album.

- **Albums you create**. Later in this chapter, you learn how to create albums for your photos and store photos in them.

Your Albums May Vary

Some apps, such as Instagram, might add their own albums to the Albums tab.

While each of these sources looks a bit different, the steps to browse them to find the photos you want to work with are similar for all three sources; this example shows using the Photos source to browse for photos:

1. On the Home screen, tap Photos.

2. Tap Photos. On the Years screen, you see photos collected by the year in which they were taken. Next to the year, you see a summary of the various locations where the photos were taken.

Start at the Beginning

If the title at the top of the screen isn't "Years," tap the back button located in the upper-left corner of the screen until it is.

3. Swipe up and down the screen to browse all the years.

4. Tap the thumbnails in the year that contains photos you want to work with. You move to the Collections screen that groups the selected year's photos based on locations and time periods.

Straight to the Map

If you want to jump directly to the map view of a group of photos, tap the heading for the period in which you are interested instead of the thumbnails it contains.

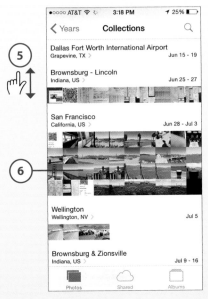

5. Swipe up and down the screen to browse all the collections in the year you selected.

6. Tap the collection that contains photos you want to see. Doing so opens the Moments screen, which breaks out the photos in the collection by location and date.

7. Swipe up and down the screen to browse all the moments in the collection you selected.

8. To see the photos in the moment based on their location, tap the moment's heading. You see a map with photos collected at the various locations.

No Map Required

If you don't want to see photos in a moment shown on the map, just tap any photo in a moment to start browsing that moment's photos.

9. Zoom in by unpinching your fingers on the map to get more detail. As you zoom, the locations of photos become more specific.

10. Tap the location that contains photos you want to see. You see a thumbnail of each photo at that location.

11. You're ready to view the photos in the group and can move to the next task.

Go Back

You can move back to the screens from where you came by tapping the back button, which is always located in the upper-left corner of the screen; this button is named with the screen it takes you back to. To choose a different source, you might have to tap the back button several times as the Photos, Shared, and Albums buttons at the bottom of the screen are only visible on the opening screen of the Photos app.

Finding Photos to Work With by Searching

Browsing photos can be a fun way to find photos, but at times you might want to get to specific photos more quickly. You can use the Search tool to get to photos quickly.

1. Continuing in the Photos app, tap the magnifying glass. The Search bar opens.

2. Type your search term. This can be any information associated with your photos, such as a date or location. As you type, collections of photos that match your search criteria are listed under the Search bar. The more specific you make your search term, the smaller the set of photos that will be found.

3. Tap the results you want to explore.

4. Browse the results to find the photo you want.

5. Tap Cancel to clear the search.

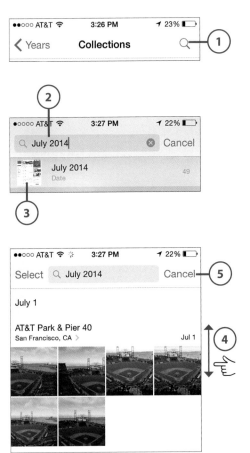

Viewing Photos Individually

The Photos app enables you to view your photos individually. Here's how:

1. Using the skills you learned in the previous tasks, open the group of photos that you want to view.

Orientation Doesn't Matter

Zooming, unzooming, and browsing photos works in the same way whether you hold your iPhone horizontally or vertically.

2. Swipe up and down to browse all the photos in the group.

3. Tap the photo you want to view. The photo display screen appears.

4. If it is a Live Photo, tap and hold on the screen to see the photo's motion.

5. To see the photo without the app's toolbars, tap the screen. The toolbars are hidden.

It's Not All Good

There's currently no way to tell if a photo is a Live Photo or not. You have to tap and hold on a photo to see. Hopefully, Apple will add some sort of icon to Live Photos so you know if a photo is a Live Photo without trying it.

6. Rotate the phone horizontally if you are viewing a horizontal photo.

7. Unpinch or double-tap on the photo to zoom in.

8. When you are zoomed in, drag around the image to view different parts of the zoomed image.

9. Pinch or double-tap on the photo to zoom out.

No Zooming Please

You can't have any zoom when you swipe to move to the next or previous photo so make sure you are zoomed out all the way before performing step 9 or 10.

---

10. Swipe to the left to view the next photo in the group.

11. Swipe to the right to view the previous photo in the group.

12. When you're done viewing photos in the group, tap the screen to show the toolbars again.

13. Swipe to the left or right on the thumbnails at the bottom of the screen to view all the photos in the current group. As you swipe, the photo you are viewing changes to be the one in the larger thumbnail at the center of the screen.

14. Tap a photo to view it.

15. When you are done viewing photos, tap the back button. You move back to the group's screen where you see the thumbnails of the photos it contains.

Photo being viewed

Using 3D Touch with Photos (iPhone 6s, 6s Plus Only)

New! You can use 3D Touch to preview and open photos as follows:

1. Browse a collection of photos in the Photos app.

2. Tap and hold on a photo in which you are interested. A Peek of that photo appears.

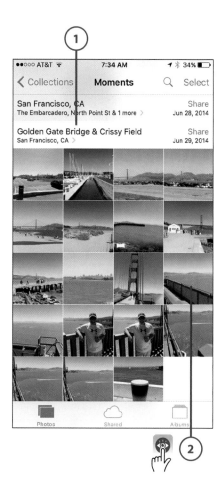

3. To open the photo, press down slightly harder until it pops open and use the steps in the previous task to view it (if you pop the photo open, skip the rest of these steps).

4. To see actions you can perform on the photo preview, swipe up the image.

5. Tap the action you want to perform, such as Favorite, to tag the photo as a favorite.

Viewing Photos in Slideshows

You can view photos in slideshows as the following steps demonstrate:

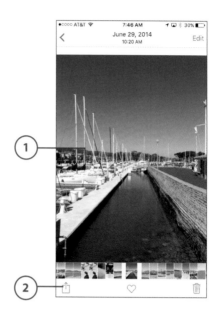

1. Using the skills you learned in the previous task, select and view the photo in a group of photos that you want to be the first one in the slideshow.

2. Tap the Share button.

It's Not All Good

When you select a photo and tap the Share button, the app indicates that one photo is selected, which is true. However, when you play the slideshow, all the photos in the group are shown. The one you selected is just the first one displayed. This is a bit confusing, but as it appears to have no bearing on what plays in the slideshow, you can safely ignore the information about how many photos are selected. If you want to choose the photos that are shown, create an album containing only those photos and view that in a slideshow instead.

3. Tap Slideshow. The slideshow begins to play.

4. You can watch the slideshow with the current options; in which case, skip to step 14, or if you want to configure slideshow options, tap the screen.

5. Tap Options.

6. Tap Theme. The theme determines how the images are displayed on the screen.

7. Tap the theme you want to use in
the slideshow.

8. Tap Music.

9. Tap the theme music you want
to use or tap iTunes Music and
then use the Select Music tool
to choose the music you want to
play during the slideshow.

10. To have the slideshow repeat
until you stop it manually, set the
Repeat switch to on (green).

11. Drag the slider to the left to slow
down the speed of the slideshow
or to the right to increase it.

12. Tap Done. You return to the
slideshow, and it plays with the
options you selected.

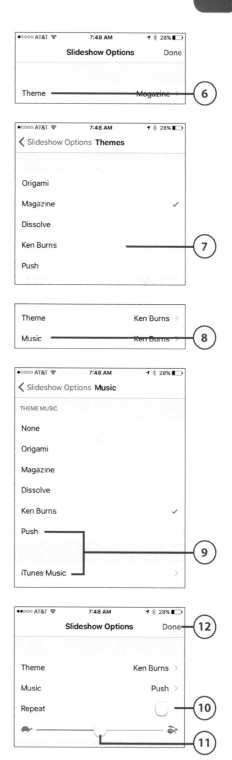

13. To hide the controls, tap the screen.

14. To stop the show before it finishes, tap the screen.

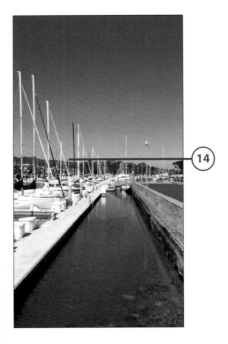

15. To pause the show, tap the Play/
Pause button.

16. To exit the slideshow, tap Done.

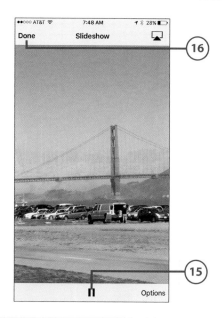

Working with Burst Mode Photos

When you use the Burst mode to take photos, the Camera app rapidly takes a series of photos. (Typically, you use Burst mode to capture motion, where the action is happening too
quickly to be able to frame and take individual photos.) You can review the photos taken in
Burst mode and save any you want to keep as favorites; your favorites become separate photos just like those you take one at a time. Here's how:

Burst mode photo

Number of photos in the series

1. View a Burst mode photo. Burst mode photos are indicated by the word Burst and the
number of photos in the burst. (You can see all of the burst photos on your phone by
opening the Bursts album.)

2. Tap Select. The burst is expanded. At the bottom of the screen, you see thumbnails for
the photos in the burst. At the top part of the screen, you see thumbnails of the photos;
the photo in the center of the previews is marked with a downward-facing arrow. Photos
marked with a dot are "suggested photos," meaning the best ones in the series according
to the Photos app.

Photo in the center of the screen

Suggested photos

3. Swipe all the way to the right to move to the first photo in the series; swiping on the thumbnails at the bottom flips through them faster.

Total number of selected photos

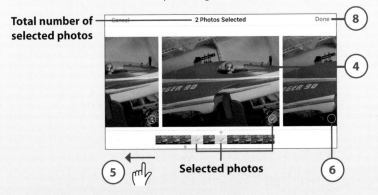

Selected photos

4. Tap a photo that you want to save. It is marked with a check mark.

5. Swipe to the left to move through the series.

6. Tap each photo you want to save.

7. Continue reviewing and selecting photos until you've gone through the entire series.

8. Tap Done.

9. Tap Keep Only *X* Favorites, where *X* is the number of photos you selected, or tap Keep Everything to keep all the photos in the burst. Each photo you keep becomes a separate, individual photo; you can work with these just like photos you take individually.

Burst Mode Photos and Uploads to the Cloud

If the Upload Burst Photos switch is set to off, burst photos are not uploaded to the cloud until you go through the steps to select and save photos from a burst. The photos you selected to keep are then uploaded to the cloud just like individual photos you take.

Editing Photos

Even though the iPhone has great photo-taking capabilities, not all the photos you take are perfect from the start. Fortunately, you can use the Photos app to edit your photos. The following tools are available to you:

- **Enhance.** This tool attempts to automatically adjust the colors and other properties of the photos to make them better.

- **Straighten, rotate, and crop.** You can rotate your photos to change their orientation and crop out the parts of photos you don't want to keep. You can also have the Photos app do this with the tap of a button.

- **Filters.** You can apply different filters to your photos for artistic or other purposes.

- **Remove red-eye.** This one helps you remove that certain demon-possessed look from the eyes of people in your photos.

- **Smart adjustments.** You can adjust the light, color, and even the black and white properties of your photos.

Enhancing Photos

To improve the quality of a photo, use the Enhance tool.

1. View the image you want to enhance.

2. Tap Edit.

3. Tap the Enhance button. The image is enhanced and the Enhance button turns blue.

4. If you don't like the enhancements, tap the Enhance button again to remove the enhancements.

5. To save the enhanced image, tap Done.

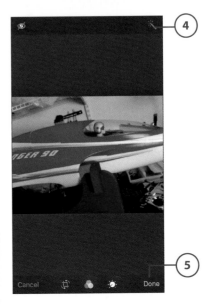

Straightening, Rotating, and Cropping Photos

To change the orientation of a photo, use the Rotate tool.

1. View the image you want to rotate.

2. Tap Edit.

3. Tap the Crop button. The Photos app attempts to straighten and crop the photo automatically.

4. If you are satisfied with how the photo is straightened and cropped, tap Done and skip the rest of these steps. If not, continue to the next step.

5. To undo the automatic straighten and crop, tap RESET.

6. To rotate the image, tap the Rotate button. Each time you tap this button, the image rotates 90 degrees.

7. To straighten the image, drag the triangle to the left or right to rotate the image.

8. When the image is straightened, remove your finger. The dial shows how much you've rotated the image.

9. To crop the image proportionally, tap the Constrain button; to crop the image without staying to a specific proportion, skip to step 11.

Photo is straightened and cropped

10. Tap the proportion with which you want to crop the image. You use this to configure the image for how you intend to display it. For example, if you want to display it on a 16:9 TV, you might want to constrain the cropping to that proportion so the image matches the display device.

11. Drag the corners of the crop box until the part of the image you want to keep is shown in the box.

12. Drag on the image to move it around inside the crop box.

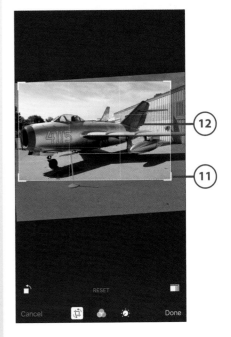

13. When the image is cropped and positioned as you want it to be, tap Done. The edited image is saved.

More on Straightening and Cropping Photos

To undo changes you've made, tap the RESET button and the photo returns to the state it was in before you started editing it. To have the app automatically straighten and crop the photo again, tap AUTO. To exit the Edit mode without saving your changes, tap Cancel.

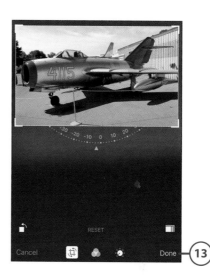

Applying Filters to Photos

To apply filters to photos, do the following:

1. View the image to which you want to apply filters.

2. Tap Edit.

3. Tap the Filters button. The palette of filters appears.

4. Swipe to the left or right on the palette to browse all of the filters.

5. Tap the filter you want to apply. The filter is applied to the image and you see a preview of the image as it will be with the filter; the filter currently applied is highlighted with a blue box. Keep trying filters until the image is what you want it to be.

6. Tap Done. The photo with the filter applied is saved.

Undoing What You've Done

To restore a photo to its unedited state, tap Revert, which appears when you edit a photo that you previously edited and saved. At the prompt, tap Revert to Original and the photo is restored to its "like new" condition.

Filter currently applied

6

Removing Red-Eye from Photos

When you edit a photo with people in it, the Red-eye tool becomes available (if no faces are recognized, this tool is hidden). To remove red-eye, perform the following steps:

1. View an image with people that have red-eye.

2. Tap Edit.

3. Tap the Red-eye button.

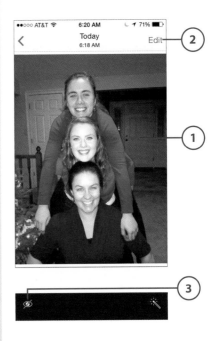

4. Zoom in on the eyes from which you want to remove red-eye.

5. Tap each eye containing red-eye. The red in the eyes you tap is removed.

6. Repeat steps 4 and 5 until you've removed all the red-eye.

7. Tap Done.

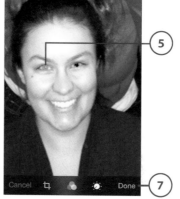

Making Smart Adjustments to Photos

You can edit your photos using the Photos app's Smart Adjustment tools. Using these tools, you can change various characteristics related to light, color, and black and white aspects of your photos.

1. View the image you want to adjust.

2. Tap Edit.

3. Tap the Smart Adjust button.

4. Tap the area you want to adjust, such as Color.

Get Straight to the Point

To jump directly to a specific aspect of the area you are adjusting, tap the downward-facing arrow along the right side of the screen. On the resulting menu, tap the aspect you want to adjust. For example, if you open this menu for Color, you tap Saturation, Contrast, or Cast to adjust those factors.

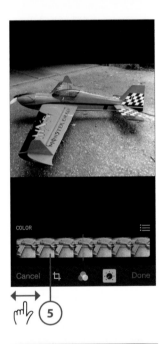

5. Swipe to the left or right to change the level of the parameter you are adjusting. As you make changes, you see the results of the change on the image.

6. When you're done adjusting the first attribute you selected, tap the List button.

7. Tap one of the options under the attribute you are already working with to adjust it; or tap the downward-facing arrow under one of the other attributes, and then tap the characteristic you want to change.

8. Swipe to the left or right to change the level of the parameter you are adjusting. As you make changes, you see the results of the change on the image.

9. Repeat steps 6 through 8 until you've made all the adjustments you want to make.

10. Tap Done to save the adjusted image.

Working with Photos

Once you have photos on your iPhone, there are a lot of things you can do with them, including:

- Emailing one or more photos to one or more people (see the next task).

- Sending a photo via a text message (see Chapter 10, "Sending, Receiving, and Managing Texts and iMessages").

- Sharing photos via AirDrop.

- Sharing photos with others via Photo Stream (covered later in this chapter).

- Posting your photos on your Facebook wall or timeline.

- Assigning photos to contacts (see Chapter 7, "Managing Contacts").

- Using photos as wallpaper (see Chapter 5, "Customizing How Your iPhone Looks and Sounds").

- Sharing photos via tweets.

- Printing photos (see Chapter 1, "Getting Started with Your iPhone").

- Deleting photos (covered later).

- Organizing photos in albums (also covered later).

Copy 'Em

If you select one or more photos and tap the Copy button, the images you selected are copied to the iPhone's clipboard. You can then move into another application and paste them in.

You'll easily be able to accomplish any actions on your own that are not covered in detail here once you've performed a couple of those that are demonstrated in the following tasks.

Individual versus Groups

Some actions are only available when you are working with an individual photo. For example, you can send only a single photo via Twitter, whereas you can email multiple photos at the same time. Any commands that aren't applicable to the photos that are selected won't appear on the screen.

Sharing Photos via Email

You can email photos via iPhone's Mail application starting from the Photos app.

1. View the source containing one or more images that you want to share.

2. Tap Select.

3. Select the photos you want to send by tapping them. When you tap a photo, it is marked with a check mark to show you that it is selected.

4. Tap the Share button.

Too Many?

If the photos you have selected are too much for email, the Mail button won't appear. You need to select fewer photos to attach to the email message.

5. Tap Mail. A new email message is created, and the photos are added as attachments.

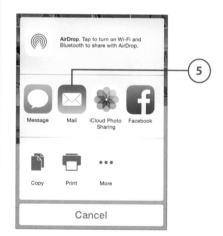

6. Use the email tools to address the email, add a subject, type the body, and send it. (See Chapter 9, "Sending, Receiving, and Managing Email," for detailed information about using your iPhone's email tools.)

7. Tap the size of the images you want to send. Choosing a smaller size makes the files smaller and reduces the quality of the photos. You should generally try to keep the size of emails to 5MB or less to ensure the message makes it to the recipient. (Some email servers block larger messages.) After you send the email, you move back to the photos you were browsing.

Images from Email

As you learned in Chapter 9, when you save images attached to email that you receive, they are stored in the All Photos or Camera Roll photo album just like photos you take with your iPhone.

Organizing Photos in a New Album

You can create photo albums and store photos in them to keep your photos organized.

To create a new album, perform these steps:

1. Move to the Albums screen by tapping Albums on the toolbar.

2. Tap the Add button.

3. Type the name of the new album.

4. Tap Save. You're prompted to select photos to add to the new album.

5. Move to the source of the photos you want to add to the new album.

6. Swipe up and down to browse the source and tap the photos you want to add to the album. They are marked with a check mark to show that they are selected. The number of photos selected is shown at the top of the screen.

7. Tap Done. The photos are added to the new album and you move back to the Albums screen. The new album is shown on the list, and you can work with it just like the other albums you see.

Playing Favorites

To mark any photo or video as a favorite, tap the Heart button. It fills in with blue to show you that the item you are viewing is a favorite. Favorites are automatically collected in the Favorites album, so this is an easy way to collect photos and videos you want to be able to easily find again without having to create a new album or even put them in an album. You can unmark a photo or video as a favorite by tapping the Heart button again.

Adding Photos to an Existing Album

To add photos to an existing album, follow these steps:

1. Move to the source containing the photos you want to add to an album.

2. Tap Select.

3. Tap the photos you want to add to the album.

4. Tap Add To. You move to the Albums screen.

5. Swipe up and down the list to find the album to which you want to add the photos.

6. Tap the album; if an album is grayed out and you can't tap it, that album was not created on the iPhone and so you can't change its contents. The selected photos are added to the album.

More Album Fun

You can change the order in which albums are listed on the Albums screen. Move to the Albums screen and tap Edit. Tap the Unlock button next to the albums you want to move, and then drag albums up or down by their List buttons. Likewise, you can delete an album that you created in the Photos app. Move to the Albums screen and tap Edit. Tap the Unlock button for the album you want to delete, tap Delete, and then tap Delete Album. When you're done making changes to your Albums, tap Done. To remove a photo from an album, view the photo, tap the Trash Can button, and then tap Remove from Album. Photos you remove from an album remain in the Camera Roll album and in your library; they are only removed from the album.

Deleting Photos

You can delete photos and videos that you don't want to keep on your iPhone. If you use the iCloud Photo Library, deleting the photos from your phone also deletes them from your photo library and from all the other devices using your library. So, make sure you really don't want photos any more before you delete them.

1. Open the source containing photos you want to delete.

2. Tap Select.

3. Tap the photos you want to delete. Each item you select is marked with a check mark.

4. Tap the Trash Can button.

5. Tap Delete X Photos, where X is the number of photos you selected. The photos you selected are deleted.

Deleting Individual Photos

You can delete individual photos that you are viewing by tapping the Trash Can button, and then tapping Delete Photo.

Viewing, Editing, and Working with Video on Your iPhone

As shown previously in this chapter, you can capture video clips with your iPhone. Once captured, you can view clips on your iPhone, edit them, and share them.

Finding and Watching Videos

Watching videos you've captured with your iPhone is simple.

1. Move to the Albums screen.

2. Tap the Videos album. Video clips have a camera icon and running time at the bottom of their icons.

3. Swipe up and down the screen to browse your videos.

4. Tap the video you want to watch.

5. Rotate the phone to change its orientation if necessary.

6. Tap Play. The video plays. After a few moments, the toolbars disappear.

7. Tap the video. The toolbars reappear.

Deleting Video

To remove a video clip from your iPhone, view it, tap the Trash Can button, and then tap Delete Video at the prompt.

8. To pause the video, tap the Pause button.

9. To jump to a specific point in a video, swipe to the left or right on the thumbnails at the bottom of the screen. When you swipe to the left, you move ahead in the video; when you swipe to the right, you move back in the video.

Current frame

Watching Slow-Motion and Time-Lapse Video

Watching slow-motion video is just like watching regular speed video except after a few frames, the video slows down until a few frames before the end at which point it speeds up again. Watching time-lapse is similar except the video plays faster instead of slower than real time.

Editing Video

You can trim a video clip to remove unwanted parts. Here's how you do it:

1. View the video you want to edit.

2. Tap Edit. If the video isn't stored on your phone, it is downloaded. When that process is complete, you can edit it.

3. Drag the left trim marker to where you want the edited clip to start; the trim marker is the left-facing arrow at the left end of the timeline. If you hold your finger in one place for a few seconds, the thumbnails expand so your placement of the crop marker can be more precise. As soon as you move the trim marker, the part of the clip that is inside the selection is highlighted in the yellow box; the Trim button also appears.

4. Drag the right trim marker to where you want the edited clip to end.

5. Tap Done.

6. Tap Save as New Clip to save the trimmed clip as a new clip or Cancel to leave the clip as it was. When you save it as a new clip, the frames outside the crop markers are removed from the clip and it is added to your library as a new clip.

There's an App for That

For more powerful video editing on your iPhone, download the iMovie app. This app provides a much more powerful video editor. You can use themes to design a video, add music, include titles and photos, and much more.

>>>Go Further
SHARING VIDEO

There are lots of ways to share your videos. View the video you want to share. Tap the Share button. Tap Next. Tap how you want to share the video. There are a number of options including Messages, Mail, iCloud, iCloud Photo Sharing, YouTube, Facebook, and Vimeo. Follow the onscreen prompts to complete the sharing process.

Using AirPlay to View Photos and Videos on a TV

Viewing photos and slideshows on the iPhone's screen is good, but seeing them on a big screen is even better. If you have an Apple TV connected to a home theater system, you can stream your photos and videos so that you can see them on your TV and hear their soundtracks via the system's audio components.

After your Apple TV is configured, your iPhone needs to be on the same network as the Apple TV so the two devices can communicate.

To view photos on your TV, do the following:

1. View a photo in the source containing the photos you want to stream.

2. Tap the Share button.

3. Tap AirPlay.

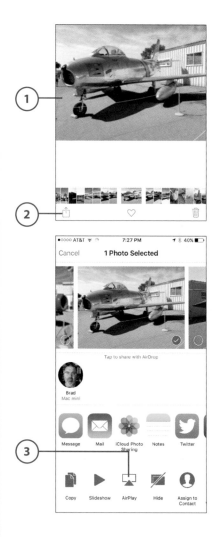

4. Tap Apple TV. The photo is streamed to the TV and you return to the photo on the iPhone; at the top of the screen, you see a blue bar indicating you are streaming. You can swipe to the left or right to move to the previous or next photo and use the other viewing tools you learned about earlier. You see the same image on the iPhone and on the TV (at very different sizes of course!).

This photo is streaming to a TV

5. To stop streaming, tap the AirPlay button.

6. Tap Turn off AirPlay.

This slideshow is streaming to a TV

Previously in this chapter, you learned how to view photos in a slideshow. You can also stream a slideshow through an Apple TV by tapping the Share button and then tapping Apple TV. Start the slideshow as you learned earlier. You see the images on the TV and hear its music on the audio device connected to the Apple TV. On the iPhone, you see the screen indicating the slideshow is being streamed. To stop the slideshow, tap the Pause button on the iPhone's screen. Exit AirPlay mode by tapping the AirPlay button and then tapping Turn off AirPlay.

Similarly, you can stream videos to an Apple TV using the same process. View the video you want to stream. Tap the Share button and tap AirPlay. Tap Apple TV. The video plays on the device connected to the Apple TV. You can control the video using the controls on the iPhone's screen.

To turn streaming off, open the AirPlay menu and tap iPhone.

Using iCloud with Your Photos

With iCloud, your devices can automatically upload photos to your iCloud account on the Internet. Other devices can automatically download photos from iCloud, so you have your photos available on all your devices at the same time. Using iCloud with your photos has two sides: a sender and receiver. Your iPhone can be both. Photo applications can also access your photos and download them to your computer automatically. Windows PCs can also be configured to automatically download photos from the cloud.

In addition to backing up your photos and having all your photos available to you, you can also share your photos and videos with others and view photos and videos being shared with you.

Sharing Your Photos

You can share your photos with others by creating a shared album. This is a great way to share photos, because others can subscribe to your shared albums to view and work with the photos you share. When you share photos, you can add them to an album that's already being shared or create a new shared album.

To create a new, empty, shared album, do the following:

1. Open the Shared source. You see the iCloud Photo Sharing screen that lists the shared albums in which you are currently participating (as either the person sharing them or subscribed to them).

2. Tap the Add (+) button.

3. Type the title of the new album.

4. Tap Next.

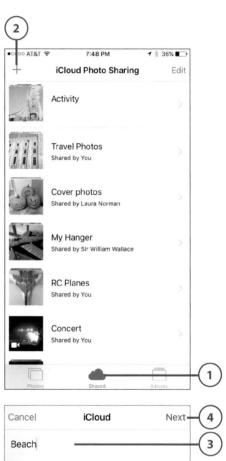

5. Enter or select the email address of the first person with whom you want to share the photos.

6. Add other recipients until you've added everyone you want to access the photos.

7. Tap Create. The shared album is created and is ready for you to add photos. The recipients you included in the new album receive notifications that invite them to join the album.

New shared album, ready for your photos

Adding Photos to a Shared Album

To add photos to an album you are sharing, perform the following steps:

1. Move to the source containing photos you want to add to a shared album.

2. Tap Select.

3. Tap the photos you want to share.

4. Tap the Share button.

5. Tap iCloud Photo Sharing.

6. Enter your commentary about the photos you are sharing. (Note, this commentary is associated only with the first photo.)

7. Tap Shared Album.

8. Swipe up and down to browse the list of shared albums available.

9. Tap the album to which you want to add the photos.

New Shared Album with Photos
You can create a new shared album with the selected photos by tapping New Shared Album.

10. Tap iCloud.

11. Tap Post. The photos you selected are added to the shared album. People who are subscribed to the album receive a notification that photos have been added and can view the new photos along with your commentary.

iCloud Account Required
The people with whom you share photos must have an iCloud account.

>>>Go Further
MORE ON iCLOUD PHOTO SHARING

Following are a few more pointers to help you use iCloud photo sharing:

- You can add comments to photos you are sharing. Open the shared album and tap the photo to which you want to add comments. Tap Add a comment. Type your comment and tap Send. People with whom you are sharing the photo receive a notification and can read your comments.

- To add more photos to a shared album, open the album and tap the Add (+) button. Use the resulting screen to select the photos you want to add, include commentary, and post the photos.

- To invite people to join a shared album, open the shared album. Tap the People tab at the bottom of the screen and then tap Invite People. Enter the email addresses of the people you want to invite and tap Add.

- You can configure various aspects of a shared album by opening it and tapping the People tab at the bottom of the screen. You can see the status of people you have invited, determine if the people with whom you are sharing the album can post to it, make the album a public website, determine if notifications are sent, or delete the shared album

- If you have Family Sharing set up (see Chapter 6), an album called Family is created automatically and shared with everyone in your sharing group automatically. Like other shared albums, you can add photos to this album to share them with your family group. Any photos added to it by the others in your group are shared with you, too.

Working with Photo Albums Shared with You

You can work with albums people share with you as follows:

1. Tap the notification you received, or tap the Shared source when you see a badge indicating you have activity.

2. Tap Accept for the shared album you want to join. The shared album becomes available on your Shared tab.

3. Tap Sharing.

4. Tap the new shared album.

5. Tap a photo in the album.

6. Tap Like to indicate you like the photo.

7. Tap Add a comment. (If you previously liked the photo, you see the number of likes for it instead; tap that number to add a comment.)

8. Type your comment.

9. Tap Send. Your comments are added to the album.

10. Tap the back button.

11. If allowed, tap the Add (+) button and post your own photos to the album you are sharing. This works just like posting to your own albums.

>>>*Go Further*

MORE ON PHOTOS SHARED WITH YOU

When you share other people's photos, keep the following points in mind:

- You can do most of the tasks with shared photos that you can with your own, such as emailing them, using them as wallpaper, and so on.

- To unsubscribe from an album, move to its People screen and tap Unsubscribe and confirm that is what you want to do. The shared album is removed from your iPhone.

- To see the activity associated with albums being shared with you, and those you are sharing, open the Activity Album on the iCloud Photo Sharing screen. You see new postings to the albums, when someone comments, and so on.

Find your way

Take a library of reading content wherever you go

Get the news you want when you want it

Listen to or watch podcasts

Manage and use store cards, credit cards, and more

Keep yourself healthy

Take phone calls on Macs and iPads, too

Use Handoff to work seamlessly across devices

16

Using Other Cool iPhone Apps and Features

In previous chapters, you learned about many of the iPhone's most useful apps, such as Phone, Mail, Messages, Safari, and Calendar. In this chapter, you learn about three more: Podcasts to subscribe and listen to or watch podcasts on your favorite topics, Maps to find and navigate to locations near and far, and Wallet to store and use information such as membership cards, boarding passes, credit cards, and more.

You also learn how to use your iPhone with Macs and iPads. The iOS Handoff feature makes it easy to work on the same projects on Macs, iPhones, and iPads. For example, you can edit a Pages document on a Mac, and see the same version on an iPad and your iPhone, too. When a phone call comes in to your iPhone, you can choose to answer it on your Mac, iPad, or Watch.

Before getting into those details, take a tour of some of the other great iPhone apps you might want to explore on your own.

Touring Other Cool iPhone Apps

The following table provides an overview of a number of other apps (all of which are installed by default) that you might find useful or entertaining:

Other Cool iPhone Apps

Icon	App	Description
	Weather	See high-level weather conditions and a forecast for any number of locations. You can use the defaults, and if you tap the List button in the lower-right corner of the screen, you can add, remove, and organize the locations you want to track. Swipe through the screens to see each area's forecast.
	Clock	Get the current time in multiple locations around the world, set alarms, use a stopwatch, or countdown time with a timer. Quickly access the Clock app by swiping up from the bottom of the screen to open the Control Center. Tap the Clock icon to open the Clock app.
	Videos	Use this app to watch movies, TV shows, and podcasts.
	Notes	Capture different kinds of information, including text notes, lists, photos, maps, and more. You can also draw in the app and attach different types of objects to notes, and then use the Attachment Manager to view them. Using online accounts with the Notes app, such as iCloud, your notes can be available on all your devices.
	Stocks	Use this one to track stocks in which you are interested. You can add any index, stock, or fund as long as you know the symbol for it, and you can even use the application to find a symbol if you don't know it. You can see current performance and view historical performance for various time periods. Rotate the iPhone to see a more in-depth view when you are examining a specific stock. You can see the current "ticker" for the items you are tracking by pulling the Notification Center down by swiping down from the top of the screen.
	iBooks	Access and organize books and PDFs so that you always have something to read. The app enables you to change how the books appear on the screen, such as making the font larger or smaller. iBooks syncs across your devices so that you can read something on your iPhone and then pick it up later at the same spot on an iPad.
	News	Read news from a variety of sources. You can search news and save items of interest to you. You can also choose your favorite news sources so that you can focus more on what you care about and avoid what you don't.

Icon	App	Description
	Health	Track and manage health-related information from multiple sources, such as other apps and devices, in one location. You can see your information on dashboards or you can drill down into the details. You can configure the information you see by selecting the sources and types of information you want to track. You can also store your vital information in the Medical ID so that emergency workers can access it from your Lock Screen in order to help you.
	Calculator	In portrait orientation, the Calculator is the equivalent of one you would get at the local dollar store. Rotate the iPhone to access scientific calculator options. Access the Calculator quickly by swiping up from the bottom of the screen to open the Control Center; then, tap the Calculator button.
	Watch	Use this app to pair and configure your iPhone with an Apple Watch. Once paired with your iPhone, you can configure how your Watch accesses content from your iPhone's apps such as Mail, Calendar, Messages, Phone, Contacts, Photos, Music, Reminders, and more.
	Compass (Extras folder)	Transform your iPhone into a compass. When you open the app for the first time, you need to calibrate it following the on-screen directions. When that is done, you can see your current location on the analog-looking compass and with precision in degree latitude and longitude. If you swipe to the right, you transform your iPhone into a level that measures on the horizontal planes along with angles. Swipe to the right to get back to the compass.
	Voice Memos (Extras folder)	Record audio notes using the Voice Memos app. Play them back, and through syncing, move them onto your computer. You can record through the iPhone's microphone or via the mic on the earbud headset.
	Find Friends (Extras folder)	See the current location of "friends" who are part of your Family Sharing group or who you add to the app manually. You can also share your location with others.
	Find iPhone (Extras folder)	Use this app to locate other iPhones, iPads, or Macs that have enabled Find My iPhone using the same iCloud account.
	Flashlight (Control Center)	This app, which is only available on the Control Center, uses your iPhone's flash as a flashlight. It's a very simple app, but also happens to be extremely useful.

Listening to Podcasts with the Podcasts App

Podcasts are episodic audio or video programs that are available on many, many topics. Using the Podcasts app, you can subscribe to and manage lots of podcasts so that you always have something of interest available to you.

Setting Your Podcast Preferences

Like most apps you've seen in this book, you can set some preferences for the Podcasts app. These preferences, which you access by opening the Settings app and tapping Podcasts on the left side, are described in the following table.

Podcasts Settings

Settings Area	Location	Setting	Description
ALLOW PODCASTS TO ACCESS	Notifications	Allow Notifications	Set to on (green) if you want the Podcasts app to notify you when new episodes are downloaded or for other events.
ALLOW PODCASTS TO ACCESS	Notifications	Show in Notification Center	When enabled, notifications from the Podcasts app are shown on the Notification Center.
ALLOW PODCASTS TO ACCESS	Notifications	Badge App Icon	When on, this switch causes the number of new episodes to be displayed on the Podcasts icon.
ALLOW PODCASTS TO ACCESS	Notifications	Show on Lock Screen	Set to on (green) if you want podcast notifications to appear on the Lock screen.
ALLOW PODCASTS TO ACCESS	N/A	Background App Refresh	To allow the Podcasts app to update itself when it is not being used, set this switch to on (green). If the general Background App Refresh setting in the General settings is turned off, this is disabled.
ALLOW PODCASTS TO ACCESS	N/A	Cellular Data	Set this to off (white) if you have a limited data plan and only want the app to refresh its data when you are using a Wi-Fi network.

Settings Area	Location	Setting	Description
PODCASTS SETTINGS	N/A	Sync Podcasts	When enabled, your podcasts sync in the Podcasts app on your iOS devices and in iTunes on computers. You can listen to the same podcasts on any synced device, and you pick up in an episode on one device right where you left off on another.
PODCASTS SETTINGS	N/A	Only Download on Wi-Fi	This switch determines if podcast episodes can be downloaded to your phone using only Wi-Fi or using Wi-Fi or cellular. With this switch on (green), episodes are only downloaded when your phone is connected to Wi-Fi. With this switch off (white), episodes can be downloaded using Wi-Fi or a cellular connection. The Cellular Data switch controls whether the app can access information, such as determining if new episodes are available, using the cellular connection. This switch controls where podcasts can be downloaded using the cellular connection or not.
PODCAST DEFAULTS	Refresh Every	Refresh Every	Tap how often you want the Podcasts app to check for, and download, new episodes.
PODCAST DEFAULTS	Limit Episodes	Limit Episodes	Tap how you want the app to keep downloaded episodes. Tap Off if you want to keep all episodes. Tap the number of most recent episodes to limit episodes based on their number.
PODCAST DEFAULTS	Download Episodes	Download Episodes	Tap the download option you want: Off, if you don't want episodes to be downloaded automatically; Only New, if you want only new episodes to be downloaded automatically; or All Unplayed, if you want all available episodes that you haven't listened to yet to be downloaded automatically.
PODCAST DEFAULTS	N/A	Delete Played Episodes	If you want the app to automatically delete episodes you have listened to, set the switch to on (green).
ACCESSIBILITY	N/A	Custom Colors	When enabled, a podcast's colors reflect its artwork.

Using the Podcasts App to Subscribe to Podcasts

You can subscribe to podcasts you want to listen to or watch so they are available in the Podcasts app. Here's how to search for podcasts from a specific organization or by topic:

1. On the Home screen, tap Podcasts.

2. Tap Search.

3. Tap in the Search bar.

4. Type your search term. As you type, the app presents podcasts related to your search term.

5. Browse the search results.

6. Tap the search you want to perform or if none of the searches are what you are looking for, type a more detailed search term and tap Search to see the entire list. The search is performed and you see the results organized into different categories, such as episodes and podcasts. You can use the tabs at the top of the screen to limit the results to one or the other.

7. Browse the search results.

8. Tap a podcast that you want to explore. You move to the podcast's screen where you see its image, title, and other information. Below the SUBSCRIBE button, you see the podcast's description.

9.   Read the description.

10. Tap More if the entire description isn't displayed.

11. To subscribe to the podcast, tap SUBSCRIBE. You are subscribed to the podcast and episodes are downloaded according to the Podcast app's settings (see table earlier in this chapter for settings and their descriptions). For example, if in the Podcast app settings you chose the 1 Month Limit Episodes setting, only the episodes released within the past month are downloaded.

12. Tap My Podcasts. You move back to your podcast library where you see the podcast to which you subscribed and it is ready for you to listen to it.

13. Tap the podcast to play it (details about finding and playing podcasts are in the following tasks).

>>>*Go Further*
MORE ON PODCASTS

As you ponder podcasts, consider the following:

- You can browse for podcasts using the Featured and Top Charts buttons. These present groups of podcasts that you can filter by tapping the Categories button at the top of the screen and choosing the category of podcast in which you are interested. You can then browse the results and explore podcasts you might wish to subscribe to just like when you search for podcasts.

- The screen for some podcasts has three tabs: Details, Reviews, and Related. These tabs are just like the tabs for apps in the App Store (see Chapter 6, "Downloading Apps, Music, Movies, TV Shows, and More onto Your iPhone").

- When you search for or browse for podcasts and you view one to which you are subscribed, you see the UNSUBSCRIBE button. To unsubscribe from a podcast without deleting all the episodes you've downloaded, tap UNSUBCRIBE.

- You can listen to or download episodes of a podcast without subscribing to it. Tap an episode to play it. To download it without playing it, tap its Download button (the cloud with the downward-facing arrow). Since almost all podcasts are free, there's no penalty for subscribing to any that you want to try. You can always unsubscribe should you decide that you don't want to listen to or watch the podcast.

- You can share a podcast by tapping the Share button, and then choosing how you want to share it (such as with AirDrop, Mail, or Messages).

- To unsubscribe from a podcast and delete all the episodes you've downloaded, tap My Podcasts. Tap the Edit button in the upper-left corner of the screen. Tap the podcast's unlock button (-) and tap Delete. The podcast and all its episodes are deleted from your library.

Choosing a Podcast to Listen To

When you're ready to listen, open the Podcasts app and tap My Podcasts. You can use the My Podcasts screen to quickly find the podcast you want to hear or see.

Podcasts to which
you are subscribed

Search bar

Swipe up or down to
browse your podcasts

Number of
unplayed episodes

Tap a podcast to
view its episodes

Tap to see
your podcasts

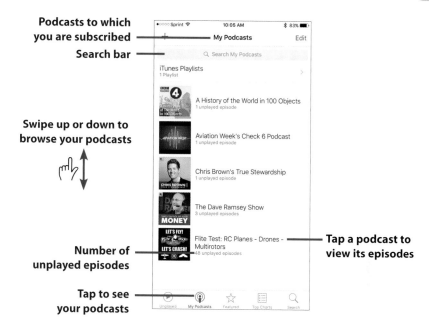

- Swipe up and down the My Podcasts screen to browse all the podcasts to which you are subscribed. You see a thumbnail for each podcast. Tap a thumbnail to see a podcast's page so you can select and play episodes (covered in the next task).

Episodes you
haven't listened to

Search bar

Swipe up or down to
browse unplayed episodes

Tap an episode to
listen to it

An episode you've
started, but not finished

Tap to see only
episodes you
haven't listened to

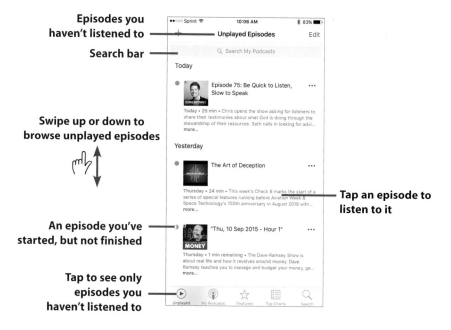

- To view a list of episodes you haven't listened to, tap Unplayed. You see the list by the date on which the episode was released. Swipe up and down the screen to find an episode in which you are interested. Tap an episode to play it (covered in the next task).

Tap and type your search term

Tap to search in the Store

Episodes of podcasts in your library that meet your search

Swipe up or down to browse results

Podcasts in your library that meet your search

Tap to select episodes to play

Tap to play episode

- You search for podcasts in your library or in the Store using the Search bar. Tap in the Search bar and type your search term. The podcasts and episodes of podcasts that meet your search criteria appear in the list of results. Tap a podcast to view and play its episodes, or tap an episode to play it. Tap Search iTunes Store to search there for podcasts related to your search.

Podcast Badge

When you see a badge on a podcast, the number indicates how many episodes you haven't viewed on a list, not how many you haven't listened to (which would make more sense).

Listening to Podcasts

The first step in listening to a podcast is to find the episode you want to listen to. You can see episodes individually, such as on a list of results from a search, or more commonly, when you view a podcast to which you are subscribed.

As you learned in the previous task, you can do this by tapping the podcast on the My Podcasts screen to open it.

When you open a podcast, you see that podcast's screen. At the top is the general information about the podcast. Below that is the list of episodes for the podcast. What you see on this screen depends on the settings for the podcast, such as how long you keep episodes. Episodes are grouped in various ways, again depending on your settings (see "Setting Your Podcast Preferences" earlier in this chapter for information on settings). You can browse the list of episodes.

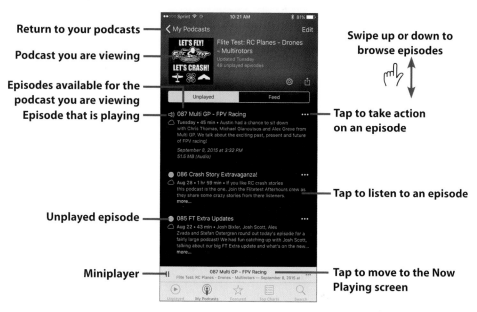

Return to your podcasts

Podcast you are viewing

Episodes available for the podcast you are viewing

Episode that is playing

Unplayed episode

Miniplayer

Swipe up or down to browse episodes

Tap to take action on an episode

Tap to listen to an episode

Tap to move to the Now Playing screen

Tap the episode to which you want to listen. If it is not currently downloaded, it downloads and starts to play as soon as enough of it has been downloaded that it can play without stopping. If it is already stored on your phone, it starts playing immediately. At the bottom of the screen, you see the Miniplayer. As the episode plays, you can view its information or pause it by tapping the Pause button.

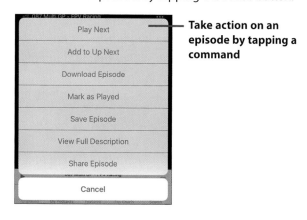

Take action on an episode by tapping a command

When you tap on the ellipsis next to an episode, you see a menu providing a number of commands you can apply to that episode, such as Play Next, Mark as Played, and so on.

Collapse Now Playing screen

Podcast you are listening to

Episode you are listening to

Repeat Last 15 Seconds

Up Next

Play/Pause

When you tap the Miniplayer, you move to the Now Playing screen. On the Now Playing screen, you have the following controls:

- Tap the downward-facing arrow to move back to the podcast's screen and display the Miniplayer instead.

- Tap the Up Next button to see a list of episodes for the podcast you are playing or if you are viewing the Unplayed list, you see the list of unplayed episodes in the order they will play (you can tap an episode from the list to play it). You can add episodes to the end of this list by using the Add to Up Next command or you can move an episode to the top of the list by using the Play Next command. Tap Done to close the Up Next list.

- Tap the Pause/Play button to pause a playing podcast or to play a paused one.

- Tap the Repeat Last 15 Seconds button to repeat the last 15 seconds of the episode.

Playhead

Playback speed

Skip Ahead 15 Seconds

Volume slider

Tap to take action on the episode

Sleep Timer

- Drag the Volume slider to the left to decrease the volume or to the right to increase it.

- To change the speed at which the podcast plays, tap the Speed 1x button; the podcast plays at 1.5 times normal speed. Tap again to play at twice the normal speed. Tap a third time to play at one-half speed, and tap once again to return to normal speed. The button reflects the current playback speed.

- Drag the Playhead to the left to move back in the podcast or to the right to move ahead in it.

- Tap the Skip Ahead 15 Seconds button to skip ahead by that amount.

- To set a sleep timer, tap the Sleep Timer button. Tap the time frame when you want the playback to stop, and tap Done. When the timer expires, the podcast stops playing. When the sleep timer is on, the Sleep Timer button is highlighted and you see the time remaining inside the button.

- Tap the ellipsis button to open a menu of commands you can apply to the episode.

Managing Podcasts and Episodes of Podcasts

Here are some pointers you can use to manage your podcasts:

Tap to manage episodes

Tap to manage the podcast

Tap to share

- To manage a podcast and its episodes, move to its screen and tap Settings (the gear button) to move to the Settings screen for the podcast.

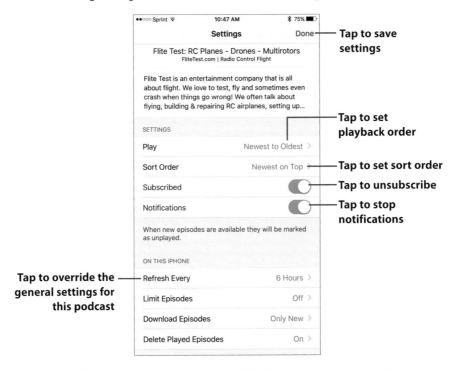

Tap to save settings

Tap to set playback order

Tap to set sort order

Tap to unsubscribe

Tap to stop notifications

Tap to override the general settings for this podcast

- The Settings tools enhance or override the general podcast preferences you set earlier. Use the Play option to set the order in which the episodes play. Tap the Sort Order option to set the order in which they appear on the podcast's screen. Set the Subscribed switch to off (white) to stop downloading episodes; set it to on (green) to resume downloads. Use the Notifications switch to stop or resume notifications for the podcast (if you've disabled all notifications for the Podcasts app, this switch is disabled). Use the controls in the ON THIS IPHONE section to override the global settings; for example, you can use the Refresh Every option to change how the podcast is refreshed. When you are done configuring the settings, tap Done.

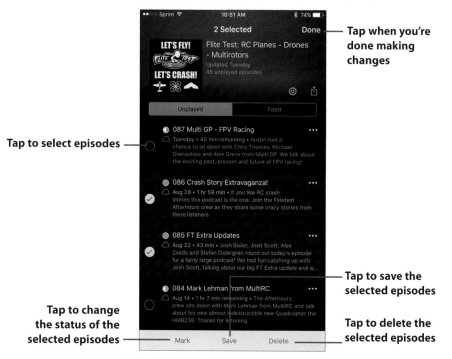

Tap to select episodes ——

Tap to change
the status of the
selected episodes ——

Tap when you're
done making
changes

Tap to save the
selected episodes

Tap to delete the
selected episodes

- To manage a podcast's episodes, move to its screen and tap Edit (shown in an earlier figure). Selection circles appear next to each episode. Tap the episodes you want to manage. Tap Mark, and then tap Mark as Played or Mark as Unplayed to change the selected episodes' status; when you mark an episode as Played, it is immediately removed from the list if the app is configured to delete played episodes. To save episodes so they won't be deleted automatically, tap Save Episodes. To unsave episodes, tap Remove from Saved. Tap Delete to delete the selected episodes. Tap Done to exit the Edit mode.

- To delete individual episodes of a podcast, swipe to the left on the episode you want to delete and tap Delete.

- When a podcast is marked with an exclamation point badge, it has a problem. Tap the podcast to see an explanation of the problem at the top of the screen. Most commonly, it is that the app has stopped downloading the podcast because you haven't listened to any episodes in a while. Tap the message to refresh the podcast.

- You can also refresh all your podcasts by swiping down from the top of the My Podcasts screen, or refresh a specific podcast by swiping down from the top of its screen.

Finding Your Way with Maps

The Maps app enables you to find locations and view them on the map. However, the real power of the Maps app is that you can then get detailed, turn-by-turn directions to those places. You can use these directions to drive, walk, or even take public transportation to the places you find.

Generating directions with the Maps app is easy and quick to do as the following steps demonstrate:

1. On the Home screen, tap Maps.

2. Tap in the Search bar, and type in the location you want to find. You can type in an address, a place name (such as Lucas Oil Stadium), or even a description of what you are looking for (for example, Starbucks near me). As you type, the app presents a list of locations that meet your search.

3. Tap the location you want to see on the map. The map appears and the location, or locations (if you do a more general search), for which you searched are marked with a pushpin.

4. If there is more than one location shown in the map, tap the pushpin for the location in which you are interested; if only one location was found, it is selected automatically and you don't need to tap it. You see a summary of the location you selected, including an estimated time to go there from your current location (the car icon indicates the time is estimated based on regular vehicle travel).

5. If you want directions from your current location to the selected location, tap the blue time estimate part of the summary pop-up and skip to step 13.

6. To generate directions starting from someplace other than your current location, tap the right-facing arrow. On the location's info screen, you see a variety of information about it, such as phone number, website, physical address, and so on (the information provided varies).

7. Browse up and down the screen to view information about the location. Links enable you to perform other actions related to it, such as tapping the phone icon to place a call to the number shown.

8. Tap Directions.

9. Tap in the top box and tap the clear button to erase the current start location.

10. Type the location for the starting point of your route. The app searches for locations based on what you type; this works just like when you started this process.

11. Tap the location where you want the route to start.

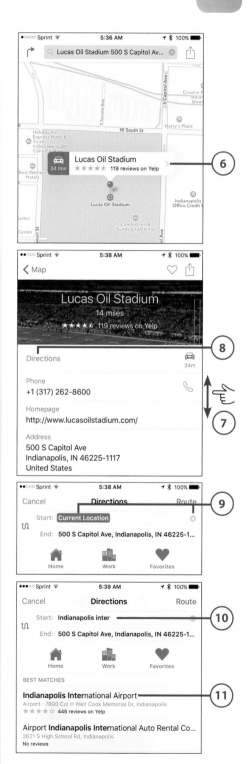

12. Tap Route. When the app determines the route you selected, you see it in dark blue on the map; alternate routes are shown in other shades (you can tap an alternate route to use it instead).

13. Tap Drive to get driving directions, Walk to get walking directions, or Transit to see routes available by public transportation.

14. Tap Start to have the app start navigating for you. The app shows you the part of the route you are on and announces when you need to do something else, such as when and where you need to turn. It gives you a "heads-up" warning when a change is coming up, such as a notice you will be exiting a highway 2 miles before the exit. The app guides you until you reach the destination. If you get off course, it recalculates the route for you automatically. This continues until you arrive at your destination.

15. As you navigate, you can tap the screen to show its controls.

16. Tap End to end the navigation before you reach the destination.

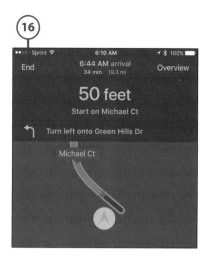

>>>Go Further

GET THERE WITH MAPS

Here are a few Maps pointers to help you along your way:

- To see an overview of your route, tap Overview. The map zooms out and you see the entire route. Tap Resume to go back to the navigation.

- To repeat the current step you are on, tap it. The app speaks the current step.

- Maps presents a 3D view of your route; tap 3D to turn this off or on. This view is difficult to describe so the best thing to do is to try it to see if you find it useful.

- To see the directions in text form, tap the List button. You see each step on the route. Tap Done to return to the map.

- To configure the voice used for navigation, tap the speaker button. You can change the volume level or set the Pause Spoken Audio switch to on (green) to temporarily stop the voice navigation. Tap Done to return to the map.

- You can use the standard zoom and swipe motions on the map to change your view. As you change the map's scale, you see the scale pop up at the top of the window. If you manipulate the map such that your current location is no longer shown, tap the arrow button to refocus the map so your location is in view. Tap it again to change into compass view so that true North "projects" from your icon on the map. You can then navigate with the map as you would with a compass.

- When you aren't navigating and are just viewing a location on the map, tap the Info button (i) to reveal options, such as Map that shows you the standard map view, Transit that shows you transit information for the location, Satellite that layers a satellite image on the map, Hide Labels and Hide Location that you can use to hide those elements, 3D Map that toggles the 3D view, and Drop a Pin that enables you to manually choose a location on a map. If Maps doesn't provide accurate information, you can tap Report an Issue to report the problem. Tap Done to close the Info screen without making changes.

- When you move into search mode, you see Nearby category buttons (for example, Food) at the top of the screen. Tap one of these to see locations in that category near you. Tap a result to see its information. If the category has sub-categories (for example, Coffee Shops when you tap Food), tap the sub-category to see locations of that type.

- Maps remembers your recent searches and presents them on the search list when you move into search mode. You can tap a recent search, such as a route, to repeat it.

- You can swap the starting and ending locations in a route by tapping the button just to the left of the Start and End fields on the search screen.

- You can tag locations as favorites and get back to them quickly by tapping Favorites on the search screen.

- As you navigate through a route, Maps identifies traffic or construction issues along the path and attempts to reroute you so that you avoid the trouble spots.

Working with the Wallet App and Apple Pay

New! The Wallet app manages all sorts of information that you need to access, from airline tickets to shopping and credit cards. Instead of using paper or plastic to conduct transactions, you can simply have your iPhone's screen scanned.

You also use the Wallet app to access your Apple Pay information to make payments when you are in a physical location, such as a store or hotel (Apple Pay is covered in detail in "Working with Apple Pay" later in this chapter). You can also use Apple Pay when you make purchases online using some apps on your iPhone.

Working with the Wallet App

You can store a wide variety of information in your wallet so that it is easily accessible. Examples include boarding passes, membership cards (to a gym for example), store cards (such as Starbucks if you are an addict like me), and loyalty or discount cards (things like loyalty cards for grocery stores or gas stations). The Wallet app eliminates the need to carry physical cards or paper for each of these; instead, your information is available to you digitally and you can enter it as needed by scanning the iPhone's screen.

Tap to open your Wallet

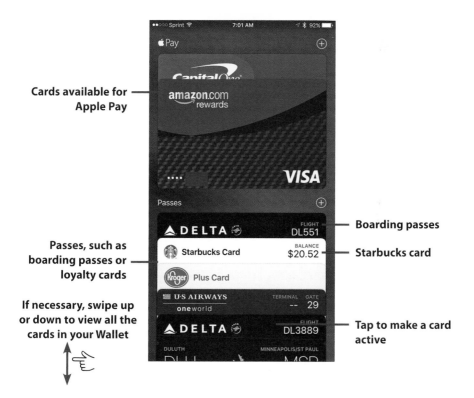

Cards available for Apple Pay

Passes, such as boarding passes or loyalty cards

If necessary, swipe up or down to view all the cards in your Wallet

Boarding passes

Starbucks card

Tap to make a card active

To open your wallet, tap the Wallet icon. The Wallet app opens. At the top, you see the Apple Pay section that shows the cards you've enabled for Apple Pay. In the Passes section, you see other cards, such as boarding passes and loyalty cards.

As you add cards and boarding passes to your Wallet, they "stack up" at the bottom of the screen. Tap the stack to see the list of items available in your Wallet. The cards expand so that you can see at least the top of each card; if you have a lot of cards installed, swipe up or down on the screen to view all of them.

Boarding pass in the Wallet app

Scan this to board the flight

Tap to share the boarding pass

Tap to configure the boarding pass

Tap to open other cards available in your Wallet

To use a card in your Wallet, tap it. It becomes the active card and you can access its information. For example, you can quickly access a boarding pass by opening the Wallet app and tapping it. To board the plane, you scan the code on the boarding pass. Even better, boarding passes start appearing on the Lock screen a few hours before the take-off time. Swipe to the right on the boarding pass on the Lock screen and you jump directly to the boarding pass in the Wallet app (you don't even need to unlock your phone).

Most passes enable you to share them or information about them by tapping the Share button and using the standard sharing tools that appear.

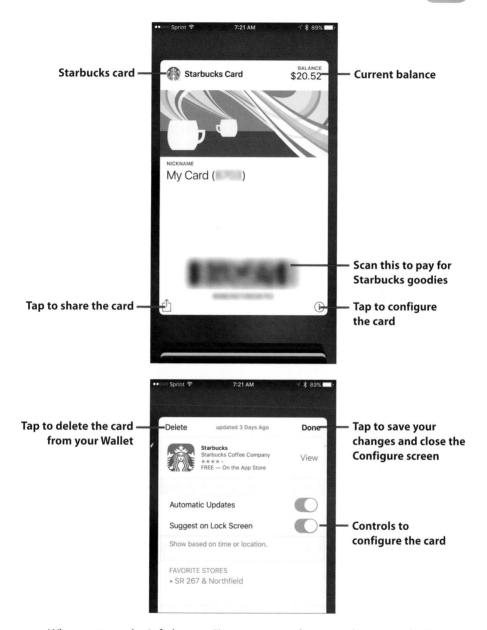

Starbucks card —— Starbucks Card

—— **Current balance**

Tap to share the card ——

—— **Scan this to pay for Starbucks goodies**

—— **Tap to configure the card**

Tap to delete the card from your Wallet ——

—— **Tap to save your changes and close the Configure screen**

—— **Controls to configure the card**

When you tap the Info button (i), you can use the controls on a card's Configure screen to adjust certain aspects of how the card works. For example, if you set the Suggest on Lock Screen switch to on (green), the card automatically appears on your Lock screen at the appropriate times. When you enable this for a card, such as Starbucks, it appears on the Lock screen when you are in close proximity to your favorite stores. And, some cards can be automatically refilled from your bank account or credit/debit card so that they always have a positive balance.

To delete a card from your Wallet (such as a boarding pass when the flight is finished), tap its Info button, tap Delete, and then confirm that you want to delete. The pass or card is removed from your Wallet.

When you're done configuring a card, tap Done. The Configure screen closes and you return to the card you were configuring.

There a couple of ways to add cards to your Wallet. The most frequent way to add a card is by using the Add to Wallet command in the app associated with the card (note that this might be called Add to Passbook in apps that haven't been updated for iOS 9 yet, but it does the same thing). In some cases, you may be able to scan the code on a card to add it.

Adding Passes or Cards to Your Wallet Using an App

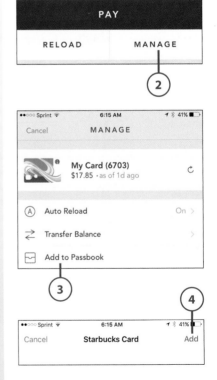

If you are a frequent patron of a particular business (perhaps you are an addicted to Starbucks coffee like I am) that has an iPhone app, check to see if it also supports the Wallet app. For example, when you use the Starbucks app configured with your account, you can add a Starbucks card to your Wallet as follows:

1. Open the app for which you want to add a pass or card to your Wallet.

2. Tap the app's command to manage its information; this command can be labeled with different names in different apps (it is the MANAGE command in the Starbucks app), or it may be accessed with an icon or menu.

3. Tap Add to Wallet or Add to Passbook.

4. Tap Add. The card or pass is added to your Wallet and is ready to use.

Wallet AKA Passbook

In prior versions of the iOS, the app now known as Wallet was called Passbook. In apps that haven't been updated for iOS 9 yet, you might see the Add to Passbook command instead of Add to Wallet. Add to Passbook does the same thing as Add to Wallet.

Finding Apps that Support the Wallet

You can search for apps that support the Wallet by opening your Wallet, tapping the Add button (+) in the Passes section, and tapping Find Apps for Wallet. This takes you into the App Store app and you see apps that support the Wallet. You can then download and install apps you want to use as described in Chapter 6.

Adding Passes or Cards to Your Wallet by Scanning Their Codes

In some cases, you can add a card or pass to the Wallet by scanning its code. To do so, follow these steps:

1. Open the Wallet app and tap the Add button (+) in the Passes section.

2. Tap Scan Code to Add a Pass.

3. Use the iPhone's camera to scan the code on the card by positioning the phone so that the white box encloses the code on the card. If the code is recognized and is available for the Wallet, the pass or card is added to the Wallet and is ready for use. If the code isn't recognized or doesn't support the Wallet, you see an error and you need to find an associated app for the card to use it with the Wallet.

Working with Apple Pay

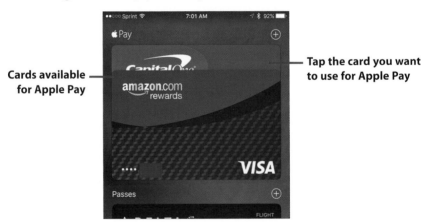

Cards available for Apple Pay

Tap the card you want to use for Apple Pay

Touch the Touch ID button to authorize payment

Apple Pay enables you to pay for things more easily and securely than with physical credit or debit cards. (Note that Apple Pay requires an iPhone 6, iPhone 6/6s Plus, or later.) When you are making a purchase in a physical store, you can simply hold your iPhone up to a contactless reader connected to the cash register and tap your finger on the Touch ID button. The iPhone communicates the information required to complete the purchase.

When you are making a transaction in an app that supports Apple Pay, tap this to pay

Apple Pay also simplifies purchases made in online stores. When you use an app or a website that supports Apple Pay, you can tap the Buy with Apple Pay button to complete the purchase.

Apple Pay is actually more secure than using a credit or debit card because your card information is not passed to the device; instead, a unique code is passed that ties back to your card, but that can't be used again. And, you never present your card so the number is not visible to anyone, either visually or digitally.

With Apple Pay, you can store your cards in the Wallet app, and they are instantly and automatically available to make purchases.

Apple Pay Support

In addition to requiring an iPhone 6 or iPhone 6/6s Plus, a credit or debit card must support Apple Pay for it to work with that card. The easiest way to figure out if your cards support it is to try to add a card to Apple Pay. If you can do so, the card is supported and you can use it. If not, you can check with the credit or debit card company to see when support for Apple Pay will be added so you can use it.

Adding Credit or Debit Cards to Apple Pay

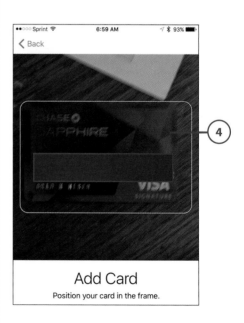

To start using Apple Pay, add a credit or debit card to it:

1. Open your Wallet.

2. Tap the Add button (+) in the Apple Pay section at the top of the screen.

3. Tap Next.

4. Position the iPhone so that the card is inside the white box. The app captures information from the card, which is highlighted in white on the screen. When it has captured all the information it can, you move to the Card Details screen.

Prefer to Type?

If you don't want to use the camera option, or if that option doesn't capture the information correctly, you can also type your card's information directly into the fields. To do this, perform step 3, and then tap Enter Card Details Manually, which is at the bottom of the Scan screen. You can use the resulting Card Details screens to manually enter the card's information.

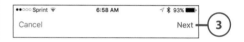

5. Use the keyboard or keypad to enter any information that wasn't captured or to correct any information that wasn't captured correctly.

6. Tap Next. The information for the card is verified. If it can't be verified, you see an error message. For example, if the card doesn't support Apple Pay, you see a message saying so. If this happens, tap OK to close the message and then wait for your card to support Apple Pay or enter a different card's information. When the card is verified, you see the Terms and Conditions screen.

7. Tap Agree.

8. Tap Agree at the prompt. The card's verification is complete and you see it in your Wallet. You are ready to use Apple Pay.

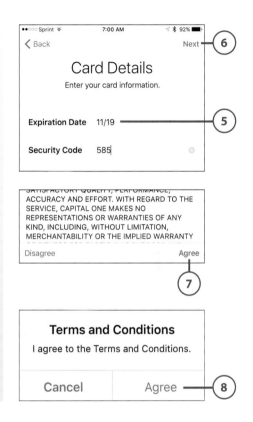

More Verification Required

In some cases, there may be an additional verification step after you tap Agree in step 8. When this is the case, the Complete Verification screen appears. Tap how you want to receive the verification code, such as via Email or Text Message, and then tap Next. The card configuration completes. You should receive a verification code. When you have the code, open the Settings app and tap Wallet & Apple Pay. Tap the card you need to verify, and then tap Enter Code. Enter the verification code you received; when you enter the correct code, the card is verified and becomes available for Apple Pay.

Managing Apple Pay

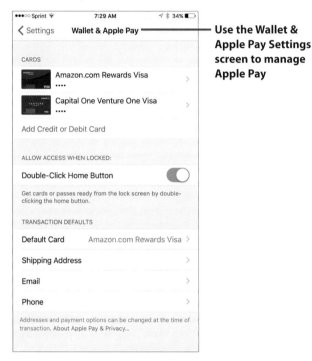

Use the Wallet & Apple Pay Settings screen to manage Apple Pay

To manage Apple Pay, open the Settings app and tap Wallet & Apple Pay. On the resulting screen, you can:

- Tap a card to configure it, such as to determine if notifications related to it will be sent. You also see a list of recent transactions for the card.

- Add a new credit or debit card.

- Use the Double-Click Home Button switch to determine if you can access the cards in your Wallet by pressing the Home button twice when the phone is locked. This makes using your Wallet even easier because you press the Home button twice and your cards appear; tap a card to use it or touch the Home/Touch ID button to pay for something with Apple Pay.

- Set your default Apple Pay card.

- Update your billing, shipping, and email addresses and phone numbers.

Ensure the Apple Pay switch is on so you can make payments using the Touch ID button

You should also make sure Apple Pay is set to use Touch ID. Open the Settings app, tap Touch ID & Passcode, and then enter your passcode. Ensure that the Apple Pay switch is on (green). This enables you to complete Apple Pay transactions by touching the Touch ID button.

Working Seamlessly Across Your Devices

Your iPhone can work seamlessly with other iOS devices running iOS 8 and later (such as iPads) and Macs running OS X Yosemite and later. This enables you to change devices and keep working on the same tasks. For example, you can start an email on your iPhone and then continue it on your Mac without missing a beat.

You can also take phone calls on iPads or Macs.

Working with Handoff

Handoff enables you to work seamlessly between iOS devices, as well as Macs running OS X Yosemite. Each device needs to be signed into the same iCloud account and have Handoff enabled. If you do not have multiple iOS devices running iOS 8 or later, or a Mac running OS X Yosemite or later, then there is no need to turn on this feature.

Enable Handoff to work seamlessly across devices

Ensure that Handoff is enabled on all the devices with which you want to use it. On iOS devices, enable Handoff by opening the Settings app, tapping General, and then tapping Handoff & Suggested Apps. Set the Handoff switch to on (green).

To enable handoff on a Mac running OS X Yosemite or later, open the System Preferences app, and then open the General pane. Ensure that the Allow Handoff between this Mac and your iCloud devices check box is checked.

Using Handoff

When Handoff is enabled on your devices, you can work on the same items on any device, as the following example of working with email shows:

1. Start an email on your iPhone (note this only works for iCloud email).

2. To work on the email on another iOS device, swipe up on the Mail icon on its Lock screen and unlock the device.

3. Work on the email on the iOS device.

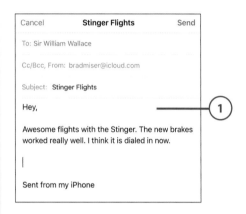

Handoff on a Mac

When your Mac detects activity associated with Handoff, an icon on the Dock appears. Click that icon to open the activity, such as an email, web page, Pages document, or other iCloud-based activity.

This works in the other direction, too. For example, if you open a web page on your Mac, you see the Safari icon on the iPhone's Lock screen. Swipe up on it and unlock your iPhone and the web page on your Mac opens on your iPhone.

Most Apple apps support Handoff and Apple has made it available to other software developers so they can add support to their apps, too.

Taking Phone Calls on Macs or iPads

A call coming in on your iPhone appears on the iPad

Tap to be reminded to return the call

Tap to decline

Tap to respond with a message

Tap to answer

When your iPhone is on the same Wi-Fi network as an iPad running iOS 8 or later, or a Mac running OS X Yosemite or later, you can take phone calls on those devices. When a call comes in to your iPhone, you see the call screen on the other devices and can take the call on one of those devices (see Chapter 8, "Communicating with the Phone and FaceTime Apps").

Configuring Devices to Share iPhone Calls

To be able to take calls to your iPhone on other devices, open the Settings app and tap Phone. Tap Calls on Other Devices. Set the Allow Calls on Other Devices switch to on (green). To allow other devices to take calls, ensure those devices' switches are on (green). To prevent calls from going to a device, set its switch to off (white).

An iPhone is easy to maintain and isn't likely to give you much trouble

In this chapter, you learn how to keep an iPhone in top shape and what to do should problems happen. Topics include the following:

→ Maintaining an iPhone's software
→ Maintaining iPhone Apps
→ Backing up your iPhone
→ Finding and securing your iPhone with Find My iPhone
→ Maintaining an iPhone's power
→ Solving iPhone problems
→ Getting help with iPhone problems

Maintaining and Protecting Your iPhone and Solving Problems

You probably noticed that this is a short chapter, and there is a good reason for that: An iPhone works very well, and you are unlikely to have problems with it, especially if you keep its software current. When problems do occur, you can usually solve them with a few simple steps. If that fails, there's lots of help available for you on the Internet.

Maintaining an iPhone's Software

Like software on computers, the software on your iPhone gets updated periodically to fix bugs, solve issues, and introduce new features. For best results, you should ensure the software you use is current to the latest releases.

There are two types of software you need to maintain: the iOS software that runs your iPhone and the apps you have installed on it. Fortunately, maintaining both types is simple.

Maintaining the iOS Software with the Settings App

You can check for updates to the iOS using the Settings app. If an update is found, you can download and install it directly on the iPhone. Here's how:

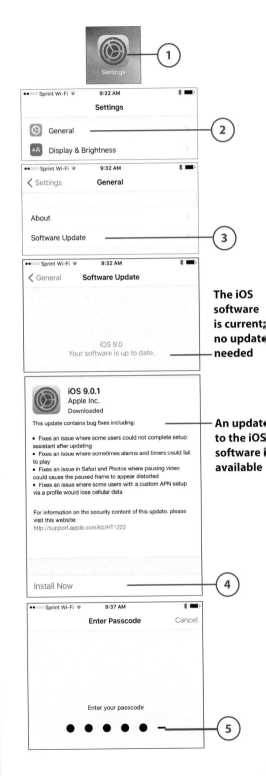

The iOS software is current; no update needed

An update to the iOS software is available

Update Notification

You may receive a notification on the iPhone when an update to iOS is available; you also see a badge on the Settings app's icon. You can tap Update in the notification to move to the Update screen (and so won't need to perform steps 1– 3).

1. On the Home screen, tap Settings.

2. Tap General.

3. Tap Software Update. The app checks for an update. If one is available, you see information about it and should proceed to step 4. If no update is needed, you see a message saying so and you can skip the rest of these steps.

4. If automatic update downloads are enabled, tap Install Now; if not, tap Download & Install. The update is downloaded if it hasn't been already and the installation process begins. Depending on your iPhone's status, you might see different warnings, such as if you aren't connected to a power supply.

5. Enter your iPhone's passcode.

6. Tap Agree.

7. Tap Agree at the prompt. The software update downloads and then installs on your iPhone. As part of the update process, the iPhone restarts. When it does, the updated software is ready for you to use.

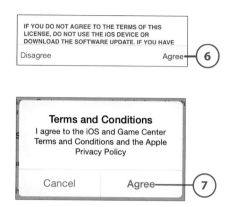

Maintaining iPhone Apps

iPhone apps are regularly updated to fix bugs or add features and enhancements. If you enabled the Automatic Downloads setting for Apps in the App Store Settings (refer to Chapter 6, "Downloading Apps, Music, Movies, TV Shows, and More onto Your iPhone," for details), you don't need to worry about keeping your apps current because the iOS does that for you automatically whenever your iPhone is connected to a Wi-Fi network. (Updates to the iOS software are also downloaded automatically, but you have to start the installation process as described in the previous task.) If you enabled the App Store app to use cellular data (refer to Chapter 2, "Connecting Your iPhone to the Internet, Bluetooth Devices, and iPhones/iPods/iPads"), the updates occur at any time your iPhone is connected to the cellular network, too (except for very large updates, which are only downloaded when your phone is connected to a Wi-Fi network).

Tap to get information about updates to your apps

Swipe up and down to browse when your apps were updated

Tap to update all your apps

Tap to update an app

When apps were updated

Tap to open an updated app

Tap to read about an update

Tap to see your updates

To see how your apps have been updated, tap the App Store app on the Home screen to open it. Tap the Updates button, and then swipe up and down to see the apps that have been updated. The updates are grouped by when the updates occurred. To see details about an update, tap its What's New link. You can open the current version of the app by tapping OPEN. If an app's update is pending, tap UPDATE to update it, or you can tap Update All to update all your apps.

>>>Go Further
MANUALLY KEEPING APPS CURRENT

If you don't want your apps to be updated automatically, turn the AUTOMATIC DOWNLOADS setting for Apps in the iTunes & App Store Settings (refer to Chapter 6 for details) to off (white). When updates are available, you see a badge on the App Store app icon showing how many updates are available. Tap the App Store app to open it, and then tap Updates. You see the available updates. Tap UPDATE for the individual updates you want to download and install, or tap UPDATE ALL to download and install all available updates.

Backing Up Your iPhone

Like all things data related, it's important to back up your iPhone's data. If you ever need to restore your iPhone to solve a problem or replace your phone with a new one, having a current backup can get you back to where you want to be as quickly and easily as possible.

There are two places where you can back up your iPhone. You can back up to your iCloud account or to your computer. In fact, you can back up to both places for maximum protection.

Ideally, you'll configure your iPhone to back up to iCloud so you can back up whenever your iPhone is connected to a Wi-Fi network that provides an Internet connection. Periodically, you can back up to your computer using the iTunes app.

To learn how to configure your iPhone to back up to your iCloud account, see "Configuring iCloud Back Up" in Chapter 3, "Setting Up and Using iCloud and Other Online Accounts." With this enabled, your iPhone is backed up automatically. You can manually back up at any time as described in the following task.

Manually Backing Up Your iPhone to iCloud

To manually back up your iPhone to your iCloud account, do the following:

1. Tap Settings.

2. Tap iCloud.

3. Swipe up the screen.

4. Tap Backup.

5. Tap Back Up Now. Your iPhone's data is backed up to iCloud. You can see the progress on the screen; however, you can continue using your iPhone because the process works in the background. You just need to start the manual back-up process, and then do whatever you want while it completes.

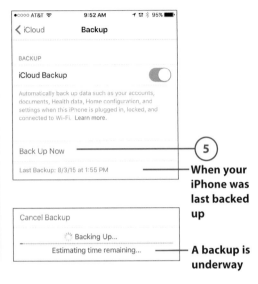

When your iPhone was last backed up

A backup is underway

Finding and Securing Your iPhone with Find My iPhone

If you lose your iPhone, you can use iCloud's Find My iPhone feature to locate your iPhone and to secure it by locking it or, in the worst case, erasing its data. Hopefully, you'll never need to use this capability, but it's good to know how just in case.

Keep It Secure

For better security, you should configure a passcode, as described in Chapter 4, "Configuring an iPhone to Suit Your Preferences." When a passcode is required, it must be entered to unlock and use an iPhone. If you don't have a passcode, anyone who picks up your iPhone can use it. This section assumes you have a passcode set. If not, go back to Chapter 4 and set one before continuing—unless you've already lost control of your iPhone. If you don't have a passcode set and lose your iPhone, you're prompted to create a passcode when you put it in Lost Mode.

After you configure Find My iPhone and use it to locate your iPhone, you can perform the following actions on it:

- **Play Sound**—This does just what it sounds like. A sound is played on the iPhone and an alert appears on its screen. This provides information to whoever has the device—such as if you've loaned the device to someone and want it back. The sound can help you locate the device if it is in the same general vicinity as you.

- **Lost Mode**—This locks the iPhone so it can't be used without entering the passcode. This can protect your iPhone without changing its data. You can also display contact information on the iPhone's screen to enable someone to get in touch with you.

- **Erase Your iPhone**—This erases the iPhone's memory as the "last chance" to protect your data. You should only do this in the worst-case scenario because when you erase the iPhone, you lose the ability to find it again using Find My iPhone.

Keeping You Informed

Whenever you use one of the Find My iPhone actions, such as playing a sound or using the Lost Mode, you receive emails to your iCloud email address showing the action taken along with the device, date, and time on which it was performed.

To use Find My iPhone, it must be enabled on your iPhone using the iCloud Settings as explained in Chapter 3 (it is enabled by default so unless you have disabled it, it should be ready for you to use when needed).

Using Find My iPhone to Locate Your iPhone

To use Find My iPhone, perform the following tasks:

1. Use a web browser to move to and log in to your iCloud website located at icloud.com.

2. Click Find My iPhone. All the devices associated with your Apple ID and on which Find My iPhone is active are located.

3. Click the All Devices menu. All your devices are shown on the My Devices list.

4. Click the device you want to locate. If the device can be located, you see it on a map. You can use the map's controls to zoom into the iPhone's location so you get the best idea of where it currently is. You also see a dialog box that enables you to perform the three actions described earlier. The details for each are provided in the following tasks.

Battery level

The iPhone's current location   **Actions you can take**

Using Find My iPhone to Play a Sound on Your iPhone

Here's how to send a sound or message to an iOS device:

1. Locate your iPhone as described in the previous task.

2. Click Play Sound.

3. To stop the sound from playing on the iPhone, unlock it and tap OK on the message prompt. (If you don't require a passcode, anyone who has the phone can do this, which is another reason requiring a passcode is more secure.)

The sound plays and the alert message appears on the iPhone

The Sound Remains the Same

When you send a sound to an iPhone, it plays even if the iPhone is muted.

Using Find My iPhone to Put Your iPhone in Lost Mode

You can put your iPhone into Lost Mode by doing the following:

1. Locate the device using the steps in the previous task.

2. Click Lost Mode. (If you haven't entered a passcode, you're prompted to create one by entering and verifying it.)

3. If you want to send a phone number to the device so that someone can call you about it, enter it at the prompt.

4. Click Next.

5. Enter the message you want to appear on the iPhone. This can be your request that whoever has the device call you, instructions for returning the device, and so on.

6. Tap Done. The iPhone is locked and the message you entered displays on the screen. While the iPhone is in Lost Mode, the Lost Mode icon on the Find My iPhone screen rotates and you see the Lost Mode indicator.

When the device enters Lost Mode, it is locked and protected with the existing passcode. The phone number and message you entered appear on the iPhone's screen. The person finding your phone can tap Call to call the number you entered.

The iPhone remains in Lost Mode until it is unlocked. You see the current status in the iPhone's window on the iCloud Find My iPhone website.

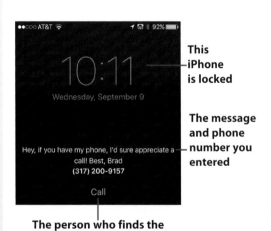

This iPhone is locked

The message and phone number you entered

The person who finds the phone can tap to call the number you entered

Using Find My iPhone to Erase Your iPhone

If you decide you've lost control of your device and want to protect the information it contains, take the following steps to erase it:

1. Locate the device using the steps in the task "Using Find My iPhone to Locate Your iPhone."

2. Click Erase iPhone.

Erase a Device

When you erase an iPhone, all its data is deleted and it is reset to factory conditions. This means you are no longer able to use Find My iPhone to locate it. Only do this when you're pretty sure the iPhone is out of your control or that you won't be getting it back any time soon.

3. Click Erase.

4. Enter your Apple ID password.

5. Click Next.

6. If you want to send a phone number to the device so that someone can call you about it, enter it at the prompt.

7. Click Next.

8. Enter the message you want to appear on the iPhone. This can be your request that whoever has the device call you, instructions for returning the device, and so on.

9. Tap Done. The iPhone is erased and the message you entered displays on the screen. The person who finds it can tap Call to call the number you entered in step 6, hopefully to return your iPhone. If it does get returned, you have to restore the iPhone using a backup from iCloud or iTunes on your computer (the steps to do this are later in this chapter).

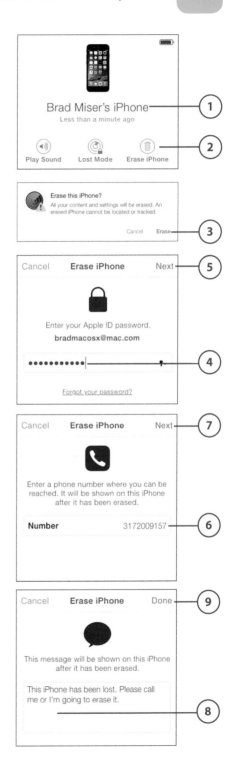

>>>Go Further

USING FIND MY IPHONE

Here are some more tips on using Find My iPhone:

- To update the locations of your devices, refresh the web page and reopen the All Devices list.

- When you send a message to an iPhone that is in Lost Mode or when you erase it, you might want to include additional contact information in the message, such as your name and where you are currently located. You could also offer a reward for the return of the iPhone. Include enough information so that if someone wants to return the device to you, she has what she needs to be able to do so.

- If you lose your iPhone, use an escalation of steps to try to regain control. Look at the iPhone's location on the map. If the iPhone appears to be near your current location, play the sound because it might help you find it again. If the iPhone doesn't appear to be near your current location or it appears to be but you can't find it, put it in Lost Mode. This hopefully prevents someone else from using it while you locate it and allows someone who finds it to contact you. If you lose all hope of finding it again, you can erase the iPhone to delete the data it contains. When you do this, you lose the ability to track your iPhone and have to rely on someone finding it and contacting you. This is a severe action, so you don't want to do it prematurely.

- Erasing an iPhone is a bit of a double-edged sword. It protects your data by erasing your device, but it also means you can't use Find My iPhone to locate it anymore. You should use this only if you're pretty sure someone has your device. After you erase it, there's no way to track the iPhone's location. How fast you move to erase your iPhone also depends on whether you've required a passcode. If you do require a passcode, you know your device's data can't be accessed without that code, so it will take some time for a miscreant to crack it, and you can be slower on going to the point of erasing it. If your iPhone doesn't have a passcode, you might want to erase it sooner to prevent someone from accessing your content.

- As you use Find My iPhone, you receive email notifications about various events, such as when a device is locked, when a message you sent is displayed, and so on. These are good ways to know something about what is happening with your iPhone, even though you might not be able to see the iPhone for yourself.

- If Find My iPhone can't currently find your iPhone, you can still initiate the same actions as when the iPhone is found, although they won't actually happen until the iPhone becomes visible again. To be notified when this happens, check the Email me when this iPhone is found check box. When the iPhone becomes visible to Find My iPhone, you receive an email and then can take appropriate action to locate and secure it.

- There's an app for that. You can download and use the free Find My iPhone app on an iOS device to use this feature. For example, you can use this app on an iPad to locate an iPhone.

Maintaining an iPhone's Power

Obviously, an iPhone with a dead battery isn't good for much. As you use your iPhone, you should keep an eye on its battery status. As long as the battery icon is at least partially filled, you're okay. As the iPhone gets low on power, the battery status icon becomes almost empty. Two separate warnings alert you when the battery lowers to 20% and then again at 10%.

Keep your eye on the battery icon so you don't run out of power

This iPhone is in Low Power Mode

New! When you see the low power warnings, you can tap Low Power Mode to have your iPhone run in this mode that reduces power use to extend the life of your battery. It does this by slowing down the phone's processor, stops automatic downloads, stops email push, and any other automatic processes. While this reduces the performance of your phone, it can greatly extend the time until your iPhone runs out of power. While in Low Power Mode, the battery status icon is yellow.

If you keep going whether you choose to run in Low Power Mode or not, the iPhone eventually runs out of power and shuts down. Once it shuts down because of a low battery, you won't be able to unlock or use it until you connect it to a charger and the battery has recharged enough for the phone to operate, which can take a few minutes. If you try to use it before it has enough power, you see the red battery icon on the screen.

This iPhone is being charged

Fortunately, it's easy to avoid running out of power by keeping your iPhone charged. Connect the phone to the charger or a computer using the USB cable, and it charges automatically. While this is occurring, you see the charging icon in the upper-right corner of the screen, and if you wake the iPhone, a large battery icon showing the relative state of the battery appears on its screen. When charging is complete, the battery status icon replaces the charging icon in the upper-right corner of the screen, the large battery icon disappears, and you see the iPhone's wallpaper if it's locked, or you see whatever screen you happen to be using if it isn't locked.

Topping Off

It's a good idea to keep your iPhone's battery topped off; this type of battery actually does better if you keep it charged rather than letting it run down all the way before recharging. Periodically, say every month or two, you might want to let your iPhone run completely out of power and then recharge it to maximize its life. The key point is, as Apple puts it, to "keep the electrons moving." So, don't let your iPhone sit with no activity for long periods of time.

Setting Low Power Mode and Getting Information About Battery Use

New! You can configure and get information about your iPhone's battery by doing the following:

1. Open the Settings app and tap Battery.

2. To manually activate Low Power Mode, set its switch to on (green); to leave it in automatic mode, skip to step 5.

3. Tap Continue; you have to do this only the first time you manually set Low Power Mode or after you reset your iPhone's warnings. The iPhone goes into Low Power Mode indicated by the yellow battery icon.

4. To return your phone to normal operation, set the Low Power Mode switch to off (white).

5. To see the percentage of charge remaining along with the battery icon, slide the Battery Percentage switch to on (green). The percentage of charge remaining appears to the left of the battery status icon at the top of the screen.

6. Swipe up the screen to see the BATTERY USAGE section. This provides information about how much power apps are using, which can come in handy when you want to make your battery last longer (see the next task for details).

7. Tap Last 24 Hours to see the power use over that time period, or tap Last 7 Days to view the power use over a seven-day time-frame. You see the percentage of total power being used by each of the apps on the list. You also see if the power is being used by background activity.

8. Tap the Clock icon to see the amount of time the app has been running to use the power it has consumed. You see this both for on screen or background activity.

9. View information about the time since the last charge that your iPhone has been in use or has been in standby.

Making the Battery Last Longer

If your iPhone's battery doesn't seem to last very long, the issue is likely that a service is very active and is requiring near-constant activity. Common causes of this problem are Push being turned on for an account that has a lot of activity, an application using GPS capabilities, and so on. Try these steps to find and stop the source of the power drain:

1. Use steps 6 through 8 in the previous task to identify apps using a large amount of power.

2. If you identify a power-hungry app that you don't want to use any more, press the Touch ID/ Home button twice to open the App Switcher.

3. Swipe to the left or right on the App Switcher until the power-hog's screen is front and center.

4. Swipe up on the app's screen to shut it down.

5. Open the Settings app, tap Mail, Contacts, Calendars, and then tap Fetch New Data.

6. Slide the status switch for Push to off (white). This disables Push functionality. To update your information, set a Fetch schedule using the controls on the bottom of the Fetch New Data screen or just open an app, such as Mail.

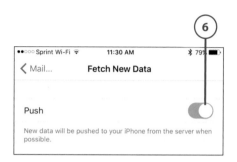

7. Turn off any transmitting and receiving functions that you aren't using, such as Bluetooth. Using the Control Center is a handy way to do this quickly.

8. Use your iPhone to see if the battery lasts longer. If it does, you know one of the changes you made was the reason; you can either leave the offending source of power drain shut down or just be aware when you are using it. If the battery still doesn't last very long, it may have a problem and you should contact Apple for assistance.

Solving iPhone Problems

Even a device as reliable as your iPhone can sometimes run into problems. Fortunately, the solutions to most problems you encounter are simple. If a simple solution doesn't work, a great deal of detailed help is available from Apple, and even more is available from the community of iPhone users.

The problems that you can address with the simple steps described in this section vary and range from such issues as the iPhone hanging (won't respond to commands) to apps not working as they should. Use the following tasks to address problems you encounter.

Restarting an App

If an app you are using locks up, displays an error, or isn't working the way it should, try shutting it down and restarting it.

1. Press the Touch ID/Home button twice. The App switcher opens.

2. Swipe to the left or right until you see the app that has frozen.

3. Swipe up on the app to shut it down.

4. Press the Touch ID/Home button to move back to the Home screen.

5. Open the app again. If it works normally, you're done. (It's generally a good idea to restart your iPhone when you've had to force an app to quit.)

Restarting Your iPhone

Whenever your iPhone starts acting oddly, restarting it should be the first thing you try. It's easy to do and cures an amazing number of problems. To restart your iPhone, do the following:

1. Press and hold the Sleep/Wake button until the slider appears on the screen.

2. Drag the slider to the right. The iPhone powers down.

3. Press and hold the Sleep/Wake button until you see the Apple logo on the screen. The iPhone restarts. When the Home screen appears, try using the iPhone again. If the problem is solved, you're done.

Can't Restart?

If your iPhone won't restart normally, press and hold the Sleep/Wake and Touch ID/Home buttons at the same time until the iPhone shuts off (about 10 seconds) and the screen goes completely dark. Then, press the Sleep/Wake button to restart it.

Resetting Your iPhone

If restarting your iPhone doesn't help, try resetting your iPhone using the following steps.

1. On the Home screen, tap Settings.

2. Tap General.

3. Swipe up the screen until you see the Reset command.

4. Tap Reset.

5. Tap the Reset command for the area in which you are having problems. For example, if you are having trouble with Wi-Fi or other networking areas, tap Reset Network Settings, or if you decide your Home screens are a mess and you want to go back to the default layout, tap Reset Home Screen Layout. If you are having lots of issues in multiple areas, tap Reset All Settings or Erase All Content and Settings (be careful because this erases everything on your iPhone).

6. If prompted to do so, enter your passcode; if you don't see a passcode prompt, skip to the next step.

7. Tap the confirmation of the reset you are doing. The reset is complete and that area of the iPhone is reset to factory conditions.

8. Reconfigure the area that you reset. For example, if you reset your network settings, you need to reconnect to the networks you want to use. If you did a Reset All Settings or Erase All Content and Settings, you'll basically start from the beginning as if your iPhone was just taken out of its box.

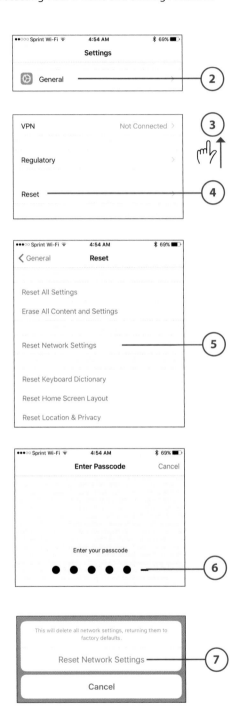

Restoring Your iPhone

The most severe action you can take on your iPhone is to restore it. When this happens, the iPhone is erased, so you lose all its contents and its current iOS software is overwritten with the latest version. If you have added information to your iPhone since it was last backed up (when you last connected it to the computer or it backed up to your iCloud account), that information is lost when you restore your iPhone—so be careful before doing this. If none of the other tasks corrected the problem, restoring the iPhone should.

Installing iTunes

If iTunes isn't installed on your computer, go to www.apple.com/itunes to download and install it.

To restore your iPhone, use the iTunes app on a computer and perform the following steps:

1. On the iPhone, turn off Find My iPhone by opening the iCloud Settings screen, tapping Find My iPhone, setting the Find My iPhone switch to off (white), entering your Apple ID password, and tapping Turn Off.

2. Connect the iPhone to your computer.

Where's the Trust?

The first time you connect an iPhone to your computer, you're prompted to trust the computer or not. Tap Trust to be able to connect it to iTunes. You also see a trust prompt in iTunes on the computer; click Continue to connect the iPhone to iTunes on the computer.

3. If iTunes didn't open automatically, launch the application.

4. Click the iPhone button. (If you have more than one device connected to iTunes, this is the Devices button; click it and select your iPhone on the list of devices.)

5. Click Summary.

6. Click Restore iPhone. Remember that you lose everything on your iPhone when you restore it, so make sure that you have all its data stored elsewhere, such as backed up on iCloud, before you do this.

7. Click Back Up. This backs up your iPhone's contents to your computer. This is a critical step because it enables you to recover the data and settings on your iPhone. If you don't do this, some of your data and settings can be lost.

Backing Up Isn't Hard to Do

iCloud is the most convenient way to back up your iPhone because it happens automatically. You can also manually back up your iPhone to your computer at any time by using these steps to access the iPhone in iTunes and then clicking the Back Up Now button. If you use iTunes regularly, it's a good idea to use it to keep your iPhone backed up on your computer, too.

---

8. Click Restore in the dialog box. The Restore process begins and iTunes extracts the software and prepares to install it.

9. Read the information about the current version of the iPhone's software, and click Next. (This step is not shown in the figures.)

10. Click Agree. (This step is not shown in the figures.) The current version of the iPhone's software is downloaded to your computer, and iTunes reinstalls it on your iPhone. You see several progress indicators along the way, both on the computer screen and on your iPhone. Early in the process, the iPhone restarts and iTunes begins reinstalling its software. (If a firmware update is needed, iTunes handles that, too.) When the process is complete, you see a message explaining what has happened.

11. Click OK. (This step is not shown in the figures.) The iPhone is restarted, and you see the Welcome to Your New Phone screen.

12. Click the Restore from this backup: radio button.

13. On the pop-up menu, ensure that your iPhone's name appears on the menu with no date and time. This indicates it is the most recent backup. If you don't see this or you want to choose to restore the phone from an earlier backup, open the menu and choose the backup you want to use to restore the phone.

14. Click Continue. iTunes restores the iPhone from the backup.

15. Click OK in the completion dialog box. The iPhone is synced according to the settings stored in the backup. When the sync process is complete, the iPhone should be back in working condition with all your content restored to it. If you have a lot of content, this process can take a while because the sync is performed starting with the iPhone's memory being "empty." You'll need to re-download any content from the iTunes Store that you've purchased to restore it, such as movies or TV shows.

Starting Over

If you want to start from the beginning, select the Set up as a new iPhone radio button in step 12 instead. Follow the onscreen prompts. When that process is complete, you're prompted to name and reconfigure the iPhone as you did when you first started using it.

How Does It Remember?

You might wonder how an iPhone can be restored. It's because critical iPhone data and settings are backed up on your iCloud account or on your computer. Each time you back up your iPhone, this information is saved so that it is available again when it is needed, such as when you restore your iPhone. iCloud backups happen automatically when your iPhone is connected to the Internet so you don't have to worry about backing it up manually. But, as described earlier, you can periodically back up your iPhone to your computer, too.

Restoring an iPhone without iTunes

You can also restore an iPhone without using iTunes. Open the Settings app, tap General, tap Reset, and tap Erase All Content and Settings. After you enter your passcode and confirm the action, the data and settings on your iPhone are erased. You can then restore your iPhone from your iCloud backup as you had the option to do when you turned on your iPhone for the first time.

Finding a Missing App

I've had more than a few emails from people on whose phones an app icon seems to have disappeared. In most cases, these were core iPhone apps that can't be removed from the iPhone, such as Settings or Photos. In almost all of these cases, the app's icon had inadvertently been moved into a folder and so was not visible in its expected location. If this happens to you, perform the following steps to restore the app to where it should be:

1. Move to the Home screen.

2. Swipe down from the center top area of the screen. The Search tool opens.

3. Tap in the Search bar and enter the name of the app that is missing. As you search, you see a list of items that match your search. If the app is found, you know it is still on the iPhone and its icon was just accidentally misplaced; you can continue with these steps to find it. Note the current location of the app, which is shown on the right side of the screen.

Current location of the missing app

If the app you are looking for isn't found, it has been deleted from the iPhone and you need to reinstall it. Download and install it again using the App Store app (don't worry, if it has a license fee, you won't need to pay for it again). (Installing apps is covered in Chapter 6.)

4. Tap Cancel. You move back to the Home screen.

5. Open the folder where the app is currently located.

6. Tap and hold on the app icon until the icons start jiggling.

7. Drag the app's icon out of the folder.

8. Place the icon back where you want it to be (refer to Chapter 5 for details of moving apps on the Home screens).

9. Press the Touch ID/Home button to lock the icons in their current positions.

Making an iPhone's Screen Rotate Again

If your iPhone stops changing from horizontal to vertical orientation when you rotate the phone, you probably have inadvertently enabled the orientation lock. Unlock it again by doing the following:

1. Look at the top of the screen. If you see the Orientation Lock icon, the iPhone's orientation is locked.

2. Swipe up from the bottom of the Home screen to open the Control Center.

3. Tap the Orientation Lock button. Note that when Orientation Lock is on, the button is white. When it is off, the button is black.

4. Confirm that the Orientation Lock icon at the top of the screen has disappeared. The iPhone now changes orientation when you rotate it.

The orientation of this iPhone is locked

Blocking Unwanted Calls, Messages, or FaceTime Requests

If you want to block calls, messages, or FaceTime requests from someone, do the following:

1. Create a contact for the phone number or email address used to send messages that you want to block. (Creating contacts is described in Chapter 7, "Managing Contacts.")

2. On the Home screen, tap Settings.

3. Tap Phone. When you block someone in the Phone app, they are blocked in the Messages and FaceTime apps, too.

4. Tap Blocked. If you have previously blocked anyone, you see them on the Blocked list.

5. Tap Add New.

6. Find and tap the contact you want to block. You return to the Blocked screen and see the person whose calls, messages, or FaceTime requests are blocked. You see each email address and phone number for that contact. Blocked phone numbers and email addresses are prevented from reaching you via the Phone, Messages, and FaceTime apps.

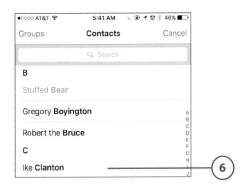

Unblock

To remove the block on a contact, move to the Blocked screen, tap Edit, tap the Unlock button for the email address or phone number you want to unblock, and tap Unblock. You will be available to the addresses or phone numbers that you unblock again.

Solving the Quiet iPhone Problem

If your iPhone stops ringing or making other sounds you believe it should, perform the following steps:

1. Make sure the iPhone isn't muted. The Mute switch on the left side of the iPhone should be in the position toward the front of the phone. If you see color in the switch, the phone is currently muted. Slide the switch toward the front of the iPhone to unmute it. You should hear sounds again.

2. With the iPhone unlocked, press the upper volume switch on the left side of the iPhone to make sure that the volume isn't set to the lowest level. As you press the button, a visual indicator of the current volume level appears on the screen. As long as you see a few "dots" on this indicator, you should be able to hear sounds the iPhone makes.

3. Make sure that the iPhone is not in Do Not Disturb mode by opening the Control Center and ensuring that the Do Not Disturb button is off (black); if it is turned on (white), tap it to turn it off. In Do Not Disturb mode, sounds are not made, such as a ring when you receive a phone call.

Do Disturb!

If Do Not Disturb was on, but you hadn't intended it to be, open the Settings app and tap Do Not Disturb to view its settings. Check to see if an automatic schedule has been set. If the Scheduled button is on (green) then a schedule for starting and stopping Do Not Disturb has been active on the phone. Slide the Scheduled switch off (white) to prevent it from automatically turning on Do Not Disturb.

4. Try a different app or task. If you aren't hearing sound from only one app and everything else sounds normal, you know there is a problem with that app. Try deleting and reinstalling it. If you still don't hear sound from any app, you know the problem is more general.

5. Move to Sounds in the Settings app.

6. Make sure the volume slider is set to at least the middle position.

7. Tap Ringtone.

8. Tap one of the default ringtones. You should hear it. If you do, you know the problem is solved. If not, continue.

9. If you aren't hearing sounds when the EarPods aren't plugged in, connect the EarPods and repeat the sound you should be hearing. If you hear the sound only when the EarPods are plugged in, try removing the EarPods and plugging them back in a few times to see if that solves the problem. If not, your iPhone needs to be serviced by an Apple authorized repair center or you can take it to the Genius bar in an Apple Store.

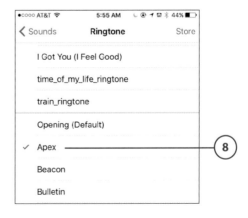

Getting Help with iPhone Problems

If none of the previous steps solve your problem, you can get help in a number of ways:

- **Apple's website**—Go to www.apple.com/support/. On this page, you can access all kinds of information about iPhones, iTunes, and other Apple products. You can browse for help, and you can search for answers to specific problems. Many of the resulting articles have detailed, step-by-step instructions to help you solve problems and link to more information.

- **Web searches**—One of the most useful ways to get help is to do a web search for the specific problem you're having. Just open your favorite search tool, such as Google, and search for the problem. You are likely to find many resources to help you, including websites, forums, and such. If you encounter a problem, it's likely someone else has too, and has probably put the solution on the Web.

- **Genius bar at an Apple Store**—All Apple Stores have a Genius bar staffed with people who will try to help you with problems. If you can't resolve a problem on your own, going to an Apple Store is often a great solution because the Apple geniuses can help you with any problem, whether it's software or hardware. In many cases, the help they provide is free, too (though you might be charged for some hardware problems). You can register for an appointment at a Genius bar by going to www.apple.com/retail/geniusbar/.

- **Me**—You're welcome to send an email to me for problems you're having with your iPhone. My address is bradmiser@icloud.com. I'll do my best to help you as quickly as I can. (I do respond to every email I receive, though at times, it might take me a few days to get back to you. I am not able to respond to FaceTime or Messages requests, so please use email to reach me.)

Index

B

J-K

N

REGISTER THIS PRODUCT
SAVE 35%*
ON YOUR NEXT PURCHASE!

How to Register Your Product

- Go to quepublishing.com/register
- Sign in or create an account
- Enter ISBN: 10- or 13-digit ISBN that appears on the back cover of your product

Benefits of Registering

- Ability to download product updates
- Access to bonus chapters and workshop files
- A 35% coupon to be used on your next purchase – valid for 30 days
  - To obtain your coupon, click on "Manage Codes" in the right column of your Account page
- Receive special offers on new editions and related Que products

Please note that the benefits for registering may vary by product. Benefits will be listed on your Account page under Registered Products.

We value and respect your privacy. Your email address will not be sold to any third party company.

* 35% discount code presented after product registration is valid on most print books, eBooks, and full-course videos sold on QuePublishing.com. Discount may not be combined with any other offer and is not redeemable for cash. Discount code expires after 30 days from the time of product registration. Offer subject to change.

quepublishing.com